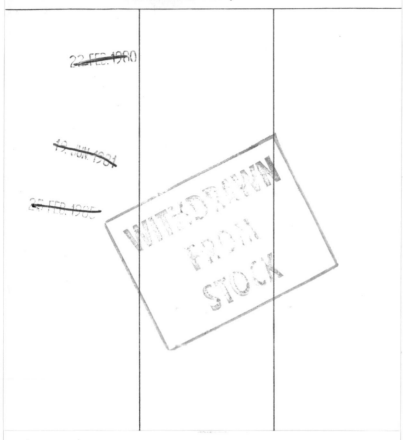

THE POLITICAL INSTITUTIONS
OF MODERN CHINA

THE
POLITICAL INSTITUTIONS
OF MODERN CHINA

by

WILLIAM L. TUNG

Professor of Political Science
Queens College, City University of New York

SECOND PRINTING

MARTINUS NIJHOFF / THE HAGUE / 1968

PRINTED IN THE NETHERLANDS

In the memory of my late mother

PREFACE

This book is prepared primarily for students who are interested in studying the constitutional development and government structure of twentieth-century China. Since the emergence of the Chinese constitutional movement at the end of the nineteenth century, political institutions in China have undergone constant changes. The first four chapters treat of constitutional development and government systems from the latter part of the Ch'ing dynasty to the re-unification of China by the Nationalist Party in 1928. The other eight chapters deal with the policies, programs, and institutions of the Nationalist and Communist governments up to 1962. While treatises on various subjects have been consulted, the sources of this book are chiefly based on the official documents from the collections as indicated in the bibliography. Materials in the first few chapters are partly drawn from my previous works on government and politics in China. Because of the immense scope of the subject and the intricacy of the problems involved, this work is not intended to be exhaustive, but is rather a brief description and discussion of each topic under consideration. As there are many valuable works on China in general as well as on her history and international relations, I have tried not to cover what has already been dealt with by others.

In my presentation of facts and views, I have endeavored to be as objective as possible, personal political convictions notwithstanding. Such an approach will inevitably invite the displeasure of those whose emotional attitudes would not tolerate any factual description of the party in opposition. However, exaggerations of either achievements or failures would not be consonant with the purpose of this book.

In my evaluation of the Nationalist institutions and their applications, I had not the slightest intention of directing criticism toward a few leaders. As a former public functionary and university professor under the Nationalist rule for many years, I share responsibility for past failures. Nor can I agree with such anti-Communist views that institutions and programs on the Mainland are not worthwhile for analytical study. For more than half a century the Chinese people have endured many civil wars and political turmoil. It is high time for the government to provide them with some political stability and economic welfare, the common aim of most revolutions throughout history. With no personal prejudice whatsoever, I venture to remind the leaders that revolution is only a means, not an end in itself.

Owing to the limitation of space and facilities, inappropriate omissions or factual errors are unavoidable. I sincerely welcome suggestions and criticism from my readers. In the completion of this book, I am deeply indebted to Dr. Raymond L. Carol, my former colleague at St. John's University, New York, to my wife Portia who reviewed the entire manuscript, and to Dr. Jeanne K. Welcher also of St. John's for her reading of the first five chapters. They all made valuable suggestions and comments. My special gratitude is to Dr. Carol whose profound knowledge of comparative government has helped me improve the exposition of ideas for the Western public and whose generous friendship has been a source of constant encouragement. Acknowledgement must also be made of the secretarial assistance of Mrs. Ruth M. Palumbo. None of them is, however, responsible for my statement of facts or views.

WILLIAM L. TUNG

QUEENS COLLEGE
of the City University of New York
Flushing, New York

TABLE OF CONTENTS

FROM AUTOCRACY TO DEMOCRACY: POLITICAL INSTITUTIONS AT THE END OF THE CH'ING DYNASTY

I. TRANSFORMATION FROM ABSOLUTE TO CONSTITUTIONAL MONARCHY

China's traditional political system

No political institution is absolutely sound at all times in all places. Its value varies with the changes in time and circumstances, which are actually the determining factors for the modern transformation from absolute monarchy into constitutional democracy. There is neither a definite standard for such transformation nor a workable rule for its success or failures. These, again, depend upon the particular background of a country, determination of the people, as well as other important elements. The uncertainty of the overall situation in modern China was the underlying reason for her frequent shifting from one government system to another.

Before the establishment of the Republic in 1912, China had traditionally been under the rule of absolute monarchy. Although some benevolent and enlightened rulers paid considerable attention to state welfare and public opinion, the government was generally under the absolute direction and control of the Imperial Court. Thus, under ruthless monarchs, there could be no guarantee whatsoever of the protection of life and property of individual citizens in the realm. This was due to the lack of a fundamental law of the state by which both the sovereign and the people should abide. It is true that, in Chinese ancient books and documents, there can be found such words as "constitution" and "constitutional law"; but they do not bear the modern meaning and significance of these terms and designate only the various laws and ordinances promulgated by the Court. Even though some of the influential philosophers in China advocated the theory that people were more important than the throne, little could be expected from those on the throne to surrender their own authorities to the rule of law.

The beginning of constitutional movement

The status of absolute monarchy in China lasted until the beginning of the twentieth century when reform toward constitutional rule was deemed by the Ch'ing dynasty as the only way to preserve the throne. To appease the discontented people, the Imperial Court took the following measures: to institute a National Legislative Council and the provincial assemblies as national and provincial representative organs of the people; to grant and promulgate the *Principles of Constitution (Hsien-fa Ta-kang)* in 1908 and the *Nineteen Articles (Shih-chiu Hsin-t'iao)* in 1911 as fundamental laws of the state; and to initiate the local self-government system as a basis for constitutional rule. However, owing to the lack of sincerity on the part of the ruling dynasty in making any real effort to bring about political reforms, revolution finally broke out in 1911 and resulted in the overthrow of the Ch'ing dynasty and the establishment of the Republic of China. Notwithstanding the tragic consequences of its failures, the "Reform Movement" during the period of Emperors Kuang Hsü and Hsüan Tung since the end of the nineteenth century was actually the vanguard of the movement toward political democracy in China. It is, therefore, proper in studying the government institutions of modern China to begin with the constitutional movement in the latter part of the Ch'ing dynasty.

2. CAUSES OF THE CONSTITUTIONAL MOVEMENT

In spite of its lukewarm interest in political reforms, preparations were still being made by the Manchu Court toward constitutional monarchy. They were propelled by two major forces of that time, namely, the unceasing revolutionary movement and the world-wide trend toward democracy and constitutionalism. In order to maintain the Manchu regime, the Imperial Court was compelled to adopt some reform measures to appease the people. But its reluctance to give up absolute autocracy and its tactics of delay in enforcing constitutional rule had convinced the intelligentsia that nothing less than the establishment of a republic through force could save the country.

Revolutionary movement

Toward the end of the Ch'ing dynasty, the Manchu government suffered corruption and inefficiency in its administration of domestic affairs, and defeat and humiliation in its dealings with foreign Powers. The weaknesses of the government were fully exposed to the people in 1885 when China was defeated in the Sino-French War. Witnessing the deteriorating situation, a young patriot, then only over nineteen years old, made up his mind to devote himself to a life-time task of over-throwing the Ch'ing dynasty and the establishment of a republic. He first started advocating his radical ideas when he studied at Po-chi Hospital School in Canton in 1886 and then at Alice Memorial Hospital in Hongkong in the following years. After his graduation, he introduced himself into Chinese society as a physician; but he devoted himself to revolutionary activities.

This young patriot was Sun Wen, also known as Dr. Sun Yat-sen. He was born on November 12, 1866,[1] in the district of Hsiangshan in Kwangtung province, China. There were three aspects of his life and environment which had important influence upon his early political ideas: (1) the control of China by the Manchus and the corruption of the Manchu regime, (2) the foreign invasions of China, and (3) his peasant parentage and early association with the members of the secret societies and the ex-Taiping soldiers.[2] An excellent organizer with a strong conviction, he soon became the leader of the revolution and was universally recognized as the founder of the Chinese Republic. His writings have since been serving as the ideological basis of the Nationalist Party (Kuomintang) and Government.

When the Sino-Japanese War broke out in 1894, Dr. Sun prepared a petition to be presented to Premier Li Hung-chang,[3] in which he reviewed the contemporary problems facing China and recommended as a solution his four-point plan: (1) the full contribution of individual abilities, (2) the full exploitation of the land, (3) the full utilization of

[1] Before the establishment of the republic in 1912, China had traditionally used her old calendar. Thus come the discrepancies of dates in many books on China, because some authors keep the original dates of the old calendar while others record the corresponding dates according to the Western calendar. To check various dates in both calendars, consult Windon Chandler Welch, *Chinese American Calendar (1849–1951)*.* Here the asterisk indicates that the work is written in English. Other sources quoted in the footnotes without * or any other sign are all in Chinese. In the bibliography can be found the publication data for each source.

[2] The Taiping Rebellion or Revolution broke out in 1850. Not till 1864 was it subdued by the Manchu regime. For twelve years, Nanking was in the hands of the rebels. Over a dozen provinces were devastated, and hundreds of cities were captured. In a score of pitched battles, the Imperial troops suffered defeat. It was evident that the Manchu generalship was not quite equal to the task before it. For details, see W.J.Hail, *Tseng Kuo-fan and the Taiping Rebellion* * (New Haven: Yale University Press, 1927). As a war measure for raising revenue during the Taiping Rebellion, the Manchu government instituted the infamous system of public sale of offices, which had been retained after the restoration of peace. See L. S. Hsü, *Sun Yat-sen: His Political and Social Ideals*,* pp. 28–29.

[3] Li's official title was Pei yang Minister or Minister of Northern Provinces.

resources, and (4) the facilitation of the distribution of goods.[1] However, Li had no intention of introducing thorough reforms and refused to receive him. Realizing that his ideas could not be fulfilled at that time, Dr. Sun left China for Hawaii and the United States for the propagation of his revolutionary principles. Meanwhile, he set up his first revolutionary organization, Hsing-chung Hui (Society for the Regeneration of China), through which he and his followers advocated the necessity and aims of revolution to the Chinese overseas.[2] In 1895, one year after the organization of the Hsing-chung Hui, his revolutionary colleagues attempted a *coup* in Canton, but it was unsuccessful. While travelling in London, Dr. Sun was kidnapped by an agent of the Manchu-Court and confined in the Chinese Legation. Owing to the efforts of his former teacher, Dr. James Cantile, and the intercession of the British government, he was subsequently released. In the next few years, he remained in Europe to study political and social institutions and to further his revolutionary propaganda among his countrymen. During that period, several attempts at revolution were made but all resulted in failures.

In 1905, Dr. Sun once again toured the world and founded his second and more important revolutionary organization, T'ung-meng Hui (The Alliance). Branches of the organization were established in Brussels, Berlin, Paris, and Tokyo. Of these, the Tokyo branch was most important, with several hundred members from seventeen provinces of China. The manifesto of the T'ung-meng Hui declared that, unlike the "hero revolutions" of the previous dynasties, the present revolution would be the "people's revolution" on the basis of liberty, equality, and fraternity.[3]

The T'ung-meng Hui aimed at the overthrow of the Manchus, the rule of the country by the Chinese, the establishment of a republican form of government, and the equalization of land ownership. This four-point program was a simplified form of Dr. Sun's later work, *The Three*

[1] *The Collected Works of Sun Yat-sen* (Shanghai: San-ming Book Co., 1937), Vol. IV, "Correspondence and Telegrams," pp. 1–17.

[2] See *ibid.*, "A History of the Chinese Revolution," p. 7; also Tsou Lu, *The Manuscript of the History of the Nationalist Party of China.* Vol. I, p. 2. There are different opinions with regard to the exact time and place of the founding of the Hsing-chung Hui. After research on this subject, Tsou Lu wrote: "Since there is a sentence in the autobiography of the late *Tsung-li* mentioning that he went to Hawaii and founded the Hsing-chung Hui, many people maintain that the Hsing-chung Hui was instituted in Hawaii. Actually, it was established in Macao. This fact can be sufficiently proved by referring to *Tsung-li's The Kidnapping in London*." (*Ibid.*, Vol. I, p. 28, footnote 1.) The word *Tsung-li* means ' General Director" or Leader, the official title of Dr. Sun Yat-sen in the party.

[3] The Manifesto of the T'ung-meng Hui can be found in all editions of *The Collected Works of Sun Yat-sen*

People's Principles, which contained the basic ideology of the Nationalist Party. The revolutionary work was to be carried out through three stages: first, military dictatorship; second, political tutelage; and third, constitutional government.[1] It should be noted here that the shifting of power from the Manchus to the Chinese as advocated by the T'ung-meng Hui meant the change from the minority rule of the Manchus to the Chinese as a whole.

The establishment of the T'ung-meng Hui marked a new epoch in the history of the Chinese revolution. Within one year, its membership had increased so rapidly that its branches were set up in all provinces of China. The attitude of foreign governments became increasingly favorable toward the Chinese revolutionists. Meanwhile, many patriots, such as Hsü Hsi-lin, Hsiung Chen-chi and Ch'iu Ch'in, began revolutionary activities independently of Dr. Sun's movement.[2] Being unable to subdue completely the spread of revolutionary ideas, the Imperial court resorted to superficial reforms in an effort to appease the people and to regain their confidence in the government. The fact that the royal decree for the preparation of a constitutional monarchy was issued just one year after the organization of the T'ung-meng Hui sufficiently illustrates the cause and effect of the revolutionary and constitutional movements.

World-wide trend toward constitutional democracy

Since the middle of the nineteenth century, Western ideas and ideals have been rapidly introduced to China through missionaries and other foreigners in China and also by the Chinese students who returned from Japan, Europe, and the United States. The Chinese intellectuals were very much impressed by the steady flourishing of democratic ideas in the different regions of the world. The newly-emerged strong powers, such as Germany, Italy, and Japan, all adopted constitutions, established representative organs, and granted political rights to the people. Though not all were in favor of using force to overthrow the Ch'ing dynasty, far-sighted Chinese began to realize that only a thorough political reform could save the fate of the country. The voices demanding a constitutional monarch had become louder with the expansion of Dr. Sun's revolutionary activities. The most im-

---

[1] For details, see Ch. V., Sec. 2, "The Outline of National Reconstruction."

[2] The members of the secret societies in China took active part in the Chinese revolution. These were the Triad or the Hung societies. For their origin and activities as well as Dr. Sun's personal connection with them, see T'ang Leang-li, *The Inner History of the Chinese Revolution,* pp. 4-9.

portant leaders of the reform movement were K'ang Yu-wei and Liang Ch'i-ch'ao, in whom Emperor Kuang Hsü entrusted the task of carrying various new measures. Their reform program, though limited at first to the spheres of administration and education, was met with strong opposition from influential officials and Manchu princes. In September 1898, the Empress Dowager, who had only recently transferred her power of regency to Emperor Kuang Hsü, resumed control of state affairs and drastically purged the reform advocates. Thus the so-called "Hundred Days' Reform" of 1898 came to an end.

Once the reactionaries surrounding the Empress had an upper hand over the reformists, they became more arrogant and ruthless and finally, through their encouragement, the Boxer Uprising in 1900 against foreigners took place. This was the most humiliating event since the Manchus came to power. The Uprising led to foreign expeditions to North China. Besides suffering severe damage to property, the Chinese people were compelled to pay higher taxes in order to discharge the heavy indemnity resulting from the rebellion. Public opinion demanded a change. K'ang and Liang, then in exile overseas,[1] were still propagating and advocating their concept of constitutional monarchy.[2] When Japan defeated Russia in the Russo-Japanese War of 1904–1905, the Chinese generally gave credit for the victory to the remarkable progress Japan had made under constitutional government. Henceforth, the demand for constitutional rule in China had become more serious than ever.

3. PREPARATION FOR CONSTITUTIONALISM

Investigation of constitutional systems abroad

In view of the revolutionary activities and constitutional demand by the people, the Imperial Court realized that its days would be numbered unless measures were taken to impress the people of its inclination toward constitutionalism. Thus, in July 1905, five commissioners were sent abroad to investigate political conditions and constitutional systems of various countries. They were all high-ranking officers: Tai

[1] Six of the constitutional reformists were executed at that time by the Imperial Court. K'ang and Liang escaped the death by fleeing to Japan.

[2] See Liang's article on "Enlightened Dictatorship," published in the *Hsin-ming Tsung Pao*. In his letter to Chinese businessmen in North and South America in June 1902, K'ang Yu-wei discussed at length the disadvantages of revolution and the advantages of a constitutional monarchy.

Tse, Tuan Fang, Tai Hung-tse, Hsü Shih-ch'ang, and Shao Ying. This was the same year that Dr. Sun organized the T'ung-meng Hui branches in the capitals of Belgium, Germany, France and Japan, with more people drawn to the revolutionary cause. On the day the five commissioners left Peking, Tai Tse and Shao Ying were wounded by a bomb thrown by a revolutionist named Wu Yueh. The two were replaced by Shang Chi-hun and Li Seng-to. Meanwhile, the Chinese envoys abroad also submitted memorials to the throne urging the adoption of a constitution adaptable to the changing circumstances. After investigating the political conditions in Japan, England, France, Belgium, Germany, Italy, Austria, and the United States, the five commissioners came back to Peking in 1906.[1] In their report, they recommended the establishment of a constitutional monarchy which, in their opinion, was the only way to avert a revolution. They also stated that the constitutional rule was an important factor contributing to the power and wealth of many countries.[2]

It was under such circumstances that, on September 1, 1906, the Imperial Court issued a momentous edict on constitutional preparations. But it was determined to prolong the preparatory period for a number of decades so that the actual constitutionalism in China would always belong to the future.

Promulgation of laws for the preliminary stage of constitutional rule

Even though unwilling to abandon its absolute rule over China, the Ch'ing regime had to pose as if it had been truly preparing for a constitutional monarchy. Once the Imperial edict was issued, something had to be done to appease public opinion. Thus followed the promulgation of a series of laws toward that end: *Principles of Constitution,*[3] *Outlines of Parliamentary Procedures, Outlines of Electoral Law, The List of Preparatory Work Prior to the Convening of Parliament, Organic Law of the National Legislative Council (Tse-cheng Yuan), Electoral Law of the National Legislative Council, Organic Law of the Provincial Assembly (Tse-I Chu),* and the *Electoral Law of the Provincial Assembly.* In order

[1] Another mission of less importance was sent out later to study the technical aspects of the constitutions in Japan, Germany, and England. This mission was composed of three persons: Ta Shou, Yu Shih-mei and Wang Ta-hsieh.

[2] See the Imperial Edict for Constitutional Preparations of September 1, 1906. The sources of all official documents referred to in this work can be found in the *Government Gazette* and various collections of laws and regulations. Unless specifically indicated otherwise, all can be found in William L. Tung, *The Government of China* (Shanghai: World Book Co., 1942, 2 vols.).

[3] For the English translation of *Principles of Constitution,* see Appendix A.

to know the overall picture of the constitutional movement in the late
Ch'ing dynasty, an analytical study of these documents is necessary.

4. THE PRINCIPLES OF CONSTITUTION, SEPTEMBER 22, 1908 [1]

Supreme power of the emperor

In September 1908, in compliance with the desires of the Imperial
Court, the Constitutional Research Bureau [2] presented to the Throne
the *Principles of Constitution* together with *Rights and Duties of the
People, Outlines of Parliamentary Procedures, Outlines of Electoral Law,*
and *The List of Annual Preparatory Work Prior to the Convening of
Parliament.* In its memorial, the Bureau emphasized that the constitution should come from the hands of the emperor and not from the
constitutional convention or parliament and specifically pointed out
the important points of a monarchial constitution:

> First, the sacred majesty of the sovereign shall not be offended against; second,
> the sovereign shall hold the supreme authority over the nation in accordance
> with the constitution; third, the rights and duties of the people shall be defined
> and guaranteed by law... Thus, in short, the constitution is that through which
> the rule of the sovereign is consolidated and the people are fully protected.[3]

It is clear that the major objective of this constitution was the
consolidation of the absolute rule of the sovereign. In the constitution,
phrases as "the sacred majesty of the sovereign" and "ten thousand
generations in succession" carried the tone of absolute monarchy. The
executive, legislative, and judicial powers all centered in the emperor.
On the other hand, the people's rights of freedom of speech, writing,
publication, assembly and association were mentioned scantily and
vaguely. As to the parliament, it was only an advisory organ to the
emperor for the enactment of laws which could not come into effect
without approval and promulgation by him. Although parliament could
impeach government officials for unlawful activities, it had no right
to interfere with their appointment and removal. Members of parliament did not even enjoy freedom of speech in parliament and could be
punished if they uttered abusive words against the throne. Furthermore, it was the emperor who had the authority to convene, adjourn,
postpone, and dissolve the parliament. Such provisions were obviously
in contrast to the parliamentary systems generally practiced in Europe

---

[1] August 27, according to Chinese traditional calendar.
[2] The Constitutional Research Bureau was reorganized from the Bureau for Political
Research, which was set up in October 1906, following the Japanese example.
[3] *Ta Ch'ing Kuang Hsü New Laws*, Vol. II, Sec. 1, pp. 25–27.

and America. In conclusion, the *Principles of Constitution* did not have the spirit of checks and balances on the basis of the separation of powers. It is important to note that, out of the twenty-three articles comprising the powers of the sovereign and the rights and duties of the people, seventeen were the same as those in the Japanese Constitution. But the latter had provisions restricting the power of the emperor and, in its application, resembled the constitutions of European and American countries. Such was definitely not the case with the *Principles of Constitution*.[1]

Delaying tactics of the Imperial Court

The *Principles of Constitution* and other subsidiary laws were only general outlines and principles for future drafting of the constitution, parliamentary procedures, and electoral laws. With respect to the preparatory period proceding the formal establishment of a constitutional monarchy, the Constitutional Research Bureau proposed that beginning with the year 1908 there should be a nine-year span of time for the organization of the National Legislative Council and the provincial assemblies, establishment of local self-government, enactment of laws, institution of courts, improvement of the economy, expansion of education, review of the census, enlargement of the police force.[2] But the general opinion at that time considered the nine-year program too long. The people's patience was limited. At the request of the National Legislative Council, the provincial assemblies, and the provincial governors, the Imperial Court finally proclaimed in October 1909 that parliament was to be convened in 1913, three years earlier than previously planned.

5. THE NATIONAL LEGISLATIVE COUNCIL (TSE-CHENG YUAN)

Establishment of the National Legislative Council

According to an imperial edict of September 20, 1907, there was to be established the National Legislative Council (Tse-cheng Yuan) to serve as the national legislative organ of the government. On July 22 of the following year, part of its organic law was drafted and approved by the throne.[3] By 1909, the *Organic Law of the National Legislative Council* and the *Electoral Law of the National Legislative Council* were ratified

---

[1] See Yang Yu-chiung, *Legislative History of Modern China*, pp. 55–56.
[2] For details, see *The List of Annual Preparatory Work Prior to the Convening of Parliament*.
[3] Ch. I on general principles and Ch. II on elections. See *Ta Ch'ing Kuang Hsü New Laws*, Vol. II, Sec. 1, p. 1.

by Emperor Hsüan T'ung, who succeeded to the throne in the same year.[1] The Council was formally convened in October 1910, with two hundred elective and appointed members, headed by a director-general and a deputy director-general in charge of routine administrative matters. Its primary objective was to function as the representative and legislative organ of the government during the transitional period and to lay down the foundation for the eventual creation of a two-chamber parliament to replace the present unicameral organ.

Functions of the National Legislative Council

The Council had jurisdiction over legislation, taxation, national revenue and expenditure, and other matters as assigned by the emperor. It was charged to make recommendations to the throne for the settlement of disputes between the provincial assembly and the governor of a province or among the provincial assemblies. In cases where the grand councillors and the ministers of the various departments had been accused of abuse of authority or violation of laws, the Council was empowered, by a two-thirds majority, to place the charges against them before the throne. If an individual person wanted to make suggestions on state affairs, he could submit to the Council a memorial sponsored by a member of the Council from his same district.[2] Thus, in accordance with its organic law, the National Legislative Council was not only an advisory organ to the throne but also had certain independent powers. In practice, the government paid little attention to the resolutions and recommendations adopted by the Council.

Distribution of Council membership

The National Legislative Council had a total membership of two hundred, with a minimum age limit of thirty, chosen from the following groups: 48 from the royal families and nobilities, 32 from among government officials, 10 well-known scholars, 10 from among the top taxpayers, and 100 from the provincial assemblies of all provinces. Strictly speaking, this last group of 100 could not be regarded as popularly elected because the governors of the provinces made the final selection from those elected by the members of the provincial assemblies. Council members from other groups were appointed by the emperor through a complicated process of nomination and recommendation.[3]

[1] They were promulgated on August 23 and October 26 respectively.
[2] See *Organic Law of the National Legislative Council*, Chs. 1, 3, 6.
[3] For details, see *Organic Law of the National Legislative Council*, Ch. 2 and also the *Electoral Law of the National Legislative Council*.

According to the intent of its electoral law, the Council was to be the foundation of the future upper house of parliament and yet retain some aspects of a lower house. This was fully explained in the memorial submitted by the Council to the throne on October 26, 1909.[1]

Relative merits of the Council

The distribution of seats and the complicated processes of election and selection of the members of the National Legislative Council were based on the practices of other countries with particular consideration of the domestic conditions in China at that time. Objectively speaking, there would have been many difficulties and abuses if direct and popular elections were held immediately. It would not be fair to say that the Manchus had not made a single move in the correct direction. Actually, during the reigns of emperors Kuang Hsü and Hsüan T'ung, there was some legislative work which deserves particular attention. It was true that, at the beginning, the Council could not function properly and freely in accordance with law. But, as time went by, it gradually commanded more respect from the government. As a matter of fact, the elected members soon assumed ascendancy in the Council which enacted *Rules governing Local Self-government* and the new Criminal Code. It should also be remembered that the Council petitioned the throne to shorten the preparatory period for constitutionalism and to adopt the cabinet system replacing the rule by the royal family. Last but not least, it prepared the historic *Nineteen Articles*. Thus due credit should be given to the National Legislative Council.

6. THE PROVINCIAL ASSEMBLY (TSE-I CHU)

Functions of the Provincial Assembly

According to the imperial edict of October 19, 1907, there was to be established a provincial assembly in each province as local representative organ. On July 22, 1908, the *Organic Law of the Provincial Assembly* and the *Electoral Law of the Provincial Assembly* were submitted by the Constitutional Research Bureau and ratified by the throne.

The chief objective of the provincial assembly was to deliberate and recommend to the provincial government important matters concerning public welfare and security in the province. Among its various functions were the following: deliberation and approval of annual

---

[1] *Ta Ch'ing Hsüan T'ung New Laws*, Vol. IX, pp. 13-14.

revenue and expenditure of the province, taxation, appropriation and budgeting, issuance of government bonds, enactment of rules and regulations, as well as matters concerning the welfare of the province and rights and duties of the people; replying to the inquires from the governor of the province and the National Legislative Council; arbitration in disputes among local self-government associations; and also acceptance of petitions from such associations or individual persons. However, no decision adopted by the provincial assembly could come into effect without the approval of the governor. If the governor did not agree with certain assembly decisions, he could have them sent back, with his dissenting opinions, to the assembly. Should the assembly insist on its original resolution, the governor would have to send the matter over to the National Legislative Council for final settlement. In a province the governor was most important as he could suspend or even dissolve the provincial assembly under certain prescribed conditions. But the governor was by no means an autocrat in a province. The provincial assembly could bring charges against him in cases of violation of law or other controversies to the National Legislative Council.[1]

Relative merits of the Provincial Assembly

By the standards of present-day Western democracy, the provincial assembly established in the late Ch'ing dynasty was far from desirable. Voters for the election of the assembly members were limited to native born male citizens of the province twenty-five years of age. Besides the sex discrimination, there were property and educational requirements. The qualifications for candidates to assembly membership were, however, not very strict. Any male citizen who was born in the province or had been a resident there for at least ten years, being thirty years of age or above, was eligible. Members of the provincial assembly enjoyed special privileges and protection for their speeches and deliberations within the assembly, for which they were not held to be responsible outside of the assembly. Except for crimes committed at the time, they could not be arrested when the assembly was in session without its permission.[2] Taking all the factors into consideration, the institution of the provincial assembly was comparatively successful. After all, this was the first time in China that the people were granted the right to vote and to be elected through express provisions of law.

[1] *Organic Law of the Provincial Assembly*, Chs. 6, 8.
[2] *Ibid.*, Arts. 3, 5–8, 39–40.

Most of the members of the provincial assemblies were genuinely enthusiastic toward democracy. They were impatient because of the undue delay in the implementation of constitutional rule, and soon organized a "Society of Petitioners for the Establishment of Parliament." Three times the Society sent delegates to Peking to make such a petition to the throne, which consequently issued an imperial edict in November 1909, shortening the preparatory period of constitutionalism as previously mentioned. Among the delegates were many distinguished citizens from various provinces, including Chang Chien, Sun Hung-yi, T'an Yen-k'ai, Tong Hua-lung, and Pu Dien-chun. Pu was one of the first to initiate the movement opposing the government's "Railway Nationalization" project in the province of Szechwan, where he was president of the provincial assembly.[1] This movement turned out to be the forerunner of the Wuchang revolution, which resulted in the establishment of the Chinese Republic in 1912.

7. THE BEGINNING OF LOCAL SELF-GOVERNMENT

Enactment of rules and regulations for local self-government

Rudimentary systems of local self-government could be traced in ancient China as early as the Chou dynasty. Further development occurred during the Han and Sung dynasties, whence the basic units of China's local autonomy had always been the *Pao* and *Chia*. The number of families which constituted such units varied at different times. Yet the modern type of local self-government only emerged in the last years of the Ch'ing dynasty. The imperial edict of August 1908 prescribing the nine-year program for constitutionalism ordered that the system of local self-government be completed within seven years so as to establish the foundation for constitutional rule. On January 18, 1909, two important documents were promulgated by the government toward that end: *Regulations for Local Self-Government in Cities, Towns and Villages* and *Electoral Rules for Local Self-Government in Cities, Towns and Villages*. Then, one year later, there followed *Regulations for Local Self-Government in Counties and Districts* and *Electoral Rules for Legislative Councils of Counties and Districts*. In view of the special status of the national capital, Peking, where ordinary rules and regulations could not be suitably applied, the government enacted

---

[1] In each provincial assembly, there were one president, two vice-presidents, and a certain number of resident members elected from the assembly members. They were in charge of the routine administrative matters of the assembly.

separately the *Regulations for Local Self-Government in the Imperial Capital* and the *Electoral Rules for Local Self-Government in the Imperial Capital*.[1] The difference in local self-government between the Imperial Capital and other cities were mainly in organization and supervision; otherwise they were similar in most respects. The above documents contained detailed provisions concerning matters on local autonomy and, therefore, could be considered as the foundation for future codification and elaboration of the rules and regulations governing local self-government in China. But the scope of functions and powers of the local autonomous units was extremely narrow, with public welfare as their main concentration, acting more or less as a subsidiary organ of the local government. Thus the sincerity of the Imperial Court in regard to the local self-governing system was seriously questioned.[2]

Self-government in cities, towns and villages

According to the prevailing laws at that time, any territorial unit that had a population over 50,000 was called "town" and those below this figure, "village." A "city" was a large "town" where a higher level government was located. In each of the cities, towns and villages, there was a legislative council as the local legislature. Its executive body was the board of trustees in cities and towns and the trustee in villages. The council members were elected from among the local citizens who met the qualifications as prescribed by law, for a term of two-years. Each council had a chairman and a deputy chairman in charge of routine matters. The council was empowered to deliberate on the following: (1) self-governing regulations and other local projects of importance, (2) collection and disposition of funds for local autonomy, and (3) punishment of employees of self-government units and settlement of electoral disputes.

City and town board of trustees had one chairman, one to three board members, and four to twelve honorary members. All were elected by the city or town legislative councils, for a term of two years. In the case of the chairman, the council was required to submit two names to the governor of the province for his final selection and appointment. The board members had to be approved by the local government before they could assume office. In practice, only the honorary members could be elected directly and independently by the council. The functions of

[1] Promulgated on February 3, 1910. For texts, see *Ta Ch'ing Hsüan T'ung New Laws*, Vol. XIII, pp. 3–22.

[2] For opinions of the Constitutional Research Bureau on local self-government, see *Ta Ch'ing Kuang Hsü New Laws*, Vol. II, Sec. 1, pp. 2–3.

the board of trustees covered four aspects: (1) election of council members and preparation for council meetings, (2) execution of matters decided by the council, (3) execution and administration of matters authorized by the local laws and regulations or ordered by the local government, and (4) deliberation of the ways and means for the execution of the above. In the villages, there were one village trustee and one deputy trustee, elected from among the native villagers by the village council and approved by the local government for a term of two years. Their functions were the same as those of the city and town boards as listed under (1)–(3). The local governments of the cities, towns and villages supervised the respective self-governing units and could, when necessary, make recommendations to the governor for the dissolution of the councils and the boards of trustees, as well as the removal of their employees.

Self-government in counties and districts

The system of local self-government during the Ch'ing dynasty was of two levels: cities, towns and villages as the lower level and counties and districts as the upper. The legislature of the upper level selfgoverning units was composed of a legislative council and a consultative council; and the local governments of the same units acted as the executive organs. The members of the legislative council were elected from the qualified candidates as prescribed by law, their number being in proportion to the population. The legislative council had a president and a vice-president whose term of office was three years, the same as that of the council members. The important functions of the legislative council were to deliberate on local autonomy finances, matters that should but could not be settled by the lower level councils, and other matters within its jurisdiction in accordance with law.

The consultative council had the head of the local government of the same area as its president. The members of the consultative council were elected by the legislative council from among the members of the latter for a term of three years. The functions of the consultative council were as follows: (1) deliberation of ways and means for the execution of matters decided by the legislative council and their order of priority, matters transferred by the legislative council, and those authorized by the local government; (2) review of the matters submitted by the local government to the legislative council for its deliberation; (3) consultation and decision on matters involving conciliation and law suits of the area; (4) arbitration of disputes concerning the local autonomy powers of cities, towns and villages; and (5) other matters properly under its jurisdiction by provisions of law.

Here the two councils were bicameral in nature. In spite of the wide scope of their functions, the head of the local government held the supreme power in the area. Whatever decisions might be made by the councils, he could either send them back for reconsideration or even nullify them if he deemed that such decisions had exceeded the authority of the councils or violated the existing laws and regulations. Furthermore, the local self-government in counties and districts was under the supervision of the governor of the province concerned and was also responsible to the related ministries of the central government. Thus the system of local self-government as practiced in China at that time had a long way to go to equal the Western standard of democracy.

8. THE REVOLUTION AND THE NINETEEN ARTICLES OF NOVEMBER 3, 1911

Successive revolutionary uprisings

As stated before, it was no secret that the Imperial Court had no sincere intention to relinquish its absolute rule in favor of constitutional monarchy. Thus dissatisfaction had been growing among the populace. Dr. Sun and his revolutionary followers had never relaxed their efforts to organize armed uprisings against the Manchu regime. During the period of 1907–1909, six uprisings were organized by the Special Committee of the revolutionists in the provinces of Kwangtung, Kwangsi and Yunnan. Dr. Sun undertook the general direction of revolutionary activities at the headquarters in Hanoi. Huang Hsing, an eminent revolutionary strategist and later Minister of War of the Provisional Government at Nanking, became the director of operations.[1] Although these struggles resulted in failures, they were extremely effective as political demonstrations against the Ch'ing dynasty.

Owing to the unsuccessful attempts, Wang Ching-wei, another important revolutionist, was so discouraged that he decided to find a quick way of overthrowing the emperor. He went to Peking and there he and Huang Fu-sheng attempted to assassinate the Manchu Regent. But the *coup* was foiled and they were arrested.[2] After many defeats, Dr. Sun was barred from French Indochina, from Hongkong, and in

---

[1] For a full description of Huang Hsing's contribution to the Chinese revolution, see Chün-tu Hsüeh, *Huang Hsing and the Chinese Revolution* (Stanford University Press, 1961).*
[2] Both were released after the Wuchang Revolution.

fact, from all places that were near China. Since he had no way of making connections with China, he entrusted all the revolutionary work in China to Huang Hsing and Hu Han-min, one of the most active leaders of the party. Dr. Sun then made another world tour to conduct a financial campaign in the interest of the revolution. Having secured sufficient funds chiefly from overseas Chinese, the revolutionists decided to proceed with their struggles at once. On March 29, 1911, an insurrection was launched at Canton, where the best of the revolutionists gathered to fight what they felt was to be the decisive battle with their enemy. As a result, seventy-two patriots were slain.[1] Their sacrifices for the country had startled the world into realization that the revolution in China had far-reaching significance.

After the collapse of the March 29 Revolution at Canton, the party members turned their attention to Wuhan. The revolutionary atmosphere in the country was already so thick that the Manchu officials were constantly in a state of terror. When a riot broke out in Szechwan as a result of the contest between the local leaders and the government in connection with the Hukuang-Szechwan Railway Loan and the nationalization decree, several regiments from the Hupei province had to be transferred there to suppress the revolt. The situation was very tense. At the same time, the headquarters of the Revolutionary Party in Wuhan were raided and thirty members were arrested. In order to save themselves, the revolutionists decided to take desperate action, with Li Yüan-hung as their temporary commander.[2] On the night of the tenth of October, 1911, they attacked Wuchang and bombarded the office of the provincial viceroy. After the defeat of the imperial forces, the viceroy and the Manchu military commander fled for their lives. On October 12, Hankow and Hanyang fell before the revolutionary army. In a few months, most of the provinces had declared their independence and joined the Revolution.

Demand for immediate constitutional rule

The news of the Wuchang revolution shocked the Imperial Court, which immediately called an emergency session of the National Legislative Council for the discussion of effective measures to save the situation. The majority of the council members demanded that the

---

[1] They were later buried in the famous historical place Huang-hua Kong. The day of March 29 had been designated by the Nationalist Government as the Memorial Day of China.

[2] Li, being a colonel in the Imperial Army, was not a member of the revolutionary organization. While waiting for Huang Hsing, who only arrived on October 20, the revolutionists induced Li to be their temporary leader.

royal cabinet be dissolved, that popular support for constitutional preparation be secured, that political prisoners be pardoned, and that the convocation of parliament be accelerated. All these were accepted by the Court. The Emperor also issued an edict of self-censure on October 30. But the revolution gained momentum and many provinces responded.

Chang Shao-tseng, Commander of the Imperial Army in Luanchow, and his deputy Lan Tien-wei cabled the Court a constitutional draft of twelve articles with the demand for its adoption. In an eleventh hour struggle, the Manchu regime took positive action. The National Legislative Council was ordered to draft a constitution. On November 2, the Council presented the hurriedly prepared *Nineteen Articles (Shih-chiu hsin-t'iao)* to the throne and they were formally promulgated the next day.[1] On November 26, the Emperor and the Prince Regent went to the Imperial Ancestral Temple to take oath that they would join the people in abiding forever by the letter and spirit of the *Nineteen Articles*.[2]

Essentials of the Nineteen Articles

The contents of the *Nineteen Articles* were quite different from the *Principles of Constitution* of 1908. According to the new constitution, the throne would have limited powers and the government would be in the form of the cabinet system. No Imperial Princes should be eligible as premier, cabinet ministers or administrative heads of provinces. The legislature would be composed of two chambers, with the National Legislative Council as the upper house and the National Assembly as the lower. The drafting and adoption of the constitution belonged to the power of the Council, while its amendment was within the jurisdiction of the Assembly. Thus the constitution was no longer granted by the throne as in the case of the previous constitution. Although the Emperor had the power of the declaration of war and conclusion of peace if the Assembly was not in session, the approval of the latter would have to be obtained afterwards. While still assuming direct control of the army and navy, the Emperor could not use these forces for internal purposes except under conditions specifically laid down by the National Assembly. In the case of the budget and the conclusion of treaties, the consent of the Assembly had to be secured. All these provisions were, in general, similar to the British parliamentary system.

---

[1] For its English translation, see Appendix B.

[2] See Li Chien-nung, *The Political History of China, 1840–1928* (Shanghai: Pacific, 1930), pp. 193–194. Here the Emperor was Hsüan T'ung (P'u Yi), who succeeded to the throne in 1908 when both Empress Dowager and Emperor Kuang Hsü died.

With regard to the relationship between the National Assembly and the Premier it was not completely satisfactory. The Assembly had the power of impeaching the Premier, but there was no provision for votes of nonconfidence as practiced in many countries with a cabinet system.

Generally speaking, the *Nineteen Articles* was a timely product which kept pace with the political currents of the world. It would be safe to say that had they been enacted and enforced ten years earlier, the tragedy of the forced abdication of the throne might have been avoided in 1912.

The overthrow of the Ch'ing dynasty

After the promulgation of the *Nineteen Articles*, the National Legislative Council, in pursuance of its eighth article, elected Yüan Shih-k'ai as Premier of the new cabinet. An extremely capable and ambitious military leader in the North, Yüan had then become a dominant figure in the country because he controlled both the army and the administration of the Imperial government. As soon as he assumed office, Yüan sent T'ang Shao-i to Shanghai to negotiate with Wu Ting-fang, the representative of the revolutionary forces. At that time, Dr. Sun was still abroad. When the Wuchang Revolution was taking place, he had just arrived at Denver, Colorado. Having learned the news, he immediately left for London to conduct diplomatic negotiations with the British government. He arrived in Shanghai on December 25. The negotiations between T'ang and Wu did not reach any fruitful conclusion because they could not agree on the form of the future government.

At that time, Tuan Ch'i-jui and several other army leaders of the Ch'ing dynasty made a joint declaration in support of the establishment of a republican form of government. Realizing that all hopes of turning the tide had vanished and that the imperial throne could not be kept any longer, the Manchu regime decided to obtain the best terms as it could from the revolutionary forces to guarantee the rights and privileges of the royal family. On February 12, 1912, the Emperor abdicated. His proclamation reads in part:

Since the revolution has spread over many provinces and brought much turmoil and suffering to the people, the government has instructed Yüan Shih-k'ai to negotiate with the representative of the revolutionary forces on matters of supreme importance concerning the convocation of parliament and a settlement on the form of government. Two months having passed, no agreement had been reached... As first declared by the Southern provinces and later supported by the military leaders in the North, the republican form of government is now the prevailing idea of the nation... And how can I, for the glory of one family, turn against the public opinion? [1]

Thenceforth the rule of the Ch'ing dynasty was ended and a new republic was established. Dr. Sun Yat-sen considered that the revolution of 1911 had brought about two important consequences in Chinese history: first, with the end of the domination of the Manchus in the country for the past two hunderd and sixty years, the equality of all races in China could be reassured; and second, the four-thousand-year old monarchial system was eliminated and replaced by a republic. [2]

With respect to the major factors contributing to the success of the revolution in 1911, it must be emphasized that the revolutionary ideas played a larger part than the armed forces. When people are desperate, they accept any kind of change. A revolution is the radical change of a regime by force. This was the situation in China in the early years of the twentieth century when the people were utterly disgusted with the Manchu regime of its suppression, discrimination, corruption, and inefficiency. Above all, as decendants from the Middle Kingdom which had been supreme in the Asiatic Mainland for four thousand years, the Chinese intellectuals could not adjust themselves to the successive humiliations from the foreign Powers since the 1840's. Through wars, threat of force, and diplomatic tricks, Japan and several Western powers had compelled China to cede and lease immense territories, pay heavy indemnities, accept extraterritoriality and uniform tariff, acquiesce in the spheres of influence, grant political and economic concessions, open ports to foreign shipping and trade, allow the stationing of foreign troops in certain areas, and conclude various unequal treaties against her territorial integrity and national sovereignty. All these happened during the latter part of the Ch'ing dynasty. Without the vigorous declaration of the Open Door Policy by the United States and the rivalries among the foreign Powers themselves, China would have been in an absolutely helpless position. A regime which disregarded the welfare of the people and suffered unceasing humiliations from without was bound to fail. So this was the destiny of the Ch'ing dynasty. [3]

---

[1] For its text, see *Government Gazette*, January, 1912.

[2] *The Collected Works of Sun Yat-sen*, Vol. IV, "A History of the Chinese Revolution," p. 10.

[3] Although it is out of the scope of this work to discuss China's foreign relations in detail, it is important to make a brief description of those directly involving her national destiny and people's interests and thus indirectly affecting her constitutional and governmental systems.

The following are important examples of China's national humiliations during the latter part of the Ch'ing dynasty:

(a) Sino-British War, 1839–1842, also known as the Opium War. Result: cession of Hong-kong, opening of five ports to foreign shipping, extraterritoriality, uniform tariff, indemnity, etc.

It should be noted that most of the rights and privileges obtained by one nation could be applicable to the others through the provision of most-favored-nation clause.

(b) Joint War of Great Britain and France against China, 1857. Result: opening of eleven new ports, navigation of the Yangtze River by foreign ships, fixing of internal transit duties, etc.

(c) Sino-Russian Treaty of Aigun, 1858. Result: cession to Russia territories north of the Amur River to its mouth.

(d) Sino-Russian Treaty of November 14, 1860. Result: cession of the territory between the Ussuri River and the Sea.

(e) First Sino-Japanese War, 1894–1895. Result: recognition of Korea's independence from China; cession of Formosa and the Pescadores, heavy indemnity, opening of four new ports to foreign shipping and trade, etc.

(f) Sino-Russian Treaty of 1896. Result: concession to Russia of the right to build the Chinese Eastern Railway in Manchuria. This can be grouped under (i) concessions. But, due to its extreme importance in the future relations among China, Japan and Russia, it is separately listed here.

(g) Leased territories: started by Germany with the lease of Kiaochow in 1898 for 99 years; followed by the lease of Port Arthur and Dairen to Russia for 25 years, Weihaiwei to England for 25 years, and Kwangchow Bay to France for 99 years, etc.

(h) Spheres of influence: England—Yangtze Valley; Germany—Shantung; Russia—Northern Manchuria and Inner Mongolia; Japan—Fukien; France—Yunnan, Kweichow and Kwangsi.

(i) Concessions: under different circumstances, China was compelled to grant various political and economic concessions to foreign Powers, including railway construction, mining exploitation, foreign settlements in Shanghai and other cities, etc. The more important was the delimitation of boundaries in favor of Russia along the Manchurian border, France along the Chinese-Annam border, and England along the Burma border.

(j) Russo-Japanese War, 1904–1905. Result: use of Chinese territory as the theatre of war, transfer of Russian acquisitions in Manchuria to Japan without China's consent, etc.

(k) Treaty of January 16, 1900, between China and the Allied Powers as a result of the Boxer Uprising. Result: heavy indemnity, suspension of civil service examinatian for five years in Boxer Uprising areas, prohibition of importing arms for at least two years, etc.

For further details, consult H. S. Morse, *The International Relations of the Chinese Empire** (New York: Longmans, Green, & Co., 1910/1918, 3 vols.); Scott Nearing, *Whither China?** (New York: International Publishers, 1927); and William L. Tung, *Imperialism and China* (Shanghai: Kuan-min Press, 1929), Pt. II.

DEMOCRACY IN EXPERIMENT: POLITICAL INSTITUTIONS DURING THE EARLY REPUBLICAN PERIOD

I. PREPARATIONS FOR A PROVISIONAL GOVERNMENT

Representative conference of the military governors

The revolution in Wuchang had inflamed many provinces. A need to discuss matters of vital importance and common interest created an increasing demand for a temporary organization to be set up in a centrally located place such as Shanghai. On November 11, 1911, Ch'eng Teh-chuan and Tong Shou-ch'ien, military governors of Kiangsu and Chekiang respectively, made a joint suggestion to that effect to Ch'en Chi-mei, the military governor of Shanghai. According to their proposal, the military governors of the provincial governments and the provincial assemblies would send one representative each to Shanghai for a conference. Prompt action was taken the following day by the representatives of Kiangsu and Chekiang through a circular telegram to the various provincial authorities. On November 15, the Representative Conference of the Military Governors held its first meeting; and, five days later, it reached a decision to recognize Wuchang as the seat of the Central Military Government of the Republic, headed by the military governor of Hupei province.

Drafting of the Organic Law of the Provisional Government

However, in the view of Li Yüan-hung, then miliatry governor of Hupei, there should be a provisional government in Wuchang to take charge of the rapidly developing affairs of state. Thus he urged the provincial authorities to send one representative from each province to Wuchang to discuss the matter. Chü Chêng and other representatives from Hupei went to Shanghai and made the same appeal to the representative conference of the military governors, which agreed to this proposal on November 24. Unfortunately, the military situation in the triple cities of Wuhan was not altogether favorable to the revolutionary forces. Hanyang had been recaptured by the Manchu army and Wuchang was under its artillery fire. Thus Hankow was temporarily chosen as the seat of the conference of the provincial representatives. At it first meeting on November 30, the conference elected T'an Jen-fung as chairman. It then proceeded to discuss the organization of a provisional government, and appointed, on December 2, Lui Fan, Ma Chun-wu and Wang Cheng-ting to draft its organic law. The draft was prepared on December 3 and was immediately adopted by the conference.[1] It became the Organic Law of the Republic of China, which was later revised on January 2, 1912.

2. ANALYSIS
OF THE ORGANIC LAW OF THE PROVISIONAL GOVERNMENT

The Executive Branch

Different from a constitution, this Organic Law only dealt with the basic features of the organization of the Provisional Government. As it was prepared in such a hurried manner, shortcomings were unavoidable. Originally there was no provision for the office of Vice Presidency, which was added when the *Organic Law of the Provisional Government* was revised on January 2, 1912. The Provisional Government was based on the presidential system, with the Provisional President as its executive. The Provisional Vice President was to perform the functions of the President if the latter was for any reason removed from office or unable to carry out his responsibilities. Both were elected by the Representative Conference of the Military Governors by a majority of two-thirds of the total ballots cast, each province having one vote. While this was not in keeping with democratic principles, it was only a temporary measure prior to the establishment of a formal government.

The executive power of the Provisional President was very wide in scope. He was the Commander-in-Chief of all the armed forces of the country. He had the power to ordain and establish the administrative system and official regulations. With the consent of the Legislative Assembly, he could declare war, make peace, conclude treaties, and set up judicial courts. His power of appointment of civil and military

[1] The *Organic Law of the Provisional Government* was signed by twenty-two representatives from the following ten provinces: Hupei, Shantung, Fukien, Hunan, Anhwei, Kwangsi, Chekiang, Kiangsu, Chihli, and Honan.

officials was practically unlimited except for that of diplomatic envoys and cabinet ministers. In the latter case, the approval of the Legislative Assembly was required. Under the direction and control of the Provisional President were nine departments, each headed by a cabinet minister: army, navy, foreign affairs, justice, finance, interior, education, industry, and communications.[1] These nine departments were actually established after the inauguration of the Provisional Government even though not specifically provided for in the revised organic law. Through the use of the Council of State Affairs, composed of the Provisional President and the ministers, they could deliberate together on matters of importance and mutual interest. This was a useful system not only from an administrative point of view but also for purposes of policy making.

The Legislative Branch

The legislative organ of the Provisional Government was the unicameral Legislative Assembly, consisting of one to three representatives from each province. Although the procedure of selecting the Assembly members was within the competence of each province, it generally followed three patterns: (1) appointment by the military governors of the provinces, (2) recommendation by the provincial asemblies, and (3) popular election. The adoption of the first two methods was probably due to the circumstances of that time. Even so, only ten provinces had been able to send representatives to the Legislative Assembly at the time of its formal convocation on January 28, 1912. The presiding officer of the Legislative Assembly was the Speaker, elected from the Assembly members by a majority of the votes cast. There was no specific provision in the Organic Law concerning the quorum of the Assembly.

Thr Legislative Assembly had a variety of functions similar to those of the legislatures of other countries. The following were more important: (1) to decide the matters within the jurisdiction of the Provisional President but requiring its approval; (2) to decide the budget of the Provisional Government, unified legislation on taxation, the currency system, public loans, and other laws and regulations during the transitional period; (3) to investigate the revenue and expenditure of the Provisional Government; and (4) to decide matters

---

[1] For details concerning the establishment of the Departments and their functions, see the *Central Executive Departments and Their Functions of the Provisional Government of the Republic of China, Government Gazette of the Provisional Government*, January 30, 1912.

submitted to it and to answer inquiries made by the Provisional President. The Provisional President could, with stated reasons, request the Legislative Assembly to reconsider its bills within ten days of their passage. However, if two-thirds of the Assembly members present voted for the original bills, he had to proclaim and execute them as laws without delay. This provision, similar to the American constitution, gave the Chief Executive an opportunity to question the measures adopted by the Legislative Assembly, and yet, at the same time, left the power of final decision to the legislative branch of the government.

3. INAUGURATION OF THE PROVISIONAL GOVERNMENT AT NANKING

Dr. Sun's diplomacy for the new Republic

When the *coup d'etat* at Wuchang took place, the United States and France were sympathetic toward the Chinese Revolution. On the other hand, Germany, Russia and Japan were not favorable to the new Republic. The attitude of the British Government was undefined. Dr. Sun felt that the key of diplomacy was Great Britain, which would determine in large measure the policy of her ally, Japan. He therefore hastened to England from the United States and laid three demands before the British Government: (1) to stop all loan negotiations with the Manchu government, (2) to prevent Japan from giving assistence to the Manchu government, and (3) to revoke all orders excluding him from British territory so that he might travel freely and return to China. The British Government acceded to all these demands. Meantime, Dr. Sun also held a preliminary conference with the president of the Consortium at London concerning the negotiation of loans to the new Republic and stopping further loan negotiations with the Manchu government. Having finished his diplomatic work in England, Dr. Sun started home by way of France.

Formal establishment of the Provisional Government

Before the Provisional Government was organized, the nation's military and political affairs were directed by Li Yüan-hung and Huang Hsing whose titles were Grand Marshall and Deputy Grand Marshall respectively. When Nanking fell into the revolutionary hands, the provincial representatives decided to choose this city as the nation's capital. The arrival of Dr. Sun Yat-sen in Shanghai on December 25, 1911, provided the leadership the revolutionary forces urgently needed.

The convention for the election of the Provisional President was called on December 29 in Nanking, attended by forty-five delegates representing seventeen provinces. Each province was to vote as one unit and had therefore one vote. Out of the seventeen votes, sixteen went to Dr. Sun who was thus elected Provisional President. On January 1, 1912, Dr. Sun began his term of office, assuming immediate charge of state affairs. Li Yüan-hung was unanimously elected Provisional Vice President on January 3, 1912, when the *Organic Law of the Provisional Government* was revised to provide for that office. On January 5, a Republican Manifesto was issued emphasizing the respect of treaty obligations and protection of foreign lives and property as the policy of the new Republic.

Prior to its convocation, the functions of the Legislative Assembly had been performed by the Representative Conference of the Military Governors. As mentioned before, the Legislative Assembly was formally instituted on January 28, 1912. Lin Sen and Wang Cheng-ting were elected as chairman and vice chairman of the Assembly respectively. From this time on, the government was beginning to take shape and the foundation of the young Republic had been firmly laid.

4. THE PROVISIONAL CONSTITUTION OF THE REPUBLIC OF CHINA (CHUNG-HUA MIN-QUO LIN-SHIH YUEH-FA), MARCH 11, 1912

Drafting of the Provisional Constitution

Any fundamental law of state should include a bill of rights, but none was stipulated in the *Organic Law of the Provisional Government*. As Parliament was to be convoked in six months, the Legislative Assembly had not had time to deliberate and formulate a permanent constitution within such a short period. It thus decided to revise the *Organic Law* into a *Provisional Constitution*. Meantime, Dr. Sun, as Provisional President, presented to the Legislative Assembly for consideration a new *Draft of the Organic Law of the Provisional Government of the Republic of China*.[1] But the majority of the Assembly members wanted to do the work by themselves, so they sent back Dr. Sun's draft without discussion on January 31. On February 7, the Legislative Assembly set up a committee to draft the *Provisional Constitution* which was hurriedly completed on March 8 and promulgated by the

[1] For its text, see Kuo Shao-chen, *A Complete History of the Chinese Revolution*, Pt. III, pp. 185–190; also the *Minutes of the Legislative Assembly* (Nanking), January 31, 1912.

Provisional President on March 11.[1] This was a very important document in China's constitutional history. It was for the purpose of supporting the *Provisional Constitution* and restoring the Parliament that a series of political and military campaigns took place under the leadership of Dr. Sun against Yüan Shih-k'ai and other warlords in the North.

Comparison between the Provisional Constitution and the Organic Law of the Provisional Government

There were seven chapters consisting of fifty-six articles to the *Provisional Constitution*, which was evidently a more comprehensive and better prepared document than the preceding *Organic Law of the Provisional Government*. The most outstanding differences between these two documents were as follows: (1) The *Provisional Constitution* had a chapter on the rights of the people which was not included in the *Organic Law*. (2) The *Organic Law* adopted the presidential system while the *Provisional Constitution* introduced the cabinet system. It was reported that Dr. Sun would resign from the Provisional Presidency so as to recommend Yüan Shih-k'ai to be his successor. The leaders of the revolutionary party, the Kuomintang, at the Legislative Assembly were alarmed by this report. Their apprehension in this matter was the primary factor of the above change. The cabinet system was therefore proposed as a precautionary measure to prevent Yüan from becoming a dictator. (3) As to the number of Assembly members sent by the provinces, the *Provisional Constitution* provided five instead of a maximum of three in the *Organic Law*. (4) The Legislative Assembly was empowered by the Provisional Constitution to impeach the Provisional President and the cabinet members and to investigate any alleged bribery or infringement of law by officials. There was no such provision in the *Organic Law*. (5) According to the *Provisional Constitution*, the Judiciary would try civil and criminal cases, but cases involving administrative affairs or arising from other particular causes would be dealt with according to special laws. The *Organic Law* failed to make such a distinction; neither did it have, as in the *Provisional Constitution*, an explicit stipulation to guarantee the independence of the Judiciary. On all five points stated above, the *Provisional Constitution* was a much more desirable document than the *Organic Law*.

---

[1] For the English translation of the *Provisional Constitution*, see Appendix C.

Comparison between the Provisional Constitution and Dr. Sun's Draft of a new Organic Law of the Provisional Government

There were also some important differences between the *Provisional Constitution* and the defunct *Draft of the Organic Law of the Provisional Government* as submitted by Dr. Sun to the Legislative Assembly. The following were the important ones: (1) The *Draft* provided that Parliament be convened in one year instead of ten months as prescribed in the *Provisional Constitution*. (2) According to the *Draft*, the Provisional President was to be elected by the convention of local representatives; while the *Provisional Constitution* assigned the function to the Legislative Assembly. (3) Although both documents adopted the cabinet system, the Provisional President had more power according to the *Draft*. (4) Unlike the *Provisional Constitution*, the *Draft* proposed that, in addition to the Legislative Assembly, the Government should establish the Examination, Control, Auditing, and Administrative *Yuan*,[1] a kind of stereotype of the later system of five-power government expounded by Dr. Sun. (5) The power of impeachment of the Legislative Assembly was applicable to the Provisional President and cabinet members according to the *Provisional Constitution*, but it was only limited to cabinet members in the *Draft*. (6) The *Draft* stipulated that every province could depute three members to the Legislative Assembly, while the *Provisional Constitution* extended the number to five.[2] Despite these differences in the two documents, the real reason behind the Legislative Assembly's rejection of Dr. Sun's proposed *Draft* was to maintain the prestige and independence of the legislative body in the government.

Evaluation of the Provisional Constitution

It is the essence of the cabinet system that the head of state should not exercise his executive power independent of his cabinet. According to the *Statute of the Cabinet* of June 26, 1912,[3] the promulgation and issuance of laws and decrees by the Provisional President were to be countersigned by the Premier or Ministers concerned or both. On principle, this was quite correct. But, if the President was strong in personality and influence, the members nominated by him would generally be subservient to his wishes. However, the Legislative Branch

---

[1] A *Yuan* in the Chinese government may consist of a number of ministries or departments.

[2] See Chen Ju-hsuan, *The Constitutional History of China*, pp. 35–36.

[3] It was supplemented by the *General Regulations of the Various Ministries* promulgated on July 18, 1912. As to the detailed organizations of the different Ministries, see *The Collection of Laws and Decrees* (Peking: Government Printing Office, 1912), No. 1, Sect. 5.

could influence his nomination of cabinet members if it were controlled by a party other than the President's. In such event, there would be constant friction between the Executive and Legislative branches of the government. All these drawbacks were evidenced in the relationship between Yüan Shih-k'ai and his cabinet members and in that between Yüan and the Legislative Assembly which was dominated by the Kuomintang members.[1] Actually there are advantages and disadvantages to both the presidential system and the cabinet system, and it is impossible to make a generalization as to which one is superior to the other. All depend upon the particular background and circumstances of the country.

According to the *Rules of Procedure of the Legislative Assembly* promulgated on April 1, 1912, members of the Legislative Assembly were respectively assigned to the general committee or committee of the whole, standing committees, and special committees. This is a common parliamentary device for the acceleration of deliberations. The defect of the Legislative Assembly was that its members were equally divided according to geographical areas and not proportional to the population of the provinces. Another shortcoming was its lack of power of overthrowing the cabinet through a non-confidence vote, which was not exactly the same as the right of impeachment as provided in the *Provisional Constitution*. Nor was the cabinet empowered to dissolve the Legislative Assembly as generally practiced in Western democracies. The failure of such provisions in the *Provisional Constitution* enabled many ambitious militarists and political opportunists to resort to expedient means to solve their own problems whenever there was a deadlock between the executive and legislative branches of the government. Moreover, the *Provisional Constitution* should have paid special attention to establishing the foundation of local self-government and clarifying the relationship between the central and local governments concerning their respective powers and responsibilities. It was unfortunate that none of these points was stressed. This negligence had far-reaching consequences in the later development of China's political institutions.[2]

---

[1] For other reasons underlying the shifting from the presidential system to cabinet system, see Ku Chung-hsiu, *A History of the Establishment of the Chinese Republic*, Pt. III, Ch. 1.

[2] For Dr. Sun's comment, see *The Collected Works of Sun Yat-sen*, Vol. IV, "A History of the Chinese Revolution," p. 12.

5. THE CHANGE OF THE PROVISIONAL PRESIDENCY AND THE SEAT OF GOVERNMENT

Yüan's succession to the Provisional Presidency

After the outbreak of the Revolution, the Provisional Government in Nanking gradually controlled in one way or another most of China. But the situation was far from being stabilized. Yüan Shih-k'ai, the last premier of the Manchu regime, still commanded a strong army in North China and dispatched a formidable force to Central China to check the revolution. Yüan was neither loyal to the Ch'ing dynasty nor inclined to the democratic form of government. His ultimate aim was to consolidate power in his own hands. In order to induce Yüan to accept the Republican form of government and shorten the war, Dr. Sun intended to recommend him as his successor on the condition that Yüan would declare his allegiance to the new Republic. There was another reason why Dr. Sun wanted to give up the Presidency. He felt that the majority of his party comrades, now that immediate victory was in sight, had forgotton the implications of their revolutionary oath and were no longer willing to submit unquestioningly to his guidance. He maintained that there were three stages to the Revolution. It was then in its first stage, that of military government, which was to be continued until the country was completely pacified and the reactionary elements rooted out. Then there would be a period of political tutelage, which would eventually be followed by the constitutional stage when the people would be well trained to practice democracy. As it seemed impossible for him, as Provisional President, to carry out his task of revolutionary reconstruction, Dr. Sun decided to resign rather than to compromise himself and his ideals.

While the peace negotiations between the South and the North were in progress, Dr. Sun, in his capacity as Provisional President, proposed five conditions to Yüan Shih-k'ai on January 22, 1912. These were vital to the political future of China. (1) Yüan should inform the foreign diplomatic envoys in Peking about the abdication of the Ch'ing Emperor and request the envoys or the consular officers in Shanghai to forward the news to the Provisional Government in Nanking. (2) Yüan should immediately make known his political beliefs and his support of republicanism. (3) Dr. Sun would resign from the Provisional Presidency as soon as the abdication of the emperor could be confirmed through the above stated channel. (4) The Legislative Assembly would then elect Yüan as Provisional President.

(5) After being elected to the Provisional Presidency, Yüan would take an oath that he would abide by the *Provisional Constitution* before assuming his office.[1] To all these demands Yüan acceded. On February 12, 1912, Emperor Hsüan T'ung abdicated as the Manchu regime was practically deserted by Yüan and his followers. Dr. Sun therefore submitted his resignation to the Legislative Assembly the following day and recommended Yüan as his successor. On February 14, Yüan was formally elected by the Legislative Assembly as the second Provisional President of the Republic. After his resignation, Li Yüan-hung was re-elected as Provisional Vice President on February 20. This completed the process of the change of Provisional Presidency.

The move of the seat of government to Peking

After the election of the Provisional Presidency, the Legislative Assembly requested Yüan to come to the South to assume his office. The Provisional Government sent Wang Ching-wei and Ts'ai Yüan-p'ei to Peking to welcome him. Yüan did not, however, want to leave his strongholds in the North. Using the riots of the soldiers of the Third Army in Peking as an excuse, Yüan maintained that he had to stay in Peking to prevent the recurrence of similar incidents. As a result, the Legislative Assembly, on March 6, agreed that the Presidential inauguration be held in Peking and that Yüan was to send the nominations for Premier and cabinet ministers to the Legislative Assembly for approval. Yüan promptly appointed T'ang Shao-i as Premier to organize a cabinet of ten ministries: foreign affairs, interior, finance, army, navy, justice, education, agriculture, industry and commerce, and communications. In April of the same year, the Legislative Assembly accepted the invitation of the Government to move to Peking with the hope that all government organs would work together more harmoniously and efficiently.

6. THE ESTABLISHMENT OF PARLIAMENT

Its convocation and importance

After the Legislative Assembly resolved to move to the North, it first met in Peking on April 29, 1912, with an attendance of one hundred and thirteen members. Wu Ching-lien and Tong Hua-lung were newly elected as president and vice president of the Assembly respectively. According to Article 53 of the *Provisional Constitution*, within ten

---

[1] Yang Yu-chiung, *Legislative History of Modern China*, pp. 60–61.

months of the promulgation of the *Provisional Constitution*, the Provisional President was to convoke the Parliament, the organic and electoral laws of which were to be enacted by the Legislative Assembly. In pursuance of this provision, the Legislative Assembly adopted the *Organic Law of Parliament, Electoral Law of the House of Representatives*, and *Electoral Law of the Senate*, all of which were promulgated by the Provisional President on August 10, 1912.

After a few months of preparation, the members of Parliament were gradually elected from the various provinces. There were 596 Representatives and 274 Senators. The formal convocation of Parliament was held on April 8, 1913 in Peking. This was the first Western-type Parliament in Chinese history and also the first bicameral legislature in the Republic. Within its short span of life, this Parliament was dissolved twice, reconvened twice, assembled in different cities to escape political prosecution, and finally met its end when Tuan Chi-jui ordered its abolition in 1925. In his military and political campaigns against Yüan Shih-k'ai and the Peking government dominated by warlords, Dr. Sun considered the restoration of Parliament as one of his major purposes. Thus its importance to the political development of modern China can be easily conceived.

Powers and functions of Parliament

The *Organic Law of Parliament* prescribed that, prior to the adoption of the Constitution of the Republic, the powers and functions of Parliament should be the same as those of the Legislative Assembly.[1] Such legislative powers and functions may be grouped as follows: (1) to pass all bills, including budgets, laws of taxation, of currency and of weights and measures, as well as measures for the calling of public loans and concluding contracts; (2) to reply to inquiries from the government; (3) to make suggestions to the government on legal or other matters; (4) to receive and consider petitions of citizens; (5) to introduce interpellations of members of the cabinet; (6) to insist on the government investigating any alleged bribery and infringement of laws by officials; (7) to impeach the Provisional President and cabinet members according to prescribed procedures; and (8) to approve actions taken by the Provisional President, such as the appointment of cabinet members and diplomatic envoys, the declaration of war,

---

[1] Art. 14.

negotiation for peace, conclusion of treaties, and the grant of general amnesty.[1]

Since there were two chambers in the Parliament, its powers and functions could not be carried out exactly in the same way as in the unicameral Legislative Assembly. Thus the following matters could be performed by each chamber independently: (1) suggestions to the government, (2) interpellations of cabinet members, (3) insistence on government investigation of unlawful conduct of officials, (4) reply to government inquiries, (5) acceptance and consideration of people's petitions, (6) permission to arrest Parliament members, and (7) enactment of procedural rules and regulations of Parliament. As the House was more representative in nature, matters concerning budget and appropriation should be discussed there first.[2] As can be seen, Parliament, in the period of the early Republic, had really become an important force to check the Chief Executive; it thus invited his extreme jealousy resulting in its successive dissolutions and eventual abolition.

Distribution of the members of Parliament

Members of the Senate and the House of Representatives were chosen differently. First, the distribution of Senators was based on geographical divisions while that of Representatives, on the basis of proportion of population. Second, Senators were elected by the provincial assemblies while the Representatives were chosen through indirect election. Qualifications for members of both chambers were the same except that the minimum age limit for House Representatives was twenty-five years, five years less than that for Senators.

According to Article II of the *Organic Law of Parliament*, the Senate was to be constituted by members chosen from the following units: (1) 10 each from the provincial assemblies of the various provinces; (2) 27 from Mongolia; (3) 10 each from Tibet and Chinghai; (4) 8 from the Central Studies Association; and (5) 6 from the overseas Chinese communities. The overseas Chinese communities were not taken as one geographical unit because they were spread all over the world. The Central Studies Association was proposed as a research institute under the Ministry of Education, composed of graduates from universities and colleges and scholars with high academic achievements

---

[1] Arts. 19, 34, 35 and 40 of the *Provisional Constitution* of 1912.
[2] Art. 14 of the *Organic Law of Parliament*.

recognized by the Association.[1] However, the Central Studies Association was never established and the eight members apportioned to it were never sent to the Senate.

The election of the members of the House of Representatives was based upon the proportion of the population of the various provinces. There was to be one Representative for every 800,000 people. However, a province could still send a minimum of ten members to the House even though its population was less than eight million. Before the completion of a new census, the distribution of members of the House was to follow the provisions contained in Articles IV and V of the *Organic Law of Parliament*. The general process of electing members of the House was to go through two stages: preliminary election in districts and then final election in larger areas composed of several districts. The eligibility of voters and the qualifications of candidates were specified in the *Electoral Law of the House of Representatives*. Generally speaking, the laws and regulations governing the election of members of Parliament, promulgated in 1912, were more reasonable than the revisions of 1918, and also more liberal in comparison with the *Electoral Law of the Legislative Yuan* of 1914.

Composition of the two Chambers

There were 274 Senators and 596 Representatives elected to the Parliament. The term of office for Senators was six years, with one-third up for re-election every two years; the members of the House of Representatives were all elected for a term of three years. In each Chamber, there were one Speaker and one Deputy Speaker elected according to its respective rules of procedure. Their term of office was two years in the Senate and three years in the House of Representatives. The functions of the Speaker were to supervise the staff, preside over sessions, keep internal order within the chamber, serve as representative of the chamber, and take charge of other routine matters. If for any reason the Speaker could not perform his functions, the Deputy Speaker would then act in his place.

In order to simplify the process of deliberation and to insure efficiency, the two chambers created general committees or committees of the whole, standing committees, and special committees. While there were some differences between the standing committees in the Senate

---

[1] For details, see the *Constitution of the Central Studies Association*, (*Government Gazette*, November 30, 1912); and *Electoral Rules of the Central Studies Association* (*Government Gazette*, March 19, 1913).

and those in the House of Representatives, they were, in general, as follows: finance, legislation, interior affairs, foreign affairs, defense, communications, education, industry, budget, petitions, and punishment.[1] This committee system originally adopted from Western countries has worked well and has since been popular in various organizations and conferences in China.

Parliamentary procedures

Members of Parliament were to assemble in their respective chambers ten days in advance of regular or temporary sessions. The convening date of Parliament was to be proclaimed by the President of the Republic. Each regular session was to last four months but could be extended if necessary. Recess during sessions could not exceed fifteen days; and one chamber could not recess more than seven days without the agreement of the other. The Speaker could call the members back into session in case of emergency.

Although the two chambers of Parliament held their joint meetings at the time of opening and adjournment, each sat separately in transaction of its business. However, resolutions could only be reached by agreement of both. Any bill defeated in one chamber could not be introduced again in the other chamber during the same session. One bill could not be presented to both chambers at the same time. Furthermore, bills introduced by the government took precedence over those by the members of Parliament and were to be considered first.

The quorum for each chamber was a simple majority. Resolutions could be adopted by a simple majority of the members present under general conditions; in case of a tie, it could be broken by the Speaker. Matters of vital importance, including legislation and finance, had to go through the procedure of three readings. However, this requirement could be waived at the request of the government and on the motion of the Speaker or ten members of Parliament. If the two chambers differed on a certain bill, each would send an equal number of members to form a joint committee to consider the bill in question; and once a mutual agreement had been reached by the committee, it could not be altered by either of the two chambers.[2]

Comparison between the unicameral and bicameral systems in China

The Legislative Assembly at the beginning of the Chinese Republic

[1] For details, see Ch'ien Tuan-sheng, *et al.*, *History of Political Institutions Under the Republic*, Vol. I, pp. 58–61.

[2] For details, see *Rules of Procedure of the Parliament*, promulgated on September 27, 1913

was unicameral, but the Parliament established in 1913 adopted the bicameral system. Opinions differed as to which worked better in China. Perhaps neither has the absolute advantages even in other countries. Generally speaking, the bicameral system has the following merits: (1) to avoid careless legislation, (2) to prevent a single legislative body from becoming arrogant and ruthless, (3) to afford room for representatives from every class of the society and thus keep a balance of the conservative and radical influences, (4) to reduce the tension between the government and one chamber of the legislature through the good offices and mediation of the other, and (5) to harmonize the two representative systems of geographical divisions and population distribution. On the other hand, among the advantages of the unicameral system the following two are specifically pointed out by its advocates: (1) to avoid obstacles resulting from the complicated procedures of the bicameral system and thus improve the efficiency of legislation and save material and human resources, and (2) to eliminate the potentially dangerous situation caused by the checks and balances of the two chambers and thereby giving the government opportunity to manipulate the parliament. These are the reasons why many countries in recent years have adopted the unicameral system and, even in bicameral countries, the upper chambers have gradually lost their past importance. It was on the basis of these controversial arguments that China had changed from one system to another.

Of course, every country has a particular background and circumstances which contribute to the success and failure of certain systems. In China, the Legislative Assembly as practiced in the early days of the Republic, though single-chambered, did not reveal any of its major weaknesses. On the contrary, it did have some of the good attributes of the bicameral system. The first Parliament achieved, to a certain extent, the advantages of a bicameral system as stated under (3) and (5). It did not, however, prove useful in restoring harmony between the Executive and Legislative branches. For, according to later experience, whenever there were serious controversies between the government and Parliament, both chambers were usually dissolved by the Chief Executive. After all, the legislative body is only a part of the government, and, as such, it cannot transcend the political reality of the time. The proper functioning of the legislature depends not only on its own system, but also on the efficiency and cooperation of other government branches. Strictly speaking, the new Republic in China was democratic only in form. Ever since its beginning, the government had been dominated by Yüan Shih-k'ai. When the Chief Executive was satisfied with nothing less than dictatorial power, the smooth operation of the political principle of checks and balances could not be expected, unicameral or bicameral system of the legislature notwithstanding.

7. THE DRAFTING OF THE CONSTITUTION AND THE ELECTION OF PRESIDENT

Political alignments in Parliament

After the convocation of Parliament, members of both chambers held, on May 1, 1913, separate elections of speakers and deputy speakers. Chang Chi and Wang Cheng-ting, both members of the Kuomintang or the Nationalist Party, were elected Speaker and Deputy Speaker of the Senate respectively; while Tong Hua-lung and Ch'en Kuo-hsiang, both members of the Progressive Party, were elected Speaker and Deputy Speaker of the House of Representatives respectively. At that time, the Nationalist Party and the Progressive Party were the two major political parties in the Parliament. The Progressive Party was a combination of the Republican Party, the United Party, and the Democratic Party. It was the party allied with Yüan Shih-k'ai even though it was a minority in Parliament. Its major policy was in favor of the centralization of the national government and the expansion of the power of the President, all of which well suited the ambition of Yüan Shih-k'ai. In opposition, the Nationalist Party, with an overwhelming majority in Parliament, laid emphasis on the power of the provincial and local governments.

While most of the small political parties in the early days of the Republic were insignificant in China's political arena, it is necessary to trace the reasons for the formation of the Nationalist Party and its relationship with Yüan Shih-k'ai in order to understand the political development during that period. Immediately after his resignation from the Provisional Presidency, Dr. Sun Yat-sen urged his revolutionary followers to leave the political field and assist him in the realization of his industrial program, in which railway construction took a prominent place. Few of them, however, followed his advice. They hoped to achieve power through their control of the Parliament. As T'ung-meng Hui, being a secret revolutionary organization, was unsuitable for parliamentary action, it was reorganized through the main efforts of Sung Chiao-jen, and opened for membership to the general public. The new organization was a combination of T'ung-meng

Hui, the United Republican Party, the Association for the Advancement of Republicanism, the People's Association for Mutual Advancement, and the All People's Party, all of which, with the exception of T'ung-meng Hui, were small political organizations with few followers and little influence.[1] After the reorganization, the Nationalist Party was given the name of Kuomintang. The present name of the Party is Chung-kuo Kuomintang or Chinese Nationalist Party; but, in common speech, it is usually called Kuomintang or the Nationalist Party. Dr. Sun was elected as the Chief Director of the then reorganized Party and Huang Hsing, Wang Ching-wei, Hu Han-min, and Sung Chiao-jen as Directors. With the new party headquarters at Peking and his nominal chief and colleagues withdrawn from active politics, Sung, a prominent parliamentarian, became the *de facto* head of the organization and the leader of the opposition party in Parliament.

Yüan Shih-k'ai, as Chief Executive, had been very jealous of the growing influence of the Nationalist Party and was afraid of its ascendancy in Parliament. He then utilized the Progressive Party, military leaders in the provinces, and other reactionary factions as his tools in opposing the Nationalist Party. It was not long before Yüan decided to test the real strength of his political enemy. On August 15, 1912, he caused the execution of two well known revolutionary generals, Chang Cheng-wu and Fang Wei. This murder created indignation in the country. The *leit-motif* of Yüan was to crush all his rivals, to which everything else was subordinate. He acquiesced in the expansion of influence of Russia in Outer Mongolia, Great Britain in Tibet, and Japan in Manchuria. In order to obtain sufficient funds for his political maneuver, he raised the so-called Reorganization Loan from the foreign Banking Consortium. Finally, for the purpose of preventing his authority from being undermined by the opposition party in Parliament, he instigated his followers to assassinate Sung Chiao-jen at Shanghai on March 20, 1913. Dr. Sun immediately urged his followers to take military action against Yüan. But the majority of them insisted on parliamentary action. It was not until Yüan had consolidated his power and purged the provinces of revolutionary influence that a punitive expedition against Yüan was launched. The expedition, generally known as the "Second Revolution," suffered a crushing military defeat. This was the turning point of the power of the Nationalist Party in the North; and the controlling influence of Yüan Shih-k'ai and other warlords in Peking continued until 1928.

[1] See Yang Yu-chiung, *op. cit.*, pp. 111–114.

The drafting of the constitution

Much has been said about the political alignment in the Parliament, which had as its first and important task the drafting of the constitution for the Republic. In pursuance of Article XX of the *Organic Law of Parliament*, the Senate and the House of Representatives were each to elect thirty members to form a "Committee for the Drafting of the Constitution." This Committee was duly organized and met, on July 12, 1913, in a palace of the "Temple of Heaven." The Nationalist Party had twenty-eight members on the Committee, a large number but with no controlling voice. According to the *Rules of Procedure of the Committee*, the quorum for holding a session was forty members and any resolution must be backed by at least thirty members before its passage. After the failure of the "Second Revolution," some members of the Nationalist Party and the Progressive Party grouped together and organized the People's Constitutional Party. Thus no single party could dominate the Committee unless it made compromises with other groups.[1]

The Committee began its task on August 2, 1913, first on the general outline and then on the articles. Yüan Shih-k'ai was afraid that the constitutional discussion carried on in the Committee might be detrimental to his objectives, so he tried in many ways to obstruct its proceedings. Finally, he prevailed upon the military governors of fourteen provinces to send a joint telegram to Parliament, demanding that the President of the Republic be elected first before drafting the Constitution. In order to ease the tension, Parliament held a joint session on September 12 and resolved that the Committee should complete the draft of the Presidential section of the Constitution within five days. Then, on October 4, the *Presidential Election Law* was adopted by the joint session of Parliament, which, as the "Constitutional Convention," promulgated it the next day. Meanwhile, for fear that Yüan might apply further pressures to obstruct its work, the Committee hurriedly completed the draft of the Constitution on October 31, generally known as the *"Temple of Heaven Draft."* This was only three days before Yüan arbitrarily and unlawfully disbanded the Nationalist Party and unseated its members in Parliament.

Essentials of the Presidential Election Law

According to the *Presidential Election Law*, promulgated on October

---

[1] For details, see Wu Tsung-chih, *Constitutional History of the Republic of China*, Pt. I, Ch. III, Secs. 18, 20.

5, 1913, any Chinese national who was fully entitled to the enjoyment of civil rights, no less than forty years old, and who had been a resident within the country for at least ten years, could be elected President of the Republic. In holding the Presidential election, members of Parliament were to form an electoral college at which a two-thirds majority of all the electors was needed to make the required quorum. The candidate who could secure three-fourths of the total votes cast through secret balloting would be elected. If no one was elected after the second ballot, the two front runners in the second ballot would continue the race and whoever could secure a simple majority of all the votes cast would be elected. The President was to hold office for five years and could be re-elected once. If for any reason the President could not perform his official functions, the Vice President would act in his place. If the same situation happened to the Vice President, an election would be held immediately and the Presidential functions were to be performed by the Cabinet headed by the Premier. As to the powers of the President, the provisions contained in the *Provisional Constitution* were to be applied for the time being until the Constitution was formally promulgated. The fundamental defect of the *Presidential Election Law* was that the President was elected by members of Parliament, which was more or less dominated by Yüan Shih-k'ai through political maneuvering and violent means.

The Presidential Election

The day after the promulgation of the *Presidential Election Law*, the Electoral College was organized by the members of Parliament and met in the House of Representatives. On the first two ballots, Yüan could not secure the required three-fourths majority of votes. It was evident that his influence in the Parliament was greatly compromised by his unpopularity. On the third ballot, the race was between Yüan and Li Yüan-hung and Yüan was finally elected. Election for the Vice President was held on the next day and Li Yüan-hung was elected. Upon their inauguration on October 10, 1913, the formal government of the Republic was established. But a government created under such circumstances was doomed to failure.

The "Temple of Heaven Draft" of 1913

By its very nature, the *"Temple of Heaven Draft,"* as a draft, had no legal effect. The Draft contained 113 articles, grouped into eleven chapters: the form of government, national territory, the citizens,

Parliament, Parliamentary Committees, the President, the Cabinet, the Judiciary, the legislation, state finance, and the amendment and interpretation of the Constitution. The important points of the Draft are as follows: (1) China as a unitary republican state, (2) a bicameral system of Parliament, (3) a cabinet system of government, (4) the election of the President by members of Parliament, and (5) the amendment and interpretation of the Constitution by a "Constitutional Convention" formed by the members of Parliament. The *"Temple of Heaven Draft"* had been severely criticized for a number of reasons including the following: First, it did not contain provisions for a system of local government. Such provision had been left out by the drafters for want of time. Second, certain Confucian dogmas had been incorporated into the Draft, an idea originated by some members of the Progressive Party and opposed by the Nationalist Party. They appeared in the Draft in a compromise form: "The philosophy of Confucius should be incorporated in the education of citizens as the fundamental principle to personal life." [1] To write into the constitution such ethical principles would either be entirely superficial without the intent of enforcement or would hamper the freedom of belief of the people. It is, indeed, one of the shortcomings of the Draft.

8. THE JUDICIAL SYSTEM OF THE NEW REPUBLIC

Constitutional provisions on the judiciary

In comparison with the executive and legislative branches and their political and legal relationships discussed so far, the judiciary was practically if not theoretically much less important in Chinese government and politics. However, law courts had long been in existence in China despite the lack of judicial provisions in the *Principles of Constitution* and the *Nineteen Articles* promulgated by the Manchu government at the end of the Ch'ing dynasty, when the sovereign had the supreme power over all matters with the exception of those conceded to the legislative organs under compelling circumstances. The separation of three powers in the government was not recognized until the establishment of the Republic. According to the *Provisional Constitution* of 1912, the law courts were to be composed of judges appointed by the Provisional President and the Minister of Justice with the function of trying civil and criminal cases. As to the cases involving administrative affairs or arising from other particular causes, these were within the

[1] Art. 19 of the *"Temple of Heaven Draft."*

competence of the administrative court in accordance with special laws.

There was much emphasis on fair trial, and judicial independence was laid in the *Provisional Constitution*. Unless public safety and order was involved, the trial of cases in the law courts was to be conducted openly. In performing their functions, the judges would be independent and not subject to the interference of government officials. During their continuance in office, their salaries could not be decreased. They could only be transferred, removed and punished in accordance with law. As to the organization of courts and the qualifications of judges, these were to be dealt with by special laws.[1] There were no essential differences in the judicial provisions in the later constitution and drafts. Thus no further analysis will be made of the judicial system in the succeeding periods of the Republic until the Five-Power-Constitution was put into practice by the Nationalist Government.[2]

The organization of Courts

Notwithstanding the radical change of the form of government, the organization of the law courts after the establishment of the Republic was more or less similar to that prevailing at the end of the Ch'ing dynasty. There was a hierarchy of four tiers of courts: (1) the primary court, (2) the district court, (3) the high court, and (4) the Supreme Court. The primary courts should have been established in every locality, but actually only a small number came into existence due to the limitations of time, budget and judicial personnel. In 1914, these courts of first instance were abolished chiefly for financial reasons and their functions were to be performed by the summary branches of the district courts. Thus the district courts took care of cases of both first and second instance. As courts of second and third instance, the high courts were established in the capitals of the provinces. The Supreme Court, as the highest tribunal of the land, dealt with appeals from the high courts and cases under its exclusive jurisdiction in accordance with law. Unlike the Supreme Court of the United States, the Chinese counterpart had not the power of constitutional review. Parallel to the law courts, there were procurators' offices on every level and these procurators were equal in rank with the corresponding judges. This system was based on the theory that it was the function of the state

---

[1] Arts. 48–52 of the *Provisional Constitution* of 1912.

[2] *Cf.* Arts. 84–89 of the "*Temple of Heaven Draft*" of 1913, Arts. 44–48 of the *Constitutional Compact* of 1914, Arts. 72–77 of the *Draft Constitution* of 1919, Arts. 97–102 of the *Constitution* of 1923, and Arts. 85–95 of the *Draft Constitution* of 1925.

to detect and prosecute crimes with the plaintiff as witness.[1] The judicial system as stated above continued in China until 1932 when a new law on the organization of the courts was promulgated.[2]

The administrative court as envisioned by the framers of the *Provisional Constitution* was not established until 1914 when the laws on the organization of the administrative court, administrative appeals, and the execution of administrative adjudication were promulgated.[3] The administrative court instituted under these laws was composed of a president and fifteen judges and was directly under the President of the Republic. Like its French counterpart, the Chinese Administrative Court was the final authority on justiciable disputes. Once a decision was reached by the administrative court, the President of the Republic would order its enforcement by the government agencies concerned. If they failed to do so, the officials in charge would be subject to censure and punishment.

The prestige and independence of the Chinese judicial system were greatly undermined by the extraterritorial jurisdiction imposed by the foreign Powers and the frequent interference by the military and civil government.[4] Financial limitations and lack of sufficient judicial personnel constituted further hindrances to the proper functioning of the judiciary. Nevertheless, the Chinese judges, especially those of the higher courts, were generally capable and competent in spite of these difficulties.

9. THE LOCAL GOVERNMENT SYSTEM

Local administration

In the early days of the Republic, the attention of the whole country was centered upon the national government and little consideration was given to the system of local government. As a result, there were diversified practices in the various provinces. It was not until January 8, 1913 that the national government issued a series of decrees to

---

[1] For details of the judicial system of the early Republican period, see the *Statute of the Courts* as revised in 1917.

[2] It did not come into effect until July 1, 1935.

[3] For details, see the *Law on the Organization of the Administrative Court* (*Government Gazette*, April 1, 1914), the *Law Governing Administrative Appeals*, and the *Law on the Execution of Administrative Adjudication* (*ibid.*, July 21, 1914).

[4] Among the many reasons justifying the existence of the extraterritorial jurisdiction, which has now been abolished, were the different conceptions and standards between the Chinese and Western civil and criminal codes. *Cf.* the statements made in the *Report of the Commission on Extraterritoriality in China* (Washington D.C.: Government Printing Office, 1926).

standardize the names and organizations of the local government.[1] Thenceforth the local government was divided into three classes, namely, the province, the prefecture and the district.

The province was the highest unit of the local government, headed by a chief administrator in charge of provincial matters. For those provinces which had not been under civil administration, the military governors would be concurrently chief administrators. The military governor was the highest military officer of the province and had the provincial army under his command. But, at that time, it was an unusual practice for the military governor to act concurrently as the chief administrator of the province.[2] The chief administrator of a province was appointed by the President of the Republic. Under him there were a bureau of general affairs and four other departments in charge of interior, finance, education and industry. However, some of the less developed provinces did not set up the four departments. Mongolia, Tibet, and Chinghai were special districts and therefore were not required to conform their administrations to the provincial system.

The prefecture was the intermediate class of the local government, headed by a civil administrator with the title of "inspector." He was also appointed by the President of the Republic upon the recommendation of the chief administrator of the province where the prefecture was located. In the inspector's office, there were a secretary and four sections in charge of the interior, finance, education and industry. The district was the basic unit of the local government; it was headed by a magistrate, who was recommended by the provincial administrator for appointment by the national government. The district magistrate, assisted by a staff, was in charge of district affairs and other matters referred to him by his superiors. Besides the province, prefecture and district, there were other local units either directly under the national government or in the immediate vicinity of the Capital. All these were reorganized so as to conform to the standardized regulations.

Such a reorganization was, indeed, an important step toward the

---

[1] The following regulations were promulgated on January 8, 1913: (a) *Regulations governing the Uniform Organization of the Provinces*, (b) *Regulations governing the Uniform Organization of the Local Government under Shun-tien Fu*, (c) *Regulations governing the Uniform Organization of the Prefectures*, (d) *Regulations governing the Uniform Organization of the Districts*, and (e) *Regulations governing the Uniform Organization of the Special Areas Directly under the National Government*.

[2] In the early days of the Republic, there were, besides the military governors, army inspectors and defense commissioners. For details, see the *Regulations governing the Organization of the Office of the Military Governor, Temporary Regulations governing Army Inspectors* (*Government Gazette*, December 21, 1913), and *Regulations governing Defense Commissioners* (*ibid.*, September 7, 1913).

unification of the Chinese local government system. But, however uniform and admirable a system might be, it should be carried out by capable and loyal administrators. The continued confusion and disorder in many provinces after the reorganization was chiefly due to the misrule of the responsible officials, who were mostly controlled by different warlords in their respective spheres of influence.

Local self-government

The local self-government system on the district level in the early days of the Republic could actually be traced back to the latter part of the Ch'ing dynasty. In every district, there were the legislative council and consultative council described in the previous chapter. Within the districts, the cities and villages retained the same organizations except certain changes of names. Thus there is no necessity to repeat the discussion here. However, the situation was different on the provincial level. During the post-revolutionary period, the original provincial assemblies were abolished and new ones were temporarily organized in different provinces. As each province operated independently, there was no uniform standard. This undesirable condition prevailed until the following laws were promulgated by the national government: *Electoral Law of the Provincial Assembly* of September 4, 1912, *Rules for the Application of the Electoral Law of the Provincial Assembly* of October 2, 1912, and *Temporary Organic Law of the Provincial Assembly* of April 2, 1913. Then the organizations and functions of the provincial assemblies became unified.

According to these newly promulgated laws and rules, a person would be eligible to vote in a provincial election if he was a male Chinese national, twenty-one years old or over, had been a resident in the election district for at least two years, and met one of the following conditions: (1) annual payment of at least two dollars of direct tax, (2) ownership of immovable property valued at least at five hundred dollars or (3) graduation from an elementary school or a school of the same standing. Since there were restrictions of sex, property and education, the suffrage was not universal. In order to be eligible to be elected to the provincial assembly, one had to be a male Chinese national and be at least twenty-five years old. The exclusion of female citizens from participation in local politics fell short of the fulfillment of democratic principles.

The election of the provincial assembly was held in two stages. In the primary election, each district was to elect twenty times the number of assembly candidates prescribed for that district. The final election was held in an enlarged area consisting of several districts. The candidates were those elected during the primary elections; those who won this final election were to be members of the provincial assembly. The number of assemblymen of each province was prescribed in the *Membership Chart of the First Provincial Assemblies of the Various Provinces*, promulgated on September 25, 1912.[1] The term of office of the members of the provincial assembly was three years with provision for reelection. At its first session, the assembly was to elect a speaker and two deputy speakers, in charge of daily routine matters.

As the legislative organ of a province, the provincial assembly had the following functions: (1) to pass laws of the province in so far as they were not in conflict with national statutes, (2) to adopt the budget of the province, (3) to decide upon provincial taxation and collection of fees if not already prescribed by law, (4) to decide upon provincial loans and contracts involving the burdens of the provincial treasury, (5) to decide upon the disposal and purchase of provincial properties and constructions, (6) to formulate the regulations on the supervision of provincial properties and construction except for those already prescribed by laws and decrees, (7) to reply to the inquiries made by the chief administrator of the province, (8) to make recommendations on matters of provincial administration and others to the chief administrator, and (9) to discuss and decide other matters under the assembly's jurisdiction in accordance with law. The chief administrator could send back the assembly's resolution for reconsideration if he deemed it necessary. But, if two-thirds of the members present insisted upon the original resolution, he must proclaim it without delay. At the same time, the provincial assembly could impeach the chief administrator, of the province in accordance with law and could also request him to investigate the conduct of other officials. Thus the assembly had, in effect, the power of supervising the provincial government.[2]

In the early days of the Republic, there were many able men in the provincial assemblies to represent the people and they made remarkable contributions to their respective provinces. It was unfortunate that their services were not utilized, because not long after their establishment, the provincial assemblies were dissolved by Yüan Shih-k'ai in November 1913 and were not reconvened until October 1916.

[1] For the chart, see *The Collection of Laws and Decrees*, 1912, No. 1, Ch. 2, Sec. 7.
[2] See Chs. 2 and 4 of the *Temporary Organic Law of the Provincial Assembly* of 1913.

MONARCHISM VS. REPUBLICANISM: POLITICAL INSTITUTIONS UNDER THE DICTATORSHIP OF YÜAN SHIH-K'AI

I. YÜAN SHIH-K'AI VS. CONSTITUTIONAL DEMOCRACY

Events leading to Yüan's abandonment of constitutional rule

Yüan Shih-k'ai's succession to the Provisional Presidency was only a stepping stone to his eventual dictatorship. However, his ambition could not be materialized immediately because Parliament was then controlled by people with republican convictions. Thus the policical institutions described in the previous chapter were still based on democratic principles, Yüan's predominance in the government notwithstanding. The murder of Sung Chiao-jen was the signal of Yüan's decision to abolish the constitutional rule. Afterwards, he had gradually developed his schemes and intensified his efforts toward the eventual change of the republican polity into monarchy. A brief examination of the successive events will show the Machiavellian character of the steps he undertook to carry out his plans.

(1) One of the most brilliant revolutionists and leader of the Nationalist Party in Parliament, Sung Chiao-jen had been known as an ardent advocate of parliamentary politics, for which he was much hated by Yüan. On March 20, 1913, Sung was assassinated at the railway station in Shanghai while he was on his way to Peking. Later investigation of the case uncovered the complicated involvement of Hung Chih-tsu, a relative of Yüan, and Premier Chow Ping-chun. It was generally believed that Yüan was the power behind the plot.

(2) When the facts of the Sung case were finally revealed, members of the Nationalist Party were outraged. Seeking a last resort to armed suppression, Yüan managed to obtain a loan of twenty-five million pounds from the Five-Nation Consortium to boost his military strength. He signed the loan agreement without previously obtaining Parliament's approval because he was afraid of its objection. This was definitely a serious violation of constitutional provisions.

(3) When the "Second Revolution" by the Nationalist Party ended in failure, Yüan acted even more ruthlessly without having to be concerned about any strong opposition. On August 19, 1913, he presented to the Committee for the Drafting of the Constitution for consideration an *Outline of the Draft Constitution* of twenty-four articles, which was prepared by his "Constitutional Studies Society." The heavy attack on the Draft by the Committee led to the execution of its member Hsü Hsiu-chun and the arrest of eight Nationalist members of Parliament among whom four were on the Committee.

(4) Once Yüan assumed the Provisional Presidency of the Republic, he planned to rid himself of the bondage of the *Provisional Constitution*. On October 16, Yüan sent a bill to Parliament recommending a thorough revision of this fundamental law. In the bill, he asked two additional powers for the President in issuing dictatorial orders and disposing of financial matters in time of emergency. He further demanded that the President need not have the consent of Parliament in declaring war, making peace, concluding treaties, setting up an administrative system and issuing official regulations, and appointing and dismissing civil and military officers. Parliament, however, after receiving the bill, maintained that there was little need for amending the *Provisional Constitution* since the Constitution was in the process of being drafted at that time. Yüan was very much disturbed by the attitude of Parliament.

(5) Yüan was displeased with the promulgation of the *Presidential Election Law* by the Constitutional Convention on October 5, 1913, but he suppressed his temper pending the Presidential election in order to avoid any possible incident. After he was sworn into office, however, he sent a letter to the Constitutional Convention on October 18, arguing that the President should be the one to promulgate the forthcoming Constitution. The Convention did not reply in view of the fact that the Constitution had not yet been completed.

(6) Since the Presidential inauguration, the Committee for the Drafting of the Constitution had made remarkable progress. Concerned that the work of the Committee might not be to his advantage, Yüan designated eight persons headed by Shih Yu and Kuo Aue to present his views to the Committee. Yüan was indignant to learn that their presence was barred by the Committee in accordance with its rules of procedure.

(7) Frustrated by the Committee's rejection of his delegation, Yüan dispatched a circular telegram on October 25 to the civil and military

leaders of the various provinces severely criticizing the Constitutional Draft. Shortly afterwards, Feng Kuo-chang, Chang Hsün and others echoed Yüan's wishes and petitioned the President to disband the Nationalist Party as the chief trouble maker of the time. This idea was undoubtedly instigated by Yüan himself.

(8) Taking the declarations of his subordinates in the various provinces as public opinion and brushing aside protests from both chambers of Parliament, Yüan ordered on November 4 the disbanding of the Nationalist Party and the disqualification of 438 Parliament members who belonged to the Nationalist Party since the "Second Revolution." This was only his preliminary step to more ruthless action. On January 10, 1914, he summarily dissolved Parliament ostensibly in compliance with the wishes of the provincial leaders, who followed the wishes of Li Yüan-hung in demanding the dismissal of the remaining members of Parliament. By then the foundation of constitutional democracy laid down in the early years of the Republic had been completely ruined. Of course, Yüan lost no time in devising a new government system to suit his own purpose.[1]

Responsibility of Li Yüan-hung

Having actively taken part in the Wuchang Revolution and having been in a high position as Vice President of the Republic, Li Yüan-hung should have done his utmost to preserve the *Provisional Constitution* and Parliament. On the contrary, he went along with Yüan when the ambition of the latter was fully unveiled. As a matter of fact, Li was personally involved in the dissolution and reconvening of Parliament twice in each case. His weakness and inability in making right decisions at the right moments had determined his own fate and, to a certain extent, that of China as well. As a typical opportunist, he only knew how to sail with the tide. Thus he was later deceived by Chang Hsün in his short-lived restoration of the Manchu monarchy even though it was promptly suppressed by anti-Monarchist forces. Finally his withdrawal from the Presidential election by the pressure of Ts'ao K'un and Wu P'ei-fu consequently led to Ts'ao's infamous succession to the Presidency by illegitimate means. To impartial observers, it is plain that Li certainly was at least partly responsible for all these occurrences.

---

[1] For details and related documents concerning Yüan's abolition of constitutional rule, see Yang Yu-chiung, *Legislative History of Modern China*, pp. 121–125, 154–184.

Dr. Sun's comment on revolutionary mistakes

When Dr. Sun turned over the office of the Provisional Presidency to Yüan Shih-k'ai, his purpose was to accelerate the unification of the country. It was his hope that Yüan could lead China onto the road of peace and order. But regrettably, what was not accounted for was "his evil nature and unpredictable personality." [1] Dr. Sun later analyzed Yüan's betrayal of the Republic in the following words:

> The first blow came at the assassination of Sung Chiao-jen. Then he was encouraged by the obtaining of a loan from the Five-Nation Consortium without Parliament's approval. The anti-Yüan coalition in the Southeast was too slow in its military action and its defeat resulted in the extinction of revolutionary forces established during the 1911 Revolution. When finally Parliament was dissolved and the *Provisional Constitution* abandoned, his betrayal of the Republic and Monarchian ambition were fully revealed. [2]

According to Dr. Sun, the course of events thus developed was actually due to the inability of the revolutionists to follow through faithfully their original plan of three revolutionary stages: first, military administration; second, political tutelage; and third, constitutional rule. The leap from the military to the constitutional stage left little opportunity to train the people in exercising their political rights. Because of that, the foundation of the Republic could not be consolidated. The gap thus created provided Yüan with the decisive advantage to precipitate his personal ambitions. In this connection, Dr. Sun frequently reiterated his painful remarks emphasizing particularly the point that no reforms could be enforced without first getting rid of the old abuses. As a result of the failure on the part of the revolutionists to follow the three-stage plan, the inevitable effect on the nation was three-fold: "First, democracy could not be realized; second, authoritarian rule was enforced under the cover of democracy; and third, even the superficial form of democracy was abandoned." [3]

Owing to his unsuccessful efforts during the "Second Revolution" and Yüan's reactionary measures against republicanism, Dr. Sun re-evaluated the efficiency of his party at the time of the national emergency. He concluded that the then existing party was really a very loose political organization without much discipline or unity of purpose, and that a thorough reorganization was absolutely necessary.

---

[1] *The Collected Works of Sun Yat-sen*, Vol. IV, "A History of the Chinese Revolution," p. 13.
[2] *Ibid.*, p. 14.
[3] *Ibid.*, p. 11.

Thus, on July 8, 1914, Dr. Sun founded the Chung-hua Ko-min Tang or the Chinese Revolutionary Party. He himself became *Tsung-li* or single head of the Party and all party members were to be responsible to him. Even though some of Dr. Sun's former adherents did not join the new party due to their objection against the oath of loyalty, the reorganization had revivified the revolutionary spirit in China.

2. YÜAN SHIH-K'AI AND THE CONSTITUTIONAL COMPACT OF 1914

The Political Conference

As Yüan Shi-k'ai was determined to abolish the democratic institutions in China, he proceeded to achieve his purpose by establishing, one after another, the Political Conference, the Constitutional Compact Conference, and the Consultative *Yuan*. All of these were set up to work out a system of government as visualized by Yüan. The Political Conference was preceded by the Administrative Conference, which was originally organized by Premier Hsung Hsi-ling to discuss local matters. When Yüan was quarreling with Parliament and looking for national support, he took the opportunity to appoint additional members to the Conference and changed its name to the Political Conference.[1] As one of Yüan's political tools, the Political Conference met on December 15, 1913. Its major functions were to make recommendations to the government and to reply to its inquiries.[2] When Yüan received the telegram sent by Li Yüan-hung and other provincial leaders demanding the dissolution of Parliament, he first requested the opinion of the Conference and virtually obtained its support. This was Yüan's maneuver to evade his responsibility for his unlawful action against Parliament, which occurred on January 10, 1914. After that, the main task of the Political Conference was to create a constitution-making body, which was destined to be the Constitutional Compact Conference. *The Organic Law of the Constitutional Compact Conference*, hurriedly drawn up by the Political Conference, was promulgated by the President on January 26, 1914.[3]

The Constitutional Compact Conference

According to its organic law, the Constitutional Compact Conference

---

[1] *Government Gazette*, November 27, 1913.

[2] See Art. 19 of the *Rules of Procedure of the Political Conference* (*Government Gazette*, December 25, 1913).

[3] For its text, see *Government Gazette*, January 27, 1914.

was composed of fifty-six members: four from the National Capital, two from each province, eight from Mongolia, Tibet and Chinghai, and four from the National Chamber of Commerce. The electors were limited to Chinese nationals, at least thirty years of age, and with one of the following four qualifications: (1) having been a high ranking government official and well experienced in public administration, (2) having passed the civil service examination and being well known in his community, (3) having graduated from advanced institutes of learning of at least three years curriculum and being well versed in science, and (4) having property valued at least ten thousand dollars and being enthusiastic in public welfare. Here the phrases "well experienced in public administration," "well versed in science", and "enthusiastic in public welfare" were all very vague and subject to the free interpretation of the government officials supervising the elections.

In order to be eligible for membership in the Constitutional Compact Conference, one had to be at least thirty-five years of age, with one of the following three conditions: (1) having been a high ranking official for at least five years and with a good record; (2) being a well known scholar whose works had been published and proved to be useful; and (3) having graduated, with law or political science as a major, from a college of at last three years curriculum, either in China or abroad, or having passed the civil service examination and since made further studies in law or political science. Here again, there were many empty terms and phrases that made the qualifications highly flexible and thus gave the government great latitude of interpretation. This kind of election was, in its essence, not different from direct appointment by the government. It was exactly Yüan's intention to have election in name and appointment in fact.

The Constitutional Compact Conference held its first meeting on February 18, 1914. Sun Yu-chun was elected chairman and Shih Yu, vice chairman. Under the practical direction of Yüan Shih-k'ai, the Conference prepared the *Constitutional Compact* on April 29 and it was promulgated by the President on May 1, 1914.[1]

Outstanding features of the Constitutional Compact

As soon as the *Constitutional Compact* was promulgated, it became the fundamental law of the country. The *Provisional Constitution*, the *Organic Law of Parliament*, and the electoral laws of the two chambers

---

[1] See Appendix D for its English translation.

of Parliament, all promulgated in 1912 and 1913, were declared to be null and void. From then on, the political system of China entered into yet another stage. There were ten chapters to the new *Constitutional Compact*, consisting of sixty-eight articles, all of which were drafted in accordance with Yüan's wishes.[1]

Among the important features of the *Constitutional Compact*, the following were most outstanding: (1) It adopted an extreme form of the presidential system, with all major powers centered in the President and with the legislature only a subsidiary organ. For all practical purposes, the Chief Executive had become a dictator. (2) On principle, the Legislature was changed to a unicameral system. The Legislative *Yuan* never came into existence and its functions were later assigned by Yüan to the Consultative *Yuan*. As the members of the latter were all appointed by the President, there was no representative organ in its true sense under the dictatorial regime of Yüan Shih-k'ai. (3) The President did not need to secure the Legislature's approval and consent in declaring war, making peace, concluding treaties, appointing and dismissing officials, and prescribing administrative systems and official regulations. Even though the Legislature's approval was required in the case of treaties affecting national territory and increasing the financial burden of the people, the President's power was unlimited especially in view of the fact that the legislative power was performed by his self-appointed Consultative *Yuan*. (4) In case of national emergency when the Legislative *Yuan* was not in session, the President could, with the concurrence of the Consultative *Yuan*, issue emergency ordinances and make urgent financial appropriations. Even though he had to request the Legislature's approval afterwards, this restriction was evidently more superficial than substantial. (5) The power of drafting the Constitution was vested in the President and the Consultative *Yuan* and that of its adoption in the National Convention.

In addition to the above features, the *Constitutional Compact* had a unique provision in Article 65, which prohibited any modification of the articles regarding the favorable treatment of the abdicated Emperor and the Imperial clan as well as the special treatment of the Manchus, Mongols, Mohammedans and Tibetans. This provision was actually

---

[1] On March 24, President Yüan sent to the Constitutional Compact Conference a memorandum recommending seven major revisions and additions, among which he demanded the expansion of the President's power to a much larger extent than what he had previously asked of the Parliament. Later he asked the Conference to include in the *Compact* the clauses concerning the favorable treatment of the national minorities and the royal family of the Ch'ing dynasty.

motivated by Yüan's shrewd move of showing kindness to the national minorities so as to gain their support for his ultimate designs.

3. THE REORGANIZED NATIONAL GOVERNMENT UNDER YÜAN SHIH-K'AI

The Consultative Yuan and the Legislative Yuan

The Consultative *Yuan* was a unique office created by Yüan Shih-k'ai for the manipulation of his personal powers. On May 24, 1914, the Constitutional Compact Conference enacted the *Organic Law of the Consultative Yuan*, which was promulgated by the President on the same day. On May 26, Yüan appointed Li Yüan-hung, the Vice President, concurrently as the chairman and seventy others as members of the Consultative *Yuan*. It is needless to say that no members of the opposition party were selected for that body. Among the members there were Liang Ch'i-ch'ao, leader of the Progressive Party, and Wong Ta-hsieh who became vice chairman of this advisory organ. On June 20, the Consultative *Yuan* was formally established whereupon the earlier Political Conference ceased to exist.

The functions of the Consultative *Yuan* can be classified into three categories:

First category, matters referred to it by the President: (1) its concurrence required by the provisions of the *Constitutional Compact*, (2) the interpretation of the *Constitutional Compact* and its auxiliary laws and (3) disputes between the executive and judicial branches of the government.

Second category, replies to President's inquiries: (1) conclusion of treaties, (2) establishment of administrative offices, (3) financial reforms, (4) promotion of education, (5) expansion of industry, and (6) other specific matters referred to it by the President.

Third category, recommendations to the President on the same matters mentioned in the second category.

The above functions properly belonged to the Consultative *Yuan*. According to Article 67 of the *Constitutional Compact*, the Consultative *Yuan* was to perform the functions of the Legislative *Yuan* before the latter's establishment. As the Legislative *Yuan* never came into being, Yüan Shih-k'ai ordered on June 29, 1914, the substitution of the Consultative *Yuan* for the Legislative *Yuan*.

The functions of the Legislative *Yuan* to be performed by the Consultative *Yuan* were as follows: (1) to give consent to the general amnesty and to the treaties affecting national territory and increasing the people's burdens; (2) to discuss and pass bills and the budget; (3) to discuss and pass or approve measures relating to the assumption of public debts and to the contracting of other liabilities to the charge of the national treasury; (4) to reply to inquiries addressed to it by the President; (5) to receive petitions from the people; (6) to initiate legislation; (7) to submit to the President suggestions and opinions relating to legislation and other matters; (8) to raise questions in regard to administration over which doubts had arisen and to request the President to reply thereon; and (9) to impeach the President in the Supreme Court of Justice if approved by a majority of three fourths or over a quorum of four fifths or over of the total number of members of the Legislative *Yuan*.[1] A number of the above functions were originally shared by the Consultative *Yuan* and some probably could not be performed by it at all. There was not the slightest chance for the Consultative *Yuan* to impeach the President who would immediately dismiss its members before the start of any proceedings in the Supreme Court of Justice.

At any rate, the Consultative *Yuan* exercised both the legislative and advisory functions of the government. It was a very influential organ at that time and later became the headquarters of Yüan's monarchial movement.

The Board of Political Affairs and the ministries

In pursuance of Article 39 of the Constitutional Compact, Yüan started to reorganize the national government. On May 3, 1914, he issued a Presidential order on the Organization of the Board of Political Affairs, whereby the existing cabinet system and the office of Premiership were abolished. The new Board of Political Affairs was headed by a Secretary of State, who was to assist the President in his administrative duties and to countersign the Presidential orders. Under the Secretary of State, there were two under-secretaries, eight councillors, and six bureaus in charge of legal affairs, confidential matters, budget and statistics, civil service examination and appointment, as well as printing and engraving. The directors of the bureaus were administrative heads and directly under the control of the Secretary of State. Hsü Shih-ch'ang, an intimate friend of Yüan's, became the Secretary of State and worked very well with the President. As a

---

[1] See Arts. 25, 28 and 31 of the *Constitutional Compact*, and also the *Organic Law of the Legislative Yuan* of October 27, 1914.

matter of fact, this Board of Political Affairs was, to a certain extent, similar to the Grand Secretariat of the late Ch'ing dynasty. By that time, Yüan, because of personal ambition and vanity, was definitely inclined to the restoration of the monarchial system.

Since the *Constitutional Compact* changed the cabinet system into the presidential system, it was natural that the status of the ministries had to be adjusted accordingly. On July 10, 1914, Yüan ordered the revision of the administrative system of the ministries, which included foreign affairs, interior, finance, army, navy, justice, education, agriculture and commerce, and communications.[1] After the reorganization, the ministries were under the direct control of the President. The ministers were appointed by the President to head the respective ministries, but they could no longer enjoy the independent positions of former days. With all the important offices of the executive branch directly under him and no representative organ to check on him, Yüan had virtually become the dictator of the country.

Revision of the Presidential Election Law

The *Presidential Election Law* was promulgated on October 5, 1913. After the Consultative *Yuan* was ordered to perform the functions of the Legislative *Yuan*, he put pressure on the former to recommend the revision of the law. Such a recommendation was duly made and referred to the Constitutional Compact Conference for consideration. On December 28, 1914, the revised text of the *Presidential Election Law* was adopted by the Conference and promulgated by the President the next day. According to the revised law, the Presidential candidate must be a male Chinese national, at least forty years of age, possessing the rights of citizenship, and having resided in China for no less than twenty years. These qualifications were much stricter than those provided in the original law. The female citizens were deprived by the new law of the right to become Presidential candidates. The Presidential Electoral College consisted of one hundred members, fifty each from the Consultative *Yuan* and the Legislative *Yuan* to be respectively elected from their own members. Thus at least one half of the members of the Presidential Electoral College were actually appointed by the President and the result of such a Presidential election could be easily foreseen.

Yet the oddest part of the revised law was the manner by which the Presidential candidates were chosen. At each Presidential election, the

---

[1] For the text of the Presidential order, see *The Collection of Laws and Decrees*, 1913, No. 4 Sec. 5.

incumbent President was to nominate three qualified candidates, write their names on a piece of specially made paper and place it in a safe in a stone walled room in the Presidential Mansion. On the election day, the President would make known the candidates he recommended. Votes could be cast, however, in favor of the incumbent President, who thus could be re-elected again and again. The term of office of the President was set at ten years, but it was immaterial because of the assurance of his reelection as provided in the revised law. All these provisions were not yet enough to meet Yüan's design, for, in Article 10, the revised law prescribed that in every Presidential election year, if the Consultative *Yuan* deemed it necessary for political reasons, it could, by a vote of two-thirds of its members, extend the incumbent President's term of office for another term. This resolution so adopted by the Consultative *Yuan* was to be proclaimed by the President himself. Thus even the formalities of election could be eliminated and a life-time Presidency was reassured.[1] Furthermore, Yüan could even recommend a member of his own family as Presidential candidate and thus found a system of hereditary Presidency. However, Yüan's ambition was then beyond the Presidency. He wanted to be an absolute monarch, betrayal of the Republic notwithstanding.

4. THE LOCAL GOVERNMENT SYSTEM UNDER YÜAN SHIH-K'AI

Local administration

Not long after the promulgation of the *Constitutional Compact*, Yüan began his program of reforms of the local government system. The *Provincial Government System, Prefecture Government System,* and *District Government System* were promulgated on May 23, 1914, and then revised on September 6. The government system of the various Special Districts was changed soon afterwards, according to a different set of rules and regulations. After this reorganization, the local government in China was still divided into three levels: the province, the prefecture, and the district. But the functions of and the relationship among the different levels had been readjusted with much more emphasis on the concentration of power in the national government. Unlike Yüan's unusual system of national government, the local administration as reorganized had no fundamental defects and lasted throughout the period of the Peking government.

The Province The province was the highest unit of the three levels

---

[1] See Arts. 3, 7, 8 and 10 of the revised *Presidential Election Law.*

of local government, headed by an inspector-general. He had control over the civil officials, and police and militia of the province. He was also empowered by the national government to supervise finance, justice, and other administrative matters within the province. For the execution of national laws and ordinances, he could enact and promulgate rules and regulations applicable only in his province. Under the inspector-general, there was a bureau of political affairs which was headed by a director appointed by him. To carry out routine administrative matters, the bureau set up four sections in charge of general affairs, interior affairs, education, and industry. This was the general organization of the provincial government.

The Prefecture The prefecture was the intermediate class of the local government, headed by a prefect to carry out the administrative duties of the prefecture. Under the direction of the provincial inspector-general, he was to supervise the finance, justice, police and militia, and other matters within the prefecture. He could also prescribe rules and regulations applicable only in his sphere of administration. Although the district magistrates were appointed by the provincial inspector-general, the prefect had the power to supervise them and could even have the power to appoint acting magistrates in case of any vacancies and pending the arrival of the new appointees. While the organization of the prefecture was determined by the provincial inspector-general, the prefect appointed his own staff. The prefect was responsible to both the provincial inspector-general and the President of the Republic.

The District The district was the lowest unit of the local government, headed by a magistrate. Under the direction of the prefect, he was in charge of the district administration, issued local regulations, supervised his staff, and commanded the police force within the district. The organization of the office of the magistrate was determined by the provincial inspector-general upon the recommendation of the prefect.

The Special Districts The special districts included Jehol, Chahar and Suiyuan. The administrative system in such areas followed the provisions of the *Regulations governing the Office of the Military Commissioner*, promulgated on July 6, 1914. In each of these special districts, there was an office of the military commissioner in charge of civil and military matters. With the authorization of the national government, the military commissioner was to supervise the finance, courts, and other matters in his special district. He was assisted by one chief of staff, two staff members, three secretaries and two aides. In his office there were two bureaus in charge of military and general affairs, each headed by a secretary. As Mongolia and Tibet had a special status, their administrative systems remained as before. Shun-tien Fu, the metropolitan area of the national Capital, was renamed Ching-tsao. Its government was also reorganized in accordance with the *Regulations governing the Administrative System of Ching-tsao*, promulgated on October 4, 1914.

Local self-government

With monarchy in mind, Yüan Shih-k'ai was not at all interested in local self-government. After the dissolution of Parliament, he ordered, on January 28, 1914, that all provincial assemblies be disbanded. On February 3, he discontinued the self-government of all levels and, three days later, he went further to abolish the "Society for Self-Government of the Capital." Henceforth, the foundation of local self-government laid down since the latter part of Ch'ing dynasty was completely destroyed. Yüan was, however, a great psychologist. In a deceptive move, he promulgated the *Experimental Regulations of Local Self-Government* on December 29, 1914.

According to the new regulations, there could be four to six self-government sub-districts in each district, and eight sub-districts in a combined area of two or more districts. This was a one-level local self-governing system, which had two categories of functions. The first category represented its proper and permanent functions, such as sanitation, charity, education, communications, agriculture, industry and commerce within the sub-district. The second category included matters authorized by the higher level governments or by the national laws and ordinances. The administration of the self-governing sub-districts was of two kinds, depending upon the population. If the population of a sub-district exceeded the average, it was to be administered by one trustee and six to ten self-government members. The trustee was appointed by the district magistrate from three candidates elected by the people of the sub-district in charge of its self-government matters. The self-government members were selected by the district magistrate from a group of candidates elected by the people of the sub-district. The number so elected was to be twice the prescribed self-government members. They were to organize a self-governing conference under the chairmanship of the trustee to discuss self-governing matters of their sub-district. But, in the sub-district where the population was below the average, there was only one trustee in charge of both deliberation and execution of matters within that sub-district. The terms of office of the sub-district trustees and self-government members were all set at two years. One half of the self-government members were to be replaced every year, but if reelected, they could serve one more term. They could be elected again after one year of the expiration of their second term. The district magistrate was the immediate supervisor of the self-governing sub-districts and had the power to promote and remove all the staff concerned.

After a few months of the promulgation of the *Experimental Regulations of Local Self-Government,* Yüan quickened the speed of his monarchial schemes. He began to worry about the progress of the self-government process, which would definitely hamper the planning institution of absolute monarchy. On April 14, 1915, he imposed some restraining measures by the promulgation of the *Procedural Rules for the Application of the Experimental Regulations of Local Self-Government.* These new rules divided the preparatory period for self-government into three stages: first, the investigation and studying of self-governing matters; second, the preparation and promotion of self-government; and third, the actual practice of local autonomy. The arbitrary division of three stages was evidently a disguised device to delay the progress of the self-governing process. Although there was, on July 21, 1915, a government order which made Ching-tsao, the metropolitan area of the national Capital, the model district of self-government, this was again a camouflage to cover Yüan's real intention against the establishment of any democratic institution in any level of government.

5. THE RISE AND FALL OF YÜAN'S MONARCHIAL MOVEMENT

The rise of Yüan's monarchial movement

The steps taken by Yüan Shih-k'ai to achieve dictatorial rule in China for the ultimate purpose of his monarchial ambition have already been described. It was time for the opportunists to advocate constitutional monarchy and create a kind of public opinion for its support. They were gratified to find a foreign scholar who made known his observation of the Chinese situation with more or less the same conclusion. In August 1915, Dr. Frank J. Goodnow, constituitonal adviser to President Yüan, contributed an article to the officially sponsored *Asiatic Daily News* on the desirability of China's restoration to monarchy.[1] Soon after the publication of this article, Yang Tu and

---

[1] For Dr. Goodnow's article, see also *Tung-fang Magazine* (Shanghai), Vol. 12, No. 10. For English texts of this article and Liang Ch'i-chao's anti-monarchical essay, see B. L. Putnam Weale, *The Fight for the Republic in China* (New York, 1917), pp. 175–185, 192–215.

others initiated an organization known as the "Society for the Preservation of Peace" *(Chou An Hui)* with the promotion of monarchism as its sole purpose. Then Liang Shih-yi and other politicians organized petition groups begging Yüan to assume the throne.

Realizing that the time had come, Yüan ordered, on August 30, that all petitions regarding the change of the form of government be dealt with by the Consultative *Yuan*, which, as expected, did not fail to meet his wishes. It immediately recommended the convocation of the "National Convention of People's Representatives" to discuss vital issues of the country and promptly prepared its *Organic Law*, which was promulgated by the President on October 8.[1] The election of the delegates to the Convention was exceptionally hurried. It was no surprise that on November 20, the 1993 delegates voted unanimously in favor of the establishment of a constitutional monarchy. Of course, they understood that the candidate for the monarch was Yüan Shih-k'ai. On December 11, the Consultative *Yüan*, on behalf of the Representatives, petitioned Yüan to ascend the throne. Acting in a highly characteristic manner, Yüan pretended to decline the request on the ground that his contribution to the country was hardly worth mentioning and that his enthronement would make him feel guilty toward the abdicated Emperor and the Republic in view of his oath at the time of his inauguration. He therefore asked the delegates to make some other choice. Though this was only a kind of gesture, Yüan must have had a guilty conscience for all his contradictions. It was understood, however, that his modest declination would simply lead to a second petition with more expressions of flattery. Compelled by the circumstances, Yüan accepted the people's request on December 12 and ordered the change of the form of government. Two days later, he appointed Shih Yu, Yang Tu and eight others to draft an imperial constitution. The Board of Political Affairs was duly reorganized to be adaptable to the imperial institutions. Henceforth he was called Emperor Hung-hsien, which means "Glorious Constitution." On December 31, he proclaimed that the New Year of 1916 should be recorded as the First Year of Hung-hsien.[2]

The fall of Yüan's monarchial movement

As soon as Yüan declared his acceptance of the monarchy, Yunnan

[1] For its text, see *The Collection of Laws and Decrees*, 1915, No. 4, Sec. 2.

[2] Immediately after he accepted the monarchy, Yüan conferred peerage titles on 128 persons headed by Lung Chi-kuang. Li Yüan-hung, the Vice President, was given the title of Prince Wu-i. But Li was astute enough to decline this dishonorable "honor."

province took the lead in armed protest and proclaimed its independence. This patriotic action, vital to the history of modern China,
was led by T'ang Chi-yao and Ts'ai Ao.[1] In the proclamation, they
enumerated various abuses committed by Yüan and stated four
objectives as their avowed goals of national reconstruction: (1) to
support whole-heartedly the republican form of government, (2) to
demarcate the powers of the national government and the local government, (3) to establish a real constitutional government in China, and
(4) to promote with utmost sincerity friendly relations with foreign
countries. Meanwhile, Dr. Sun returned to China from exile. His
personal presence at this troubled time gave a powerful impetus to the
"Save the Republic" movement. As the anti-monarchist armies moved
toward the north, other southwestern provinces followed suit.

On May 5, 1916, the joint forces eventually established at Chao-ching
a Military Council as headquarters of the "National Protection Army."
This supreme organ of the anti-Yüan movement firmly declared that
Vice President Li Yüan-hung should succeed to the Presidency and
that, before Li could actually perform the Presidential duties, the
Military Council was to assume control over all matters internally and
externally. The Military Council had one commander, one deputy
commander, one chief commissioner of political affairs, and a number
of commanders and political commissioners.[2] T'ang Chi-yao and
Ch'en Ch'un-hsüan were elected commander and deputy commander
respectively. Under the direction of the Council and with the cooperation of other patriotic elements, the anti-Yüan movement had
become so strong that Yüan was compelled to give up his monarchial
dream.

Actually, Yüan foresaw his downfall much earlier. Realizing the
unpopularity of his imperial intrigue and unwilling to relinquish
completely his political career, he shrewdly ordered, on March 23, the
cancellation of his monarchial schemes and thereby restored himself
to the office of the Presidency.[3] On April 22, he reorganized the Board
of Political Affairs and a cabinet system was reestablished with Tuan
Ch'i-jui, who had stood aloof in all the monarchial turmoils, as Premier.
In a spirit of self-criticism, Yüan even accused himself of "lack of

[1] On December 5, 1915, Dr. Sun's followers made an unsuccessful attempt to seize a
government warship in the port of Shanghai. This was definitely a sign of the revolutionary
defiance against Yüan.

[2] For details, see the *Organic Law of the Military Council*, 1916.

[3] To his great disappointment, Yüan unexpectedly received a joint telegram from Feng
Kuo-chang and his four other generals, urging him to abandon monarchism to pacify the
people.

virtue." But all these measures were too late. The anti-Yüan forces insisted on his resignation on the ground that his extreme unreliability and shameful abuses made him undeserving of the office of Presidency. The agony of frustration and disgrace had severly damaged Yüan's health. He died on June 6, 1916, and was succeeded by Li Yüan-hung the next day.

Objectively speaking, Yüan was not undeserving of some praise in his opportunistic decision to desert the Manchu regime after the outbreak of the Wuchang Revolution in 1911. The part he played did avoid bloodshed and speeded up the unification of the country. But, his contribution to the nation was limited and yet his personal ambition had no bounds. His unwise attempt to restore the abandoned monarchy and do away with a republican form of government had not only met strong resistance from the revolutionaries but also invited deep suspicion and opposition from other enlightened people. Liang Ch'i-ch'ao, the leader of the Progressive Party, was one of the outstanding figures of the latter group. Disregarding Yüan's inducements and threats, Liang wrote an article which was openly against monarchism. Worst of all, Yüan had no definite political convictions which would command respect from his compatriots. Admittedly he was most skillful in using tactics to win friends. But his tactics alone were not sufficient for statesmanship because people could not be deceived all the time. His eventual downfall was due not only to the resolute action of the anti-monarchist forces, but also to the animosity of public opinion, the unanimous decision of the so-called national convention of people's representatives to the contrary notwithstanding[1]

The attitude of foreign powers was another important factor which determined the fate of Yüan Shih-k'ai. When Yüan succeeded to the Provisional Presidency, he was favorably considered by Japan and Western nations as the strong man of China. The "reorganization loan" granted by the Five-Nation Consortium was signed under the strong protest of the Nationalists. Yüan was extremely pleased with his diplomatic success and used the loan to suppress his opponents instead of reorganizing the administration as originally planned. When his monarchial movement was in full sway, the Western powers were busily occupied with World War I and left the Chinese situation to the mercy of Japan. Taking advantage of the national confusion created by Yüan's personal ambition, Japan sent

---

[1] For a comprehensive survey of Yüan's political career, see Jerome Ch'en, *Yüan Shih-K'ai* (Stanford: Stanford University Press, 1961).*

to the government in Peking the Twenty-one Demands on January 18, 1915. The terms laid down by Japan were so strict and severe that, if accepted, China would degenerate into a Japanese protectorate. Eager to win Japan's support but worrying about public opinion, Yüan really faced a dilemma. On May 7, Japan delivered an ultimatum insisting on accepting her revised demands,[1] which were acquiesced in by Yüan without the approval of Parliament.

As to foreign attitudes toward Yüan's monarchial plan, Japan first expressed her extreme concern and then indicated her opposition to it in December. France, Russia, Great Britain and Italy followed suit. It was clear that, with the ascendancy of the anti-Yüan movement, Japan would not like to back the wrong horse and incur the resentment of the people of China. In spite of his later efforts to change the Japanese attitude, Yüan was compelled to give up all hope of foreign support. This was perhaps another serious miscalculation on the part of Yüan in the planning of his monarchy. Thus, in his last days, Yüan was a broken-hearted man, deserted both domestically and internationally.

---

[1] The Twenty-one Demands may be briefly grouped under five heads:

Group I. Demands of railway, mining and concession rights in Shantung.

Group II. Insistence upon extension to ninety-nine years of the leases of Port Arthur, Dairen, the South Manchurian Railway, the management and control of the Kirin-Changchun Railway for ninety-nine years; and other exclusive railway and mining rights, and priority in investments.

Group III. Program for the control of China's main source of iron and coal in Central China.

Group IV. Demands dealing with the entire Chinese coast.

Group V. Insistence that China should have Japanese police and that China should employ Japanese advisers in financial, political and military matters.

Since these demands were never ratified by the Chinese Parliament, they had no binding force upon China. For details, see B. L. Putnam Weale, op. cit., pp. 88–144.

SPLIT BETWEEN THE NORTH AND THE SOUTH: POLITICAL INSTITUTIONS DURING THE PERIOD OF INTERNAL DISSENSIONS

I. DEVELOPMENTS UNDER THE REGIME IN PEKING

The restoration of the Provisional Constitution and Parliament

Prior to his death, Yüan Shih-k'ai willed that Vice President Li Yüan-hung be the Acting President in accordance with Article 29 of the *Constitutional Compact*. The succession of Li to the Presidency had been advocated by the anti-Yüan forces, but they insisted that such a step should be based on the *Provisional Constitution*.[1] It will be seen that Dr. Sun and his followers had persistently upheld the validity of the *Provisional Constitution* of 1912 throughout the period of internal dissensions between the North and the South. On the other hand, Premier Tuan Ch'i-jui maintained that since the *Provisional Constitution* had long been abrogated, it could not be legally restored simply by a government decree.[2] After much discussion, the views of the South finally prevailed. On June 29, 1917, President Li proclaimed the formal restoration of the *Provisional Constitution*, the *Presidential Election Law* of 1913 and the first Parliament, which should be reconvened beginning with August 1, 1917. Satisfied with Li's measures, the Military Council in the South dissolved itself on July 14 and the nation was thus reunited.

With the restoration of the *Provisional Constitution*, the government reverted to the cabinet system and the ministries were reorganized in accordance with the 1912 laws governing the administrative systems. Statutes and ordinances enacted under the regime of Yüan Shih-k'ai and in conflict with the *Provisional Constitution* were henceforth declared null and void. Meanwhile, Feng Kuo-chang was elected by

---

[1] Art. 42.
[2] For details, see *Government Bulletin*, June 24, 1916.

Parliament as Vice President of the Republic. It seemed that after all the turmoil China would go back to normalcy.

Amendment of the "Temple of Heaven" Draft

As always, Parliament was again preoccupied with the work of constitutional drafting. It proceeded to reexamine the "Temple of Heaven" Draft, which was not yet completed at the time of its dissolution. As a result of the reexamination, some recommendations were made for its amendment, including the abolition of the Standing Committee of Parliament and the emergency powers of the President as well as the prohibition of Parliamentary members from cabinet posts. The Standing Committee as provided in the original Draft was to take charge of the routine matters of Parliament during the period of its adjournment. It was to be composed of forty members, twenty each elected respectively among the members of the two chambers themselves.[1] No final decision could be reached with regard to the provincial system and the conditions under which Parliament might be dissolved.[2]

The second dissolution of Parliament

At that time, the Peking government was actually in the hands of Tuan Ch'i-jui even though Li was President of the Republic. In May 1917, a dispute arose between Parliament and the cabinet over China's policy during World War I. Tuan urged the declaration of war against Germany. His advocacy was said to be a carefully planned step toward the achievement of a major ambition. He hoped to obtain funds from Japan, ostensibly for the purpose of financing an expedition against Germany but, in reality, with the object of crushing his opponents. Tuan followed the policy, "to declare but not wage war on foreign countries; to make but not delcare war on internal enemies." Having learned of Tuan's plan, Parliament declared itself against the war. On the other side, the Anfu militarists supported Tuan and persisted in their war agitation. President Li dismissed Tuan as a result of the controversy. But later, under the pressure of the militarists and at the advice of Chang Hsün, an unreformed warlord of the Ch'ing Dynasty, Li dissolved both chambers of Parliament on June 12.[3]

---

[1] Arts 51 and 53 of the "Temple of Heaven" Draft.

[2] For various opinions on the provincial system, see Wu Tsung-chih, Constitutional History of the Republic of China, Vol. I, pp. 279–281, 297–299, 301–303.

[3] The Presidential order of the dissolution was published in the Government Gazette, June

The plot to restore the Manchu Emperor

When the situation went from bad to worse, Chang Hsün made capital of this opportunity. On June 14, he entered Peking with his troops. Then he launched a *coup d'etat* at the Capital and proclaimed the restoration of the Manchu Emperor to the throne on July 1. Faced with this grave crisis, President Li reinstated Tuan Ch'i-jui to the office of Premier. The combined forces of Tuan and Feng Kuo-chang defeated Chang on July 12.[1] Thus the Republic was restored. Taking the responsibility for the whole incident upon himself, Li resigned from the Presidency. Feng Kuo-chang, the Vice President, succeeded Li as President. Tuan remained as Premier.

Thereafter, there were serious controversies between the Peking government on the one side and the revolutionaries and parliamentarians on the other. China had to go through another period of internal dissensions and hostilities. The split between the North and the South thus created lasted until 1928 when the nation was united again by the Nationalist Party.

2. THE NEW PARLIAMENT
AND THE NEW CONSTITUTIONAL DRAFT

The election of a new Parliament

With the restoration of the Republic and the resignation of President Li, Parliament should have been re-convoked because it had been illegally dissolved by Li under the pressure of the militarists. But, owing to his long and bitter clashes with the first Parliament, Tuan did not want it to function again. By an ingenious device, the government decided to set up, in accordance with the *Provisional Constitution* of 1912, the Legislative Assembly, which would revise all the laws concerning the election and organization of the two chambers of Parliament. Then the government would call for a national election for a new Parliament. According to the government decree of September 29, 1917, all the provinces, Mongolia, Tibet and Chinghai were to send their respectively prescribed members of the Legislative Assembly to the Capital within a month's time. The new Legislative Assembly was convoked on November 10, and, before long passed the *Revised Organic Law of Parliament*, *Revised Electoral Law of the Senate* and

---

13, 1917. When Parliament was dissolved for the second time, part of the *Draft* had not yet gone through the procedure of second reading.

[1] For details, see *Tung-fang Magazine*, Vol. 14, No. 8, "Major Events in China."

Revised Electoral Law of the House of Representatives. All these laws were promulgated by the President on February 17, 1918.

The revised laws were essentially different from the original ones in the following points. (1) The total membership of the Senate was reduced from 264 to 168. (2) The apportionment of the membership of the House of Representatives was on the basis of one member to each one million population instead of the previous 800,000, thus reducing the total membership of the House from 556 to 378. (3) Formerly the Senators were elected by the provincial assemblies; according to the revised laws, the provincial assemblies were replaced in this case by local election conventions composed of primary electors with strict qualifications. (4) The qualifications of the primary electors for the election of the House of Representatives were also stricter than before.

Only fourteen provinces held elections for a new Parliament in accordance with the revised laws; while others, such as Kwangtung, Kwangsi, Yunnan, Kweichow and Szechwan, protested strongly against the election. However, regardless of the objections of the Southwestern provinces, the new Parliament was convoked on August 12, under the manipulation and direction of the Anfu Club, Premier Tuan's political clique.

The new President and the new split between the North and the South

According to the *Presidential Election Law* of 1913, the term of office of the President was five years. If for any reason the President could not perform his functions, his office would be taken over by the Vice President until the current term expired.[1] Yüan Shih-k'ai became President in October 1913. He was succeeded by Li Yüan-hung who was in turn succeeded by Feng Kuo-chang. The five-year term would expire in October 1918. Therefore a new election was in order. In this case, the new Parliament acted promptly and elected Hsü Shih-ch'ang as President of the Republic on October 10. Since the death of Yüan Shih-k'ai on June 6, 1916, the Presidency of the Peking government had been changed three times within a short period of two years and four months. This marks the extreme instability of the political situation in Peking. Fortunately, the administrative system of the national government was not much affected by the change of the head of state. As for the substitution of a new Parliament for the old one, it was bitterly resented by the Southwestern provinces. In the ensuing years, the South, under the leadership of Dr. Sun Yat-sen, carried out

[1] Arts. 3 and 5.

a number of military expeditions against the North in the name of protecting the *Provisional Constitution* and restoring the old Parliament.

The new Constitutional Draft of 1919

The new Parliament abandoned the *"Temple of Heaven"* Draft. For the purpose of drafting a new constitution, a committee of sixty was set up in Parliament, thirty each elected respectively among the members of the two chambers. With surprising speed, the Committee finished the work on August 12, 1919. Thus another *Draft Constitution of the Republic of China* was added to Chinese constitutional history. The provisions of the new Draft were very much the same as its predecessor except the following items.

(1) The new Draft prohibited members of Parliament to be concurrently civil or military officials, while the *"Temple of Heaven"* Draft made an exception to this in the case of cabinet ministers.

(2) There was no provision for the Standing Committee in Parliament to take charge of the routine matters during the period of its adjournment.

(3) The new Draft omitted the requirement as provided previously that the dissolution of the House of Representatives by the President must secure the concurrence of two-thirds of the Senators present.

(4) The required quorum for both chambers was changed from a simple majority to a one-third majority in the new Draft.

(5) The organization for the interpretation of the constitution, as provided in the old Draft, was the Constitutional Conference constituted of members of both chambers; while, in the new Draft, it was to be composed of the two Speakers of both chambers, the Chief Justice of the Supreme Court, the presidents of the Administrative Court and the Auditing *Yuan*.

The 1919 Draft also adopted the cabinet system of government and the bicameral system of Parliament, which were basically the same as those provided in the old Draft. At the time of the completion of the new Draft in 1919, there was some possibility of reconciliation between the North and the South. When the negotiations for rapprochement were going on, the work on the constitution was temporarily suspended. Then in July 1920, two military cliques, Chihli and Anhwei, started war against each other. Premier Tuan Ch'i-jui, leader of the Anhwei or Anfu clique, was defeated and the new Parliament perished with him. On October 30, President Hsü Shih-chang instructed the various provinces to elect once again new Parliament members in pursuance of the electoral laws of 1912 to form a new "New Parliament." Thereby the *Revised Organic Law of Parliament, Revised Electoral Law of the Senate* and *Revised Electoral Law of the House of Representatives*, promulgated in 1918, were no longer effective.

3. PARLIAMENT'S SECOND RESTORATION
AND ITS ADOPTION OF THE 1923 CONSTITUTION

Second restoration of the old Parliament

Since President Hsü Shih-chang was elected by the so-called New Parliament deemed by the Southwestern provinces as unconstitutional, it was natural that they defied the Presidential order of October 30, 1920. As a result, only eleven provinces held Parliamentary elections. Then Hsü himself became involved in an armed conflict in the North. Suspected by the winning Chihli military clique of favoring the defeated Fengtien military clique, Hsü had to resign from the Presidency on June 2, 1922. Sharing his fate, the so-called new "New Parliament" miscarried. At that time, the Chihli clique adopted an anti-Hsü policy by advocating the restoration of the old Parliament, which met again in Peking on August 1. Early on June 11, ex-President Li Yüan-hung was welcomed to Peking as the head of the state once more. The overthrow of Hsü should have pleased the Southwestern provinces. However, Dr. Sun was disturbed by the refusal of the reconvened Parliament to seat the members elected by the Constitution-Protecting Parliament which was instituted by him and his followers in the South to fight for the restoration of the *Provisional Constitution* and the old Parliament.

Election of a new President

At that time, Ts'ao k'un, the leader of the Chihli clique, set his eyes on the Presidency himself. He was strongly supported by his faithful subordinate, Wu P'ei-fu, who was in command of a substantial force in North China. Under such circumstances, Li could not possibly stay long in office and was forced out a year later. Then Ts'ao proceeded to bribe a large number of the members of Parliament to hold a new Presidential election on October 5, 1923. Ts'ao K'un was elected as President by a large majority of votes cast by Parliamentary members.[1]

---

[1] On that day, 593 members of Parliament signed their names on the attendance sheet. Out of the 590 votes cast, Ts'ao K'un got 480, more than the required number of three-fourths of the total votes cast. According to the provisions of the *Presidential Election Law* of 1913, Ts'ao was thus elected as President.

The acceptance of bribes by the people's representatives in the Presidential election was universally condemned. Parliamentary politics in Peking thus went bankrupt. Despite protests from various quarters, Ts'ao assumed the office of Presidency on October 10 and managed to remain a year until his forced resignation on November 2, 1924.

The completion of the first Constitution

In order to atone for the bribery involved in the Presidential election, the members of Parliament made a serious attempt to complete the unfinished work of the constitutional drafting. The Constitutional Conference of Parliament held its first meeting on October 4 to re-examine its original draft, and with unusual speed, passed and promulgated the Constitution on October 10, 1923. It was the first Constitution of the Republic of China after years of drafting by Parliament. Yet, owing to the circumstances of its creation, this Constitution was not respected by the people, nor were any sincere efforts made to enforce it. When Tuan Ch'i-jui went to Peking to head the government on November 24, 1924, he promulgated the *Organic Law of the Provisional Government System*. This new Law, for all practical purposes, superseded the 1923 Constitution.

Essentials of the 1923 Constitution

In spite of the undesirable circumstances surrounding its enactment, the 1923 *Constitution* had a few outstanding features.[1] First, it added one chapter on public or government powers dividing those belonging to the national government and the local government respectively,[2] and included another chapter on local government system dealing with the division and organization of local areas and the relationship between the province and the districts.[3] Second, even though the *Constitution* stated in Article I that "the Republic of China shall be a united Republic forever," implying a unitary form, there was a clear division of powers between the central and the local governments, thus having, to a certain extent, the nature of the constitution of a federal government. This was different from all the previous constitutional drafts. Third, the *Constitution* adopted the cabinet system of government. Besides the appointing and dismissing of the Premier, all other Presi-

---

[1] For the English text of the 1923 *Constitution*, see Appendix E. For an evaluation of the Parliament, see Ku Tun-jou, *The Legislative History of China*, Ch. XV.
[2] Ch. V.
[3] Ch. XII.

dential decrees and other documents relating to national affairs could not be effective unless countersigned by one of the cabinet ministers. One important feature was that the appointment of the Premier had to have the concurrence of the House of Representatives.[1] Fourth, it adopted a bicameral system of Parliament. The right to impeach the President and the cabinet ministers belonged exclusively to the House of Representatives; while the Senate, besides its right to concurring to the dissolution of the House of Representatives, also had the power of trying the impeached President and cabinet ministers. Another significant point was that the House of Representatives could cast a vote of non-confidence. Evidently the two chambers had different functions and were not on equal footing.[2]

The 1923 *Constitution* in comparison with previous drafts had definitely incorporated certain improvements. Although some Parliamentary members who helped to create it had wrongfully accepted bribes in the Presidential election, the Constitution itself had no fundamental defects. However, the prevailing circumstances of the nation made it practically unenforceable.

4. THE CONSTITUTION-PROTECTING GOVERNMENT IN THE SOUTHWEST

The Emergency Session of the old Parliament

After the second dissolution of the old Parliament, its Nationalist members went to Shanghai from Peking and worked for its restoration. At the time when Chang Hsün's *coup* to reinstall the Manchu dynasty was crushed, they issued a declaration demanding the punishment of the monarchists and the reconvening of the old Parliament. These demands were ignored by President Feng Kuo-Chang and Premier Tuan Ch'i-jui of the Peking government. Instead, the northern leaders set out their own schemes. Therefore, as leader of the revolution and founder of the Chinese Republic, Dr. Sun Yat-sen now took upon himself the duty of protecting the constitution of 1912 and led these Parliament members south to Canton. He questioned the legality of the government in Peking and was determined to use force for the restoration of constitutional legitimacy. On August 18, 1917, more than one hundred thirty members of the old Parliament gathered together in Canton and adopted a resolution that an Emergency Session of Parliament be convened. This Emergency Session met on August

[1] For details, see Ch. VIII.
[2] Arts. 60–63.

25 and, four days later, enacted the *Organic Law of the Emergency Session of Parliament.*

According to this law, the Emergency Session was constituted by the members of the old Parliament and would remain in existence until domestic peace and the Provisional Constitution of 1912 had been restored. Deliberations were conducted through the joint session of the Senate and the House of Representatives and a quorum was to require the presence of the members representing at least fourteen provinces. In this respect, Mongolia, Tibet, Chinghai, and the overseas Chinese communities were classified as each to have the status of a province. The Speakers and Deputy Speakers of the Emergency Session were elected from the incumbent Speakers and Deputy Speakers of the two chambers of the old Parliament.

The Military Government in the Southwest

On August 30, 1917, the Emergency Session enacted and promulgated the *Organic Law of the Military Government.* As the supreme organ of the Constitution-Protecting forces, the Military Government was to be headed by a Generalissimo as the Chief Executive and representing the Republic of China in foreign relations. Under the Generalissimo, there were two marshals to assist him in the administration of the state affairs. The Generalissimo and the marshals were elected separately by the Emergency Session of Parliament by a simple majority vote. Within the Military Government there were six ministries: foreign affairs, interior, finance, army. navy and communications. The minister was elected by the Emergency Session of Parliament and appointed by the Generalissimo. On September 1, the Emergency Session elected Dr. Sun Yat-sen as the Generalissimo and Lu Jung-ting and T'ang Chi-yao as marshals. When Dr. Sun assumed his office on September 10, he issued a declaration of his avowed determination to restore constitutional legitimacy in China.

In spite of Dr. Sun's enthusiasm for the Constitution-Protecting movement, there were opportunists within the Military Government including Marshall Lu Jung-ting who secretly negotiated for peace with President Feng and Premier Tuan of the Peking Government. In January 1918, these opportunists joined together with the powerful militarists of the Southwest to organize the so-called Joint Constitution-Protecting Conference of the Southwestern Self-governing Provinces.[1]

---

[1] This Conference proclaimed the *Rules of the Joint Conference of the Constitution-Protecting Provinces of the Republic of China.* See *Tung-fang Magazine,* Vol. 15, No. 2.

Meanwhile, they prevailed upon the Emergency Session of Parliament to reorganize the Military Government to suit their purposes. Under such circumstances, Dr. Sun resigned from the office of the Generalissimo. Opportunism was the dominant factor underlying the reorganization of the Military Government.

According to the *Revised Organic Law of the Military Government* promulgated on May 10, 1918, the Military Government adopted a collective system by replacing the office of the Generalissimo with a Board of Governors in charge of war and peace negotiations. However, the peace terms could not come into effect without the concurrence of the joint session of the two chambers of Parliament. The number of Governors was to be decided by the joint session of Parliament. At each meeting, the Board of Governors was to elect a Chairman, who was to assume the office as Chief Executive and perform the functions of the President as prescribed in the *Provisional Constitution* of 1912. The Chairman was, however, directly responsible to Parliament, which could impeach him with the concurrence of a simple majority of the members present. Under the Board of Governors, there were the Political Council, the Military Commission, and the General Staff Headquarters. On May 20, the Emergency Session of Parliament elected seven Governors of the Military Government including Dr. Sun Yat-sen and Ch'en Ch'un-hsüan. Since Dr. Sun realized at this time that Ch'en Ch'un-hsüan and other influential members of the Board of Governors were not determined to protect the Constitution, he was not enthusiastic for his election to the new post.

The drafting of a constitution by the Constitution-Protecting Parliament

On June 22, 1918, the Emergency Session of Parliament resolved to call for a formal session in continuance of the second regular session held in 1917. But the number of Parliament members in Canton still could not constitute a quorum. According to Article 7 of the Rules of Procedure of Parliament of 1913, members of Parliament could be disqualified if they failed to report to Parliament after it had been in session for one month. It was by the enforcement of this rule that a few hundred Parliament members were disqualified and their seats were filled by alternate members. Once the quorum was secured for a regular session, the Emergency Session of Parliament was renamed the Constitution-Protecting Parliament.

On several occasions, the Constitution-Protecting Parliament issued declarations against the New Parliament in Peking and the President elected by it as unconstitutional and detrimental to national unity.[1] It proceeded to complete the unfinished work of the constitutional draft left by the old Parliament. Beginning with September 28, 1918, the constitutional conference discussed the chapter on the local government system. However, because of the peace negotiations which had taken place in Shanghai between the governments of the North and the South in February 1919, many members of Parliament had left Canton and thus the deliberation on the draft was delayed. The negotiations reached a deadlock in August. When the discussion of the constitutional draft was resumed on November 18, controversies arose on the power to dissolve Parliament and the functions of the provincial governors. Consequently some Parliament members who belonged to a political faction called the Tseng-hsueh Society refused to attend the meetings. As the members present were not enough to constitute a quorum, Speaker Lin Sen announced a temporary adjournment of Parliament on January 24, 1920. Thus no real progress was made in constitutional drafting by the Parliament members in Canton.

The Chinese Revolutionary Party renamed as the Nationalist Party of China

It was mentioned before that Dr. Sun Yat-sen considered his failure against Yüan Shih-k'ai largely due to the loose organization and lack of discipline of the Nationalist Party (Kuomintang). For this reason, he decided to found the Chinese Revolutionary Party (Chung-hua Ko-min Tang) on July 8, 1914, with the purpose of reviving the revolutionary spirit in China. However, many members failed to join the new party owing to their objection to the oath of loyalty even though they were still enthusiastic toward the revolutionary cause. Besides, after the party reorganization in 1914, many overseas branches continued to use the traditional name, "the Nationalist Party," in order to avoid registration difficulties with the local governments. As a matter of expediency, the name of the party was changed back on October 10, 1919. But the formal title of the party since 1919 has been the Nationalist Party of China (Chung-kuo Kuomintang), even though it is commonly known as the Nationalist Party (Kuomintang). Dr. Sun remained as the Director-General (Tsung-li) of the renamed party, with the assistance of a number of departments and commissions which had undergone minor changes in 1920 and 1923.[2] The major reorgan-

---

[1] See Yang Yu-chiung, *Legislative History of Modern China*, pp. 260–262.
[2] For details, see William L. Tung, *The Government of China*, Vol. I, p. 387.

ization of the party was, however, not made until 1924 as fully described in the following chapter.

Ch'en Ch'un-hsüan vs. Parliament in the Southwest

In the spring of 1920, the situation in the Southwest was on the verge of total collapse. Ch'en Ch'un-hsüan and his colleagues had secretly negotiated peace terms with the North. For fear that Parliament might frustrate his endeavors, Ch'en decided to get rid of it by suspending the payment of its expenses. Under the deteriorating situation, members of Parliament gradually left Canton. Speaker Lin Sen denounced Ch'en's malicious action by an open statement. On June 3, 1920, Dr. Sun and three other Governors of the Military Government challenged Ch'en's peace negotiations as unconstitutional. Thus the Board of Governors had a wide split and could not perform its proper functions.

In August of the same year, the two chambers of Parliament met in the capital of Yunnan province in an emergency session with the intent to set up a government there. This was opposed by T'ang Chi-yao, Governor of that province. In September, Parliament moved to Chungking in Szechwan province, but it had to leave in the following month due to the power struggle there. It was only after Ch'en Ch'un-hsüan had been ousted that Parliament was able to meet again in Canton in January 1921. Thus the history of the Constitution-Protecting Parliament was short but eventful.

The organization of a formal government and the election of the President

Ch'en Ch'un-hsüan's opportunistic measures in the Southwest also met strong opposition from Ch'en Ch'iung-ming, who led his army back to Canton from Fukien province. Unable to fight against this enemy force, Ch'en Ch'un-hsüan fled Canton and, on October 24, announced his resignation from the Military Government. In order to continue the Constitution-Protecting task, Dr. Sun Yat-sen returned to Canton soon afterwards. On December 1, he announced the convocation of a Political Affairs Conference. The wandering Parliament members also came back to Canton and met again on January 12, 1921. With little more than two hundred members, not sufficient to constitute a quorum, the meeting was called the Emergency Session. Realizing the inadequacy of the Military Government, the Emergency Session of Parliament decided to establish a formal government in Canton and thus enacted the *Organic Law of the Government of the Republic of China* on April 7, 1921. Dr. Sun was elected by the Emergency Session as

President of the new government. When he was sworn into office on May 5, he solemnly declared his determination to unify the country and strengthen the foundation of the Republc.

According to the *Organic Law* of the new government, the President was the Chief Executive and Commander-in-Chief of the armed forces. He had the power to appoint and dismiss civil and military officers and to issue orders. He was to represent the Republic in foreign affairs. As to the relations between the President and Parliament, there was no express provision except Article 2, which provided that "the President is to be elected by the Emergency Session of Parliament." Under the President, there were several ministries in charge of foreign affairs, finance, army, navy, interior, and justice. Each ministry was headed by a minister. In practice, one could concurrently hold two ministerial posts.[1]

The headquarters of the Generalissimo

Once the constitutional arrangements had been settled, Dr. Sun turned his attention to the task of the Northern Expedition. His policy was not actually supported by Ch'en Ch'iung-ming who, seemingly obedient to his command, was secretly planning his own course. While the expeditionary forces were gaining in Kiangsi province, Ch'en staged a *coup d'etat* in Canton on June 16, 1922, which "left the government in ruins and Parliament dispersed." [2] Dr. Sun barely escaped with his life. Then he set up his temporary headquarters on board a warship and was later joined by Chiang Kai-shek. Since the reinforcements could not reach the area in time, he left Canton for Shanghai on August 9. Early in 1923, the northern expeditionary force turned back toward Canton and defeated Ch'en Ch'iung-ming. Upon his return to Canton on February 11, Dr. Sun set up the Headquarters of the Generalissimo to replace the formal government during the period of emergency. The reorganization was completed on March 2. The Generalissimo was to be in charge of all civil and military matters. He had the power to appoint and dismiss all civil and military officers. Under the Generalissimo, there were four ministries in charge of interior, foreign affairs, finance and reconstruction. In addition, there were the Supreme Court and the Office of the Prosecutor-General in Canton.[3]

[1] For example, Wu Ting-fang was concurrently foreign minister and finance minister, and Ch'en Ch'iung-ming was concurrently minister of the army and minister of the interior.

[2] Dr. Sun's *Declaration of the Second Constitution-Protecting Movement* (*The Collected Works of Sun Yat-sen*, Vol. IV, "Political Declaration Through the Years," pp. 21–26.

[3] See Tsou Lu, *The Manuscript of the History of the Nationalist Party of China*, Vol. II, p. 1077; and also Ch'ien Tuan-sheng, *et al.*, *History of the Political Institutions under the Chinese Republic*, Vol. I, p. 166.

At that time, Ts'ao K'un was elected President by the Parliament in Peking through bribery. Dr. Sun was strongly opposed to Ts'ao's government, but the Canton regime was not strong enough to wage a war immediately against the North. He first consolidated his control in Kwangtung province, then proceeded to reorganize the Nationalist Party so as to strengthen the revolutionary organization, and finally led the armies northward against the Peking regime. When Ts'ao K'un was eventually thrown out of power by his enemy forces in the North and replaced by Tuan Ch'i-jui as Chief Executive of the Peking Government, Dr. Sun left Canton for Peking in November 1924, to discuss state affairs with Tuan and other northern leaders. But the Headquarters of the Generalissimo remained in existence until July 1, 1925, when the Nationalist Government was established in Canton.

5. THE PEKING GOVERNMENT
UNDER PROVISIONAL CHIEF EXECUTIVE TUAN

The organization of the Provisional Government in Peking

In the winter of 1924, another civil war broke out in the North between Ts'ao K'un and Wu P'ei-fu of the Chihli military clique on one side and Chang Tso-lin of the Manchurian clique on the other. As a result of the Chihli defeat, Ts'ao K'un was forced to step down from the Presidency. As the defection of Feng Yü-shiang from the Chihli clique was the determining factor of Chang's victory, Feng and Chang formed a temporary alliance. At their invitation, Tuan Ch'i-jui, a former prime minister, went to Peking on November 24, 1924, and assumed the title of the Provisional Chief Executive. On the same day, he promulgated the *Organic Law of the Provisional Government of the Republic of China.*

As head of the Provisional Government, the Chief Executive was to hold supreme authority over civil and military affairs of the state and to represent the country in foreign relations. Under him there were ministers of foreign affairs, interior, finance, army, navy, justice, education, agriculture and commerce, and communications. There being no provision for a prime minister, the Chief Executive was to preside over cabinet meetings. All government decrees and related documents had to be countersigned by one or more of the ministers. This requirement was not as important as it seemed to be, because the Chief Executive had the power to appoint and dismiss the ministers without any restraint. Legally, the Chief Executive had combined in himself the powers of the President, Parliament and the cabinet; but practically, his freedom of action was much restrained by the constant interference of the military leaders.

When Tuan came back to power in 1924, he was determined to eliminate the old constitutional system. At the cabinet meeting of December 13, 1924, it was decided that the Government should issue three orders: (1) to nullify the *Constitution* of 1923, (2) to abrogate the *Provisional Constitution* of 1912 and (3) to dissolve the Parliament. These orders were withheld for a while for fear that there would be strong objections especially from the South against the abrogation of the *Provisional Constitution* of 1912; but they were finally carried out on April 24, 1925. As Chang and Feng had their own ambition to dominate the government, Tuan's position became untenable in the winter of 1925. He had to reorganize the government to meet the changing situation. By revising the *Organic Law of the Provisional Government of the Republic of China* on December 26, he created a cabinet system with a premier at its head. The premier was to preside over cabinet meetings and to sign government decrees and related documents with the countersignature of one or more of the ministers. Tuan used the premiership as a buffer office to ease his relationship with the military leaders.

Tuan stayed in the office as Provisional Chief Executive until April 20, 1926, when Chang and Feng broke up their alliance and the former took direct control of the Peking government.

The Reorganization Conference

After the fall of Ts'ao K'un and Wu P'ei-fu in 1924, Dr. Sun Yat-sen was invited to go to Peking by Feng Yü-hsiang, Chang Tso-li and Tuan Ch'i-jui. Before his acceptance of their invitation, he issued a statement, urging the convocation of a People's Convention as a consultative organ. In his view, that Convention should be preceded by a preparatory meeting composed of representatives from all civic groups, the military forces against the Chihli clique, and all the political parties. However, Tuan as Chief Executive of the Peking government wanted to hold a Reorganization Conference and, without obtaining Dr. Sun's consent, promulgated the regulations governing its organization on December 23, 1924. The objectives of the Conference were to discuss military reforms and national finance and to draft rules for the People's Convention. The Conference was constituted by the following: (1) those who had made great contributions to the nation; (2) the military commanders against the Chihli clique; (3) chief civil and military officials of the provinces of Mongolia, Tibet and Chinghai; (4) those selected by the Chief Executive from the nations's best known scholars. Contrary to Dr. Sun's wishes, the civic groups were not represented at the Conference.

In spite of the strong objection of the Nationalist Party under the leadership of Dr. Sun, the Reorganization Conference was convoked in February 1925. At its first session on February 13, Chao Erh-hsün and Tong Yi were elected chairman and vice-chairman respectively. The Conference continued in session until April 20, and adopted the Regulations governing the People's Convention, the Military Reorganization Commission, and the Financial Reorganization Commission. These Regulations were all promulgated by the Provisional Chief Executive on April 24.[1] Each of the two Commissions was composed of a president, two vice-presidents and a number of commissioners, all appointed by the Chief Executive. But the People's Convention, which was supposed to adopt a constitution for the nation, was never convoked.

The Provisional Political Council

An important organ of the Provisional Government under Tuan Ch'i-jui, the Provisional Political Council, was set up on July 30, 1925. Its purpose was to create positions for the former members of the Reorganization Conference and also to show the public Tuan's democratic inclination by having a semi-legislative organization. According to the *Regulations governing the Provisional Political Council* promulgated on May 1, 1925, the Council was composed of representatives from the following categories: (1) those appointed by the chief military and civil authorities of the various provinces and special areas; (2) those appointed by the Provisional Chief Executive from Mongolia, Tibet, Chinghai, the minority groups, the overseas Chinese, and other qualified individuals; (3) chairmen of the provincial assemblies; and (4) one elected among the various associations of the provinces in accordance with law. The council had a chairman and a vice-chairman appointed by the Provisional Chief Executive from the Council members.

The Provisional Political Council served as an advisory organ to the Chief Executive, but did not possess independent legislative powers. The Chief Executive could refer the following matters to the Council for deliberation: (1) the promotion of provincial autonomy and, prior

[1] For their texts, see *Government Bulletin*, May 25, 1925.

to the promulgation of national and provincial constitutions, the enactment of temporary regulations governing provincial self-government; (2) the execution of resolutions passed by the Reorganization Conference, the Military Reorganization Commission, or the Financial Reorganization Commission; (3) the prevention and mediation of disputes between or within the provinces; (4) the declaration of war, negotiations for peace, and conclusion of treaties; (5) the flotation of domestic and foreign loans and the increase of taxation; and (6) other matters that the Chief Executive might deem fit to submit to it for consideration. If the Chief Executive should disapprove any measure passed by the Council, he might, within twenty days, return it to the Council for reconsideration; but he should execute it accordingly if the Council maintained the original decision after reconsideration. This relationship is similar to that between the executive and legislative branches in the democratic countries. The difference is that members of the Council were not elected and it was therefore less likely they would do anything contrary to the wishes of the Provisional Chief Executive.

The Provisional Political Council was originally scheduled to exist until the formal government was established. Unfortunately, it vanished at the same time as did the power of Provisional Chief Executive Tuan in 1926.

The Draft Constitution of 1925

With the abrogation of the *Provisional Constitution* of 1912 and the *Constitution* of 1923, Tuan Ch'i-jui planned to draft a new constitution to be submitted to the People's Convention for final approval. The drafting task was entrusted to the National Constitution Drafting Commission of seventy members who were appointed by the Provisional Chief Executive and by the military and civil authorities of the provinces and special areas. The Commission met on August 3, 1925, and, on December 12, another *Draft Constitution of the Republic of China* was adopted.

The *Draft Constitution* of 1925 consisted of five parts, fourteen chapters, one hundred sixty articles, and most of its contents were similar to the Constitution of 1923. The following were its outstanding features. First, it added two chapters on "People's Livelihood" and "Education." Second, it specifically enumerated the various provinces and special areas as national territories of China. Third, it made a clear demarcation of the powers between the national and local governments.

Fourth, the members of the House of Representatives were to be elected through direct elections and could be recalled by the voters. Fifth, the important powers of Parliament were more concentrated in the House of Representatives. Sixth, the amendment of the constitution was to be made by a special Constitutional Convention. Technically speaking, there were some improvements in the *Draft Constitution* of 1925; but the planned People's Convention had never been convoked to deliberate on its adoption as a national constitution.

The Peking Military Government after the fall of Tuan Ch'i-jui

When Tuan Ch'i-jui lost the support of Chang Tso-lin, the Manchurian warlord, and was compelled to retire to Tientsin on April 20, 1926, the Government of the Provisional Chief Executive came to an end. Meanwhile, the National Revolutionary Army in the South had started its Northern Expedition and was advancing rapidly. Under these circumstances, Chang Tso-lin first assumed the office of the Commander-in-Chief of the National Security Army to resist the revolutionary army and later, at the request and support of his followers, organized the Military Government with himself as the Generalissimo on June 18, 1927.[1]

The Generalissimo was to hold the highest authority of the Republic. Under him there was a cabinet which was composed of a premier, and ministers of foreign affairs, interior, finance, justice, education, industry, agriculture and labor, and communications. The following matters were to be discussed at the cabinet meetings: (1) government mandates; (2) declaration of war, negotiations for peace and conclusion of treaties; (3) budget and special appropriations; (4) military organizations; (5) appointment of high-ranking officials; (6) disputes between the ministeries; and (7) other matters submitted for discussion in accordance with law or at the wishes of the premier and the ministers. The government in Peking at that time was actually under a military dictatorship. It was overthrown when Chang Tso-lin was defeated by the revolutionary army of the Nationalist Party and retreated to Manchuria in June 1928.[2]

---

[1] For the organization of the Military Government in Peking, see *Government Bulletin*, June 19 and July 13, 1927.

[2] His train was blown up by a mine on June 4 and he was fatally wounded. After his death, the Manchurian army was commanded by his son, Chang Hsueh-liang, generally known as the Young Marshal. On December 31, 1928, the Young Marshal changed his allegiance to the Nationalist government. Thus the nation was united again.

6. THE LOCAL GOVERNMENT SYSTEM

Legal provisions

The local government system during this period generally followed the classification of 1914: the province, the prefecture and the district. There were only slight variations. The Hunan and other provincial constitutions adopted since 1920 and the national *Constitution* of 1923 had some different provisions on the local government system, but they were either applicable only to limited areas or had never come into effect at all. As for the Special Areas of Jehol, Chahar, and Suiyuan, the Peking government promulgated the *Temporary Regulations governing the Office of the Military Commissioner* on February 22, 1928. These new regulations were a little different from those of 1914, but the three Special Areas were soon changed into the status of provinces. With respect to the local self-government, some progress had been made during this period, for example, the restoration of provincial assemblies and the promulgation of a series of rules and regulations concerning the local self-government of districts, cities and villages. The more outstanding features of the local government system during this period are described below.

The provincial system

Two new departments under the office of the governor – After the death of Yüan Shih-k'ai in 1916, the Peking government made some changes in the provincial government system. By the decree of July 6, 1916, the title of the head of the province was changed from inspector-general to governor. This was followed by a decree of August 14, ordering the provinces to restore the provincial assemblies. On September 6, 1917, the President promulgated the *Temporary Regulations concerning the Establishment of the Departments of Education and Industry*. The provincial authorities were instructed to create the two departments as substitutes of the original two sections with corresponding functions under the Bureau of Political Affairs of the Office of the Governor. While directly under the control of the governor, the two departments were supervised by the ministries of education and industry of the national government respectively.

The provincial consultative council – After the promulgation of the *Regulations governing the Provincial Consultative Council* on June 23, 1921, such councils were gradually set up in the various provinces as auxiliary organs to the provincial administration. A council was composed of twelve members with the provincial governor as its chairman. The council members came from the following categories: three appointed by the governor from his department commissioners and bureau directors, three selected by the governor from the natives of the province, and six elected by the provincial assembly. The functions of the consultative council were as follows: (1) to consider matters relating to local improvements and administration; (2) to plan and reorganize the provincial properties, construction, public equipment and other financial matters; (3) to examine and discuss the budget, appropriations and other items referred to the provincial assembly by the governor; (4) to determine whether or not recommendations made by the provincial assembly could be executed; (5) to discuss the governor's replies to inquires made by the provincial assembly; (6) to appear, at the request of the governor, before the provincial assembly to make explanations of the bills submitted by the governor; (7) to settle disputes arising from the local self-government units and other difficulties; (8) to deliberate on the means of execution of the resolutions adopted by the provincial assembly; (9) to recommend to the governor or reply to his inquiry on questions concerning national administration; and (10) to consider other local matters that were not specifically provided by law as being within the jurisdiction of the national government. After the restoration of the provincial assembly and the creation of the consultative council, the authority of the province was vested in three organs. This was an important feature of the provincial system during this period.

The provincial constitutions – The provincial-constitution movement started in 1920. Having realized the remoteness of the adoption of a national constitution to be observed throughout the country, Hunan and other provinces set out to draft their own provincial constitutions. Their objectives were first to start their provincial self-governments and then to organize a joint conference with the purpose of drafting a national constitution for the ultimate unification of China. This movement was generally known as the "united provincial self-government." On November 2, 1920, Hunan province took the lead in enforcing local self-government and in drafting a provincial constitution. The *Hunan Provincial Constitution* was adopted by a popular vote of the province on December 11, 1921, and was promulgated on January 1, 1922. Chekiang, Kwangtung and Szechwan provinces followed suit and drafted their own provincial constitutions.[1] Other provinces, such as

---

[1] On September 9, 1921, the provincial government of Chekiang promulgated the Chekiang

Yunnan, Kwangsi, Kweichow, Shansi, Kiangsu, Kiangsi, Hupei and Fukien, had also favored such a movement but never made it a reality.

According to the *Hunan Provincial Constitution*, the chief administrator of the province was the governor and the provincial legislature was the provincial assembly consisting of members directly elected by the people of the province. There were many significant points of the self-government system in Hunan province: universal suffrage without distinction of sex; the rights of initiative, referendum and recall; and the election of the governor by popular vote from four candidates chosen by the provincial assembly. These provisions had indeed the true spirit of democracy. As the other constitutions and draft constitutions were not as outstanding as the Hunan constitution, it is unnecessary to discuss them here. The *Constitution* of 1923, which provided a provincial government system similar to that of the Hunan constitution, permitted the individual provinces to enact their own self-government regulations if they were not in conflict with the national constitution and statutes.[1] As the *Constitution* of 1923 was never enforced throughout the country, the individual provinces retained their own systems without the necessity of any revision.

The district system

The district government in general – The district government system during this period was largely based on that instituted in 1914. Organizational changes were made in 1921. The chief administrator of the self-governing district was called the magistrate, who was either appointed by the governor upon the recommendation of the district convention or selected and commissioned by the governor from the nominees chosen by the district assembly and approved by a popular vote. According to the *Constitution* of 1923, the magistrate was to be directly elected by the people of the district. With the assistance of the district consultative council, the magistrate was to take charge of the administration of the district. The popular election of the magistrate

Provincial Constitution, commonly known as "9/9 Constitution." Before it could be put into practice, the Chekiang provincial assembly raised an objection. According to the opinion of the assembly, since it had never been voted upon by the citizens of the province, it should be deemed as one of the many drafts submitted by the citizens and all these drafts should be reviewed by the "Provincial Constitution Commission." The Commission finally chose three drafts to be voted upon by the citizens of the province on August 1, 1923 and planned to adopt the one that secured the most votes as the provincial constitution of Chekiang. This scheduled voting was, however, never carried out. As to the texts of the *Draft Provincial Constitution of Kwangtung* and the *Draft Provincial Constitution of Szechwan*, see *The China Year Book* (Shangai: Commercial Press), 1924, pp. 120–145.

[1] See Arts. 125–127 of the *Constitution* of 1923.

could, however, be applied only to those districts where judicial independence had been established and local autonomy had been completed.

New rules and regulations concerning district autonomy – When local self-government was suspended in March 1914 by the order of President Yüan Shih-k'ai, the district assemblies were abolished. Thus, for a long period, there were no legislative organs in the districts. In January 1917, a movement started in Parliament for the revival of the local self-government; it was well received by the executive branch. By the Presidential decree of January 19 for the enforcement of local self-government, the ministry of interior was instructed to pay serious attention to the enactment of rules and regulations concerning the subject. A few months later, however, Parliament was dissolved and the promotion of local self-government was once again put aside. It was not until September 8, 1919 that the Peking government promulgated the *District Self-government Regulations*. On January 17, 1920, the President ordered the provinces to carry out the self-government program seriously and thoroughly. This was followed by the convening of the "Local Administration Conference" from May 4 to June 8, 1920. The Conference drafted the *Procedural Rules for the Application of the District Self-government Regulations* and the *Electoral Rules of the District Assembly*, which were all promulgated on June 18, 1921. The *City Self-government Regulations* and the *Village Self-government Regulations* were also drafted by the Conference and promulgated on July 3, 1921. All these new rules and regulations concerning local self-government superseded those promulgated by Yüan Shih-k'ai, including the *Experimental Regulations of Local Self-government* and the *Procedural Rules for the Application of the Experimental Regulations of Local Self-government*. It should be noted here that under Yüan's regime local self-government had one level only, the sub-district. With the enforcement of the new system, there were two levels, the district and the city or village.

Functions of the district self-government – According to the provisions of the *District Self-government Regulations*, the territory of the district self-government was the same as the existing district boundary and the prefect was its direct supervisor. The district self-government was to take charge of matters concerning the district in general and those beyond the capabilities of the lower units: (1) education; (2) communications, irrigation and other constructions; (3) industry and public enterprises; (4) sanitation and public welfare; and (5) other matters within the jurisdiction of the district self-government as prescribed by law.

The district assembly – As the legislature of the self-governing district, the district assembly was composed of ten to thirty members elected by the people of the district. It had a chairman and a vice-chairman. The following matters were to be discussed and decided by the district assembly: (1) matters concerning local autonomy financed by funds of the district self-government; (2) the charter of the district self-government; (3) the district budget; (4) the assessment of taxes and fees within the district; (5) the purchase and disposition of immovable properties; (6) the management and disposition of property, construction and public equipment of the district; and (7) other matters within the jurisdiction of the district assembly in accordance with law.

The district consultative council – The district consultative council was to assist the magistrate in carrying out the administrative work of the district. With the magistrate as its chairman, the council was composed of four to six members, half of whom were appointed by the magistrate and the other half elected by the district assembly. The chief functions of the council were as follows: (1) to execute the resolutions adopted by the district assembly; (2) to handle matters relating to district assembly elections; (3) to submit bills to the district assembly; (4) to enact rules and regulations concerning the self-government of the district; (5) to administer or supervise the property, construction and public equipment of the district self-government; (6) to administer the revenue and expenditures of the district self-government; and (7) to collect taxes and fees in accordance with law and the resolutions of the district assembly.

Enforcement of district autonomy – The above *District Self-government Regulations* were never universally applied to all the provinces. During the period from September 1921 to March 1922, the Peking government had prescribed dates and areas for the enforcement of these regulations; but such orders were never strictly carried out. Nevertheless, since 1920, district assemblies had been established in Hunan, Chekiang Kwangtung and Yunnan provinces in accordance with their respective self-government laws and regulations. Provisions for the establishment of district assemblies were also made in the *Constitution* of 1923.

The Municipal system

Early practices in individual cities – The city government system had not received public attention until 1920, when it was incorporated into the provincial constitutions of Hunan, Chekiang, Kwantung and Szechwan. The *Hunan Provincial Constitution* classified the cities into three classes on the basis of their population. The municipal assembly was to be the legislature and the mayor was the chief administrator, both elected directly by the people of the city. A city commission was created as an auxiliary organ to the city administration, with the mayor as its chairman. One half of the members of the city commission were to be elected by the municipal assembly and the other half selected and appointed by the mayor from the various professional groups.

In February 1921, a new form of city government was introduced in Canton. The municipal government of Canton was under the direct control of the provincial government. It had a mayor and a city commission in charge of administration and a municipal council as its legislative organ. The municipal government also had six bureaus in charge of finance, engineering, public safety, sanitation, public works and education. In 1925, Shanghai was elevated to the status of special municipality and began preparations for self-government. The municipal government of Shanghai had the municipal assembly as the legislature, the mayor as the chief administrator, and the municipal board of trustees as the auxiliary organ to the city administration. The above is only a brief account of the municipal systems in the various parts of the country.

Unified system of municipal government – The nation did not have a unified system of municipal government until July 3, 1921, when the *City Self-government Regulations* were promulgated. These regulations were amended on July 4, 1922 and later supplemented by the *Procedural Rules for the Application of City Self-government Regulations* of September 9, 1922. According to the above provisions, the territory of city self-government was to be identical with the existing administrative boundary, and any area with a population below 10,000 was to be administered in accordance with the *Village Self-government Regulations*. There were two kinds of municipalities, the special and the ordinary, depending upon the importance and population of the cities. In each municipality, there were a municipal assembly as the legislature, a municipal self-government as the administrative organ, and a municipal consultative council as the latter's auxiliary.

Municipal legislature – The municipal assembly consisted of ten to twenty members elected by the citizens of the city. It was presided over by a chairman elected from the assembly members. The following matters were discussed and decided by the municipal assembly: (1) the city charter; (2) city improvements and matters related thereto; (3) municipal self-government matters financed by city funds; (4) the city budget and appropriations; (5) the assessment of taxes and fees within the city; (6) the flotation of public bonds and negotiation of contracts involving financial burdens of the people; (7) the purchase, sale and disposition of city immovable property; (8) the administration and disposition of city property, construction and public equipment; (9) matters relating to the employment of city personnel; (10) replies to inquiries made by the municipal administration or other supervisory offices; and (11) other matters within the jurisdiction of the municipal assembly in accordance with law.

Municipal administration – The municipal self-government had the mayor as the chief administrator. He was elected from those people qualified to be members of the municipal assembly. The mayor was to execute resolutions passed by the municipal assembly, to handle municipal elections, and to administer the municipal revenue and expenditure, public properties and other matters relating to city management. The municipal consultative council consisted of the mayor, an assistant, borough trustees and honorary councillors. The mayor served as its chairman. All city bills submitted to the municipal assembly had to be decided first by the municipal consultative council, which was an auxiliary organ to the city administration.

Government control vs. municipal autonomy – The three municipal organs mentioned above were in charge of city government. If properly co-ordinated, they could carry out their respective functions efficiently. But the self-governing cities had been subject to constant interference from their supervisory offices. The ordinary municipalities were to be directly supervised by the district magistrates, while the national capital and special municipalities were under the direct supervision of the ministry of interior. Sometimes, the supervisory offices exercised such an extensive power that government control had almost overshadowed the local autonomy. With the exception of the national capital and Tsingtao, both of which had seriously enforced the *City Self-government Regulations*, most of the cities during this period were administered by their superior governments rather than by the local officers elected by the people.

The village system

The village legislative and administrative organs – According to the *Village Self-government Regulations* of 1921, the territory of the village self-government was to be identical with that of the existing administrative boundary. If a certain village could not become an independent self-government unit for reasons of inadequate territory, small population or unsound financial conditions, it might be combined with the neighboring village or villages of the same district for the purpose of self-government. In each self-governing village, there were a village assembly as the legislature and a village self-government office as the administrative organ. The village assembly consisted of six to ten members, elected by the citizens of the village. It had a chairman to preside over the assembly meetings. With the exception of items (6), (9) and (10), the functions of the municipal assembly were applicable to the village assembly. The village self-government office had a village administrator, who was appointed by the district magistrate upon the recommendation of the village assembly. The qualifications of the village administrator were the same as those of the members of the village assembly. The powers and functions of the village administrator corresponded to those of the mayor of a city. When necessary, one or two village trustees could be named to assist him. The district magistrate had extensive supervisory power over the village within his district. He could even impose penalties against the village assembly and village self-government office should they violate the law or exceed their powers.

Evaluation of village self-government – Village self-government during this period existed more in word than in deed. Because the education of the people and their political training were not advanced enough for self-rule, it was next to impossible to expect actual progress of local autonomy. Nevertheless, some provinces, such as Shansi and Yunnan, where political and economic situations were relatively stable, had formulated their own programs for self-government with considerable success. In this connection, the village system as practiced in Shansi province was the most outstanding example.[1]

---

[1] See Ch'ien Tuan-sheng, *et al., op. cit.,* Vol. II, pp. 660–664.

CHAPTER V

THE NATIONALIST PARTY IN POWER:
UNIFICATION OF CHINA
UNDER KUOMINTANG PROGRAMS

I. THE REORGANIZATION OF THE NATIONALIST PARTY IN 1924

Reasons for the reorganization

According to Dr. Sun Yat-sen, the revolutionary program of China would be divided into three stages: first, military administration; second, political tutelage; and, third, constitutional government. As the Nationalist Party's development has been the source of power in Chinese politics, especially during the periods of military administration and political tutelage, a comprehensive analysis of the various phases of the Party is necessary for a clear understanding of modern China. A brief description has already been made of the different organizations of the party at different times: Hsing-chung Hui (Society for the Regeneration of China) in 1894, T'ung-meng Hui (The Alliance) in 1905, the Nationalist Party (Kuomintang) in 1912, the Chinese Revolutionary Party (Chung-hua Ko-min Tang) in 1914, and the Nationalist Party of China (Chung-kuo Kuomintang) in 1919.

The Nationalist Party in 1919 was still a loose organization, largely made up of intellectuals. In order to undertake the revolutionary task of overthrowing the rule of the militarists and the domination of the imperialist powers in China, the Party had to be established on a broader basis with mass support. Dr. Sun fully realized the far-reaching consequences of the student movement in 1919[1] and the increasing influence of the workers after 1922. Disappointed with the Western

---

[1] When the Versailles Peace Conference in 1919 decided to transfer former German rights and interests in Shantung to Japan despite China's strong protest, the students in Peking were angry with the Peking government because of its diplomatic failure. On May 4, 1919, they attacked some of the cabinet ministers and made various efforts to stir up nationalist sentiment among the populace throughout the country. For the significance of the new intellectual movement in China, see *Bulletin* No. 6 of the Chinese National Association for the Advancement of Education. The most comprehensive description of this movement was made by Chow Tse-tsung in his book, *The May Fourth Movement: Intellectual Revolution in Modern China.*

democracies for their unsympathetic attitude toward China's demands at the Versailles Peace Conference, he was hopeful that Nationalist cooperation with Soviet Russia would help carry out his revolutionary programs.

Dr. Sun's cooperation with Soviet Russia – As early as 1918, Chicherin, Soviet Commissar of Foreign Affairs, announced the Soviet intention to relinquish Russian rights and privileges acquired by Czarist Russia in China. A formal note to open negotiations toward that effect was sent to the Chinese Foreign Minister in Peking of October 27, 1920. Then the Bolsheviks sent, one after another, Yurin, Paikes, and Joffe to China. Like Paikes, Adolph A. Joffe could not settle with the Peking government the two important questions of Outer Mongolia and the Chinese Far Eastern Railway. However, his successful establishment of political relations with Dr. Sun was a very important event in Chinese history. In December 1922, he initiated conversations with Dr. Sun in Shanghai. On January 26, 1923, Sun and Joffee issued a joint manifesto, which read, in part, as follows:

Dr. Sun Yat-sen holds that the Communistic order or even the Soviet system cannot actually be introduced into China, because there do not exist here the conditions for the successful establishment of either Communism or Sovietism. This view is entirely shared by Mr. Joffe, who is further of the opinion that China's paramount and most pressing problem is to achieve unification and attain full national independence, and regarding this great task he has assured Dr. Sun Yat-sen that China has the warmest sympathy of the Russian people and can count on the support of Russia.[1]

This manifesto became the foundation of the cooperation between the Nationalist Party and Soviet Russia. The disavowal of a major concept of Lenin and the Comintern by Joffe in the manifesto was certainly in accordance with the instructions from Moscow in order to win the confidence of Dr. Sun. In July 1923, Dr. Sun sent his trusted military aide, Chiang Kai-shek, to Russia to study Soviet military and political conditions. After several conversations with Chiang, Chicherin wrote to Dr. Sun on December 4, 1923:

We think that the fundamental aim of the Kuomintang Party is to build up a great powerful movement of the Chinese people and that therefore propaganda and organization on the biggest scale are its first necessities. Our example was significant: our military activities were successful because a long series of years had elapsed during which we organized and instructed our followers, building up in this way a great organized party throughout the whole land, a party capable of vanquishing all its adversaries. The whole Chinese nation must see the differ-

---

[1] This manifesto is included in *The Collected Manifestos of the Nationalist Party*, published by the special committee of the mass meeting at Nanking on the memorial day of Dr. Sun in 1928. See also *The China Year Book*,* 1924, p. 863.

ence between the Kuomintang, a popular organized mass party, and the military dictators of the various parts of China.[1]

Obviously, Chicherin stressed the advisability of slow and deliberate organizational activity among civilians and emphasized party preparation for the revolutionary mission. The absence in Canton of a permanent and responsible representative from the Soviet government had long been felt at Moscow. Thus early in the fall of 1923, Michael Borodin was appointed to take charge of this important mission. Borodin arrived in Canton in October 1923. He became the political adviser of Dr. Sun, with the special task of assisting in the reorganization of the Nationalist Party.

The First National Congress of the Nationalist Party

The reorganization of the Nationalist Party took place in January 1924, when its First National Congress was held at Canton. There were one hundred and ninety-nine delegates representing the party branches both in China and overseas. In his speech delivered at its opening ceremony on January 20, Dr. Sun emphasized the importance of party discipline in order to correct past mistakes. The Congress adopted a new constitution and set up a new form of organization. Before its adjournment, an important manifesto was issued reaffirming the "Three People's Principles" as the cornerstone of the Chinese revolution.

According to the newly-adopted party constitution, the highest organ of the Nationalist Party was to be the National Congress meeting once a year. During its recess, the authority of the Congress was to be delegated to the Central Executive Committee and the Central Supervisory Committee. The members of both committees were to be elected by the delegates to the National Congress. However, the supreme authority of the Party was still vested in Dr. Sun, who was elected to the office of Tsungli (Director-General). As Leader of the Party and concurrently chairman of the two committees, he even had the power to veto the decisions of the National Congress.

As the plenary session of the Central Executive Committee met only a few times each year, a standing committee was set up to deal with all matters of a routine nature. The party organization in the provinces, municipalities, and districts consisted of local branches which were responsible to their respective superior organs. Any five members could form a "nucleus," which was under the control of the sub-district party

[1] Louis Fischer, *The Soviets in World Affairs,* Vol. 2, p. 635.

branch. Political opinions could be expressed freely within the party meeting, but a decision once made had to be obeyed by all members. In order to maximize the influence and power of the organization, strong discipline was maintained within the Party. The importance of political training was stressed, and party members were urged to carry on energetic propaganda for the principles and programs of the party and to qualify themselves for leadership in the popular movements so as to facilitate the success of the revolution.

The three great policies of the reorganized Nationalist Party

Among the momentous decisions adopted by the First National Congress of the Nationalist Party were the three great policies: (1) cooperation with Soviet Russia, (2) admission of the Chinese Communists to the Nationalist Party, and (3) emphasis on the organization of peasants and workers. Dr. Sun's purpose in cooperating with Soviet Russia was to get Soviet support against imperialism. The Nationalist Party expected to adopt the Russian method of revolutionary organization, but had no intention of instituting the Communist system in China, as had been pointed out by the Sun-Joffe manifesto of 1923. Of course, Soviet renunciation of acquired rights and interests in China was at that time another attraction to Nationalist Party members even though it has never been fulfilled.

The Chinese Communist Party was founded on July 1, 1921, in Shanghai, where twelve delegates held its first national congress. Ch'en Tu-hsiu was elected as Secretary-General of the newly formed party. It was because of the Comintern policy of establishing a united front in China that the Chinese Communists indicated their willingness to join the Nationalist Party. In this connection, Dr. Sun clearly pointed out: "The Communists are joining our Party in order to work for the national revolution.... In any case, if the Communists betray the Kuomintang, I will be the first to propose their expulsion." [1]

The Central Executive Committee of the reorganized Nationalist Party set up a department in charge of labor and peasant movements, headed by Liao Chung-k'ai. In the opinion of Dr. Sun, the task of the Chinese labor movement was not to attack the capitalists but to support the "Three People's Principles." [2] As to the peasant problem in China, he deemed that it could be solved through peaceful cooperation

---

[1] T'ang Leang-li, *The Inner History of the Chinese Revolution,** p. 178.

[2] See Dr. Sun's Labor Day speech in 1924 under the title, "The Sufferings of the Chinese Workers from Unequal Treaties," which is contained in *The Collected Works of Sun Yat-sen* (Shanghai: New Cultural Press, 21st ed., 1929), Vol. III, pp. 189–196.

among the government, farmers, and land owners, rather than through conflict and destruction.[1] Various mass organizations were rapidly established throughout the country by students, workers, peasants, and businessmen. Undoubtedly, the Communists played a leading role in all these activities which will be fully described later.[2]

Mention should be made here about the establishment of the Whampoa Military Academy in May 1924, with Chiang Kai-shek as President and Chou En-lai as head of its Political Department. It was organized along Russian lines for the purpose of training officers for the Party Army, which, a few years later, became the backbone of the Northern Expeditionary Forces for the unification of China. General Galens was appointed as military adviser of the new army.[3]

2. BASIC PRINCIPLES AND PROGRAMS OF THE NATIONALIST PARTY

The basic principles and programs of the Nationalist Party, which have been and remain the guiding rules of the Nationalist Government, are contained in the following writings of Dr. Sun Yat-sen:

(1) *The Three People's Principles* (or *San Min Chu I*),

(2) *The Five-Power Constitution* (or *Wu Ch'uan Hsien Fa*),

(3) *The Program of National Reconstruction* (or *Chien Kuo Fang Lo*),

(4) *The Outline of National Reconstruction* (or *Chien Kuo Ta Kang*), and

(5) *The Manifesto of the First National Congress of the Nationalist Party*.

The importance of these writings to the Nationalist Party and Government was emphasized in the last will of Dr. Sun. In his will, *The Five-Power Constitution* was not specifically mentioned, because it was included in *The Three People's Principles*. These writings are briefly presented below.

The Three People's Principles

The Three People's Principles includes three parts: the principle of

---

[1] See his speech on August 23, 1924, before the Government Institute for the Training of Workers for the Peasant Movement at Canton, *ibid.*, pp. 337–342. The English texts of most of Dr. Sun's Writings and important speeches can be found in L. S. Hsü's *Sun Yat-sen: His political and social Ideals**.

[2] Ch. VII, Sec. 1.

[3] Galens was later known as Marshal Blücher while leading the Soviet Far Eastern Army after the outbreak of the Sino-Japanese War. Both Galens and Borodin had to leave China for Russia after the split between the Nationalists and the Communists in 1927.

nationalism, the principle of democracy, and the principle of livelihood. It was delivered in a series of lectures at the National Kwangtung University in Canton by Dr. Sun, the original manuscripts being destroyed by fire in 1922. The third part was uncompleted when he died in 1925.

The principle of nationalism has two implications: first, the over-throw of the Manchu rule and the domination of the imperialist powers in China; and second, the equality of all races in China. Dr. Sun's principle of democracy is based on the demarcation of the five governing powers of the government and four political rights of the people, to be explained under *The Five-Power Constitution*. There are two essential points in his principle of livelihood: the equalization of land ownership and the regulation of capital. His land policy stresses a fair system of taxation in order to avoid one important cause of economic inequality in traditional China. With respect to the regulation of capital, its purpose is to prevent private capital from dominating public economy. Thus big enterprises, such as railways and steamship lines, should be operated by the state.[1] The application of these two phases of the principle of livelihood is elaborated in *The Outline of National Reconstruction*, to be described later.

The Five-Power Constitution

The five-power constitution is a unique contribution of Dr. Sun to political theory. According to this constitutional system, there are five independent powers exercised by the government, namely, the executive, the legislative, the judicial, the examining, and the supervisory. Its significance is in the independence of the examining and supervisory powers from the other three as generally practiced in Western nations. He explained the reasons for the extreme importance of civil service examinations, which have long been practiced in China: "Without the examination system, there was no way of determining who were trained and talented; a condition such as this resulted in many capable men not being employed by the government. At the same time, a great many ignorant and incapable people, who were anxious to become officials, found their way into the government

---

[1] For a detailed analysis of *The Three People's Principles*, refer to Chou Fu-hai, *The Theoretical System of The Three People's Principles*; also William L. Tung, *What Are The Three People's Principles?* (Shanghai: Kuo-min Press, 1929). For the English translation of *The Three People's Principles*, see Frank W. Price, *San Min Chu I: The Three Principles of the People** (Shanghai: Commercial Press, 1927).

service through corrupt means."[1] As to the supervisory power, another remarkable feature of the traditional system of the Chinese government, it was vested in the powerful censors appointed by the emperor. In Chinese history, there is a long list of famous officials in charge of impeachment, who even admonished the emperors for their misdeeds. Parallel to the five governing powers exercised by the government, the people have four political rights: suffrage, recall, initiative, and referendum. Thus, if the government with five powers is considered as a great machine, the four rights of the people constitute checks and balances on this powerful machinery.[2]

The Program of National Reconstruction (Chien Kuo Fang Lo)

There are three books which constitute what Dr. Sun calls *The Program of National Reconstruction* (or *Chien Kuo Fang Lo):*
(a) *The Philosophy of Sun Wen* (or *Sun Wen Hsuen She)*,
(b) *The Primer of Democracy* (or *Ming Ch'uan Ts'u Pu)*, and
(c) *The International Development of China* (or *Shih Yeh Chi Hua)*.

These three books contain the fundamental programs for the reconstruction of China. They are also called by Dr. Sun "The Program of Psychological Reconstruction," "The Program of Social Reconstruction," and "The Program of Material Reconstruction," respectively.

The Philosophy of Sun Wen – This book was written by Dr. Sun in Shanghai in 1918, when he was planning his future course of revolutionary work. Several of his outstanding ideas are to be found here. It is a review of the traditional philosophy of Chinese life, in which he severely criticized the old Chinese expression that "knowing is easy and doing more difficult." According to him, the truth is that knowing is more difficult than doing. He urged this psychological change as the prerequisite of political, economic and social reforms in China, because he considered the failure of the Chinese Revolution thus far due largely to wrong thinking by his fellow-revolutionists. In his preface to this book, he wrote:

---

[1] These remarks were made by Dr. Sun Yat-sen in his series of lectures in July 1921, before a group of the party members at the party headquarters in Kwangtung. See *The Collected Works of Sun Yat-sen* (Shanghai: Tai Chuan Co., 1929), Vol. II, Pt. 3 of "The Program of National Reconstruction," p. 109.

[2] The five governing powers of the government will be exercised by five *Yuan*. The office of *Yuan* is a unique system of the Chinese government, higher than a department or a ministry in the Western countries. Under a *Yuan*, there may be a number of departments or ministries. For Dr. Sun's description of the exercise of the four rights of direct democracy, see *ibid.*, p. 112.

It was, in their understanding, the idea that "doing is difficult, and knowing easy." This view was first expressed by Fu Kueh, under Emperor Wu-Ting of the Shan dynasty, two thousand years ago. Since that time, it has taken root so deeply in the mind of the Chinese people that now it is seemingly impossible to eradicate. My whole plan for the reconstruction of China was paralyzed by this saying.[1]

The Primer of Democracy – This book is mainly on parliamentary law, written by Dr. Sun in 1917, as a guide for the conduct of public meetings. In his opinion, Chinese citizens ought to understand the parliamentary procedure in the practice of democracy. This book has nothing to do with the program of social reconstruction as indicated by its title.

The International Development of China – This book outlines an elaborate plan for the material reconstruction of China. It included extensive construction of railways and highways, vast exploitation of mineral resources, and large-scale production of consumer goods. Dr. Sun laid the plan before several Western powers after World War I with the suggestion that they render assistance for the development of China. Since the Western governments were anxious to reconstruct their own countries. Dr. Sun's hope was not fulfilled. [2]

The Outline of National Reconstruction (Chien Kuo Ta Kang)

After the reorganization of the Nationalist Party in January 1924, Dr. Sun began to devise the fundamental steps of the modernization of China. As a result, he wrote *The Outline of National Reconstruction* consisting of twenty-five articles,[3] in which he stated that the reconstruction of the Republic of China should be based on *The Three People's Principles* and *The Five-Power Constitution*. The work of reconstruction was three-fold and would be carried out in three periods. The following is a summary of *The Outline*.

Three phases of national reconstruction – There are three phases or steps of national reconstruction: (1) advancement of the economic well-being of the people, (2) promotion of democracy, and (3) development of nationalism. As the first step, the government will develop agriculture to give the people an adequate food supply,

---

[1] *The Philosophy of Sun Wen* is included in *The Collected Works of Sun Yat-sen* in all three editions referred to in this work.

[2] The English text of *The International Development of China** was published in 1922 (New York: Putnam's Sons).

[3] Dr. Sun personally wrote two copies of *The Outline*, one being kept at Mme. Sun's place and the other at Sun Fo's. This showed his emphasis on this *Outline*, which was published in April, 1924. Sun Fo, son of Dr. Sun Yat-sen, had played an important role in the National Government.

promote textile industries to solve their clothing problem, institute large-scale housing projects to provide them with decent living quarters, and build roads and canals to improve transportation. All these are considered as the four great necessities of life, namely, food, clothing, housing and transportation. For the promotion of democracy, the government will educate the people and give them the necessary political training for the exercise of their rights of suffrage, initiative, referendum, and recall. Under the third phase, the government will give assistance to the minorities and make them capable of self-government and self-determination. Meanwhile, the government will take measures to prevent foreign aggression and revise the unequal treaties concluded with foreign powers. Of course, all the three phases of work can be carried out simultaneously.

Three periods of national reconstruction – According to the *Outline*, the reconstruction program will be divided into three periods: (1) the period of military administration, (2) the period of political tutelage, and (3) the period of constitutional government. However, the success or failure of national reconstruction depends largely on the work accomplished during the period of political tutelage.

Period of military administration – During the period of military administration, all political machinery will be placed under the direct control of the military government. In order to bring about national unification, the government will overcome internal discord by military force on the one hand and awaken the people through propaganda on the other. When a province has been completely brought under military control, the period of political tutelage begins and the period of military administration ends.

Period of Political tutelage – During the period of political tutelage, the government will send to different districts (*hsien*) qualified experts, who have satisfactorily passed the required civil service examinations, to assist the people of the different districts in establishing systems of local self-government. The work will begin with a census throughout the district and a survey of its land areas and boundary lines. When the people in the district have been trained to exercise their four rights of self-government and are capable of performing their duties of citizenship and willing to carry out the revolutionary principles, they will be permitted to elect their own magistrate and legislators. The district will then become completely self-governing. In a completely self-governing district, the people will have the direct rights of suffrage, recall, initiative and referendum.

Local self-government during the period of political tutelage – After local self-government has been established, each district is to elèct one representative to the Representative's Assembly for participation in the affairs of the Central Government. Only those who have been examined by the Central Government and have fulfilled the necessary qualifications can become candidates for public office, whether appointive or elective, both in the Central Government and in the local government units. When all the districts in a province have evolved a working self-government, the province is to pass into the period of constitutional government. The Representative's Assembly will elect a provincial governor to supervise the provincial self-government. In matters within the sphere of national administration, the governor will receive orders from the Central Government. The district will be the unit of self-government and the province will be a link of effective cooperation between the Central Government and the district. The powers of the Central Government and the provincial governments will be equally divided. Matters of national interest will be entrusted to the Central Government; and those of a local character will be entrusted to the local administration. Neither centralization nor decentralization will be favored.

Economic policy during the period of political tutelage – When a district reaches the stage of self-government, an assessment will be made of all private land under its dominion by first requiring the landowners to report to the government the location, size, and value of their land. The local government may tax or, if necessary, buy the land according to the assessed value. Should the land increase in value due to political reform or social improvement after registration, such unearned increment as accrued will belong to the people of the district as a whole; it will not be considered the private property of the individual owners. Land profits, unearned increments from land, products of public land, products from forests and waterways, mineral resources, and water power will be owned by the local government; and they will be used to pay for public improvements, charitable work, and other kinds of public service. The development of natural resources and the establishment of big industries, which go beyond the power of the district and need external assistance, will be subsidized by the Central Government. The net profits thus obtained will be divided equally between the Central Government and the local government. Each district is to support the Central Government to the extent of not more than fifty percent of its annual income. The exact percentage will be determined by the people's representatives each year.

The Central Government at the beginning of the period of constitutional government – The Central Government will establish five separate *Yuan* to administer the five political functions, namely, the Executive, the Legislative, the Judicial, the Examining, and the Supervisory *Yuan*. The Executive *Yuan* is to consist of the following ministries: (1) interior, (2) foreign affairs, (3) military affairs, (4) finance, (5) agriculture and mining, (6) labor and commerce, (7) education, and (8) communications. Before the promulgation of the constitution, the Presidents of the five *Yuan* are to be appointed, controlled and dismissed by the President of the National Government.

Period of constitutional government – On the basis of this *Outline* and the actual experience during the periods of political tutelage and constitutional government, the Legislative *Yuan* will draft a constitution. When the majority of the provinces has reached the period of constitutional government, a National Assembly will be held to consider and adopt the constitution. When the constitution is promulgated, the highest political power of the Central Government is to be vested in the National Assembly. This Assembly will exercise the rights of initiative and referendum. A national general election will be held in accordance with the provisions of the constitution. The National Government will be dissolved three months after the national election and its powers will be handed over to the Government elected by the people themselves. This will be the succesful completion of the program of national reconstruction.

The Manifesto of the First National Congress of the Nationalist Party

The most important statement of the policies of the Nationalist Party is contained in the Manifesto of its First National Congress, held in January 1924 at Canton. It is divided into two sections, dealing with external and internal policies to be followed by the Nationalist Party and Government. Although this manifesto was not written by Dr. Sun, its essential points were incorporated in *The Outline of National Reconstruction*. In his last will, it was emphasized equally with his other works. The following is an analytical description of the policy section of this important document.

External policy on unequal treaties – According to the *Manifesto*, all unequal treaties are to be abolished and substituted by new treaties on the basis of equality and reciprocity. The unequal treaties are those providing for leased territories, extraterritoriality, foreign control of customs tariffs, and the exercise of foreign authority over Chinese territories. All countries that are willing to abandon their special privileges and the unequal treaties will be accorded most-favored-nation treatment.

Repayment of foreign loans – Foreign loans which do not impair China's sovereign rights will be properly secured and repaid. A conference consisting of delegates from commercial and social organizations will be called to devise ways and means for the repayment of such loans. However, the people of China will not be responsible for the repayment of foreign loans contracted by the Peking regime to maintain the power and interests of the selfish militarists.

Division of powers between the Central and local governments – The principle of equilibrium will be observed in the division of powers between the Central and local governments. Matters that require uniform standards for the whole nation will be alloted to the Central Government; those that are peculiar to a locality and require particular treatment will be alloted to the local governments. The people of each province may draw up their own constitution and elect their own governor, who will be in charge of the provincial administration under the direction of the Central Government and will supervise the local autonomy within the province. The district (*hsien*) is to be the unit of local self-government. The people of every self-governing district have the rights of election, recall, initiative and referendum. The national constitution is to be the supreme law of the land. Any provisions of the provincial constitutions which may be in conflict with the national constitution shall become null and void.

Rights and duties of the people – The people will be guaranteed by law to have freedom of assembly, association, speech, publication, domicile and worship. Universal suffrage will be established without any property qualifications. The people may enter the public service through both election and competitive examinations. Equality between the sexes will be recognized in legal, economic, educational and social fields. Energetic efforts will be made for universal education and for the development of a better educational system. On the other hand, it is the duty of the people to pay taxes and serve in the military forces. A system of conscription will be established to replace the traditional mercenary troops.

Economic policy – The means of increasing food production will be studied to meet the demand of the people on the basis of a new census and a resurvey of the cultivated land. Laws will be enacted to improve the labor and agricultural conditions and to protect their organizations. The state will also promulgate laws governing land, the use thereof, its expropriation, and the tax on land values. Land owned by private individuals will be assessed and reported to the government by the landlord. The government will levy a tax according to the declared value, and, in case of necessity, may purchase it at the price declared. The land tax, the tax on increments of land value, the products of public land, and all profits therefrom will be placed at the disposal of the local governments for developing local enterprises, relieving the poor and the aged, supporting orphans, carrying out famine relief, and safeguarding public health and public projects. All other prevailing taxes which are detrimental to national economy will be abolished.

Enterprises of monopolistic nature unsuitable for private undertakings, such as railways and steamship lines, will be owned and managed by the state. The development of natural resources and the operation of big industries beyond the power of the local governments will be undertaken by the state. The profits from such undertakings will be equally divided between the Central and the local governments. With regard to the expenditure of the state, each district will pay to the national treasury a certain percentage of its revenue. Such percentage will be not less than ten percent nor more than fifty percent of its total revenue.

Evaluation of Dr. Sun's political theory

The above presentation is only a brief sketch of Dr. Sun's political theory, which has been fully dealt with by many Chinese and foreign writers. From his programs and policies for China's national reconstruction, a clear comparison can be made with the later application by the Nationalist government. In the analysis of Dr. Sun's political thought, different views have been expressed: "A German Marxian showed Sun to be a forerunner of bolshevism; an American liberal showed Sun to be a bulwark against bolshevism. A Chinese classicist demonstrated Sun's reverence for the past; a Jesuit father explained much by Sun's modern and Christian background." [1] However, none of these interpretations represents the whole picture of his ideology. In order to obtain a precise conception of his works, a review of the background of his political theory is advisable.

The peculiar environment of China since the middle of the nineteenth

---

[1] Paul M. A. Linebarger, *The Political Doctrines of Sun Yat-sen, an Exposition of the San Min Chu I*, p. 8.

century and the world trend toward democracy are the important factors which contributed to his formulation of "The Three People's Principles." Inasmuch as China was invaded by the imperialist powers and suppressed by the Manchus, he worked out the principle of nationalism. In the "Manifesto of the First National Congress of the Nationalist Party," special emphasis was laid on the abolition of unequal treaties imposed upon China. Isasmuch as great merits have been demonstrated by the democratic system of Western governments in comparison with the autocratic rule of China, he advocated the principle of democracy in which the good part of Chinese political traditions was incorporated. He was aware of the unpreparedness of the Chinese people to practice Western democracy at once and hence was very cautious in the promotion and eventual application of constitutional government in China by paving a solid foundation through the preparatory stages of military administration and political tutelage. Detailed steps were carefully planned in "The Outline of National Reconstruction" and the "Manifesto of the First National Congress of the Nationalist Party."[1] Inasmuch as capitalism had created, to a certain extent, undesirable social conditions in Western industrial countries, he expounded the principle of livelihood to avoid a possible social revolution in China in the future by regulating private capital and land ownership. According to Dr. Sun, "The Three People's Principles" was a sound program for national salvation with a view to elevating China to an equal position in the international community.

There is no doubt that Dr. Sun's political thought was influenced by the political and economic theories of the West. Such an influence can be traced, among others, to his acquiescence in Montesquieu's theory of the separation of powers, his opposition to unearned increment probably derived from Henry George,[2] and his agreement with Maurice William's idea of rejecting the materialistic interpretation of history.[3] Dr. Paul M. A. Linebarger considered that "Sun was in all probability a more assiduous and widely read student of political science than any

---

[1] In 1920, Dr. Sun wrote *Methods of Applying Local Self-Government* for the guidance of the nation's endeavor toward that direction.

[2] He knew of Henry George before the establishment of the T'ung-meng Hui, which advocated the redistribution of land in its platform. However, the redistribution would not prohibit the private ownership of land.

[3] Maurice William's view in this respect was fully discussed in his book, *The Social Interpretation of History** (New York, 1921). Dr. Sun commented that Mr. William's interpretation sounded perfectly reasonable and fitted in with his principle of livelihood.

other world leader of his day except Wilson." [1] At the same time, Dr. Sun laid great emphasis on the traditional value of Confucianism and China's old social order. He even went so far as to caution the Chinese people to keep their old virtue as a psychological basis of national reconstruction. In *The Philosophical Basis of the Theory of Sun Wen*,[2] Tai Chi-t'ao, a leading member and scholar of the Nationalist Party, explained in detail the influence of Chinese philosophy on Dr. Sun's ideology.

Dr. Sun's antagonistic attitude toward Marxism is evidenced by his express repudiation of the materialistic interpretation of history and the class war theory. After carefully examining the writings of Marx, he concluded: "What Marx gained through his studies of social problems was a knowledge of diseases in the course of social progress. Therefore, Marx can only be called a social physiologist."[3] The misconception of the influence of Marxism on Dr. Sun's political thought is largely due to the verbal tone of the latter's lectures.[4] Even though there are some similarities between Communism and the principle of livelihood, the difference of methods make them incompatible.

3. THE NORTHERN EXPEDITION AND THE UNIFICATION OF CHINA

Dr. Sun's trip to the North and his death in Peking

It was mentioned in the previous chapter that, at the invitation of Tuan Ch'i-jui and other leaders in the North, Dr. Sun left Canton for Peking in November 1924. Before his departure, he issued a statement explaining his immediate plans to the people.[5] He urged the convocation of a National People's Convention to discuss the internal difficulties of China and her relations with foreign Powers. He also suggested that, before the Convention assembled, a preliminary conference be held to study certain basic problems. In spite of the popular approval of Dr. Sun's proposal, Tuan decided to summon the Reorganization Conference as described before.

Immediately after his arrival at Tientsin on December 4, Dr. Sun

---

[1] Paul M. A. Linebarger, *op. cit.*, p. 6.
[2] Published in Canton, 1925.
[3] Frank W. Price, *op. cit.*, p. 391.
[4] Sometimes Dr. Sun used the term "Communism" simply to mean "great similarity", which, in Chinese classics, indicates that all people work together for their common good in a world of complete harmony.
[5] See "The Manifesto on Going to Peking," November 10, 1924, included in *The Collected Works of Sun Yat-sen*.

fell ill and was unable to leave his room. Nevertheless, he wrote a letter to Tuan, insisting on the wisdom of his policy, and warning Tuan that in the Reorganization Conference "the representation of influential elements seems to be overstressed and of popular organizations almost completely ignored," and, further, that "this Conference will not be able to correct old mistakes or initiate a new political era." [1] Despite his physical weakness, Dr. Sun later went to Peking. His health continued to decline. Many party members came to Peking to see him for the last time. On March 11, 1925, he signed his final testaments, one addressed to the Nationalist Party and another to his family. On March 12, 1925, he died. With his death, the Chinese Revolution lost its greatest leader. [2]

His last will was considered so important that the Party decreed it should be recited at the opening of every meeting whether political in nature or not. It reads as follows:

---

[1] For details, see *ibid.*, "A Letter to the Chief Executive Tuan, concerning the Reorganization Conference, February 17, 1925."

[2] Dr. Sun Yat-sen is still revered as one of China's great revolutionary heroes in the Communist controlled Mainland. At the time of the founding of the People's Republic of China on October 1, 1949, Chairman Mao Tse-tung stated: "For over a century, our predecessors have never paused in their unflinching and unswerving struggle, including the 1911 revolution led by Dr. Sun Yat-sen, the forerunner of the Chinese revolution, against foreign and domestic oppressors. Our predecessors instructed and requested us to fulfill their behest. We are doing it now." (*Sun Yat-sen Commemorative Album**, Peking, 1956, p. 17.) At the 90th anniversary of the birth of Dr. Sun Yat-sen, on November 12, 1956, the Chinese people on the Mainland were allowed to hold huge meetings and conduct other forms of activities in Peking and other cities to pay tribute to this great revolutionary leader. Attending the commemoration meeting in Peking were party and government leaders, including Mao Tse-tung and Chou En-lai. The opening words of Mao's speech were: "Let us pay tribute to the memory of our great revolutionary predecessor, Dr. Sun Yat-sen!" Condemning great-power chauvinism and emphasizing the importance of modesty, Mao commended Dr. Sun as follows:

" Dr. Sun was a modest man, I heard him speak on many occasions and was impressed by the grandeur of his mind. The way in which he devoted himself to the study of China's historical conditions and contemporary social conditions, and of the conditions in foreign countries, including the Soviet Union, shows that he was a man of great modesty.

"His whole life was devoted heart and soul to the rebuilding of China. Of him it could be said that he gave of his best, gave his all till his heart ceased to beat." (*Dr. Sun Yat-sen: Commemorative Articles and Speeches by Mao Tse-tung, Soong Ching-ling, Chou En-lai and Others**. Peking: Foreign Languages Press, 1957. pp. 9, 11.)

In his opening address to the same meeting, Chou En-lai paid tribute to the contribution Dr. Sun made to the Chinese revolution in the following manner:

"Today is the 90th anniversary of the birth of Dr. Sun Yat-sen. Reverently, in respectful remembrance, we pay tribute to this outstanding forerunner of the democratic revolution in modern China. Dr. Sun was a valiant fighter who led the struggle to overthrow the feudal monarchy and to build up a democratic republic. He was a patriot who fought against imperialist aggression and for the independence and freedom of China. In his later years, he went a step further. He adopted the three cardinal policies of alliance with Soviet Russia, cooperation with the Communists and assistance to the workers' and peasants' movement, thus developing his old Three People's Principles into the new Three People's Principles. He was a great revolutionary and a great statesman." (*Ibid.*, p. 22.)

For forty years I have devoted myself to the cause of National Revolution, the aim of which is to secure for China a position of independence and equality among nations. The accumulated experience of these forty years has fully convinced me that to attain this goal, it is necessary to awaken the mass of our own people and associate ourselves with those peoples of the world who treat us on a footing of equality in the common struggle.

At present, the work of the Revolution is not yet achieved. Let all my comrades follow my writings, "The Program of National Reconstruction," "The Outline of National Reconstruction," "The Three People's Principles," and "The Manifesto of the First National Congress of the Party," and work unceasingly for their ultimate realization. Above all, the convocation of a National People's Convention and the abolition of unequal treaties, which I have recently advocated, should be accomplished within the shortest possible time. This is my last will.

Consolidation of Kwangtung and the Northern Expedition

After the death of Dr. Sun, the party members worked hard for the realization of party principles and programs, even though the political future of the party sometimes seemed very dark. Among the most prominent members in Kwangtung were Chiang Kai-shek, Wang Ching-Wei, Hu Han-min, and Liao Chung-k'ai. Borodin was still a high adviser of the Party and remained a powerful figure in party activities.

Under pressure of urgent necessity, Chiang Kai-shek organized a model regiment, commonly known as the Party Army, the officers of which were instructors and graduates of the Whampoa Military Academy. Notwithstanding the fact that the soldiers were professional mercenaries, they had received both military and political training. The Party Army finally defeated all the undesirable military elements in Kwangtung, which was consolidated as the stronghold of the imminent Northern Expedition.

In order to deliberate on party, governmental and military affairs, a plenary session of the Central Executive Committee of the Nationalist Party was held in June 1925. A Central Political Council and a Military Council were created to take charge of political and military affairs respectively. On June 14, the Central Political Council decided to reorganize the Headquarters of the Generalissimo at Canton into a formal government. Thus, on July 1, 1925, the National Government was established with Wang Ching-wei as Chairman.

Meanwhile, the internal dissensions among the Party members and the conflict between the Nationalists and the Communists had become acute. After the assassination of Liao Chung-k'ai, Hu Han-min was compelled to leave Kwangtung. Borodin induced him to take a trip to Soviet Russia. Then the three divisions of Hsü Ch'ung-chih proved unreliable. When Chiang had them disarmed, Hsü petitioned for a leave of absence to go to Shanghai. Despite these setbacks, the Nationalist Party emerged victorious from the dangers which surrounded it in Kwangtung.

On January 1, 1926, the Second National Congress of the Nationalist Party was convoked at Canton. It formally accepted the last will of Dr. Sun as the fundamental charter of the Party, amended the constitution of the Party, reiterated the aims of the Chinese Revolution, and passed resolutions supporting mass organizations. With regard to the Communists, it was decided that the Party would continue to admit them, but only as auxiliaries. The number of Communists in any committee or council of the Party was restricted to not more than one-third of the total. The Party programs put forward by this Congress were identical to those adopted by the First National Congress. It was further decided that no new *Tsungli* (Director-General or Leader) would ever be designated.

Immediately after the adjournment of the Second National Congress, Chiang was appointed Inspector General of the military forces in Kwangtung with a view to preparing for a Northern Expedition. Because of the political dissensions between Chiang and Wang Ching-wei, the latter retired from the National Government and went abroad. At that time, all the armies under the Military Council had been mobilized and were ready to break the unfavorable status quo. On May 28, 1926, the National Government at Canton appointed Chiang Commander-in-Chief of the National Revolutionary Forces for a Northern Expedition against the warlords.

The National Revolutionary Forces at the disposal of Chiang consisted of seven Armies.[1] In the North, Feng Yü-hsiang and Yen Hsi-shan were both on the side of the Nationalist Party. Owing to the strict discipline and the political training of the army, the popular sympathy with the Nationalist cause, and the military ability of Chiang and other commanders, they won one victory after another. On October 10, Wuhan was captured, and Wu P'ei-fu's army was entirely destroyed. The National Government then moved to Wuhan. No less powerful than Wu in Central China was Sun Chuan-fang, the overlord of the five provinces of Kiangsi, Kiangsu, Fukien, Anhwei and Chekiang. Chiang's campaign against Sun Chuan-fang was short and decisive; the five provinces were conquered successively. Nanking and

---

[1] First Army — Ho Yin-ch'ing, Second — T'an Yen-k'ai, Third — Chu Pei-teh, Fourth — Li Chi-tsen, Fifth — Li Fu-lin, Sixth — Ch'eng Ch'ien and Seventh — Li Tsung-jen.

Shanghai fell in March 1927.[1] Less than one year after the start of the Northern Expedition, the forces of Wu and Sun Chuan-fang were crushed, and almost half of China was under the control of the Nationalist Government.

The split in the Nationalist Party and the purification movement

In view of the success of the military campaign, leaders of the Nationalist Party became very hopeful that the teachings of Dr. Sun might be soon realized. The facts did not, however, justify this optimism. Because of Chiang's preoccupation with the Northern Expedition, party affairs had gradually fallen into the hands of the Communists. Acting under instructions from the Third International, Borodin planned vigorous projects to establish Communism in China. He tried to use Hsü Ch'ien and other important members of the Nationalist Party as the instruments of his policy.[2] With the arrival of Wang Ching-Wei at Wuhan on April 10, 1927, the situation became still more complicated.

As the Nationalists and Communists could not cooperate wholeheartedly, Chiang was determined to expel the Communists from the Nationalist Party. Since the Central Executive Committee of the Party and the National Government at Wuhan were controlled by the Communist Party, he went to Nanking together with Wu Chih-hui, Li Shih-ts'eng, Chang Ching-chiang, Ts'ai Yüan-p'ei, Ch'en Kuo-fu[3] and several other leaders to organize another Central Executive Committee and a new National Government on April 18. At the same time, the Purification Movement against the Communists was inaugurated. Many of them were arrested and prosecuted.

The Wuhan government disagreed with Chiang's policy. Under the chairmanship of Wang Ching-wei, the Central Executive Committee of the Party at Wuhan decided on April 17 to expel Chiang and those participating in the Nanking government. The conflict between Nanking and Wuhan became more and more serious. T'ang Sheng-chih

---

[1] The Communists claimed that the fall of Shanghai on March 22 was largely through the efforts of the General Labor Union under their leadership. See Harold R. Isaacs, *The Tragedy of the Chinese Revolution** (2nd ed.), pp. 137–141.

[2] Hsü Ch'ien was one of the intimate friends of Borodin. Having just returned from Soviet Russia, he was very enthusiastic about Russian institutions, and, for a while, became a very powerful figure in Wuhan. He turned against the Communists when the conflict between the two parties become intense in Wuhan.

[3] Chen Kuo-fu was a nephew of Chen Chi-mei, one of the most important revolutionists who overthrew the Ch'ing dynasty in 1911. He and his brother Li-fu were in charge of the Party organization for a long time.

was appointed Commander-in-Chief of the Army in place of Chiang.[1] At that time, Chang Tso-lin, warlord of Manchuria, was in control of the North. Although both Nanking and Wuhan forces marched northward against Chang, they were antagonistic toward each other. With the reinforcement of Feng Yü-hsiang's troops, the Nationalist forces finally defeated Chang Tso-lin, who ordered all his armies to retreat north of the Yellow River. Yet the victory did not rescue the Nationalist Party from its dangerous position, nor reconcile the inner dissensions between the Wuhan and Nanking factions.

Before the split between Wuhan and Nanking, a group of the so-called "Old Comrades" was already breaking away from the Party. They were usually called the "Western Hills Faction," among which were Chang Chi, Hsien Ch'in, Tsou Lu, Lin Shen and Wu Chih-hui.[2] From the very beginning of the party organization in 1924, they were strongly Anti-Communistic and opposed to the Russian orientation of the Party and, especially, to the admission of the Communists. After 1925, they organized another Central Executive Committee of the Nationalist Party at Shanghai. Because they sympathized with Chiang's anti-Communistic attitude, it was not difficult to reach a compromise between Chiang and the Western Hills Faction.

Reconciliation between Wuhan and Nanking

The situation in Wuhan was very turbulent. The result of the activities of the Communists was such that all the factories at Wuhan were closed and conflict between the employers and the employees took place daily. Privately owned factories were confiscated. Furthermore, the agrarian question arose, especially with regard to the confiscation of farm lands. Borodin persisted in his Communistic schemes. Wang Ching-wei and the other "pure" Nationalist members initiated an attempt to counteract the activities of the Communists. However, their efforts could succeed only if the unity of the Nationalist Party was restored.

The anti-Communist riot engineered by Nationalist troops at Changsha in Hunan province on May 21, 1927, hastened the separation of the Nationalist members from the Communists at Wuhan and the departure of Borodin from China. Through a lengthy period of negotiation, Wang and others decided to cooperate with Nanking. For

[1] Originally T'ang Sheng-chih belonged to the army of Wu P'ei-fu. He later joined the Nationalist Party and distinguished himself in the Northern Expedition.

[2] The name derived from a conference which they held before the tomb of Dr. Sun Yat-sen in the temple on the Western Hills near Peking.

a short time, Chiang resigned his duties as Commander-in-Chief of the Army and gave up his other important offices. A special Committee was organized, representing all the factions of the Party, to carry on the party activities. Regardless, the confusion and dissensions continued. As a result of Chiang's resignation, there were many obstacles in the path of the military expedition against the North. Not until Chiang's return to Nanking was the period of compromise among all the factions inaugurated. The so-called Nanking-Hankow-Shanghai cooperation, including the Western Hills Faction, was then formally realized. [1]

As a result of the compromise, the Fourth Plenary Session of the Second Central Executive Committee of the Party was convened at Nanking on February 1, 1928. In principle, the Party was declared to be anti-Communist and devoted to the welfare of no single class, but of all people. The Purification Movement was pushed forward by every possible means. Chiang was re-appointed Commander-in-Chief of the Nationalist Army. Plans were perfected for a combined advance to Peking by Chiang, Feng and Yen. The Nationalist drive on Peking was well under way by the middle of April, and the Northern armies offered little resistance.

Nationalist unification of China

The unification of China under a strong central government had been considered by Japan as a fundamental menace to her expansion. Japan's jealousy of the rapid progress of the Nationalist cause became manifest when the revolutionary forces were marching through Southern Shantung. On April 19, 1928, five thousand soldiers were ordered to proceed to Tsingtao by the Japanese Government, which declared that "though the Japanese Government has absolutely refrained from supporting any party or faction in the civil wars in China, the Government will be compelled to take adequate self-defense measures in case peace and order in districts where Japanese are residing is disturbed..." [2] When the main body of the Nationalist troops entered Tsinan, capital of Shantung province, early on May 1, the Japanese Commander chose to regard their entry as a cause of war. On May 3, serious street fighting broke out. The result of this Japanese move was the murder of Ts'ai Kung-hsi, the Chinese commissioner of foreign affairs in Shantung, and

---

[1] Hankow is one part of the triple city of Wuhan where the National Government was once located.

[2] Foreign Policy Association, Information Service, *The Rise of the Kuomintang** (Vol. IV, No. 8), p. 182.

the burning of the building occupied by the Bureau of Foreign Affairs.[1]

Furthermore, the Japanese Government advised the Japanese commander to lay the following demands before the National Government at Nanking: (1) a formal apology for the incident from Chiang Kai-shek; (2) punishment of General Ho Yao-tsu and others responsible for the outrages; (3) suspension of hostilities, propaganda, and warlike activities within seven miles of Tsinan, Tsingtao and the railway. Here the main purpose of Japanese intervention was to prevent the growth of the Nationalist movement, which would undoubtedly resist further Japanese invasion of China. In order not to hamper the advance against the Northern militarists, the Ministry of Foreign Affairs of the National Government finally yielded.

Notwithstanding the Tsinan incident, the Nationalist forces made steady progress toward Peking, which was finally captured. On May 18, 1928, Japan addressed the Peking and Nanking governments on Japanese policy in Manchuria. The National Government was warned that should the Nationalist Army pursue Chang Tso-lin's forces, Japan would disarm the troops of both sides before allowing them to enter Manchuria. Moreover, Manchuria as a part of Chinese territory should not have concerned Japan, whose intervention was manifestly a violation of the rules of international law.

It was generally understood that the Japanese ambition was to expel all Chinese forces from Manchuria. The bombardment of Chang Tso-lin's train near Mukden during his retreat was an obvious Japanese intrigue designed to promote this objective. Returning secretly to Mukden, Chang Hsueh-liang succeeded to the command of his father's forces. He was strongly warned by Japan that he should not join the Nationalist cause. This warning he disregarded. On December 31, 1928, the Nationalist flag was hoisted over the Three Eastern Provinces (Manchuria), marking the complete unification of China under the Nationalist Party.

4. THE BEGINNING OF POLITICAL TUTELAGE

The functions of the Central Executive and Supervisory Committees of the Nationalist Party

The organization of the Nationalist Party as laid down in its constitution adopted at the First National Congress in 1924 has been briefly described. Minor changes of the constitution were made at the

[1] *Ibid.*, pp. 183–184.

Second National Congress in 1926 and the Third National Congress in 1929. No amendments were adopted by the Fourth and Fifth National Congresses in 1931 and 1935 respectively. The office of *Tsungtsai* (Director-General or Leader) to exercise the power of *Tsungli* was not provided in the constitution until the Emergency Party Congress in 1938,[1] which deemed it necessary to concentrate party power in a sole leader to carry out the war against Japan. Thus, at the early stage of political tutelage from the unification of China in 1928 to the war against Japan in 1937, the prevailing Party constitution was the one amended at the Third National Congress in 1929.

According to that constitution, the highest organ was the National Congress, composed of delegates from the local branches. Its functions were as follows: (1) to adopt and approve the reports of the National Government; (2) to revise the platform and the constitution of the party; (3) to formulate new policies and new programs to enable the National Government to meet new situations; and (4) to elect all the members of the Central Executive and the Central Supervisory Committees.[2] The constitution further provided that the National Congress was to be convened every two years. However, it could be postponed by the Central Executive Committee under special circumstances. A special congress could be called if necessary, in accordance with the provisions of the constitution.

When the National Congress was not in session, the highest authority of the party was vested in the Central Executive and the Central Supervisory Committees. These two Committees were of equal rank and wholly independent of each other. Their functions were as follows:

Central Executive Committee:

(1) To represent the Party in its external relations;

(2) To carry out the resolutions of the National Congress;

(3) To organize Party headquarters in the several provinces and districts;

---

[1] It is evident that "*Tsungtsai*" has the same meaning as "*Tsungli*," but in a different word. The Emergency Congress was held at Wuchang, March 29-April 1, 1938.

[2] All new members of the two Committees were inducted by means of the following oath, repeated with the right hand raised:

"I solemnly swear that I shall faithfully observe the last will of the *Tsungli* [Sun Yat-sen], believe in the principles of the Party, abide by the Party discipline, obey the orders of the Party, keep the secrets of the Party, and never form or take part in any other political organization. Nor shall I be selfish and let my personal feelings interfere with the execution of my duties. If I violate my oath, I shall be willing to accept the severest punishment of the Party."

(4) To organize the Central Party headquarters; and

(5) To allocate Party funds from whatever source derived.

Central Supervisory Committee:

(1) To decide on the punishment of members violating Party discipline;

(2) To audit the accounts of the Central Executive Committee;

(3) To review the progress of Party affairs; and

(4) To supervise the conduct of the National Government and decide whether its policies and records conform to the policies of the Party.

The Central Executive and the Central Supervisory Committees were required to hold plenary sessions at least once every six months. Each committee elected a Standing Committee from its own number. When the full committees were not in session, the Standing Committees transacted routine business.

The importance of the Party to the National Government is evidenced in the functions of the National Congress in adopting and approving the government reports and in guiding the government by formulating new policies and new programs. These functions were to be performed by the Central Executive Committee when the National Congress was not in session. In addition, the Central Supervisory Committee was to supervise the conduct of the National Government and decide whether its policies and records conformed to the policies of the Party. Such kind of supervisory power was also applied to the supervisory committees of lower party levels in their relationship with the governments of corresponding levels. Detailed procedures were provided in the *Rules Governing the Party Supervisory Committees in Their Examination of Policies and Records of the Governments of Corresponding Levels,* promulgated on December 19, 1929. The supervisory committees could demand explanations from and make investigations of the governments of corresponding levels. The transmission of messages was generally through the executive committees of the same levels. In case of serious government deviations from party policies, the supervisory committee could even recommend impeachment of the officers concerned to the higher-level government for action through its higher-level supervisory committee. Through this device, the government could be constantly under the direction and supervision of the party. In order to avoid unnecessary misunderstandings, government officers were sometimes appointed as members of party committees at the same level. In spite of frequent personal contacts, friction and disputes between the party and government were common phenomena.

The Central Political Council as a link between the Party and government

Under the Central Executive Committee of the Nationalist Party, there was a Central Political Council, to which was delegated the power of formulating important policies to be executed by the National Government. It served as a link between the Central Executive Committee and the National Government. The Council was first established on July 11, 1924, as an advisory organ to Dr. Sun Yat-sen when he was General-issimo of the Military Government at Canton. After his death in March 1925, the Council decided, at its meeting on June 14, 1925, to set up formally a national government for the execution of its policies and the administration of government affairs.[1] Then the Council became an effective instrument of the Party to control the government. The members of the Council were nominated by the Central Executive Committee. While its name and organization underwent many changes,[2] the chief function of the Council was to discuss and decide the following matters: (1) fundamentals of legislation, (2) principles of legislation, (3) administrative policies, (4) general plans for national defense, (5) financial programs, and (6) selection of the Presidents and members of the five *Yuan* and other specially appointed officials of the National Government.

The exact relationship between the Party and the National Government was defined in the *Fundamental Principles of Political Tutelage*, which were first adopted by the Standing Committee of the Central Executive Committee and then approved by the Central Executive Committee on October 3, 1928.[3] As these principles prescribe the respective spheres of functions of the Party and the National Government, a translation of the full text is reproduced below:

Art. 1. During the Period of Political Tutelage, and until the National People's Assembly can be called into being, the National Congress of the Party shall act for the Chinese people in the exercise of their political rights.

Art. 2. When the National Congress of the Party is not in session, the political rights shall be exercised by the Central Executive Committee of the Party.

Art. 3. The people shall gradually be taught to exercise the rights of suffrage,

[1] The National Government was formally established on July 1, 1925, in accordance with the decision of the Council.

[2] For details, see William L. Tung, *The Government of China*, Vol. I, pp. 391–394; and Ch'ien Tuan-sheng, *The Government and Politics of China**, pp. 139–145, 475–476.

[3] The adoption of these Principles by the Standing Committee of the Central Executive Committee was confirmed on March 19, 1929, by the Third National Congress of the Party.

recall, initiative and referendum, as provided in Dr. Sun's *The Outline of National Reconstruction*, in order to prepare the way for constitutional government.

Art. 4. The exercise of executive, legislative, judicial, examining and supervisory powers shall be delegated to the National Government, so as to lay the foundations for representative government in the Constitutional Period.

Art. 5. The direction and control of the National Government in the administration of important state affairs shall be entrusted to the Central Political Council of the Central Executive Committee of the Party.

Art. 6. The Organic Law of the National Government of the Republic of China may be amended and elucidated by resolution of the Central Political Council of the Central Executive Committee of the Party.

From the above provisions, it is clear that the Central Political Council was an all powerful organ of the Party. As a sub-committee of the Central Executive Committee, it virtually directed the National Government and formulated all the important national policies, foreign and domestic, to be executed by the National Government. All political officials of the first and second rank were appointed and could be dismissed by the Council. Thus the National Government in exercising the five governing powers was responsible to the Central Political Council, which, in exercising the four political rights on behalf of the people, was responsible to the Central Executive Committee of the Party. Therefore, the Central Political Council was "the highest political organ in China and the pivot on which the whole system of the Party Government moves." [1]

Shortcomings of the Party organizations and operations

As the National Government was practically controlled by the Party during the period of political tutelage, any shortcomings of the organizations and operations of the Party were definitely reflected in the national administration. The most notable characteristic of the organization of the Nationalist Party was its reliance on committees. Those in favor of the committee system considered it as an evidence of the Party's democratic inclination in deliberation. Every Party member could freely express his opinion in Party meetings, though he had to submit to a majority decision. As all members were on equal footing, neither any individual nor any faction could dictate what the others must do. Thus the fruits of mature deliberation were achieved on the basis of the ideal of democracy. In fact, the Party organizations and operations were not as democratic and efficient as expected. Its committee system was most frequently criticized on the following grounds:

First, the committee system had the fundamental defect of divided

[1] Wang Ching-wei, *China's Problems and Their Solutions**, p. 89.

responsibility which, in reality, meant no responsibility. Utilization of the committee system often prevented that assignment of rights and duties to individuals which was necessary if action was to succeed deliberation. Hence confusion and inefficiency were the natural result.

Secondly, in consequence of the faulty demarcation of rights and duties among the committee members, inner dissension and friction had often arisen, especially in local party branches. Whatever selfishness there might be in the nature of men was sharpened by the faults of the system. The suspicions and jealousies thus engendered hampered the more unselfish and impersonal members. As a result, obstruction and even deadlock often occurred.

Thirdly, as a corollary to deliberate consideration, discussions usually took more time than necessary. Furthermore, the necessity of compromise often led to action which was less satisfactory than the bolder propositions which could not win acceptance.

Lastly, Party meetings, both national congresses and many less important gatherings, were often described as "discussion without resolution; and resolution without execution." While this criticism was somewhat exaggerated, it was not entirely without foundation.[1]

In addition to the defects of the committee system, another problem was raised respecting the admission of members to the Party. It was said that the procedure of admission was too easy. Remnants of the following of former politicians and militarists had made their way into the Party in the hope of obtaining some government offices, a practice which was detrimental to party discipline and good spirit. Consequently, many progressive and faithful members were disappointed with the Party organization. These critics concluded that, with all the shortcomings of system and membership, little success could be expected from the Nationalist Party in performing its responsibilities during the period of political tutelage. However, it must be remembered that the failure of the Party in many respects was due also to national calamities and foreign interference.

---

[1] At the Fourth and the Fifth National Congresses of the Party, several delegates submitted proposals for the immediate execution of the resolutions adopted by the former Party sessions but not yet put into effect. While these proposals were adopted, not all such resolutions have been executed to date.

THE FIVE-POWER CONSTITUTION AT WORK: POLITICAL INSTITUTIONS DURING THE PERIOD OF POLITICAL TUTELAGE

1. THE NATIONAL GOVERNMENT BEFORE 1928

The Organic Law of July 1, 1925

As stated before, the National Government of the Republic of China was first established in Canton, on July 1, 1925. With only ten articles, the first *Organic Law of the National Government* had three characteristics:

(1) Party control. Article 1 stipulated that the National Government was to be in charge of the national affairs under the direction and supervision of the Nationalist Party.

(2) Collective leadership. The National Government was composed of sixteen state councilors, who were to dispose of important state affairs as a collective body. The Chairman and five Standing Members, elected from among themselves, were to take charge of routine matters.

(3) Simple organization. The National Government had only three Ministries: military affairs, foreign affairs, and finance.

At the military stage, it was the established policy that the Party should control the government. Since the death of Dr. Sun, no one could immediately build up such a high prestige as to assume the sole responsibility of state affairs. Located in a small area and having limited functions, there was no necessity of setting up a complicated organization on the basis of *The Five-Power Constitution*.

Minor revisions of the Organic Law of 1925

With the rapid advancing of the Northern Expedition forces and the transfer of the government seat to Wuhan in accordance with the resolution of the plenary session of the Central Executive Committee of the Nationalist Party on March 10, 1927, the *Organic Law* was revised by increasing the number of state councilors to twenty-eight and abolishing the office of Chairman.[1] The elimination of a nominal head of the Government further indicated the mounting jealousy of power among the leaders. Minor changes in internal organization were again made when Chiang Kai-shek established another National Government in Nanking. During the period from September 20 to December 28, 1927, the Nationalist Party was represented by a Central Special Committee as a result of the compromise among the different factions representing Nanking, Wuhan and Shanghai. As the Committee itself was temporary in nature, it did not bother to make any fundamental change in the National Government except increasing the state councilors to forty-three. On February 13, 1928, a new *Organic Law of the National Government* provided one Chairman, five to seven Standing Members, and a total number of forty-six state councilors.[2] In addition to several ministries, the National Government was to set up a Supreme Court and a Bureau of Auditing; these units never came into existence during the effective period of this law.

2. THE NATIONAL GOVERNMENT SINCE 1928

Enactment of an Organic Law of the National Government on the basis of the Five-Power Constitution

The official unification of the country was considered as the end of the first stage of the revolutionary program as advocated by Dr. Sun. Having brought the revolution from the military period to the period of political tutelage, the Party leaders deemed it necessary to construct a framework for the government on the basis of *The Five-Power Constitution* with a view to developing the capacity of the people for the exercise of political powers. On the proposal of Hu Han-min and Sun Fo, an *Organic Law of the National Government of the Republic of China* was drawn up by the Fifth Plenary Session of the Second Central Executive Committee of the Party and promulgated on October 8, 1928. This law had undergone several revisions,[3] and the one revised on December 30, 1931 was the prevailing law governing the organization of the National Government during the prewar period.

---

[1] For its text, see *The Current Laws of the National Government* (Bureau of Legal Affairs of the National Government, 1928), pp. 2–3.

[2] The Chairman and Standing Members were elected from among the forty-six state councilors.

[3] It was revised on November 24, 1930 and again on June 15, 1931.

The Essentials of the Organic Law of the National Government of December 30, 1931

According to the 1931 Organic Law, the National Government was to exercise all the governing powers of the Republic of China under the direction and supervision of the Nationalist Party. It was composed of one Chairman, twenty-four to thirty-six state councilors, and five *Yuan*, namely, the Executive, the Legislative, the Judicial, the Examining and the Supervisory. Each *Yuan* was headed by a President and a Vice-President, all of whom were appointed from among the state councilors. The Chairman was only a nominal head of the Government, the actual executive power being vested in the Executive *Yuan*. He had a term of two years and could remain in office for another term. The State Council, consisting of the state councilors, was to carry out the functions not belonging to any individual *Yuan* and to settle matters referred to it by two or more of the *Yuan*. As the Nationalist Party was to hold the supreme authority during the period of political tutelage, all the above-mentioned high-ranking officials were nominated by the Central Executive Committee of the Party.

The Executive Yuan – The highest executive organ of the National Government was to be the Executive *Yuan*, which was to establish ministries to perform various executive and administrative tasks, appoint commissions to take charge of specific state matters, and introduce in the Legislative *Yuan* laws dealing with matters within its competence.[1] The ministers, political and administrative vice-ministers and the chairmen and vice-chairman of the various commissions were appointed and could be removed by the National Government at the instance of the President of the Executive *Yuan*. The following matters were to be decided at the meetings of the Executive *Yuan*, attended by the President, Vice-President, the Ministers of the various ministries, and the Chairmen of the various commissions: (1) bills on legislative matters to be introduced in the Legislative *Yuan;* (2) budgets to be submitted to the Legislative *Yuan;* (3) amnesties to be submitted to the Legislative *Yuan;* (4) declarations of war, negotiations for peace, conclusion of treaties, and other international matters, to be submitted to the Legislative *Yuan;* (5) appointment or dismissal of government

---

[1] During that period, the Executive *Yuan* generally had the following ministries: interior, foreign affairs, military affairs, navy, finance, communications, industries, railways and education. There were a few commissions on Mongolian and Tibetan affairs, overseas Chinese affairs and other matters. The National Reconstruction Commission, the National Military Council and the National Economic Council were directly responsible to the National Government.

officials above the rank of *chien jen;* [1] (6) all matters which could not be settled between the various ministries and commissions of the Executive *Yuan;* and (7) all other matters which, according to law or in the opinion of the President of the Executive *Yuan*, should be decided at the meetings of the Executive *Yuan*.

The Legislative Yuan – The highest legislative organ of the National Government was to be the Legislative *Yuan*, which was to decide upon legislation, budgets, amnesties, declaration of war, negotiations for peace, conclusion of treaties and other important international affairs. The Legislative members, from fifty to one hundred, were to be appointed by the National Government at the instance of the President of the said *Yuan* for a term of two years. [2] Members were not permitted to hold concurrently administrative offices in other branches of the Government. The President of the Legislative *Yuan* presided over its meetings.

The Judicial Yuan – The highest judicial organ of the National Government was to be the Judicial *Yuan*, which was authorized to supervise judicial administration, discipline officials, and adjudicate administrative cases. [3] Such matters as the granting of pardons and reprieves and the restitution of civil rights were to be submitted by the President of the Judicial *Yuan* to the National Government for its approval and action. It could also introduce in the Legislative *Yuan* bills on matters within its own competence.

The Examining Yuan – The highest organ of the National Government was to be the Examining *Yuan*, which was to conduct examinations and determine the qualifications for entry in the public service. [4] No public functionary could be appointed until he had passed an examination and fulfilled the requirements for admission to the civil service as determined by law. It might also introduce in the Legislative *Yuan* bills on matters within its own competence.

The Supervisory Yuan – The highest supervisory organ of the National Government was to be the Supervisory *Yuan*, which was to

---

[1] *Chien jen* is the fourth rank of Chinese government officials; *shan jen* being the first rank, *dai jen*, the second; *chain jen*, the third; and *wain jen*, the fifth.

[2] According to the 1931 *Organic Law of the National Government*, one half of the Legislative members was to have been elected by the people. But this provision had never been carried out during the effective period of that law.

[3] The Judicial *Yuan* was, at that time, composed of the Ministry of Justice, the Supreme Court, the Administrative Court, and the Commission for the Disciplinary Punishment of officials. The Ministry of Justice was sometimes shifted under the Executive *Yuan* on the ground that it was administrative in nature.

[4] The Examining *Yuan* was to be composed of the Examination Commission and the Board of Personnel.

exercise the power of impeachment and that of auditing.[1] It was to be composed of from thirty to fifty members and a number of supervisory commissioners, all of whom were appointed by the National Government at the instance of the President of the Supervisory *Yuan*. Like the Legislative members, they could not concurrently hold any other office in any of the organs of the Government. It might also introduce in the Legislative *Yuan* bills on matters within its own competence.

The above are the essential features of the organization and functions of the National Government as provided in the 1931 Organic Law. The number of state councilors, and Legislative and Supervisory members were different under different organic laws. The 1928 Organic Law provided for twelve to sixteen state councilors, who were later increased from sixteen to thirty-two under the Organic Law of June 15, 1931. In accordance with the provisions of the 1928 Organic Law, there were forty-nine to ninety-nine Legislative members and nineteen to twenty-nine Supervisory members. These were only minor changes. The major differences of the different organic laws were the powers of the Chairman of the National Government and the President of the Executive *Yuan*.

Reasons underlying the revisions of the organic laws of the National Government

The shifting of the powers of the Chairman of the National Government and of those of the President of the Executive *Yuan* had been determined largely on the consideration of the occupants of the respective offices. Chiang Kai-shek was the Chairman of the National Government under the 1928 Organic Law. Even though the organization of the government was based upon the spirit of collective leadership, the Chairman had actual executive power and was concurrently Commander-in-Chief of the armed forces. T'an Yen-k'ai, Hu Han-min, Wang Tsun-hui, Tai Chi-t'ao and Ts'ai Yüan-p'ei were the Presidents of the Executive, the Legislative, the Judiciary, the Examining and the Supervisory *Yuan* respectively.[2] After the death of T'an Yen-k'ai in September 1930, Chiang was concurrently President of the Executive *Yuan*. As a result of the revision of the Organic Law on November 24, 1930, the powers of both the Chairman of the National Government and the President of the Executive *Yuan* had

---

[1] The Board of Auditing has been under the direct control of the Supervisory *Yuan*.

[2] The Examining and Supervisory *Yuan* were not established at the same time as the other three *Yuan*. The Supervisory *Yuan* did not come into existence until February 2, 1931, when Yu Yu-jen succeeded Ts'ai Yüan-p'ei as its President.

been increased. Following the promulgation of the *Provisional Constitution of the Republic of China for the Period of Political Tutelage* on June 1, 1931, the Organic Law was revised on June 15, 1931. The Chairman became the Chief Executive of the National Government. The Presidents of the five *Yuan* were appointed on the recommendation of the Chairman. Chiang remained as the Chairman of the National Government and the President of the Executive *Yuan*. Technically, his power far exceeded that of the President of the United States; but actually, his freedom of action was rather restricted due to the complicated situation of the country and the increasing number of dissidents both within and without the Party.

The ascendency of Chiang's power was a result of his political and military victory over his enemies within the Nationalist Party, who organized an "Enlarged Conference" representing almost all the dissident elements and started a civil war in 1930. Wang Ching-wei, Feng Yü-hsiang, and Yen Hsi-shan all joined forces against Chiang. With the fall of these influential leaders, Chiang had the opportunity to consolidate his power for the reconstruction of the nation; but, on May 27, 1931, the Nationalist leaders in Kwangtung declared their independence from Nanking and proceeded to set up another National Government in Canton. Chiang was then accused of being a dictator. The reconciliation between Canton and Nanking had not been reached until the Japanese invasion of Manchuria on September 18, 1931. The compromise was the revision of the *Organic Law of the National Government* in December 1931 by reducing the power of the Chairman and thus making him a nominal head of the government. Lin Sen served as Chairman of the National Government until his death in September 1943. Inasmuch as military power has been dominant in Chinese politics and Chiang has been directly or indirectly in control of the armed forces of the country, his voice has been predominant in the National Government whether he was the Chairman, the President of the Executive *Yuan* or the Chairman of the National Military Council.

3. THE NATIONAL PEOPLE'S CONVENTION AND THE
PROMULGATION OF THE PROVISIONAL CONSTITUTION OF THE
REPUBLIC OF CHINA FOR THE PERIOD OF POLITICAL TUTELAGE

The demand for a provisional constitution for the period of political tutelage

There was no unanimous opinion among the Nationalist leaders concerning the promulgation of a provisional constitution for the period of political tutelage. The Fifth Plenary Session of the Second National Congress of the Party, held in August 1928, adopted a resolution that a provisional constitution be promulgated during the period of political tutelage in accordance with the teachings of Dr. Sun Yat-sen. On the other hand, Hu Han-min, then President of the Legislative *Yuan* and a senior leader of the Nationalist Party, considered it unnecessary because he believed that Dr. Sun's teachings should be the basis for political tutelage. The subject was no longer under serious discussion after the Third National Congress of the Party decided in March 1929 to ratify the *Fundamental Principles of Political Tutelage*, to pass a resolution for the *Confirmation of Dr. Sun Yat-sen's Writings as the Fundamental Laws of the Republic of China during the Period of Political Tutelage*, and to adopt the *Rules concerning the Exercise of Governing Powers*. However, the "Enlarged Conference" in Peiping [1] raised a strong objection to the delay of the promulgation of a provisional constitution and set up an independent government on September 1, 1930. The next day, Wang Ching-wei and six others were appointed to draft a provisional constitution for the period of political tutelage. They started to work on September 15 and completed a draft on October 27. At that time, Chang Hsueh-liang, Commander of the armed forces in Manchuria, decided to side with the National Government in Nanking and made his entry into Peiping. Thus the rebels had to retreat to Taiyuan, where the final stage of the drafting work was done. This was the reason why it was known also as Taiyuan Draft of the Provisional Constitution.

Characteristics of the Taiyuan Draft of the Provisional Constitution

In spite of the military defeat of the "Enlarged Conference," the Taiyuan Draft had certain worthwhile characteristics. It accepted Dr.

[1] "Peking" and "Peiping" are used interchangeably in many Western books. When the Nationalists established the Capital in Nanking, they changed the name Peking (Northern Capital) into Peiping (Northern Peace). Being the seat of the central government again, Peking was restored to its original name by the Communists.

Sun's *Outline of National Reconstruction* to be the fundamental principles for political tutelage. The individual rights of the people were directly protected by the Provisional Constitution instead of by laws as in many other constitutions. There was a clear demarcation between the powers of the Central Government and those of the provincial governments, which could have their own provincial constitutions. The organization and functions of the National Government were similar to those provided in the 1928 Organic Law, but more emphasis was laid on the popular election of the Legislative and Supervisory members. There was a provision for a national representative organ to serve in a consultative capacity of the National Government during the period of political tutelage. The representative organs in the provinces and districts were stipulated in great detail. A compulsory system of education was adopted. The Draft paid special attention to the protection of labor and the restriction of the development of capitalism. In the declaration promulgating the Draft, the "Enlarged Conference" accused the National Government in Nanking of its delay of promulgating a provisional constitution for the period of political tutelage as contradictory to Dr. Sun's teachings and thus resulting in political tutelage in name but individual dictatorship in fact.[1] Such kind of accusation could not escape the attention of the people, even though it was largely a political weapon in the long series of power struggles among the Nationalist leaders.

The National People's Convention of 1931

On October 3, 1930, Chiang Kai-shek cabled the Central Party Headquarters in Nanking with the request it convoke a National People's Convention for the adoption of a provisional constitution for the period of political tutelage. He was then conducting the military campaign against the rebels in the North and was reasonably sure of an early victory. In November 1930, the Fourth Plenary Session of the Third National Congress of the Party adopted his proposal and decided to hold the Convention on May 5, 1931. Thus the National Government promulgated the *Electoral Rules of the National People's Convention* on January 1, 1931. Tai Chi-T'ao and Sun Fo were appointed in charge of matters concerning the election of representatives to the National People's Convention, which was completed by the end of April.

According to the *Electoral Rules of the National People's Convention*, the total number of representatives was 520, to be distributed as

[1] See Tientsin *Ta Kung Pao*, November 29, 1930.

follows: (1) 450 from the various provinces, (2) 22 from the various municipalities, (3) 12 from Mongolia, (4) 10 from Tibet, and (5) 26 from overseas Chinese communities. With the exception of the representatives elected from Mongolia, Tibet and overseas Chinese communities in accordance with special regulations, all others were elected from the following legally registered organizations in various provinces and municipalities: (a) peasant associations; (b) labor unions; (c) chambers of commerce; (d) industrial organizations; (e) educational societies, national universities, universities registered at the Ministry of Education and associations of liberal professions; and (f) local branches of the Nationalist Party. There were certain restrictions concerning candidates' qualifications. Persons who belonged to any one of the following categories were not qualified to be elected: (a) having committed anti-revolutionary activities; (b) having been convicted of corruption in public service; (c) having been deprived of civil rights which had not yet been restituted; (d) being mentally ill or having bad habits; [1] and (e) having been expelled or suspended from the Nationalist Party.[2]

Besides the 520 representatives through election, members of the Central Executive and Supervisory Committees of the Nationalist Party and State Councilors were qualified to attend the Convention and had the right to vote. The alternative members of the two powerful Committees, heads of the five *Yuan* and ministries, and those having special permission from the Presidium of the Convention, could also attend its meetings but without voting.[3] From the foregoing, it is clear that the Nationalist Party could directly or indirectly control the Convention.

The Convention was formally opened on May 5, 1931, with an attendance of more than 450 representatives. Members of the Central Executive and Supervisory Committees of the Party and also the State Councilors were present at the opening ceremony on May 5, 1931. A Presidium of nine persons was elected. The Presidium members were to preside over the Convention meetings, which were eight in all from May 8 to May 17. It adopted many resolutions, the most important of which was the enactment of the *Provisional Constitution of the Republic of China for the Period of Political Tutelage.*[4] This Convention was the

---

[1] This is an expression traditionally used in Chinese law to apply to addicts of opium and other drugs.

[2] See the *Electoral Rules of the National People's Convention*, Arts. 1, 5, 7, 8, and 13.

[3] Art. 3 of the *Organic Law of the National People's Convention*, promulgated by the National Government on April 24 and revised on May 4, 1931.

[4] For its English translation, see Appendix F.

first assembly attended by people's representatives since the beginning of the period of political tutelage. In his address, President Chiang Kai-shek pointed out that the main purpose of the Convention was, on the one hand, to consolidate peace and national unification as well as to map out plans for national reconstruction; and, on the other, to pave the way for the inauguration of the era of constitutional government, when political power would be restored to the people.[1]

Essentials of the Provisional Constitutions of 1931

The Provisional Constitution consisted of eighty-nine articles grouped into eight chapters: first, general principles; second, rights and duties of the people; third, essentials of political tutelage; fourth, people's livelihood; fifth, education of the citizens; sixth, division of power between the Central and local governments; seventh, organization of the governments; and eighth, an annex. The provision on the rights and duties of the people was similar to that in most of the Western democratic constitutions. People's livelihood was much emphasized here and the State would afford every encouragement and protection to the private enterprises. As to the education of the citizens, *The Three People's Principles* were prescribed as the basic principles of education in the Republic. This rigid stipulation would preclude the freedom of academic research and study of other political ideologies to a large extent. Of course, it must be remembered that this Provisional Constitution was designed for the period of political tutelage when the Nationalist doctrines should still prevail.

The most important part of this Provisional Constitution was the chapter on the essentials of political tutelage. It described clearly the relations between the Party Government and the people. The National Congress of the Party was to exercise the governing powers during this period on behalf of the people, who should be trained how to exercise the four political rights of election, initiative, recall and referendum. Meanwhile, the National Government was to be under the direction and supervision of the Nationalist Party. The Provisional Constitution further provided that when a majority of the provinces in the country were to reach the period of constitutional government, that is, when district autonomy was to be completely instituted throughout each of such provinces, the National Government would summon a National Assembly to decide upon the adoption and promulgation of the

---

[1] For details of the National People's Convention, see *The Minutes of the National People's Convention* (Nanking: Central Headquarters of the Nationalist Party, 1931).

Permanent Constitution. Accordingly, a draft of the Permanent Constitution should be prepared by the Legislative *Yuan* on the basis of *The Outline of National Reconstruction* and practical achievements.

The principle of equilibrium was adopted in the division of power between the Central and local governments. However, local laws and regulations would be deemed null and void if they were in conflict with those promulgated by the Central Government. Only general principles on the organization of the governments were provided in the Provisional Constituiton, as the powers and functions of the government organs were separately provided in the organic law of the National Government as discussed before. As to the interpretation of this Provisional Constitution, the power was vested in the Central Committee of the Nationalist Party.

As this constitution was provisional in nature to be effective within a limited period of time and was prepared by the Nationalist Party, it could not be expected to be as comprehensive and democratic as a permanent constitution.[1] Yet it should still be the fundamental law of the country during the period of political tutelage. Facts proved that many provisions, such as people's livelihood and education, had never been effectively enforced by the government. There were many cases of government infringement of private rights and restrictions on personal liberty. When the *Organic Law of the National Government* was revised and promulgated on December 30, 1931, its provision on the powers and functions of the Chairman of the National Government was in conflict with that in the Provisional Constitution. Strictly speaking, this *Organic Law* should have been declared null and void according to Article 84 of the Provisional Constitution. If the latter was considered unrealistic because of the change of internal circumstances of the

---

[1] The National People's Convention created a special committee to examine the various proposals submitted by the representatives for inclusion in the Provisional Constitution. The author's primary recollections, as a member of that committee, are of the many sharp and enlightening debates. Compromises were the usual results. For example, because during the period of the Peking Government educational funds were regularly diverted to other purposes with a consequent adverse effect on the progress of education, some members of the committee strongly urged the independence of the educational funds. On the other hand, others condemned this suggestion as unreasonable on the following grounds: first, the Nationalist Government would never repeat the abuses of the Peking Government, and so such provision was by no means necessary; secondly, there were many other matters no less important than education, such as communications, economic reconstruction, and the like, and if educational funds should be isolated in the national treasury, why should not the others be similarly treated, an arrangement which would result in the Ministry of Finance having nothing to do. As the only means of ending the prolonged debate and of forcing a conclusion, a compromise was reached — Art. 52 of the Constitution: "The Central and local governments shall provide adequate funds for necessary educational expenses and shall also safeguard the security of funds which are by law specially set apart [for educational purposes]."

country, resort could have been made to its amendment through legal procedures. But no step had been taken in either direction.

4. NATIONALIST EFFORTS TO CARRY OUT PARTY PRINCIPLES AND PROGRAMS

Domestic reconstruction and abolition of unequal treaties

Since its unification of China in 1928, the Nationalist Party had endeavored to carry out the party principles and programs. In the field of material reconstruction, there was notable progress, especially in its improvement of communications. But considerable achievements could not be expected from the National Government, which had to fight continuously against the Nationalist dissidents, Communists and Japanese. As mentioned before, the Provisional Constitution of 1931 stipulated that *The Three People's Principles* should be the basic principles of education during the period of political tutelage. It was with this in mind that the Nationalist Party promoted the work of political tutelage through the educational institutions and party branches. Early in 1928, the National Government ordered that the college instructors of all the required courses on Dr. Sun Yat-sen's political theories be specially examined and certified by a special committee composed of the Central Executive Committee of the Party and the Ministry of Education. Among the qualifications were membership in the Party for at least five years with good records and publication of treatises with special contributions to Dr. Sun's political theory. Through education the National Government aimed also to cultivate national consciousness, patriotism and intelligent participation in government by the citizenry. As to the main task of training people to exercise political rights for the preparation of local self-government, it fell on the shoulders of the party workers and will be discussed more fully elsewhere in this work.

In the field of international relations, the National Government had been conciliatory toward foreign Powers. There were a few minor incidents involving foreign nationals and interests in several cities, which were taken over by the Nationalist forces during the course of the Northern Expedition. The Nanking incident was more serious but was settled peaceably. The Shantung incident was deliberately created by Japan for the purpose of obstructing the nationalist unification of the country as stated before. It was beyond the expectation of the Nationalist Party and Government that Japan should start her invasion of

Manchuria in 1931, followed by a series of open hostilities in North China and Shanghai, and then developing into a full-scale war in 1937. The Sino-Japanese War, which became part of World War II in December 1941 and did not end until September 1945, had far-reaching consequences in the domestic situation of China.

The immediate objective of the National Government was the termination of unequal treaties and the conclusion of new ones on the basis of equality and mutual benefit. Instead of resorting to unilateral abolition of the former, the National Government carried on negotiations with the interested Powers toward that end. The Sino-American Treaty of July 25, 1928, established the principle of complete tariff autonomy, which was followed by the treaties with other countries. Thus tariff autonomy, one of the most important aspirations of the National Government, was restored to China within a short period. No less important than tariff autonomy was the relinquishing of the system of extraterritoriality, which had prevented the Chinese Government from exercising its judicial power over foreigners within its territory. On December 28, 1929, the National Government declared its determination to restore its inherent jurisdictional sovereignty. Serious steps were also taken to reform its own judicial system as well as the civil and criminal codes. Regulations governing the exercise of jurisdiction over foreign nationals in China were promulgated on May 4, 1931; but the date of its enforcement was postponed indefinitely by a decree issued on December 29 of the same year. The main reason for the postponement was the Japanese invasion of Manchuria in September 1931, when the National Government decided to avoid any possible friction with other Powers and to concentrate all its efforts to protect China's territorial integrity. World War II changed the foreign relations between China and the major Powers, and the problem of extraterritoriality was finally settled through mutual understanding. By a treaty with China on January 11, 1943, the United States surrendered its extraterritorial rights. Great Britain signed a similar treaty on the same day.

The foreign concessions and leased territories in China were major obstacles to the integrity of Chinese sovereignty. Through years of negotiations with the related Powers, the National Government regained some of these territories. Among them were the British Concessions at Tientsin and Kuling as well as the territory of Weihaiwei which was leased to Great Britain in 1898. Other special rights and privileges obtained by foreign Powers through unequal treaties were also abolished through years of prolonged negotiations. On the whole, the National Government was fairly successful in its efforts to terminate unequal treaties imposed on China by the foreign Powers since the middle of the nineteenth century.

Administrative reforms

The administrative and judicial reforms to be discussed here were largely the work of the Executive, Judicial, Examining and Supervisory *Yuan*. However, the Legislative *Yuan* deserved no less merit than the others, because it not only showed an excellent spirit of cooperation with them but also enacted all the necessary laws and regulations for the enforcement of these reforms.

The administrative reforms were achieved largely through the system of civil service examination, the exercise of impeachment, and emphasis upon administrative efficiency. With the inauguration of the Examining *Yuan*, public examinations had been prescribed as the proper avenue of entrance to the civil service. These examinations were of three kinds: (1) ordinary, held in the provinces or other designated places; (2) higher, held in the national capital, either annually or biennially; and (3) special, held at any time deemed necessary. Certificates were issued by the Examination Commission to the successful candidates entitling them to appointment in the different branches of the civil service.

The Examining *Yuan* further performed the following functions: (1) registration of the present civil service personnel as well as all successful candidates; (2) review of the efficiency rating records of functionaries in all central, provincial and local government offices, their appointments and dismissals, their promotions, demotions and transfers, as well as the records required of them concerning their qualifications, scholarship and experience; and (3) execution of the prescribed scale of salaries, the pension law and retirement allowances, the provision of facilities for the further training of civil servants and general supervision of their working conditions. It is believed that through the examination system, competent personnel could possibly be provided for the entire government machinery. By means of various supervisory processes exercised by the Examining *Yuan* as described above, incompetent persons could be prevented from entering the government service and the former practice of favoritism and bribery as a road to civil service might be eliminated.

In order to free the government offices from corruption and extravagance, the Board of Auditing was established under the direct control of the Supervisory *Yuan*. It performed the following functions: (1) examination of the budgets and financial statements of all government offices; (2) supervision of the execution of the budgets of all government offices; (3) certification of statements concerning revenues and expenditures, and of the disbursement orders of all government offices; and (4) investigation of cases of dishonesty or corruption, as well as waste or extravagance, in government offices. When a government officer violated the law or abused his authority, any member of the Supervisory *Yuan* could present an impeachment bill to the Government. It should be accompanied by relevant documentary evidence, which must be examined by three other members of the said *Yuan*, to be designated by its President. If the impeachment bill was unanimously passed by this examination committee, the person impeached would be punished or removed from office according to the nature of his offence. Even high officials were not spared. In this way, the immediate effect was to put the officials in constant fear of impeachment and made them watchful of their steps.

Since public administration is a branch of expert or technical knowledge, nothing is more important than efficiency. One of the most persistent complaints against the Chinese bureaucracy was the constant and exasperating delays in the handling of official matters. With a view to instituting necessary reforms concerning the transaction of government documents, the Executive *Yuan* held a conference to study the problem, attended by representatives of fourteen government organs. After deliberate consideration, reforms were made so as to eliminate dilatoriness and unnecessary duplication, to lay down a uniform system of punctuation, and to provide for regular and systematic checks on documents. Other possible improvements were studied for the purpose of making the administrative branch of the government as efficient as possible. In spite of all these efforts, inefficiency was still characteristic of a number of government branches.

Judicial reforms

After the establishment of the National Government at Nanking, the judicial system was reformed from the ground up, with the Judicial *Yuan* as the highest organ. The Judicial *Yuan* consisted of: (1) the Ministry of Justice,[1] (2) the Supreme Court, (3) the Administrative

---

[1] The Ministry of Justice was originally a component part of the Judicial *Yuan*. A change took place on January 1, 1932, when it was placed under the jurisdiction of the Executive

Court, (4) the Commission for the Disciplinary Punishment of Officials; and (5) the Judicial Officers' Training School. The Ministry of Justice exercised general control over judicial administration throughout the country. The Supreme Court was reorganized on November 16, 1928. The Court had a President in charge of the supervision of all matters relating to judicial administration and consisted of seven divisions for civil cases and nine divisions for criminal cases. In order to become better acquainted with local conditions in other parts of the country, the Supreme Court, on July 18, 1935, adopted the policy of calling to Nanking, at intervals of three months, a group of twelve High Court judges from the provinces. These judges were thus given an opportunity to familiarize themselves with the working of the highest tribunal of the land.

Following the precedent of Continental Europe, the Chinese judiciary consisted of three grades of courts: the District Court, the High Court, and the Supreme Court. The District Court was the Court of the first instance for all cases, civil or penal, excepting a few criminal cases relating to offenses against the internal or external security of the country. The High Court or Provincial Court was to hear all appeals from the District Courts. The Supreme Court dealt almost exclusively with appeals from the lower courts on points of law. Unlike that of the United States, it had no power to decide on the constitutionality of a law or an ordinance. Divisional Districts Courts, Divisional High Courts and Divisional Supreme Courts could be established as the size and population of the different provinces might require.

The Administrative Court was established in Nanking in June 1933. It had jurisdiction over cases in which appeals were made against allegedly illegal administrative acts. The decisions rendered by the Court were binding upon the administrative offices concerned. The Commission for Disciplinary Punishment of Officials commenced work on June 1, 1932. It was to exercise jurisdiction over disciplinary matters in all cases where those were not dealt with by special laws. The Judicial Officers' Training School was established with a view to preparing a body of students competent to interpret and apply the laws and ordinances.[1] The National Government paid great attention to this problem. The faculty of the School consisted of experienced members

---

Yuan. In October 1934, it was returned to the Judicial *Yuan.* These changes reflect a series of decisions adopted by high Party officials, who, throughout this period, were frankly puzzled with regard to the form of organization indicated.

[1] The School was originally under the supervision of the Ministry of Justice; but, since November 17, 1934, it was placed under the direct control of the Judicial *Yuan.*

of the legal profession. Graduates of the School were appointed by the Ministry of Justice as "prospective" judges or procurators in the various District Courts.

One of the most important judicial reforms instituted by the National Government was the creation of machinery for the selection of a better type of judicial personnel. According to the *Organic Law of the Judiciary* promulgated on October 28, 1932, and effective July 1, 1935, candidates for appointment as judge or procurator were required to meet at least one of the following conditions: (1) having passed the judicial officials' examination and undergone the prescribed training; (2) having served as a teacher of the required law subjects in a public university or college or in a registered private university or college for more than two years; (3) having served as a judge or procurator for more than one year; (4) having practiced law for more than three years; or (5) having graduated from a law college (either in China or abroad) which has been recognized by the Ministry of Education, and having made a notable contribution to legal science. Stricter qualifications were required for the judges and procurators of the High Courts and Divisional High Courts, the judges of District Courts who were concurrently presidents, and the chief procurators of District Courts. The judges or procurators of the Supreme Court were chosen even more strictly than those mentioned above.[1]

Special emphasis was placed by the National Government on the codification of Chinese law. The Legislative *Yuan* made an appropriate contribution to this important task. Within a few years, a new civil code, a new criminal code, a complete code of commercial law and a new trade union law were promulgated. The National Government had therefore carried out its program of providing China with a complete *corpus juris*.

Prison reform also received particular attention. For the purpose of investigating prison conditions and aiding the authorities concerned in devising measures for further improvement, special officers were sent out from time to time to provinces and districts. Modern prisons were constructed. Prisoners were made to work and were taught simple handicrafts to enable them to earn a living after their release. In a word, all known methods of rehabilitating criminals were applied.

[1] See *The China Year Book*, 1936, p. 325.

5. THE PREPARATION FOR CONSTITUTIONAL RULE IN CHINA

The question of the early termination of political tutelage

According to the Party program, the stage of military administration ended at the time of the unification of China in 1928. With the beginning of the stage of political tutelage, the question arose about the duration of this period. In June 1929, this problem was discussed at the Third Plenary Session of the Second National Congress of the Nationalist Party. It was finally decided that the period of political tutelage be limited to six years, ending in 1935. However, on account of internal disputes within the Party, the task of tutelage was not accomplished effectively. After the Japanese invasion of Manchuria on September 18, 1931, there was an increasing criticism of the policies of the National Government and demand for the early termination of Party rule. As there was no representative organ in the government, dissenting opinions of different circles could not be effectively expressed. When the nation was suffering both from internal disturbances and external crisis, dissatisfaction toward the government and wide-spread blame on party rule were inevitable. It was difficult for the Nationalist Party and Government to decide whether they should terminate the period of political tutelage while the foundation for constitutional government was not yet well laid.

The process of gradual transition from political tutelage to constitutional government was provided in *The Outline of National Reconstruction:* "After local self-government has been established, each district is to elect one representative to the Representative's Assembly, to participate in the affairs of the Central Government." [1] Since local self-government of districts could not be completed in the near future, the organization of a Representative's Assembly by the people was out of sight. Although the *Organic Law of the National Government* of December 30, 1931 prescribed the popular election of one half of the members of the Legislative and Supervisory *Yuan*, this provision had never been put into practice. Thus the voice of the people could not be heard through their own representatives.

When Japan invaded Shanghai in 1932, the National Government and the Party Headquarters temporarily moved to Loyang. In order to consolidate the country to meet the increasing national crisis, the Second Plenary Session of the Fourth National Congress of the Party met in March and resolved to convene a National Emergency Confer-

[1] Art. 14.

ence. The National Government selected from different circles of the nation four hundred thirteen people as members of the Conference, which opened at Loyang on April 7 of the same year.[1] The Conference, attended by about one third of the selected members, lasted for seven days. It adopted a number of important resolutions concerning national preservation, among which was to urge the government to terminate political tutelage within the prescribed period and set up a representative organ in the meantime.[2] The Party leaders were then perplexed by the complicated situation and could not reach an immediate decision as to whether the period of political tutelage should be terminated earlier so as to start with the period of constitutional government.[3]

It was not until the meeting of the Third Plenary Session of the Fourth National Congress in December 1932 that a resolution was passed to convene a National Assembly in March 1935 for the purpose of adopting a permanent constitution and, prior to that, set up a People's Political Council as a representative organ in 1933.[4] In spite of this resolution, the People's Political Council was not established until 1938 when the war against Japan was already in full swing.[5] Because of the war emergency, the convocation of the National Assembly was indefinitely postponed. In accordance with the previous decision of the Party in 1929, the period of political tutelage was to end in 1935. However, the local self-government of districts, a prerequisite for constitutional rule, had not been completed. Therefore, the immediate commencement of constitutional government would be in contradiction with *The Outline of National Reconstruction* and would create abuses due to the lack of preparation as originally planned. On the other hand, the time for the actual enforcement of local self-government would still be far away in accordance with the *Principles for the Improvement of Local Self-Government* promulgated in 1934.

---

[1] See the *Rules governing the Organization of the National Emergency Conference*, promulgated by the National Government on March 17, 1932. (*The Collected Laws and Regulations of the Republic of China*, edited by the Legislative *Yuan* and published by Chung-hwa Book Co., 1934, Vol. I, Pt. 2, p. 1086.)

[2] For details, see *The Minutes of the National Emergency Conference* (edited and printed by the Executive *Yuan*, 1932), p. 76.

[3] See, for example, Sun Fo, "Draft Principles of National Salvation," *Shih-shih Hsin Pao*, April 27, 1931; Yu Yu-jen, "The Abandonment of Political Tutelage and the Danger of the Chinese Revolution," *The Central Daily News*, May 5. 1932.

[4] For details, see *The Minutes of the Third Plenary Session of the Fourth National Congress of the Nationalist Party*, edited and published by the Secretariat of the Central Headquarters of the Nationalist Party, 1932.

[5] The full-scale war between Japan and China started with the Lukou-ch'iao Incident on July 7, 1937. It was generally agreed that Japan purposely planned an armed conflict with the Chinese soldiers in that place so as to use it as a pretext for the furtherance of her invasion of China.

Then how much longer should the people wait for the beginning of constitutional rule in China? This was, indeed, a dilemma for the leaders of the Nationalist Party and Government.

The Draft Constitution of May 5, 1936

In accordance with the provisions of *The Outline of National Reconstruction*, the constitution of the Republic of China was to be drafted by the Legislative *Yuan*, made known to the public, and decided by the National Assembly for its adoption and promulgation at the beginning of the period of constitutional government.[1] A resolution to that effect was passed by the Third Plenary Session of the Fourth National Congress of the Party in December 1932. In January of the following year, Sun Fo became President of the Legislative *Yuan* and started the drafting of the constitution immediately. A drafting committee of forty-two members was appointed by him on January 20, with himself as chairman and Chang Tse-ben and Wu Ching-hsiung as his deputies. After twenty-four meetings, the preliminary draft was completed on February 24, 1934.[2] The Legislative *Yuan* then made it public on March 1.

On the basis of various proposals and comments, the Legislative *Yuan* revised the preliminary draft and, on October 16, adopted the *Draft Constitution of the Republic of China*. This Draft was then submitted to the National Government for its transmittal to the Party. On October 17, 1935, the Central Standing Committee of the Nationalist Party decided that the Draft should be revised according to the following five principles: (1) the Draft should be based on the fundamental principles of *The Three People's Principles*, *The Outline of National Reconstruction*, and the *Provisional Constitution of the Republic of China for the Period of Political Tutelage;* (2) the organization of the government should be based on practical political experience with a view to establishing a system which could consolidate the national strength without too rigid restrictions on its actual operation; (3) the Draft should only make general provisions on the Central and local government systems, leaving the details to be decided by law; (4) as to certain provisions which should be included in the constitution but could not be enforced at once or throughout the country, the date and

---

[1] Arts. 22–23. For a summary of the opinions on constitutional problems in China by Dr. Sun Yat-sen and Sun Fo, then President of the Legislative *Yuan*, see Wu Ching-hsiung and Huang Kung-chiao, *A History of the Constitution-making in China*, Vol. II, p. 637-792.

[2] At the first meeting of the drafting committee on February 9, Chang was designated to be the principal writer of the preliminary draft. Later Chang resigned and Wu succeeded him.

manner of their coming into force should be prescribéd by law; and (5) simplicity and clarity should be the characteristics of the contents of the Draft. The Draft was revised once more by the Legislative *Yuan* in accordance with the Party instructions.

In November 1935, the Sixth Plenary Session of the Fourth National Congress of the Party voted to submit the revised Draft to the Fifth National Congress, which was meeting at Nanking at that time. Then the First Plenary Session of the Fifth National Congress of the Party, in December 1935, appointed a committee of nineteen to review the Draft and decided May 5, 1936 as the date of its promulgation. Upon the suggestion of the committee, the Central Standing Committee of the Party decided to refer to the Legislative *Yuan* the Draft for its reconsideration and revision of twenty-three points. This long awaited *Draft Constitution of the Republic of China* was finally revised and passed by the Legislative *Yuan* on May 2, and promulgated by the National Government on May 5, 1936. It was generally known as the Draft Constitution of May 5,[1] consisting of one hundred forty-eight articles divided into eight chapters: (1) general provisions, (2) rights and duties of the people, (3) National Assembly, (4) Central Government, (5) system of local government, (6) national economy, (7) education, and (8) enforcement and amendment of the Constitution. On the whole, this was a well written document even though the drafting period was comparatively short. This Draft formed the basis of the *Constitution of the Republic of China of 1946*, which will be discussed later.

6. THE LOCAL GOVERNMENT SYSTEM
DURING THE PERIOD OF POLITICAL TUTELAGE

The two-level system and its variations

During the period of political tutelage, the local government system had been changed from the previous three-levels into two-levels, with the province as the higher unit and the municipality, district (*hsien*), or an area corresponding to a district, as the lower. As to the municipality directly under the control of the Executive *Yuan*, it was considered an independent unit by itself with the status similar to a province. The former intermediate unit of the local government system, the prefecture, was abolished by a decision of the Central Political Council of the Party in 1930. The office of "administrative inspector" later

[1] For the various drafts, see Wu Ching-hsiung, *et al.*, *op. cit.*, Vol. II, pp. 793–978.

came into existence under the Nationalist regime with the function to direct and supervise a few districts as designated by the provincial government. But this office was neither permanent in nature nor universally instituted in all the provinces. It only served as an auxiliary organ of the province and could not be considered as an intermediate unit. The National Government had set up, one after another since 1931, the Political Council in Peiping, the Political Council for the Southwest and the Political Council for Hopei and Chahar provinces.[1] These Councils were to meet the need of certain special circumstances in a few particular regions of China and stood between the Central and a few provincial governments, but they were in existence only for a short period and in certain limited areas with no effect on the local government system. The status of a province was granted by the National Government after 1928 to the following localities which were formerly classified as "special areas" and administered under special laws: Jehol, Chahar, Suiyuan, Chinghai and Sikang.[2] This change had simplified the local government system to a certain extent.

Legal basis of the local government system

Since the establishment of the National Government in 1925, various rules and regulations were promulgated governing the organization and functions of the local government in substitution for the old ones.[3] *The Provisional Constitution of the Republic of China for the Period of Political Tutelage* of 1931 laid down the basic principles of the local government system. In each province, a provincial government would be established in charge of the administration of provincial affairs under the direction of the National Government. It was only when a province reached the period of constitutional government that the People's Representative Assembly of that province would elect a governor. In each district *(hsien)*, a district government would be established in charge of the administration of district affairs under the direction of the provincial government. In localities where industry and commerce, population or other special conditions might warrant, municipalities could be established. As to the system of local government in Mongolia and Tibet, it was to be determined separately by law.[4] It should be

---

[1] Hopei province was originally under the name of Chihli. Another change of name was applied to Liaoning province, formerly known as Fengtien.

[2] The provincial government was not immediately set up in Sikang.

[3] For the territorial divisions of the various provinces, see *The Year Book of Internal Affairs* (Nanking: Ministry of Interior, 1935), pp. B8–B45.

[4] Arts. 78–83.

emphasized here that the concentration of power in the Central government has been the characteristic of the political system of China. Thus the local government was always under the direct control of the Central government and had no reserved power whatever before reaching the period of constitutional rule.

As to the local self-government during the period of political tutelage, the National Government also enacted new laws and regulations to substitute for those promulgated by the Peking regime. *The Outline of National Reconstruction* prescribed clearly that the completion of district self-government should be the determining factor of the transition from political tutelage to constitutional rule.[1] Both local administration and local self-government are to be separately discussed below.[2]

The provincial government

On the date of its own inauguration in Canton on July 1, 1925, the National Government promulgated the first organic law of the provincial government. Accordingly, the Kwangtung provincial government was established two days later. Through a number of revisions at different times. the organic law of March 23, 1931, was the prevailing law during the period of political tutelage.[3] The unique feature of the provincial government under the Nationalist regime was the commission or council system on the basis of collective responsibility. According to the early laws, each province had a number of commissioners, who, in turn, elected a chairman from among themselves. After October 1927, the provision concerning the chairman was changed and he was thereafter designated by the National Government. Besides the chairman, there was, for a time, a provision for standing commissioners who were elected from among themselves to take charge of routine matters.[4] The following description of the organization and functions of the provincial government was based on the organic law of March 23, 1931.

The provincial government was the highest organ in the province. Within its competence and without conflict with national laws, it could enact and promulgate rules and regulations applicable in that province.

[1] Arts. 16–23.

[2] For a brief description of the government system of Mongolia and Tibet, see William L. Tung, *The Government of China*, Vol. II, p. 693.

[3] The dates of revisions are as follows: (1)November 11, 1926; (2)July 8, 1927; (3) October 25, 1927; (4) April 27, 1928; (5) February 3, 1930; and (6) March 23, 1931. For the texts of the organic laws of 1925 and 1931, see *ibid.*, Vol. II, pp. 697–701.

[4] The Organic Law of November 11, 1926.

However, approval of the National Government was required for those rules and regulations which would restrict the freedom or increase the financial burden of the people residing therein. The provincial government was to be administered by a council of seven to nine members appointed by the National Government, which would also designate one member as chairman. The importance of the chairman in a provincial government depended on his personal ability, influence and relationship with the leaders of the National Government. According to the provisions of the organic law, he was to take charge of the routine and emergency matters of the provincial government, call and preside over the meetings of the provincial council, and execute its resolutions thereof. In practice, his influence went far beyond those functions and sometimes reached to the extent that collective responsibility as a basic feature of the provincial government existed in name only.

The following matters were to be discussed and decided by the provincial council: (1) the issuance of ordinances, enactment and promulgation of rules and regulations, suspension and abolition of ordinances issued and actions taken by the lower-level government agencies; (2) the increase or revision of financial burdens of the people; (3) the decision and alteration of administrative divisions within the province; (4) the budget and financial statement of the province; (5) the disposition of provincial properties and planning of provincial enterprises; (6) the execution of all matters entrusted to it by the National Government; (7) the supervision of local self-government; (8) the institution or alteration of administrative areas and organizations of the province; (9) the application for and transfer of the national army units stationing within the province as well as the preservation of law and order by the local military, police and militia forces; (10) the appointment and dismissal of provincial officials; and (11) other matters deemed by the provincial council necessary for its discussion and decision. However important the provincial council seemed to be, it was chiefly an organ of deliberation. The execution and administration of provincial affairs were largely the responsibility of the various departments and the secretariat under the direction of the chairman of the provincial government.

Most of the provinces had four departments in charge of civil affairs, finance, education and reconstruction. When necessary, a province might have a department of industry independent from that of reconstruction and also other agencies, such as the headquarters of the provincial security forces. The chairman of the provincial government was concurrently the commander of such security forces. The head of each department was appointed by the National Government from among the council members of the provincial government in charge of the affairs of the department and its subordinate agencies. The secretariat was headed by a secretary-general in charge of all other matters not within the jusrisdiction of the departments. Generally, the extent of the power of the secretary-general depended largely upon his relationship with the chairman.

Since 1931, there had been much talk about the change of the provincial system. Among the proposals were the reduction of provincial areas and the restoration of the former system of having a governor as chief administrator of a province. In practice, the prevalent system of collective responsibility existed in name only, the actual power being concentrated in the chairman. However, no steps were taken to bring about these proposed reforms. In July 1934, the Nanchang Headquarters of the National Military Council directed the provinces under its control during the military campaign against the Communists to set up a combined office for all government organs in a province. This device was supposed to achieve efficiency and economy. Due to its evident success, the Executive *Yuan* promulgated on October 24, 1936, temporary regulations to extend this practice to other provinces. All these measures were, however, of temporary nature and did not affect the basic system of the provincial government.

The office of administrative inspector

Prior to the promulgation of the *Temporary Regulations concerning Provincial Administrative Inspectors* by the Executive *Yuan* on August 6, 1932, different agencies with similar functions were established in several provinces without the approval of the National Government.[1] At the same time, the Honan-Hupei-Anhwei Military Headquarters enacted the same type of regulations for temporary establishment of the office of administrative inspectors in areas where there were armed conflicts between the Government and Communist forces.[2] Both regulations were latter superseded by the *Temporary Regulations governing the Office of Administrative Inspectors*, promul-

---

[1] The provinces were Anhwei, Kiangsu, Chekiang, Kiangsi, Kwangsi, Kwangtung and Sinkiang. For details, see Ch'ien Tuan-sheng, *et al.*, *History of Political Institutions under the Chinese Republic*, Vol. II, pp. 518–526.

[2] The authority of this Military Headquarters to enact local rules and regulations was delegated by the National Government.

gated by the Executive *Yuan* on October 15, 1936. Even though more provinces had provided for administrative inspectors as time went on, the system itself was of temporary nature. In other words, the office of administrative inspector only served as an auxiliary organ of the provincial government and did not constitute an intermediary level of government between the province and districts.

Appointed by the Executive *Yuan* and under the direction of the provincial government, an administrative inspector was to supervise all the administrative matters of the districts and municipalities within his territorial jurisdiction. The following were his specific functions: (1) to plan and review their administrative programs and important works; (2) to examine their budgets, financial reports, rules and regulations; (3) to supervise local administration and self-government; (4) to examine the records of local functionaries and matters concerning their promotion, demotion and discipline; (5) to call administrative conferences; (6) to settle disputes among the districts and municipalities within his territorial jurisdiction; and (7) to carry out the orders of the provincial government.

Generally, the administrative inspector was concurrently commander of the local security forces within his area of jurisdiction and also magistrate of the district where his office would be located. Since its institution in 1932, this temporary system had served some useful purpose, especially in the maintenance of peace and improvement of administrative efficiency. Due to the extensiveness of provincial areas, an auxiliary agency like this did have many advantages both in theory and in practice.

The municipal government

The municipal system in the cities was not standardized until July 3, 1928, when the National Government promulgated the organic laws regulating special and ordinary municipalities.[1] However, not long after their coming into force, these laws were criticized as unrealistic and lacking provisions for self-government. With a view to correcting these shortcomings, the Central Political Council of the Party adopted six principles as the basis for the enactment of new legislation by the Legislative *Yuan*.[2] Thus came the new Organic Law Governing Municipalities of May 20, 1930.[3]

---

[1] For their texts, see *Government Gazette*, No. 72 (July 7, 1928).
[2] At its meeting on February 12, 1930. See *Official Journal of the Legislative Yuan*, No. 15.
[3] Various proposals for its revision were made since 1932. The Legislative *Yuan* even prepared a revised draft to that effect. See *Official Journal of the Legislative Yuan*, Nos. 46, 84.

There were two categories of municipalities. One was under the direct jurisdiction of the Executive *Yuan* and on an equal footing with provincial governments; while the other, under the jurisdiction of the provincial governments and on an equal footing with the district governments. The standard of classification was based upon the size, population and political and economic importance of the various municipalities.[1] At the head of a municipal government was a mayor, who was to administer all the affairs of the municipality and to supervise the working of local self-government. The municipal government generally consisted of a secretariat and a number of bureaus, such as finance, public safety, social affairs, public works, public health, land and education. The secretary-general and bureau chiefs were all under the direction of the mayor in charge of their respective offices. Similar to the provincial council of a provincial government was the municipal council, which was composed of the mayor, bureau chiefs and three representatives from the municipal assembly if already established. The functions of the municipal council to a municipality was the same as those of the provincial council to a province.

The district government

The district government in China was traditionally under the responsibility of a chief administrator, generally known as the magistrate. For a short period after October 1926, a committee system was adopted. The provincial government appointed a number of committee members in charge of different bureaus and designated one as chairman. The practice of collective responsibility in the lower units of government was not suitable to the existing circumstances of China and inevitably created many abuses and frictions. Thus the National Government ordered, on June 9, 1927, that all the district governments be restored to the magistrate system. However, throughout the period of the Northern Expedition, the organization of district governments was quite diversified and had not been standardized until the promulgation of the *Organic Law of Districts* on September 15, 1928.[2] It was revised on June 5, 1929 and supplemented by the *Procedural Rules for the Applictaion of the Organic Law of Districts* on October 2. Further revisions of the Organic Law and the Procedural Rules were made on July 7, 1930.

---

[1] For the various municipalities under the two categories, see Tung, *op, cit.*, Vol. II, pp. 680, 694.

[2] For its text, see *Government Gazette*, No. 92 (September 1928).

The district government was headed by a magistrate, who was assisted by a secretary and several sections or bureaus in charge of different functions. The districts were classified into three ranks according to their size, population and financial rating.[1] In the district government, there was a district council composed of the magistrate, secretary, and section or bureau chiefs. The functions of the district council were similar to the provincial and municipal councils in their respective territorial jurisdictions. Under the magistrate, there were generally four bureaus according to the *Organic Law of Districts* of 1930: public safety, finance, reconstruction and education. Because of increasing criticism on the over-developed organization of the district government, the Ministry of Interior of the National Government and the Nanchang Military Headquarters of the National Military Council, then engaging in military campaigns against the Communists, seriously considered the reduction of the size of bureaus by changing them into three smaller sections. The proposed change was put into effect on December 31, 1934,[2] first in Honan, Hupei, Anhwei, Kiangsi and Fukien provinces and later extended to Szechwan, Kansu, Kweichow, Shensi and Chekiang provinces.[3] Mention must also be made of the district assembly, which was to be the legislative body of the district; but it would not be established until the district reached the stage of self-government. One of the important prerequisites for the constitutional rule of the country was the completion of district self-government, which had not been fully carried out during the period of political tutelage. The lack of well equipped experts in district government, largely due to meager pay and little chance of promotion, was one of the serious factors contributing to its inefficiency and stagnation.

Legal provisions for local self-government

The fundamental principles of local self-government during the period of political tutelage were based on *The Outline of National Reconstruction* and *Methods of Applying Local Self-Government*, all written by Dr. Sun Yat-sen and endorsed by the Nationalist Party. At its Third National Congress in March 1929, the Party decided four points as the basic procedure for the application of local self-government. They were

---

[1] Formerly there were various ranks of districts according to the classifications of different provinces. See also the *Rules for the Classification of Districts*, December 23, 1929.

[2] For details, see *The Complete Collection of Laws and Regulations of the Republic of China* (Shanghai: Commercial Press, 1936), Vol. I, pp. 538–542.

[3] For model districts and areas preparing for the establishment of district governments, see Tung, *op. cit.*, Vol. II, pp. 682–683.

(1) to promote local self-government, with the district as a unit;
(2) to enact laws and regulations for self-government in such a way
as to fit in the political and economic organization of the local unit for
the ultimate realization of the principles of democracy and livelihood;
(3) to send well-trained party members by the government to help the
district people in the preparation of self-government; and (4) to adopt
gradual steps in the enforcement of self-government, with the fulfillment
of all required conditions and the completion of elections as the final
aim.[1] Upon the recommendation of the Ministry of Interior of the
National Government in January 1930, the Central Political Council
passed the time schedule for the completion of local self-government,
beginning with 1929 and ending in 1934. Unfortunately, none of the
provinces had fulfilled its duty in the promotion of self-government
according to the ideal schedule.

As described before, the *Organic Law of Districts* was promulgated
in 1928 and revised in 1929. With the enactment of the *Organic Law of
Municipalities* in 1930, the self-government of lower units in both
districts and municipalities was provided. Detailed procedures were
prescribed in regulations governing the self-government for sub-
districts and other lower units, promulgated on September 18, 1929
and revised on July 7, 1930. The organic laws and electoral rules of the
district and municipal assemblies were also promulgated on August 10,
1932, although the date of their enforcement was postponed to March
12, 1933. Altogether, there were approximately fifty rules and regulations promulgated by the National Government during a short period
for the promotion of local self-government. However, in April 1934,
the National Government reversed its former policy and the movement
for local self-government suffered setbacks.

The municipal or district assembly

The municipal assembly was the representative organ in a municipality. Its chief functions were to deliberate on the following: (1) preparation for the election of the heads of sub-districts and other matters
concerning self-government; (2) enactment of municipal rules and
regulations; (3) municipal budget and financial report; (4) municipal
revenue, loans and other matters involving the increase of the financial
burden of the people; (5) managing and planning of municipal properties and enterprises; (6) people's livelihood and relief; (7) promotion

---

[1] See the resolution concerning the procedure for the enforcement of local self-government
as the foundation of political reconstruction (Tung, *op. cit.*, Vol. II, pp. 754–756).

of education and culture; (8) examination of measures initiated by the people; (9) matters submitted by the mayor for consideration; and (10) other matters concerning the municipality. The decisions of the municipal assembly were to be carried out by the mayor, who might request the assembly to reconsider certain items deemed not desirable. In case the assembly, by a vote of two-thirds majority, upheld the same resolution which the mayor again refused to execute, the issue was to be settled by popular vote in accordance with law. Furthermore, the municipal assembly could appeal to the superior government agency for the mayor's inaction or improper action in the execution of its decisions. The functions of a district assembly and its relation to the magistrate were similar to those discussed.

Due to its early preparation for self-government since 1928 and its prestige as the cultural center of the country, Peiping was the first municipality to establish the municipal assembly elected by the people. Thirty-seven members were elected by the qualified voters of the municipality on March 26, 1933, and, in turn, they elected from among themselves one chairman and one deputy-chairman of the assembly. Since its inauguration on August 1, 1933, the Peiping municipal assembly faced many difficulties. First, the laws and regulations promulgated by the National Government governing its organization, functions and relations with the municipal government were over-simplified to the point of ambiguity.[1] Secondly, there were constant conflicts between the municipal assembly and the municipal government and most of the efforts for reconciliation were in vain. Although the conflicts were mainly due to the legal ambiguity regarding their respective functions and relations with each other, personal prejudice was also one of the causes. Thirdly, the majority of the people in Peiping were so busy with economic pursuits that there was almost no time for them to exercise the four political rights – initiative, referendum, election and recall. Lastly, the majority of the people and even the members of the assembly were not well equipped for the exercise of political powers. In other words, their education and training had not quite prepared them for the practice of democracy. Whatever short-comings were evidenced in Peiping would inevitably be found in other places. Among others, the municipalities of Canton, Nanking and

---

[1] A long supporter of the local self-government movement, the author was elected as the first chairman of the Peiping municipal assembly. He found it necessary to spend almost four months at Nanking, capital of the National Government, in long consultation with the Executive *Yuan*, Legislative *Yuan*, and the Ministry of Interior, pleading for a revision of the laws and regulations in relation to the municipal assemblies.

Shanghai had followed Peiping's example. Yet most of these municipal assemblies were provisional in nature, because the assembly members were selected by the respective mayors for a temporary period. Due to Japanese encroachments in North China and the uncertainty of its political situation, the Peiping municipal assembly was suspended after the expiration of its one-year term.

Local self-government after 1934

The Japanese invasion and internal conflicts in China had interrupted the work of local self-government to a large extent. The accomplishments in this respect of the sub-districts and other lower-level units were strictly limited.[1] In order to correct the extreme rigidity of legal provisions which could not possibly be adaptable to all localities and to meet the changing situation of the nation, the Central Political Council decided, on February 21, 1934, that local self-government be divided into three periods: (1) preparation for self-government, (2) the beginning of self-government, and (3) the completion of self-government. During the first and second periods, the mayor or magistrate was to be appointed by the government. While all the assemblymen were to be elected by the people during the second period, the mayor or magistrate could nominate up to one half of them during the first period. When the third period came, all the government officials and assemblymen of the municipality or district would be elected by the people, who would actually exercise the rights of suffrage, initiative, recall and referendum. The district assemblies established since 1934 in Kweichow, Kansu, Chahar and Yunnan provinces were based upon the regulations resulting from the 1934 decision.[2] After the full-scale war against Japan in 1937, new rules were promulgated for the creation of temporary assemblies in different localities as representative organs of the people. Throughout the period of political tutelage, the laws and regulations were too numerous and the changes were so rapid that the people could scarcely follow the complicated development. Without the solid foundation of local self-government, the constitutional government established after the war could not be expected to be the same as that advocated by Dr. Sun Yat-sen.

---

[1] For a full discussion of the municipal and district assemblies and the application of local self-government to lower-level units, see Tung, *op. cit.*, Vol. II, pp. 686–691.

[2] See *ibid.*, pp. 691–693.

COMMUNISM VS. NATIONALISM: THE CHINESE COMMUNIST PARTY AND SOVIET REGIMES (1921–1945)

I. THE FORMATION OF COMMUNIST ORGANIZATIONS IN CHINA

Early promoters of Marxism

The Russian Revolution and the sympathetic attitude of the Soviet Union toward China created a favorable impression among the Chinese intellectuals, who, thoroughly dissatisfied with the existing conditions of the country, had searched diligently for new principles and programs for national salvation. While the Nationalist Party under the leadership of Dr. Sun Yat-sen had a large following, it did not attract many radicals to its camp. Among the radicals, Ch'en Tu-hsiu, a professor at Peking University, was the leading figure. In 1915, he had issued a periodical under the name *New Youth (Hsin Ch'ing Nien)*, in which he advocated cultural re-evaluation. This re-evaluation would be a critical testing of both the traditional standards of the Chinese and the new ideas of the West. His colleague, Li Ta-tsao (Li Ta-chao), was one of his chief contributors. It was under Li's guidance that Marxist study groups were formed at Peking University in the spring of 1918. This was about a year before the meeting of the First World Congress of the Communist International in Moscow and the May Fourth demonstrations, which were led by the patriotic and progressive students in Peking. While this student movement was not organized by the Communists, it had accelerated the spread of revolutionary ideas in China.[1]

The failure of the Paris Peace Conference to satisfy the Chinese demand for the restoration of Shantung to China was contrasted by the first Karakhan Declaration on July 25, 1919, in which the Soviet government indicated its readiness to relinquish Russian rights and

[1] For the Communist evaluation of the May Fourth movement, see Hu Chiao-mu, *Thirty Years of the Communist Party of China**, pp. 5–7.

privileges acquired by the Czarist regime in China.[1] Even though this Soviet promise was later proved to be an empty gesture, it did inspire the Chinese public at a time of desperation. Then followed actual contacts between the Communist agents and the radical elements in China. In May 1920, the Communist International sent Voitinsky to China to help organize the Marxism Society in Shanghai with branches in Peking and in several of the provinces.[2] The important leaders in charge of organizing various Communist groups at that time were Ch'en Tu-hsiu in Shanghai, Li Ta-tsao in Peking, and Mao Tse-tung in Hunan. In France, Chou En-lai, Li Li-san, and Ch'en Yi carried out similar activities among the Chinese in France with the purpose of propagating Communism.

The Creation of the Communist Party and the Youth Corps

The Second World Congress of the Communist International, held in Moscow and Petrograd in the fall of 1920, decided to intensify the Communist movement in China. Through its representative, G. Maring, the Chinese Socialist Youth Corps was founded in Shanghai in August of the same year.[3] Chou En-lai and several others set up the same organization in Paris in the following February. When the Third Comintern Congress met in Moscow, June 22–July 12, 1921, the Communist Party of China was formally born. Its Founding or First Congress, held in Shanghai on July 1, was attended by twelve delegates including Mao Tse-tung, Chang Kuo-t'ao, and Tung Pi-wu.[4] The Communist International was represented at the Congress by Maring. At that time, the total number of Communist members throughout the country was no more than sixty. Ch'en Tu-hsiu was then in Canton, but he was elected as first Secretary-General of the Communist Party. In October of the same year, Mao Tse-tung became the Secretary of its Hunan branch.

The expansion of the Communist movement

Following the establishment of the Communist Party, the labor movement in China grew steadily. The Secretariat of the Chinese Labor Union was set up in Shanghai with Chang Kuo-t'ao as its head. The

---

[1] For its text, see Jane Degras, *Soviet Documents on Foreign Policy**, Vol. I, pp. 158–161.

[2] They were Hunan, Hupei, Chekiang, Anhwei, Shantung, and Kwangtung.

[3] At its Third Congress in February 1925, the Corps was renamed the Chinese Communist Youth.

[4] The other delegates were Chou Fu-hai, Ch'en Kung-po, Ch'en Wang-tao, Ch'en T'an-ch'iu, Li Han-chun, Li Ta, Ho Shu-heng, Liu Jen-ching, and Pao Hui-seng.

First Congress of the All-China Labor Federation, held in Canton in May 1922, was attended by 170 delegates representing 100 unions with approximately 200,000 members. Meanwhile, the First National Congress of the Socialist Youth Corps, with a membership of more than 4,000, met in Peking. However, the Communist Party itself did not expand as fast as its mass organizations. There were only 123 members at the time of its Second Congress, held in July 1922 and attended by 20 delegates. The Congress stressed anti-imperialism, anti-warlordism, labor reforms, and "democratic revolution." In its manifesto, the Communist Party adopted a moderate policy of benevolent criticism toward the Nationalist Party.[1] One important decision of the Second Congress was that the Chinese Communist Party should join the Comintern so as to become an integral part of the world revolution. The delegates at the Second Congress were more united in principles and objectives than those attending the first one. Ch'en Tu-hsiu was re-elected Secretary-General of the Party and Chairman of the Political Bureau.

2. THE FIRST UNITED FRONT
OF THE NATIONALISTS AND COMMUNISTS

Important aspects of the collaboration

As early as January 1922, when the Conference of the Toilers of the East was held in Moscow and Petrograd, the idea of a united front was advanced. In his speech to the Conference, Zinoviev, Chairman of the Comintern, emphasized the importance of an alliance between the Communist-led workers and the non-proletarian toilers in China. At the Special Plenary Session of the Central Committee of the Communist Party in August 1922, Maring urged the adoption of a resolution to work with the Nationalist Party, against the original wishes of the Committee members. The necessity of such an alliance was formally recognized at the Comintern's Fourth Congress in Moscow, November 5- December 5 of the same year. As stated before, the joint declaration by Dr. Sun Yat-sen and A. Joffe issued in Shanghai on January 26, 1923, laid down the foundation for cooperation between the Nationalist Party and Soviet Russia. At its Third Congress at Canton in June, the Communist Party proclaimed its intention to cooperate

---

[1] For the resume of this manifesto, see Conrad Brandt, *et al.*, *A Documentary History of Chinese Communism**, pp. 63–65. Most of the Chinese texts of the manifestoes and programs of the Chinese Communist Party can be found in Hu Hua, *Source Materials of the Chinese Revolution under China's New Democracy*.

with the Nationalist Party. Ch'en Tu-hsiu remained in the leading position of the party. Mao Tse-tung was elected a member of its Central Committee.

The policy of a united front was actually implemented at the First National Congress of the Nationalist Party in Canton in January 1924. This important Congress adopted resolutions admitting Communists into the Party, cooperating with Soviet Russia, and stressing the workers and peasants' movement.[1] As a result, a number of important Communists were elected to the Central Executive Committee of the Nationalist Party: Li Ta-tsao, T'an P'ing-shan and Yu Shu-te as regular members; Mao Tse-tung, Chang Kuo-t'ao, Ch'u Ch'iu-pai, Lin Tsu-han, Han Lin-fu and Yu Fang-chou as alternate members. In his memorandum stating the reasons for Communist membership in the Nationalist Party, Li Ta-tsao said that, looking around the country, they found that the Nationalist Party was the only revolutionary party with history, principles and leadership. Concerning the future relationship between the two parties, his opinion was as follows:

> Before joining it, we have made a detailed study both of the theories and of facts. Dr. Sun has given us permission to retain our relationship with the China branch of the Third International. Consequently, our joining this Party and at the same time keeping our membership in the Communist Party is an open and honorable action, not a surreptitious move. On the contrary, since we have joined the Party and so long as we remain its members, we shall carry out its political program and abide by its constitution and by-laws. We shall obey the disciplinary measures or punishment imposed by this Party in case we fail to do so.[2]

It can be seen from Li's statement that the future relationship between the two parties was bound to be intricate and uneasy. The Communists were determined to expand their influence not only among the masses but also in the armed forces. When Whampoa Military Academy was founded with Chiang Kai-shek as commandant, Chou En-lai was appointed as head of its political department. The Communist infiltration of the Academy had far-reaching consequences. Some of its graduates became distinguished generals of the Communist army later on.

The aggressive steps of the Communist Party

Under the direction of the Communists, the mass movement was greatly intensified. The peasant associations in Hai-lu-feng, Kwantung,

---

[1] For details, refer to "The three great policies of the reorganized Nationalist Party," under Ch. V, Sec. 1.

[2] Chiang Chung-cheng (Chiang Kai-shek), *Soviet Russia in China**, p. 27.

organized since 1921 by P'eng Pai, were expanded to a membership of 134,000 by the middle of 1924. A year later, the All-China Labor Federation convened its second congress in Canton, with 281 delegates representing 166 unions. Lin Wei-min was elected as Chairman of its Central Executive Committee and Liu Shao-ch'i and Liu Wen-sung as Vice-Chairman.

Meanwhile, the Comintern never relaxed its world movement of Communism. Less than a year after its Fifth Congress, the Sun Yat-sen University was instituted in Moscow in May 1925. A number of important leaders of the Chinese Communist Party were trained there and in other institutions in Russia. The leadership of the Comintern in its attack on world imperialism was emphasized in the manifesto issued by the Fourth Congress of the Communist Party in January 1925. The Congress also resolved to push forward the labor, peasant, women and youth movements. The Communists played an important role in the General Strike and anti-British and anti-Japanese demonstrations aggravated by the May Thirtieth Incident in Shanghai, where a number of students were killed by the British police. Consequently, the membership of the Communist Party increased from 900 to 57,900.[1] With Li Li-san as Chairman, the Shanghai Federation of Labor Unions was then organized by the 200,000 local workers. At the same time, Mao Tse-tung started the peasant organizations in Hunan. Soon afterward, the Great Strike of Hongkong and Canton broke out involving 250,000 workers. Under Communist instigation, 130,000 workers returned to Canton and organized patrols to blockade Hongkong.[2]

The break-up of the first united front

Deeply concerned with the rapid expansion of Communism, the Western Hills Faction of the Nationalist Party urged its party headquarters in Canton to dismiss the Soviet advisers. Such a demand was turned down by the Communist-infiltrated Second National Congress, held in January 1926. Instead, the Nationalist Party Congress elected seven Communists as members and twenty-four as alternate members of its Central Executive Committee. However, the relationship between the two parties underwent a rapid change on March 20, 1926, when a plot against Chiang Kai-shek occurred on the Gunboat *Chungshan* in Canton. The Communists worked out a plan to

[1] Hu Chiao-mu, *op. cit.*, p. 16.
[2] See Harold R. Isaacs, *The Tragedy of the Chinese Revolution,** pp. 70–72, 106–107.

seize Chiang on board the Gunboat *Chungshan* on his way back from Canton to the Military Academy at Whampoa, of which he was the Commandant. According to Chiang, the Communists would have sent him to Vladivostock as a prisoner, thus removing a major obstacle to their eventual scheme of proletarian dictatorship. Chiang immediately arrested Captain Li Chih-lung, a Communist Acting Director of the Naval Forces Bureau, and some fifty other Communists.[1] The Central Executive Committee of the Nationalist Party adopted a resolution on May 15, barring Communists from top positions in the Nationalist organizations. Unwilling to break with Soviet Russia at that time, Chiang reached a truce with the Communists before the Northern Expedition was launched.[2]

By the end of 1926, a new strategy toward China was formulated by the Seventh Enlarged Plenary Session of the Executive Committee of the Comintern, which dispatched M. N. Roy to Wuhan as its representative. Meanwhile, a number of Chinese Communists returned from Russia to China. including Yeh T'ing, Wang Jo-fei, and Ch'en Yen-nien. Mao Tse-tung was then busily occupied in organizing peasant associations in Hunan. At the beginning of 1927, their membership increased to more than two million. His well known *Report on An Investigation into the Peasant Movement in Hunan* was the result of his survey, from January 4 to February 5, of the peasant movement in Changsha and other places of that province. The labor movement was simultaneously pushed forward. It was said that the armed occupation of the British Settlement in Hankow by the workers on January 3 was under the direction of Liu Shao-ch'i. As previously described, the workers' riot in Shanghai on March 21 paved the way for the Nationalist conquest of the city.

The extensive activities of the Communists created serious friction with the Nationalists. On April 12, Chiang Kai-shek started his anti-Communist drive in Shanghai and Nanking. Communist organizations were disbanded and many Communists were executed.[3] In spite of the conciliatory attitude adopted by the Fifth Congress of the Communist

---

[1] Chiang Chung-cheng, *op. cit.*, pp. 37–41.

[2] For a brief history of the Chinese Communist Party up to 1926, see C. Martin Wilbur and Julie Lien-ying How, *Documents on Communism, Nationalism, and Soviet Advisers in China,* 1918–1927*, Doc. 1, pp. 41–77; also Hu Chiao-mu, *op. cit.*, Sec. 1.

[3] On April 6, 1927, the Peking Government under the control of Chang Tso-lin ordered an armed search of the Soviet Embassy in Peking. More than sixty Communists were arrested including Li Ta-tsao, who was later executed. The action taken by Peking had, however, no connection with that of the Nationalists in the South.

Party in Hankow in April-May 1927,[1] the Nationalist Left-Wing in Wuhan ordered, on June 13, the withdrawal of the Chinese Communists from office and the dismissal of Borodin and other Soviet advisers. Roy was soon replaced by Lominadze, who could not save the situation either. On July 15, the Wuhan Government finally decided upon the expulsion of the Communists from the Nationalist Party. Thus the break between the Communists and the Nationalists became complete. The Sino-Soviet relations were subsequently severed.[2]

3. ARMED UPRISINGS AND THE CHANGE OF LEADERSHIP

From the August First Uprising to the establishment of the Kiangsi base

As a result of the split between the Nationalists and the Communists, the latter resorted to armed uprisings in various areas. Yeh T'ing and Ho Lung jointly launched the "August 1 Uprising" in Nanchang, Kiangsi, with approximately 30,000 soldiers.[3] Chu Teh, Chou En-lai and other Communist leaders participated in this riot, which marked the birth of the Chinese Red Army. On August 7, 1927, six days after the Uprising, an Emergency Conference of the Communist Party was held. Ch'u Ch'iu-pai, Mao Tse-tung, Li Li-san, Hsiang Chung-fa, Jen Pi-shih, Su Chao-cheng, Teng Chung-hsia, and several other leaders were present. Ch'en Tu-hsiu was charged with all the past failures because of his opportunistic policies and was replaced by Ch'u Ch'iu-pai as Secretary-General of the party. Actually, Ch'en took all the orders from the Communist International, which was represented at the Conference by Lominadze. This "August 7 Conference" adopted a radical platform of armed uprisings and agrarian rebellion against the Nationalist Government.

The famous "Autumn Harvest Insurrection" was engineered by Mao Tse-tung in Hunan on September 5–18, 1927. The purpose of the insurrection was to organize a peasants and workers' army and establish a Communist regime in Hunan. After its failure, Mao was dismissed from the Provisional Politburo and also from the Hunan Provincial Committee. In October 1927, Mao led his defeated forces to the

---

[1] This Communist Congress was attended by more than 100 delegates representing more than 50,000 members. Elected to its Political Bureau were Ch'en Tu-hsiu, Ts'ai Ho-shen, Li Wei-han, Ch'u Ch'iu-pai, Chang Kuot'ao, T'an P'ing-shan, Su Chao-cheng, Li Li-san, and Chou En-lai.

[2] For the relations between the Communist and Nationalist Parties during the period of the Northern Expedition, see Wilbur and How, *op. cit.*, Docs. 43–50; also Ch. V, Sec. 3.

[3] Hu Chiao-mu, *op. cit.*, p. 26.

Chingkang Mountains on the Kiangsi and Hunan border, where the first Communist base was established.

There were several other armed uprisings in the following months. Yeh T'ing and Ho Lung occupied Swatow for a week. Short-lived Soviet regimes were set up in Hai-lu-feng in Kwangtung and Ch'a-lin in Hunan.[1] The workers uprising in Canton, known as the Canton Commune, was ordered by the Comintern. Yeh T'ing, Chang T'ai-lai,[2] Su Chao-cheng, P'eng Pai, Yeh Chien-ying, and Yun Tai-ying took part in this riot, which only lasted three days.[3] Chu Teh, Lin Piao, and Ch'en Yi then led the South Hunan Uprisings of peasants, miners and soldiers; but they suffered the same fate as the others. In May 1928, Mao and Chu joined forces in the Chingkang Mountains and formed the Fourth Red Army, with Chu as Army Commander and Mao as Party Commissioner. There were only ten thousand men and two thousand rifles. On July 21, P'eng Teh-huai and Huang Kung-lieh led an outbreak in P'ingkiang, Hunan. They organized the Fifth Red Army, with P'eng as Army Commander and T'eng Ta-yuan as Party Commissioner. During that period, the Fourth and Fifth Red Armies were the strongest units among the Communist forces. The other Communist armies were much smaller in size and some of these units never had more than one thousand men.[4]

Failure of Ch'u Ch'iu-pai and Li Li-san

The Sixth Congress of the Communist Party, held in Moscow in July 1928, paid the utmost attention to the agrarian revolution under proletarian leadership. Ch'u Ch'iu-pai was condemned for his putschism and replaced by Hsiang Chung-fa as Secretary-General of the Party. Mao Tse-tung was not among the 170 delegates present at the Moscow meeting; he remained with his forces in the Kiangsi base, but he was re-elected to the Central Committee. Chou En-lai, Li Li-san, Liu Shao-

[1] It was said that the Communist regime in Ch'a-lin (Tsalin, in the Chingkang Mountains of the Hunan border) was the first Soviet Government. However, the general opinion was that the regime set up at Hai-lu-feng was the first one. The Hai-lu-feng riot was led by P'eng Pai, who was arrested and executed by the Nationalist Party in Shanghai on August 30, 1929. Hai-lu-feng is a joint name for Hai-feng and Lu-feng. See Shinkichi Eto, "Hai-lu-feng—The First Chinese Soviet Government," *The China Quarterly*, No. 8 (Oct.-Dec., 1961) and No. 9 (Jan.-Mar., 1962).

[2] Chang was killed in action.

[3] For a full description of the Canton Commune, see Harold R. Isaacs, *op. cit.*, pp. 282–292. For its fundamental programs issued on December 11, 1927, see Hu Hua, *op. cit.*, pp. 223–224.

[4] The other Red armies during that period were as follows: the First in the Honan-Hupei-Anhwei border under Chang Kuo-t'ao, the Second in western Hupei under Ho Lung, the Third in western Kiangsi under Lo Ping-hui, and the Twenty-Sixth in northern Shensi under Liu Tsu-tan and Kao Kang.

ch'i, P'eng Pai, and Hu Weng-chiang were all elected to responsible positions.[1] Ch'u was sent to Moscow as representative to the Comintern. At that time, Ch'en Tu-hsiu led various opposition groups against the policies of the Central Headquarters in Shanghai. On November 15, 1929, this founder of the Communist Party and several others were dismissed from the party.

In spite of party dissensions and reorganization, Communist uprisings were numerous. In the summer of 1928, there was an important riot in northern Shensi, led by Liu Tsu-tan (Liu Chih-tan).[2] This armed venture marked the Communist expansion into Northwest China. From July 27 to August 5, 1930, Changsha, Hunan, was occupied by the Communist forces but was recaptured by the Nationalist Army before long. This was also a period of intensified riots under the banner of Li Li-san line. Due to his repeated failures, Li was severely criticized for his putschist policy at the Third Plenary Session of the Sixth Central Committee of the Party at Lushan in September 1930. The anti-Li movement was led by Ch'en Shao-yu (Wang Ming), who had returned with other Moscow-trained students a few months previously.[3] Condemned by the Comintern, which was represented in China by P. Mif, Li resigned from the Political Bureau in November. Soon afterward, he was ordered to Moscow for consultation.

By that time, Chiang Kai-shek fully realized the serious nature of the Communist riots. Beginning on November 2, 1930, he started a series of "annihilation campaigns" against the Communists and eventually captured Juichin, the Communist capital in Kiangsi, on November 11, 1934.

Further change of Party personnel

Communist leadership was changed again at the Fourth Plenary Session of the Sixth Central Committee, which was held in Shanghai in January 1931. Li Li-san, Ch'u Ch'iu-pai, Li Wei-han, and Ho Ch'ang were replaced by Ch'en Shao-yu, Chang Wei-t'ien, and Shen Tse-min. Hsiang Ching-fa remained Secretary-General. One of the most important decisions was to hold a Congress of Soviets in Kiangsi, which led to the eventual establishment of the Chinese Soviet Republic at Juichin in November 1931.

[1] They were in charge of various Bureaus: Chou, Organization; Li, Propaganda; Liu, Labor; P'eng, Peasant; and Hu, Military.

[2] Liu was later killed in combat with the Nationalist Army in Shansi in April 1937.

[3] They included quite a number of prominent leaders of the Communist Party, such as Chang Wen-t'ien (Lo Fu), Ch'in Pang-hsin (Po Ku), Shen Tse-min, and Wang Chia-hsiang.

After the arrest of Hsiang Chung-fa and others by the Nationalist Party,[1] Ch'en Shao-yu was elected as Acting Secretary-General in June 1931. In October 1932, the National Government arrested Ku Shun-chang, head of the Communist Special Service Department, and won him over for the Nationalist cause. This event made Shanghai absolutely unsafe for the Communist leaders. Thus Ch'en Shao-yu, Chou En-lai, Ch'u Ch'iu-pai, Chang Wen-t'ien, Ch'in Pang-hsien, and others fled to Mao's headquarters at Juichin. Soon afterward, the National Government arrested Ch'en Tu-hsiu and other Chinese Trotskyites in Shanghai.[2] Ch'en Shao-yu was then replaced by Ch'in Pang-hsien as Secretary-General and sent to Moscow as representative to the Comintern.

The Communists never relaxed the expansion of their armed forces. In May 1932, Hsü Hsiang-ch'ien and Chang Kuo-t'ao organized the Fourth Front Army in northern Szechwan. Their scattered forces, if combined, would have been potentially formidable. A possible strong ally was the 19th Route Army, which revolted against the National Government on November 20, 1933. Under the leadership of Li Chi-tsen, Ch'en Ming-shu, Chiang Kuang-lai, and Ts'ai T'ing-kai, a "People's Government" was set up in Foochow, Fukien. However, their regime was suppressed by Chiang Kai-shek so soon that the Communists did not have time to join forces with them.

In January 1934, Chang Wen-t'ien succeeded Ch'in Pang-hsiu as Secretary-General and Liu Shao-ch'i became Chairman of the All-China Labor Federation. Mao had been Chairman of the Chinese Soviet Republic since November 1931. After the Second All-China Congress of the Soviets, held at Juichin in January 1934, he remained in that position.

4. THE ESTABLISHMENT OF SOVIET REGIMES IN CHINA

The Chinese Soviets

The first Soviet regime was established in Hai-feng and Lu-feng, Kwangtung, in November 1927, and lasted until the following February. This was the result of the peasant uprising organized by P'eng Pai. In the meantime, a Soviet regime emerged at Ch'a-lin, Hunan. The Canton Commune, set up by the workers, existed only a few days in

---

[1] They were later executed in Shanghai.

[2] It was in January 1931 that a Trotskyite group was founded in Shanghai, with Ch'en Tu-hsiu as Secretary-General and Chairman of the Political Bureau. Ch'en died at Kiangtsin, near Chungking, on May 28, 1942.

December of the same year.[1] In July 1928, the P'ingkiang Soviet was established in Hunan by P'eng Teh-huai. However, the strong base of the Communists was found in southeastern Kiangsi, where Mao and Chu Teh established a Soviet regime in August 1929. In May of the following year, an important conference, represented by the delegates from various Soviet regions, was held in Shanghai. This conference adopted resolutions for the establishment of a Central Soviet Government in China and enactment of the land and labor laws. The same decisions were reached at the Fourth Plenary Session of the Central Committee in January 1931.

The Japanese invasion of Manchuria on September 18, 1931, did not interrupt the determined efforts of the Communists to set up a regime separate from the National Government in Nanking. The First All-China Congress of the Soviets had its opening session at Juichin on November 7, 1931. It was attended by 290 delegates, including Ch'en Shao-yu, Chou En-lai, and Chang Kuo-t'ao. The all-powerful Congress proclaimed the establishment of the Chinese Soviet Republic with Juichin as its capital, formulated its Constitution, enacted land and labor laws, and elected the Central Executive Committee of the Chinese Soviet Republic. Then, on November 27, the Central Executive Committee held its first meeting and elected Mao Tse-tung as Chairman, Hsiang Ying and Chang Kuo-t'ao as Vice-Chairmen, and Chu Teh as Commander-in-Chief of the Red Army.

There were six scattered areas under the control of the Chinese Soviet Republic during the period of 1930–34. Among these, the "Central Soviet District" along the Kiangsi-Fukien border was most important. With seventeen *hsien* (districts) and three million of population under its control, it lasted from 1930 to 1934. The other Soviet districts were much smaller and less permanent, located along the borders of Hupei-Hunan, Hunan-Kiangsi, northern Kiangsi, Honan-Hupei-Anhwei, and Hupei-Hunan-Kiangsi.[2] Even though all the Soviet areas were surrounded by the Nationalist forces, the Provisional Central Government of the Chinese Soviet Republic issued a declaration of war against Japan on April 15, 1932. The Communists never failed to seize any convenient opportunity of gaining public support through propaganda.

---

[1] The exact period was from December 11 to 13, 1927.
[2] For details, see Harold R. Isaacs, *op. cit.*, Appendix, pp. 323–349; also Victor A. Yakhontoff, *The Chinese Soviets** (New York: Coward-McCann, 1934).

The Communist Constitution of November 7, 1931

The Constitution of the Chinese Soviet Republic was adopted and promulgated by the First All-China Soviet Congress on November 7, 1931.[1] It was a comparatively simple but comprehensive document, which stipulated the form of the state and the organization of the government, rights and duties of the people, the eventual abolition of imperialism and capitalism, the reform of land and labor conditions, and the protection of minorities in China. The following were the essential points.

The form of the state and the organization of the government – The Chinese Soviet Republic was established on the basis of the democratic dictatorship of the workers and peasants. Its highest authority was vested in the All-China Congress of the Soviets, composed of the deputies chosen from workers, peasants, and soldiers. When the Congress was not in session, the supreme power was held by the All-China Central Executive Committee of the Soviets. Nevertheless, government affairs were actually conducted by a Council of People's Commissars appointed by the Central Executive Committee. This set-up was similar to that in Soviet Russia.

Rights and duties of the people – The political rights and freedoms would be enjoyed by all workers, peasants, Red soldiers, and the entire toiling population; but they were denied to the militarists, bureaucrats, landlords, the gentry, village bosses, monks, and all other exploiting and counter-revolutionary elements. All the toiling people, attaining the age of sixteen, were entitled to vote and to be voted for in the elections of the Soviets. It was only those people who would enjoy freedom of worship and also free universal education. The emancipation and protection of women were specially emphasized. To bear arms was considered a privilege which could only be granted to workers, peasants, and the toiling masses. On the other hand, enlistment in military service would undoubtedly be deemed as the supreme duty of the toiling masses.

Self-determination of national minorities – The Constitution recognized the right of self-determination of the national minorities in China. The Government would encourage the development of their own cultures and languages. Theoretically, each national minority could form an independent state and separate itself from China. The national minorities as listed in the Constitution were Mongolians,

[1] For its English text, see Conrad Brandt, *et al., op. cit.*, pp. 220–224.

Tibetans, Miao, Yao, and other racial groups living in China.[1]

Domestic programs – As socialism was to be the final goal of the Soviet regime, various measures would be taken to restrict the development of capitalism in order to eliminate the capitalist exploitation of the toiling masses. The improvement of the living conditions of the working class would be the basis of labor legislation. Land laws were to be enacted with a view to ultimate nationalization of the land, which would be confiscated from the landlord and distributed to the poor and middle peasants.[2]

External policies – The Chinese Soviet regime would take steps to free China from the yoke of imperialism by abolishing all the political and economic privileges previously obtained by foreign Powers in China through unequal treaties. All foreign enterprises would be confiscated and nationalized if they were not in conformity with the Chinese laws. However, all alien toilers living in China would be protected by law. Furthermore, all foreign revolutionaries could take asylum in China and receive material assistance for their revolutionary cause. It was emphatically stipulated in the Constitution that the Chinese Soviet regime would be ever ready to form a united revolutionary front with the proletariat and all oppressed peoples of the world. Naturally, Soviet Russia was specified as China's loyal ally.

The Communist Constitution of 1931 was superseded by that of 1954, which will be fully discussed later.[3]

---

[1] According to the *Handbook on People's China** (Peking: Foreign Languages Press, 1957), the Hans constituted 93.94 percent of the population, numbering 547,283,057. The other nationalities, with a total of 35,320,360, were only 6.06 percent of China's population. The people in Taiwan (Formosa) and overseas Chinese were not included in the above figures. The national minorities and their main centers of habitation were listed as follows: Chuang (6,600,000) in Kwangsi province; Uighur (3,700,000) in Sinkiang Uighur Autonomous Region; Hui (3,600,000) in Kansu and Chinghai provinces; Yi (3,300,000) in Liangshan Mountains on Szechwan-Yunnan borders; Tibetan (2,800,000) in Tibet and Chamdo Area and Chinghai province; Miao (2,500,000) in Kweichow and western Hunan provinces and other regions in central, south and south-west China; Mongolian (1,500,000) in Inner Mongolian Autonomous Region, Kansu and Chinghai provinces, and Sinkiang Uighur Autonomous Region; Puyi (1,250,000) in south-western part of Kweichow province; and Korean (1,100,000) in Yenpien Korean Autonomous *Chou* in Kirin province. (pp. 14–15.) In addition, there are several national minorities with smaller populations: T'ung (600,000) in Southeastern Kweichow and northern part of Kwangsi; Yao (600,000) in Kwangsi, northern Kwangtung, and southern Hunan; and T'ai (500,000) in border regions of Yunnan. (*People's China*, June 1, 1954.) The population figures of national minorities in China vary slightly in different sources.

[2] For the English text of the Land Law of 1931, see Conrad Brandt, *et al., op. cit.,* pp. 224–226. *Cf. The Agrarian Reform Law* of June 30, 1950. (*The Agrarian Reform Law of the People's Republic of China and Other Relevant Documents**. Peking: Foreign Languages Press, 1959.)

[3] Chs. XI, XII.

The long March and the firm establishment of Mao's leadership

The "annihilation campaigns" conducted by Chiang Kai-shek had finally brought results. Having been hard pressed by the Nationalist Army, the Communist forces started their evacuation of the Kiangsi base in October 1934 and began the famous 6,000-mile Long March to Yenan. During the course of their retreat, they held an important conference at Tsunyi, Kweichow, on January 13, 1935. Mao Tse-tung was elected at the conference as Chairman of the Central Committee and Politburo and thus formally assumed party leadership.[1]

At a strategic conference in Maoerhkai, northwestern Szechwan, in the fall of 1935, it was decided that the major forces led by Mao should march toward Northwest China while the Fourth Front Army under Chu Teh, Chang Kuo-t'ao and Hsü Hsiang-ch'ien should be left in Szechwan temporarily. Probably Chang's disagreement with Mao as to their final destination of retreat led to their eventual breakup. In October 1935, a year after the beginning of the Long March, Mao and Chou En-lai joined forces with the local guerilla units in northern Shensi under Liu Tzu-tan and Kao Kang. One month later, they attacked Yenan, which became Communist headquarters in the following years. However, it was not until October 1936 that Chu Teh and Lo Ping Hui united their Second and Fourth Red Armies with the Communist main forces in the Northwest. The tragic situation of the Communists at that time was well described by Mao himself in the following words:

> As a result, all the revolutionary bases were lost except the Shensi-Kansu border area, the Red Army was reduced from 300,000 to a few tens of thousands, the membership of the Chinese Communist Party was reduced from 300,000 to a few tens of thousands, and the Party organizations in Kuomintang areas were almost entirely wiped out.[2]

5. THE SECOND UNITED FRONT
AND EXPANSION OF THE COMMUNIST REGIMES

Communist call for the Second United Front

It was the consistent strategy of the Communists that, when they were relatively weak, a united front policy would be advanced in order to consolidate their strength. On January 15 and March 4, 1933, the

---

[1] Ch'u Ch'iu-pai was left behind. He was arrested and executed by the National Government on June 18, 1935. Benjamin I. Schwartz's *Chinese Communism and the Rise of Mao** (Harvard University Press, 1961) is a brief but most systematic treatise, analyzing the change of leadership in the Communist Party.

[2] *Mao Tse-tung: Selected Works** (New York: International Publishers, 1954) Vol. I, p. 193.

Chinese Communists made repeated statements in favor of the formation of a united front against Japan. Then, on April 15, they issued a "Manifesto on Anti-Japanese United Front." On August 1, 1935, the Maoerhkai conference proclaimed the urgency of the formation of an Anti-Japanese People's United Front. This policy was approved by the Seventh World Congress of the Comintern and reiterated by the Central Political Bureau of the Communist Party on December 25 of the same year.

In January 1936, the Communists urged Chang Hsueh-liang, Commander of the Northeastern Army stationed in Shensi with the mission to annihilate the Reds, to discuss matters concerning united action against Japan. To go one step further, the Central Committee of the Communist Party addressed the Nationalist Party on August 25, calling for the cooperation of the two parties. The letter reads in part:

> The Chinese Communist Party and the Chinese Red Army hereby solemnly declare: We approve of the establishment of a unified democratic republic for the whole country; approve of the convocation of a parliament elected by universal suffrage; support an anti-Japanese national salvation congress representative of all the people and all the anti-Japanese armed forces in the country, and a unified national defense government for the whole country. We hereby declare: As soon as a unified democratic republic is established for the whole of China, the Red areas will become one of its component parts, the representatives of the people of the Red areas will attend the all-China parliament, and the same democratic system will be set up in the Red areas as in other parts of China.[1]

On the basis of past experience, the National Government was very skeptical of the sincere intentions of the Communist Party. Receiving no Nationalist response to the letter, the Communists issued another declaration for a united Democratic Republic in the ensuing month. In spite of these political maneuvers, the Nationalist-Communist relationship did not change materially until the Sian Incident on December 12, 1936.

The Sian Incident

The Sian Incident was the turning point of the formation of the Second United Front between the two parties against Japanese invasion. On December 12, 1936, Chiang Kai-shek was forcibly detained by two Nationalist generals, Chang Hsueh-liang and Yang Hu-cheng, who were originally ordered by the National Government to exterminate the Communists in the Northwest. The underlying factors contributing to the incident were complicated. The soldiers under

---

[1] *Ibid.*, Vol. I, pp. 324–325.

Chang's command came from Manchuria and longed for home. Yet Manchuria could not be recovered without fighting a decisive war against Japan. For some time, the personal relationship between Chiang and the two generals had been deteriorating. Chiang was hesitant to wage a full-scale war against Japan while the nation was still divided. The Communists took advantage of the situation and tried to deepen the dissensions between the National Government and its armed forces in Shensi.

At that time, Moscow was in favor of forming a new united front in China against Japan under the leadership of Chiang Kai-shek. The policy of Soviet Russia was solely motivated by the consideration of her own security. After the conclusion of the Anti-Comintern Pact between Germany and Japan, Soviet Russia had been in constant danger of being attacked from both East and West. Inasmuch as a strong China as Japan's enemy would be an effective measure to keep the latter from undertaking a military venture against Siberia and the Chinese Communist Party was not yet in the position of leading the, nation in a foreign war, both Stalin and Mao considered it expedient to have Chiang released.[1] On the other hand, any personal danger to Chiang would lead to a bloody war against the Communists and might result in their disaster. The National Government had already prepared for armed attack against the rebels and the Communists if persuasion and negotiation should not produce Chiang's release. It was due to these factors that Chiang was finally set free after two weeks of detention in Sian.

Chiang denied that he had ever made any conditions with the rebels and the Communists in Sian. It was probable, however, that they discussed how they might unite the nation against their common enemy. In his statement made after his departure from Shensi, Chiang declared vaguely that all promises would be kept and actions resolutely taken. Mao claimed, on December 28, that Chiang did accept the following terms:

(1) to reorganize the Kuomintang and the National Government by expelling the pro-Japanese clique and admitting the anti-Japanese elements;
(2) to release the patriotic leaders in Shanghai and all other political prisoners and to guarantee the freedoms and rights of the people;
(3) to end the policy of "annihilating the Communists" and to enter into an alliance with the Red Army to resist Japan;

[1] See H. H. K'ung, "A Memoir of the Sian Incident," in *The Collection of Speeches of H. H. K'ung*, Vol. II, pp. 657–704. K'ung was then Acting President of the Executive *Yuan* of the Chinese Government.

(4) to convoke a national salvation conference of all parties, all groups, all circles, and all armies to decide on the line for fighting Japan and saving the nation from extinction;

(5) to establish relations of cooperation with countries sympathetic to China's resistance to Japan; and

(6) to adopt other specific ways and means for national salvation.[1]

In any event, the unceasing aggression of Japan in North China required the National Government to take effective steps to form a new united front of all the elements in the country for the defense of its territorial integrity.[2]

The Consolidation of Communist regimes

On February 10, 1937, the Communist Party made another appeal to the Nationalist Party, similar to its letter of August 25, 1936. Meanwhile, it lost no time in consolidating its power in Communist controlled areas. On March 3, the Shensi-Kansu-Ninghsia Soviet Government was set up with Chang Kuo-t'ao as Chairman and Yenan as capital. After the outbreak of war between China and Japan on July 7, the National Government recognized the status of the Shensi-Kansu-Ninghsia Border Region. This compromise was arranged as a result of the negotiations between Chiang Kai-shek and Communist representatives at Lushan.[3]

With the conclusion of the Sino-Soviet Treaty of Non-Aggression on August 21, the relations between the National Government on the one hand and Soviet Russia, the Comintern and the Chinese Communist Party on the other were improved. On the following day, the Red Army was reorganized into the Eighth Route Army, with Chu Teh and P'eng Teh-huai as commander and deputy commander respectively.[4] This reorganized Red Army soon made advances toward northern Hopei and Shansi against the Japanese invaders. Meanwhile, the Shensi-Kansu-Ninghsia Soviet Government was renamed the Shensi-Kansu-Ninghsia Border Region Government. On September 22, the Communist Party declared its intention to abolish the Chinese Soviet

---

[1] *Mao Tse-tung: Selected Works**, Vol. I, p. 255.

[2] The Sian Incident was described in detail by Chiang Kai-shek and Madame Mei-ling (Sung) Chiang in *General Chiang Kai-shek; the Account of the Fortnight in Sian When the Fate of China Hung in the Balance** (Garden City: Doubleday, Doran & Co., 1937). This book was originally published in Chinese under the title, *Sian: a Coup D'etat*. See also Chiang Chung-cheng, *Soviet Russia in China**, pp. 72–79.

[3] The Communist representatives were Chou En-lai, Ch'in Pang-hsien, and Lin Tsu-han.

[4] Lin Piao, Ho Lung, and Liu Po-ch'eng were appointed as divisional commanders of the Eighth Route Army.

Republic and Red Army, renouncing all Communist programs, and pledging adherence to the Three People's Principles as advocated by Dr. Sun Yat-sen.[1]

In October, the National Government reorganized the Communist forces in Kiangsi and Fukien into the New Fourth Army with Yeh T'ing and Hsiang Ying as commander and deputy commander respectively. Later, it moved to Kiangsu and Anhwei to carry out guerrilla war against the Japanese army. Before the end of the year, the Shansi-Hopei-Chahar Border Region was established under Communist control. On January 10, 1938, the Provisional Administrative Committee of the Border Region was instituted at Fup'ing in western Hopei.

In view of the intensified war against Japan and their own domestic problems, both Chiang and Mao concentrated on consolidating their powers in the areas which they respectively controlled. The Nationalist-Communist relations in that year were comparatively conciliatory. As a result of his disagreement with Mao, Chang Kuo-t'ao fled to the Nationalist territory and was expelled by Mao from the Communist Party. Further advances were made by the Communist forces in Honan, Shantung, Suiyuan, Hopei, and Chekiang. The Nationalist Party held an Emergency Congress at Hankow on April 1. Several decisions of major importance were adopted by the Congress, including the election of Chiang as Director-General *(Tsungtsai)* of the Party, the creation of the *San Min Chu I* (The Three People's Principles) Youth Corps as a subsidiary organization to the Nationalist Party, the establishment of the People's Political Council as a representative organ of the various segments of the nation, and the formulation of important programs for national reconstruction and armed resistance against Japan. The first session of the People's Political Council was held in Chungking, China's war-time capital, on July 6. It was attended by seven Communist delegates, including Chou En-lai, Ch'in Pang-hsien, Wang Jo-fei, and Ch'en Shao-yu.[2] It was in this same year that Mao published his *On Protracted Warfare* and made a report, "On the New Stage," before the Enlarged Sixth Plenum of the Communist Party at Yenan.

In the ensuing January, the First People's Council of the Shensi-Kansu-Ninghsia Border Region met and elected Kao Kang as Chairman of the Council and Lin Tsu-han as Chairman of this Border Region

[1] This Communist declaration was handed to the National Government on July 15, but it was released by the Central News Agency on September 22.
[2] Ch'en returned from Moscow in the spring of 1938.

Government. The realtions between the two parties were then deteriorating. The Communists protested in the summer that the National Government had virtually imposed a strict blockade of the Border Region. Thus armed conflicts became imminent.

In spite of his internal and external burdens, Mao had been busy writing. On December 15, he issued a pamphlet, *The Chinese Revolution and the Communist Party*, explaining the necessity of a transitional stage of a democratic united front during the war period. Then, on January 19, 1940, he published his well-known work, *On the New Democracy*, in which he considered "new democracy" as an expedient step toward eventual Communism in China. It was perhaps on the basis of "new democracy" that Mao announced the so-called Three-Thirds system into all political and administrative organs in the areas under Communist control. In other words, each organ would be represented by one-third Communists, one-third Nationalists, and one-third independents.[1] Nevertheless, this system of proportional representation had not been actually carried out.

Protracted negotiations and military conflicts

The Communist relations with the National Government turned from bad to worse when the New Fourth Army Incident occurred in January 1941. As a result of its armed conflict with the government forces, the Fourth Army commander, Yeh T'ing was captured and its deputy commander, Hsiang Ying, killed in action. As a measure of military discipline, the National Government ordered its disbandment; but its remnants under the command of Ch'en Yi fled to northern Kiangsu and Shantung. Then, to the great disappointment of the National Government, Soviet Russia concluded, on April 13, a five-year neutrality pact with Japan.

Mao continued to consolidate his power in the Communist dominated areas in order to strengthen the party's position in its negotiations and armed conflicts with the Nationalists. At the opening ceremony of the Central Party Academy in Yenan, on February 1, 1942, Mao inaugurated the *Cheng-feng* (party rectification) movement. In his speech, "Reform in Learning, the Party, and Literature," Mao emphasized the importance of correcting the erroneous tendencies in the Party, Army,

---

[1] Hu Chiao-mu described this "tripartite representative system" as follows: "This was a system whereby Communists (representing the working class and the poor peasants), progressives (representing the petty bourgeoisie), and middle-of-the-roaders (representing the middle bourgeoisie and enlightened gentry) each contributed one-third of the leading government personnel." (*Thirty Years of the Communist Party of China**, p. 66.)

and Administration. In the following February, he launched another movement, "Increase Production," for the ultimate realization of self-sufficiency in the Communist areas. Meanwhile, he took another step of major importance by appointing his trusted lieutenant, Liu Shao-ch'i, as Secretary of the Central Secretariat of the Communist Party.

The following years marked a period of protracted negotiations between the two parties. In May 1944, Lin Tsu-han was sent to Sian to discuss with the Nationalist representatives various issues concerning political democratization and military reorganization. Then Chou En-lai went to Chungking to conduct negotiations with the purpose of forming a coalition government. Mao presented a report, "On Coalition Government," to the Seventh Congress of the Communist Party, which met in Yenan from April 23 to June 11, 1945, not long after the Yalta Conference. The Congress revised the Party Constitution drafted by Liu Shao-ch'i and resolved, in no uncertain terms, to follow Mao's thought as the guide of the Communist Party.

By that time, events turned rapidly toward the conclusion of World War II. Soviet Russia hurried to declare war against Japan on August 8. In compliance with the terms of the Yalta Conference, the National Government signed the Sino-Soviet Treaty of Friendship and Alliance at Moscow on August 14, the same date of Japan's surrender. Of course, that alliance and friendship was short-lived and, in fact, has never materialized.

The United States had sincerely hoped that there would be a unified and prosperous China after the war. Thus the American Government lost no time in mediating between the two parties. Upon the urging and in company of American Ambassador Patrick Hurley, Mao flew to Chungking, on August 26, to confer with Chiang on the complicated problems. They issued a joint statement for peace and unity on October 11.[1] Yet, before the end of the month, military hostilities broke out in eleven provinces. Communist forces penetrated deep into Manchuria and other areas, including Hupei, Honan, Shantung, eastern Hopei, northern Shansi, Suiyuan, Chahar, and Jehol. Thus peace and unity remained the longed-for but unattainable hope of the Chinese people.

[1] See Chiang Chung-cheng, *op, cit.*, pp. 138–139.

CHAPTER VIII

CHINA AT WAR:
POLITICAL INSTITUTIONS DURING THE PERIOD
OF THE SINO-JAPANESE WAR

I. THE HOSTILITIES BETWEEN CHINA AND JAPAN

Japan's aggressive policy against China

The expansionists in Japan had long held the opinion that China's unity was Japan's disaster. In the mind of the Japanese militarists, a unified and strong China would block their aggressive designs in Asia. It was to their great disappointment that the Nationalist unification of the country was achieved in spite of their well-planned Tsinan Incident in May 1928, when the Japanese soldiers fought against the advance of the Nationalist troops in Shantung.[1] Japan's determination to take direct action in Manchuria could be traced back to the winter of 1928, when Chang Hsueh-liang, virtual leader in Manchuria after the death of his father, failed to comply with Japanese wishes to maintain a semi-independent status of Manchuria. Instead, he sided with the Nationalist Government in Nanking. On September 18, 1931, the Japanese army finally executed its long and carefully planned invasion of Manchuria in violation of the Covenant of the League of Nations, the Nine-Power Treaty of 1922, and the Kellogg-Briand Pact.

China immediately appealed to the League of Nations to take necessary action against the Japanese aggression. The League called upon Japan to refrain from aggravating the dispute, but it failed to impose sanctions against the aggressor. The Great Powers were not solidly behind the League decisions. Secretary Stimson's policy of non-recognition of forcible change of status did not receive support from Great Britain and France and thus was of little practical value. Japan disregarded the American policy and created the puppet state of "Manchukuo," on February 18, 1932. The League Assembly passed a resolution on March 11, endorsing the American non-recognition

---

[1] See Ch. V, Sec. 3, "Nationalist unification of China."

principle. It also sent the Lytton Commission of Inquiry to investigate the situation in the disputed areas. In its report of September 4, the Commission repudiated Japan's justification of the use of force in Manchuria and her creation of "Manchukuo" contrary to the wishes of the Manchurian people. In conclusion, the report recommended the establishment of a special administration in Manchuria under Chinese sovereignty.[1] Japan's answer to the report was her official recognition of "Manchukuo" on September 15 and her notification of withdrawal from the League.

The Japanese militarists were not satisfied to confine their activities to Manchuria. By the spring of 1933, they occupied Jehol and penetrated into Hopei province, where a demilitarized zone was set up by the Tangku truce. In 1935, they even attempted to push autonomous movements in Hopei, Shantung, Shansi, Chahar, and Suiyuan. Negotiations between China and Japan for a peaceful settlement were conducted in 1936. Unfortunately, no agreement satisfactory to both countries could be reached and thus the two neighboring giants in the Far East were destined to fight a prolonged and destructive war.

The full-scale war, 1937–1945

The full-scale war between the two countries broke out on July 7, 1937, at Lukou-ch'iao (Marco Polo Bridge) near Peiping. On that night, the Japanese troops in that area demanded entrance to Wanping at the southern end of Lukou-ch'iao on the pretense of searching for a missing soldier. Upon the refusal of the Chinese local commander, they opened fire and started the eight-year war. On October 6, the League Assembly declared Japan's action as a violation of the Nine-Power Treaty of 1922 and the Kellogg-Briand Pact. Nineteen nations having interests in the Far East met at Brussels in November 1937, and reaffirmed the principle of the Nine-Power Treaty guaranteeing China's sovereignty and territorial integrity.[2] Japan was, however, determined to use force to crush China's resistance. The Japanese troops occupied Nanking and Hankow in December and Canton in the following year. By that time, China had lost all the principal ports,

---

[1] For the Report of the Commission, see League Doc. C. 663. M. 320. 1932. VII*. For a brief analysis of the League efforts to settle the Sino-Japanese dispute through conciliation, see William L. Tung, *China and Some Phases of International Law** (New York: Oxford University Press, 1940), pp. 164–168.

[2] The stationing of a limited number of Japanese troops along the Peiping-Tientsin Railway was permitted by the treaty as a result of the Boxer Uprising in 1900.

coast cities, and railway lines.[1] Meanwhile, Japan set up puppet regimes in Peiping and Nanking to take charge of the administration of her occupied areas.[2]

China's foreign relations during the War

China and the United States – After the outbreak of World War II, Great Britain and France were busily occupied by their own defense in Europe. The United States and Soviet Russia were the only major powers which could possibly render assistance to China. The American attitude toward China had been sympathetic from the very beginning of the war. The United States took parallel action with the League of Nations throughout the period of Sino-Japanese hostilities. President Roosevelt's quarantine speech of October 5, 1937, clearly pointed at Japan. Although American military aid was limited due to insurmountable difficulties of transportation, the United States Government extended both loans and credits to China in addition to the lend-lease assistance.

After Pearl Harbor, the United States and Great Britain became full-fledged allies of China. As an expression of their friendship to China and in recognition of her great-power status, the two countries, by their treaties with China on January 11, 1943, abolished their extraterritorial jurisdiction in China. In the same year, the United States repealed the Chinese exclusion laws. Chiang Kai-shek was invited to take part in the Cairo Conference, which issued the important Cairo Declaration dealing with post-war situation in the Far East on December 1, 1943. However, the Chinese people deeply resented the decisions of the Yalta Conference at the expense of China without her previous knowledge and consent.

China and Soviet Russia – The Japanese invasion of Manchuria in 1931 constituted a direct threat to the security of Soviet Russia. After Stalin's failure to reach an understanding with Hitler in 1934, Soviet policy sought collective security by joining the League of Nations and directing the Communists in different countries to advocate united-front governments. It was quite evident that Soviet Russia could not

---

[1] For a full description of the Sino-Japanese War, see Chinese Ministry of Information, *China Handbook, 1937–1945** (New York: Macmillan Co., 1947), pp. 299–322; Ho Ying-chin, *A Description of the Eight Years' War of Resistance* (Chinese Ministry of Defense, 1955). Ho was Chief of Staff and concurrently Commander-in-Chief of the Chinese Ground Forces during the war.

[2] Peking Provisional Government in 1937; Reformed Government of the Chinese Republic in Nanking in 1938. Since 1940 until the Japanese defeat, Wang Ching-wei headed the Nanking puppet regime.

possibly fight against two formidable enemies in both East and West at the same time; furthermore, the establishment of diplomatic relations between the United States and Soviet Russia did not materially affect the situation in the Far East. As the Chinese Eastern Railway (CER) in Manchuria, jointly owned by China and Russia, was an important cause of tension between Moscow and Tokyo, the Soviet Government, on March 23, 1935, made a substantial retreat by selling the railway to "Manchukuo," China's strong protest notwithstanding. History proved that the policy of appeasement could never satisfy the ambitions of an aggressor. When the Japanese troops made advances in Inner Mongolia in 1935, the security of Outer Mongolia was endangered. Moscow's relations with Tokyo turned from bad to worse when Japan signed the Anti-Comintern Pact with Germany on November 25, 1936.

Soon after the outbreak of the Sino-Japanese War, Soviet Russia signed a Non-aggression Pact with China on August 21, 1937. Moscow followed the pact by extending economic and military aid to China. Nevertheless, Stalin cherished no friendship with Chiang. Their short-lived cooperation during the early part of the war was solely motivated by the Soviet desire to keep China continuously fighting against Japan so as to reduce the chance of the latter's attack on Siberia. At the Yalta Conference, Stalin exacted a very high price for Soviet entrance into the Far Eastern war from Roosevelt and Churchill, who paid it in a most generous manner with Chinese coin. The Sino-Soviet treaty of August 14, 1945, was merely a confirmation of what had been secretly arranged at Yalta. China agreed to recognize the independence of Outer Mongolia, the special status of Dairen and Port Arthur, and the joint management of the Chinese Changchun Railway. In return, Soviet Russia promised to support the National Government as the central government of China. Of course, that vague promise was never kept by the Soviet Government.

Wartime measures of the Nationalist Party and Government

In order to carry out the prolonged war of resistance against Japan, the Nationalist Party and Government took serious steps to consolidate China's national strength. Among the important wartime measures, were the following: establishment of a strong leadership under Chiang Kai-shek, reconciliation with the Chinese Communist Party, cooperation with other political parties and groups, and institution of representative bodies on both national and local levels. The relationship between the two major parties was discussed in the preceding chapter. All other measures are briefly described below.

2. THE FORMAL ESTABLISHMENT
OF CHIANG KAI-SHEK'S LEADERSHIP

Chiang's position in the Nationalist Party

The ascendancy of Chiang's power had encountered the constant jealousy of the senior members of the Nationalist Party, Hu Han-min and Wang Ching-wei in particular. Before the war, his dominating influence in the party had been exercised through his control of the army. The establishment of Chiang's formal leadership in the party had long been discussed by his followers but did not materialize until 1938. After the outbreak of the Sino-Japanese war in July 1937, the situation was completely changed. As Commander-in-Chief of the armed forces, Chiang concentrated in himself all the war powers. Hu was then dead. Wang alone could not challenge Chiang's position. It was under these circumstances that Chiang was elected as leader of the Nationalist Party and of the newly created Youth Corps.

The election of Chiang as Tsungtsai of the Nationalist Party

When the Extraordinary Congress of the Nationalist Party was held at Wuchang, March 29–April 1, 1938, the office of *Tsungtsai* (Leader or Director-general) was instituted. For all practical purposes, *Tsungtsai* has no distinction from *Tsungli*, which was held by Dr. Sun Yat-sen during his life-time. After the death of Dr. Sun in 1925, the Second National Congress of the Nationalist Party in 1926 adopted a resolution that, to do honor and reverence to the Party's late leader, he be always in the position of *Tsungli* of the party but that its functions be exercised by the Central Executive Committee. In order to evade any conflict with this resolution, the Extraordinary Congress decided to set up the office of *Tsungtsai*, which was to exercise the power of *Tsungli* in his absence.[1] The Extraordinary Congress also decided to provide an office of Deputy *Tsungtsai*, which had no actual power whatsoever. Chiang and Wang Ching-wei were elected *Tsungtsai* and Deputy *Tsungtsai* respectively.[2] Thus, since April 1938, Chiang has become the sole leader of the Nationalist Party both in name and in fact.

[1] These two Chinese terms have the same meaning; this was one of the most interesting manipulations in Chinese politics.
[2] Wang eventually left Chungking to head the Japanese puppet regime in Nanking. He later died in Japan.

Chiang as leader of the San Min Chu I Youth Corps

One of the most important resolutions adopted by the Extraordinary Congress was the creation of the *San Min Chu I* (The Three People's Principles) Youth Corps, which was independent of the regular organization of the Nationalist Party. The important reason for its formation was to recruit young people into the party, in competition with the constant expansion of the Communists. Its organization was along the same line as the regular party, with the *Tsungtsai* as the leader of the Corps. As it developed, the Corps was not composed of young people only and thus became overlapped with the regular party organization. Chiang was quite disappointed with their friction and rivalry, and finally ordered their amalgamation in September 1947.

Chiang as sole leader of all factions in the party

Each of the different factions within the Nationalist Party, although faithful to Chiang, attempted to exercise dominant influence upon the leader. According to some observers, Chiang was not entirely displeased with the checks and balances among his followers. However, the unity of the party was undoubtedly undermined by factional dissensions. It was said that, besides the different political groups composed of dissidents in the party, there were three important factions among his own followers. They were: (1) the Organization Group, party members connected directly or indirectly with the Organization Department of the Party, having a controlling voice in the party; (2) the Army Group, mostly graduates of the Whampoa Military Academy, having predominant influence in the party organization of the army and in the *San Min Chu I* Youth Corps; and (3) the Political Study Group, mature politicians surrounding Chiang, exercising power through him but not in the party itself. While there were different affiliations among Chiang's followers, speculations about factional alignments were not all based upon facts. Exaggerations of such a nature in the political arena were unavoidable during a tumultuous period.

3. WARTIME PARTY ALIGNMENTS

The early attitude of the Nationalists toward other political parties

The existence of different political parties is the fundamental feature of a democratic system of government in its Western sense. In the early years of the Chinese Republic, there was a number of small

parties and political groups. Chiefly because of their limited membership, loose organization, as well as lack of leadership and policies,
most of them either vanished or were merged with others.[1] The
Nationalist Party alone weathered the political storms of the Republic
and became the ruling party of China until the advent of Communist
power on the Mainland.

When the Nationalist Party re-united China through military force,
the activities of other political parties were not sanctioned prior to the
Sino-Japanese hostilities. The Communist Party had to resort to arms
in order to carry out its programs. The Chinese Youth Party could
maintain its existence by seeking protection from local warlords, who
were beyond the control of the National Government. Under the
circumstances of one-party dictatorship, there was little opportunity
for people to organize political parties against the policies and
programs of the Nationalist Party.

Less antagonism after 1931

The Japanese invasion of Manchuria on September 18, 1931, was the
turning point of China's inter-party relationships. People from different quarters were dissatisfied with the government position of virtual
non-resistance against foreign aggression. Led by college students, mass
meetings and demonstrations were held everywhere.[2] Slogans against
Japan were mixed with those against the ruling party and government. Facing a formidable enemy from without, the Nationalist Party
and Government could not afford to antagonize the dissidents within
the country. Thus moderate activities by political parties and groups

[1] See Ch. II, Sec. 7, "Political Alignments in Parliament."
[2] On the morning of September 19, 1931, the day after the Mukden Incident, a mass
meeting presided over by the author was held on the open ground in front of the former
Imperial Palace in Peiping. It was attended by more than one hundred thousand people,
including students, workers, peasants, merchants, party members, and government employees. After its adjournment, about three thousand, largely students, marched to the
Peiping Headquarters of the National Military Council. Chang Hsueh-liang, Commander of
the Manchurian forces, was then stationed in Peiping as Chiang's deputy in charge of the
Military Headquarters. The demonstrators demanded arms because they wanted to fight
against the Japanese invaders. In order to avoid a bloody incident, an understanding was
reached with Chang that he would receive ten representatives from the marchers at his official
residence. After learning the difficulties of the government position as explained by Chang,
the representatives promised to explain the facts to their compatriots. When the demonstrators finally dispersed, it was already six o'clock in the afternoon. This unique mass
meeting, still so vivid in the memory of the author, was an evidence of the patriotic sentiment
of the general public and of their anxiety over government reluctance to fight against the
foreign invaders. Throughout the winter and the following year, there were mass meetings
and demonstrations all over the country. Although some of these resulted in mob violence
and caused personal injuries and property damages, the Nationalist Party and Government
maintained a tolerant attitude toward the patriotic extremes.

other than the Communist Party were tolerated to a certain extent.

Inter-party relationship during the war

When the Sino-Japanese war broke out in July 1937, China was still technically under the political tutelage of the Nationalist Party. The Extraordinary Congress in 1938 adopted the Program of Armed Resistance and National Reconstruction, under which the nation's power was concentrated in the Nationalist Party and its leader. Yet the country was in imminent danger and the war of resistance could not be carried out efficiently without the united efforts of all segments in China. The formation of the second united front between the Nationalist and the Communist parties was already described. In order to solicit the support of all political parties and groups, the Nationalist Party created the National Defence Advisory Council immediately after the war started. According to the organic law enacted by the Supreme National Defense Council on August 10, 1937,[1] the Advisory Council was an important organ for defense purposes. The leaders of different parties and groups were invited to join the Council. Even though it was only advisory in capacity, the Council helped exchange ideas and promote understanding among the leaders of different political beliefs.

The useful purpose served by the National Defense Advisory Council was further advanced in July 1938, when the People's Political Council came into being with representatives from various parties and groups in the country. Despite their constant criticism of the ruling party's unwillingness to practice democracy, the minor political parties and groups stood behind the government in the prosecution of war. At the same time, the Nationalist leaders had shown their sincere intention to make concessions to the opposition parties with a view to achieving national unity. At the time of the San Francisco Conference for the establishment of the United Nations in 1945, the Chinese Delegation appointed by the government included Tung Pi-wu of the Communist Party, Li Huang of the Chinese Youth Party, and Carsun Chang of the China Democratic Socialist Party.

The Chinese Youth Party

The Chinese Youth Party (Chung-kuo Ch'ing-nien Tang) was first founded in Paris on December 23, 1923, by a group of Chinese students

[1] The Supreme National Defense Council was established as a result of the reorganization of the Central Political Council, to be fully discussed in the following section.

in France.[1] Some traced its origin dating to 1918, when the Young China Study Association was organized by students in China and Japan. The party stood for nationalism and democracy and was anti-Communistic in nature. Among its leaders were Tseng Chi and Li Huang. When the Nationalist Party came into power, the Chinese Youth Party was outlawed. The party leaders sought the protection of the local leaders in Szechwan and the Northeastern Provinces, which were then not entirely subservient to the National Government. Thus its party congresses were all held in Mukden, political center of the Northeastern Provinces, during the period of 1928–1931.

The organization of the Chinese Youth Party was similar to that of the Nationalist Party. The party was made up largely of landlords, school teachers, and businessmen. After the outbreak of the Sino-Japanese war, it supported the Nationalist Party. Their cooperation was formally cemented by an exchange of letters between the leaders of the two parties in April 1938.

The China Democratic Socialist Party

The China Democratic Socialist Party (Chung-kuo Min-chu She-hui Tang) had its origin in 1931, when a periodical, *National Renaissance (Tsai-sheng)*, was published by a group of university professors and students. In 1934, they formed the Nationalist Socialist Party under the leadership of Carsun Chang (Chang Chun-mai). The present name was adopted as a result of its later amalgamation with the Chinese Democratic Constitutionalist Party, which was organized by overseas Chinese in North America.[2] The programs of the party were not much different from those of the socialist democratic parties in other countries. Due to internal dissensions, the party was not well organized and had a limited membership. Like the Chinese Youth Party, it decided to cooperate with the Nationalist Party in April 1938 by an exchange of letters between the party leaders.

The National Salvation Association of the Chinese People

There were other groups and associations which were of a political nature but did not call themselves parties. The National Salvation Association of the Chinese People (Chung-kuo Jen-min Chiu-kuo Hui)

---

[1] Under the name of China Nationalist Youth Corps at its initial stage, the party adopted the present title at its fourth national congress in September 1929. It is also known in English as the Young China Party. See *China Handbook, 1960–61**, p. 100.

[2] The origin of this party could be traced way back to the Emperor-Preservation Association of K'ang Yu-wei and Liang Ch'i-ch'ao at the end of the Ch'ing dynasty.

was one of them. Organized in 1936 by a group of professors, newspaper editors, and former politicians, it was anti-government and extremely effective in agitating student demonstrations. Because of this, seven of its leaders were arrested. After the Sian Incident, the Government released them upon the demand of the Communists and as a move toward national unity against Japanese aggression.

The Liberation Action Committee of the Chinese People

The Liberation Action Committee of the Chinese People (Chung-hua Min-tsu Chieh-fang Hsing-tung Wei-yuan Hui) was formed under the leadership of Chang Pai-chun. It originated from the so-called "Third Party," which was organized by Teng Yen-ta in 1927 at Wuhan. Adhering to the principles and policies of the Nationalist Party before its split with the Communists, Teng set up the Provisional Action Committee of the Kuomintang in 1929. He was later arrested by the National Government and died in prison at Nanking in 1931. After its reorganization and renaming, the Committee gradually lost the reason for its original existence. After the outbreak of the war, Chang Pai-chun, as leader of the Committee, was invited to join the National Defense Advisory Council.

The Chinese Rural Reconstruction Group

The leader of the Chinese Rural Reconstruction Group (Chung-kuo Hsiang-ts'un Chien-she Hsien-hui) was Liang Shu-min, who had long advocated rural reconstruction as the foundation of national progress. He put his belief into practice in 1930 by establishing the Shantung Research Institute of Rural Reconstruction, which subsequently merged with other organizations of similar nature to form the Rural Reconstruction Group. During the war, he actually worked in the war area and had a keen interest in promoting political and social reforms.

The Chinese Vocational Education Association

Founded in 1917, the Chinese Vocational Education Association (Chung-hua Chih-yeh Chiao-yu She) was chiefly interested in the promotion of educational services. Huang Yen-p'ei, leader of the Education Association of Kiangsu Province, was the dominant figure of this semi-political group. Because of its previous connections with local warlords, the National Government did not tolerate its activities until the outbreak of the Sino-Japanese war. When all political groups expressed their willingness to support the National Government for the prosecution of the war, this Association was invited to be represented at the National Defense Advisory Council. Nevertheless, its leaders, mostly educators and professional people, remained very critical of national affairs.

The Chinese Democratic League

The name of the Chinese Democratic League (Chung-kuo Min-chu T'ung-meng) was formally adopted in October 1944; but it was actually organized in 1939 and called the Association of Comrades for Unification and Reconstruction (T'ung-i Chien-kuo T'ung-chih Hui). It was composed of all the small political parties and groups with the hope of exercising as much influence upon national affairs as the two major parties in China.[1] It was reorganized in 1941 for further consolidation and its name was changed to the League of Chinese Democratic Political Groups (Chung-kuo Min-chu Cheng-t'uan T'ung-meng). Tso Shun-sheng of the Chinese Youth Party was elected as Secretary-general of the League. Individual members were also admitted.

After its reorganization in 1944 under the present name, the League elected Chang Lan as Chairman. Its political program was built upon the practice of democracy and the abolition of one-party rule. With participating members of diversified political convictions, the League was a very loose organization. Under these circumstances, it could not be expected to become a strong and united party. The final break occurred in 1945, when the Chinese Youth Party and the China Democratic Socialist Party left the League.[2] Then a new political alignment emerged in China: the two small parties allied with the Nationalist Party and the other associations and groups took sides with the Communist Party.[3]

4. THE SUPREME NATIONAL DEFENSE COUNCIL — THE HIGHEST ORGAN OF WARTIME CHINA

The forerunner of the Supreme National Defense Council

The importance of the Central Political Council as the highest policy-making body was described above.[4] When war broke out in July 1937,

[1] Among the leading figures of the Association at that time were Carsun Chang, Tso Shun-sheng, Chang Pai-chun, Lo Lung-chi, Shen Chun-ju, and Tsou T'ao-fen.

[2] Due to the pressure of the Nationalist Party, the League declared its dissolution in 1947 officially, but continued to carry out its activities as the Communist ally.

[3] For further details of Chinese political parties, see Ch'ien Tuan-sheng, *The Government and politics of China**, Chs. XIII, XXIV; for other political groups emerging ɜa a later date and working together with the Communist Government in the Mainland, see Ch. X.

[4] Ch. V, Sec. 4, "The Central Political Council as a link between the Party and Government."

the Party leaders deemed it imperative to set up a smaller organ than the Central Political Council in charge of national defense. In August, the Standing Committee of the Central Executive Committee of the Nationalist Party decided to convene the Supreme National Defense Conference. According to article 7 of its organic law, the Chairman of the Supreme National Defense Conference could dispose of all party, political, and military affairs during the period of war by decrees, in accordance with expediency and regardless of normal procedures. The Chairman of the National Military Council was designated concurrently as Chairman of this newly created Conference, which was, in principle, still responsible to the Central Political Council. When the Central Political Council suspended its functions after its sixty-fourth meeting, the decisions of the Conference were submitted directly to the Standing Committee of the Central Executive Committee for approval.

The organization of the Supreme National Defense Council

On January 29, 1939, the Supreme National Defense Conference was reorganized into the Supreme National Defense Council, which was directly responsible to the Central Executive Committee of the Party. The *Tsungtsai* of the Party was designated concurrently as the Chairman of the Council. This change was more technical than real, because Chiang Kai-shek would remain Chairman of this supreme organ either in his capacity as *Tsungtsai* of the Party or as Chairman of the National Military Council.

The Supreme National Defense Council was a large organization, including members of the Standing Committees of the Central Executive and Supervisory Committees of the Party, the Presidents and Vice-Presidents of the five *Yuan*, members of the National Military Council, and others recommended by its Chairman and approved by the Standing Committee of the Central Executive Committee. As the organization of the Supreme National Defense Council was too bulky, a Standing Committee was created to facilitate the transaction of the Council's manifold duties.[1] There were eleven members of the Standing Committee, appointed by the Chairman of the Council according to the following proportions: Party, three; Government, six; and military, two. The Standing Committee of the Council met once every two weeks

[1] In practice, the Supreme National Defense Council was empowered to do whatever work its Chairman might deem necessary. For example, as a counsellor of the Council, the author was once on a committee of three to codify all the administrative laws of the country in 1942.

and could be attended by all the members of the Central Executive and Supervisory Committees as well as the Secretary-General of the Nationalist Party. The members of the Central Executive Committee in charge of important party, political, and military affairs might be designated by the Council's Chairman to attend its meetings. The administrative office of the Council was the Secretariat, which was composed of a Secretary-General, counsellors, technical experts, and a number of sections.

The functions of the Supreme National Defense Council

The Supreme National Defense Council had not only the powers and functions of the Supreme National Defense Conference but also those of the Central Political Council. All the Party, political, and military organs were under the direction of the Supreme National Defense Council, the Chairman of which could dispose of all matters by decrees without the limitation of regular procedures during the period of war. Through its regular meetings, the Council gradually became a liason center of the Party, political, and military organs. As Chiang headed many important organs at the same time, he usually exercised his multiple powers through different offices. In fact, matters of national defense were not necessarily concentrated in the Supreme National Defense Council.[1]

5. THE TRIPLE-LINKED ADMINISTRATIVE SYSTEM

Essential features of the system

The Nationalist Party and Government instituted in wartime China the so-called Triple-linked Administrative System, which included three stages of planning, execution, and evaluation. The idea was originated by Chiang Kai-shek and adopted by the Seventh Plenary Session of the Fifth Central Executive Committee of the Party in January 1940. In pursuance of the party resolution, two new agencies were to be established, under the direction of the Supreme National Defense Council. They were the Central Planning Board responsible for planning and the Party and Government Work Evaluation Commission in charge of evaluating. As to execution, it was the function of all the Party and government departments.

---

[1] After the war, the Central Political Council was ordered to resume its activities and the Supreme National Defense Council was abolished.

The Central Planning Board

The Central Planning Board was created in October 1940. At its head was a Director-General, a position concurrently held by the Chairman of the Supreme National Defense Council. Under the Director-General, there were a Secretary-General and other staff members. As a planning agency, the Board created a Planning Council with a large number of planners. These planners were chosen from various party, government, educational, and professional fields. The Board also had an Investigation and Research Department and a number of committees in charge of political planning, economic affairs planning, as well as Taiwan (Formosa) and Northeastern Provinces investigation.

The chief function of the Central Planning Board was to study and formulate plans concerning political and economic reconstruction. From 1940 to 1948, the Board worked on various projects among which were: a Three-Year Wartime Reconstruction Plan, a Government Administrative Program for 1942-45, a Postwar Five-Year National Defense and Economic Reconstruction Plan, an Outline of the Demobilization Plan, and a Ten-Year Plan for the Development of the Northwest. Although the contents of the plans were not all practical, they represented the serious preparations of the Nationalist Party and Government in the prosecution of the war and reconstruction of postwar China.

The Party and Government Work Evaluation Commission

In September 1940, the Standing Committee of the Central Executive Committee of the Nationalist Party decided to institute the Party and Government Work Evaluation Commission. As one part of the Triple-linked Administrative System, the Commission came into being in January 1941. It had a Chairman, two Deputy Chairmen, and eleven members. The Presidents of the five *Yuan* and the Secretaries-General of the Central Executive Committee, Central Supervisory Committee, and Supreme National Defense Council were *ex-officio* members. All the members were appointed by the Supreme National Defense Council. Chiang was concurrently Chairman of the Commission. Therefore, the work of planning, execution, and evaluation was actually under one leader. The Commission had a Secretary-General in charge of its administrative matters.

The chief function of the Commission was to check on the party and government work of all levels, their financial and personnel administration, progress of economic reconstruction, as well as the enforcement of laws, orders, and approved plans. The Commission had two sections, one in charge of the evaluation of the Party and the other of the Government. Each section was headed by a Deputy Chairman of the Commission. Investigation parties were sent out by the Commission to inspect various party and government agencies, which were required to make all files available for their examination and evaluation. From 1941 to 1948, the Commission had prepared voluminous evaluation reports.

Evaluation of the system

Many critics questioned the value of the system. According to their observation, little had been done in planning and executing and hence there was no need of evaluation. This generalization was not quite true. This Triple-linked Administration System served substantially to remedy previous lack of coordination and cooperation of the party and government agencies. Chiang's leadership in all the three phases of the system had both advantages and disadvantages. Through him, the work of planning, execution, and evaluation could be linked together. On the other hand, the merits of checks and balances could not be expected from a system with the three branches all headed by one person. There was nothing wrong in the system itself, but its actual operation was too superficial in many respects. Worst of all, both the Nationalist Party and Government were not resolute enough in correcting mistakes pointed out by the evaluation reports.

6. THE WARTIME NATIONAL GOVERNMENT

The President and the State Council

After the outbreak of the Sino-Japanese war in July 1937, the national power was concentrated in Chiang Kai-shek in his capacity as Commander-in-Chief of the armed forces and *Tsungtsai* or leader of the Nationalist Party. The President of the National Government was nominally head of the state, but had no actual power. It was not until 1943 when Chiang succeeded Lin Sen as President that the power and prestige of the Presidency was considerably enhanced.[1]

The State Councillors were nominated by the Central Executive Committee of the Nationalist Party or its Standing Committee and appointed by the President of the National Government. Generally, they were important members of the Nationalist Party. The State Council was supposed to be the most powerful organ in the National

[1] For details, see the Organic Law of the National Government of September 15, 1943.

Government; but, in fact, it had little voice in decisions on state affairs. As the majority of State Councillors were party members and bound to obey the leader by party discipline, no resolutions against Chiang's wishes could be adopted.

The National Military Council

To concentrate national strength against the Japanese invasion, the National Government decided at the beginning of the war to expand the power of the National Military Council. As General Headquarters of the Commander-in-Chief of China's armed forces, the Council was in charge not only of military affairs, but also of party, political, economic, and propaganda matters. This unique status lasted from August 1937 to January 1938, when the non-military matters were gradually transferred to other appropriate government agencies. However, the transfer was limited only to insignificant functions.

Because of the extraordinary situation caused by the war, the National Military Council exercised powers far beyond the military field. This was especially true in the war areas. Its Political Department not only took charge of the indoctrination of the armed forces but also extended its activities to cultural, educational, and other spheres. The Office of Counsellors of the National Military Council dealt with all problems of foreign affairs. Their opinions were bound to influence the decisions of the Ministry of Foreign Affairs. The most unique feature of the Council was its Office of Aides, which had three important sections. Only the First Section administered military matters. The Second Section was in charge of all confidential matters for Chiang and soon became the all-powerful channel of communications between Chiang and other organs and individuals. The Third Section was empowered to investigate and recommend candidates for public office for Chiang's appointment in various party, government, and military agencies. Thus the actual powers of the Second and Third Sections of the Office of Aides far exceeded their nominal positions.

Above all, the position of the Chairman of the National Military Council was predominant throughout the war. According to the Organic Law of the National Military Council of January 17, 1938, its Chairman was the Commander-in-chief of the armed forces of the nation and had the power to direct the people throughout the country to do whatever necessary for national defense. Even though the Council was composed of seven to eleven members, they were only in a subordinate position to the Chairman.

The Executive Yuan

As mentioned before, the National Government adopted the Five *Yuan* system: the Executive, the Legislative, the Judiciary, the Examining, and the Supervisory.[1] To meet the demands of the war and to increase the efficiency of the administration, the Executive *Yuan* underwent many changes during the period of the Sino-Japanese hostilities. Among these changes the following were more important:

(1) the abolition of the Ministry of Navy in January 1938 and the transfer of naval affairs to the Naval Headquarters of the National Military Council;

(2) the expansion of the Ministry of Industry to include various economic and other matters and the change of its name to the Ministry of Economic Affairs in January 1938;

(3) the transfer of the National Health Administration from the Ministry of Interior to the Executive *Yuan* in January 1938;

(4) the creation of the National Relief Commission in February 1938, in charge of national relief affairs until its abolition in July 1945;

(5) the transfer of the Ministry of Social Affairs from the Nationalist Party Headquarters to the Executive *Yuan* in 1939;

(6) the establishment of the Ministry of Agriculture and Forestry in July 1940;

(7) the creation of the Economic Council in January 1941 to coordinate economic activities of the different government agencies;

(8) the institution of the Land Administration in June 1941;

(9) the establishment of the Ministry of Food in July 1941;

(10) the creation of the National General Mobilization Council to take the place of the Economic Council and carry out the functions as prescribed in the *National General Mobilization Act* of March 29, 1942 until its abolition in March 1945;[2]

(11) the transfer of the Ministry of Justice from the Judicial *Yuan* to the Executive *Yuan* in November 1942;

(12) the establishment of the Ministry of Conscription in September 1944;

(13) the institution of the War Production Board in November 1944;

(14) the creation of the National Relief and Rehabilitation Administration in January 1945; and

(15) the transfer of the Ministry of Information from the Nationalist Party Headquarters to the Executive *Yuan* in accordance with the

[1] Ch. VI, Sec. 2.
[2] *The National General Mobilization Act* was enforced in May 1942.

resolution adopted by the Sixth National Congress of the Party in May 1945.

The Executive *Yuan* took various steps to reduce the non-essential government offices and staff. On March 9, 1945, it ordered the abolition of 120 administrative units and their branch offices, involving 21,927 public functionaries. This was definitely a drastic measure toward economy and efficiency at a time when the war was near its end.[1]

The Legislative Yuan

The proper exercise of the functions of the Legislative *Yuan* was considerably restricted during the war, because a large part of its legislative power was taken over by the Supreme National Defense Council. In 1942, a readjustment of the organization and functions of the Central Government was made. Henceforth all bills not urgent in nature were to be deliberated at the Legislative *Yuan*, which was also to be notified by the Supreme National Defense Council of those urgent bills promulgated by it directly. The Legislative *Yuan* met once every week. After April 1938, its meeting was held once every two weeks. In spite of all the limitations, the Legislative *Yuan* during the period of war enacted 463 laws and regulations, 297 budgetary bills, and 328 other kinds of bills. It approved 30 treaties and made one declaration of war.[2]

The Judicial Yuan

Notwithstanding all the difficulties during the war, the Judicial *Yuan* and the courts continued to carry out their functions in the free area of China. In November 1942, the Ministry of Justice was transferred from the Judicial *Yuan* to the Executive *Yuan*, which contended that judicial administration should be integrated with the Executive. With this change, there was not much left to be performed by the Judicial *Yuan*. The power of interpreting the Constitution and laws by the Grand Justices was not given to the Judicial *Yuan* until the 1946 Constitution came into force.

However, in the field of the training of judicial officials and the promotion of legal knowledge, the Judicial *Yuan* made no small contribution during the war. At the time of its closing in June 1943, the

---

[1] See *China Handbook, 1937–1945**, p. 101.

[2] All these were enacted during the period from November 18, 1937 to March 15, 1945. The members and staff were quite serious in their work. Even though only one-third of the members were required to constitute a quorum, usually the attendance came to two-thirds according to the author's recollection as a member of the Legislative *Yuan* at that time.

Judicial Officials' Training School of the Judicial *Yuan* had trained 1,795 judicial officials.[1] Beginning in 1942, the training program had been carried out in various universities and colleges with the assistance of the Ministry of Justice. The President of the Judicial *Yuan* and a number of judges in Chungking had also led the movement promoting legal studies in wartime China through the activities of the China Law Society.[2]

The wartime court system in China remained the same, three grades of courts and three trials. While the courts in enemy areas were compelled to evacuate, new ones were established in the interior provinces. In July 1945, the courts actually functioning were the following: the Supreme Court in Chungking, 24 high courts, 81 branch high courts, and 328 district courts. For the convenience of litigants, the circuit court system was instituted in nine war-stricken provinces.[3]

With the abolition of extraterritorial jurisdiction in 1942, a set of regulations was promulgated by the National Government to provide for proper court jurisdiction for foreigners in China. On April 5, 1945, the *Advocates Act* was revised to permit foreign nationals to practice law in China. To represent poor defendants involving criminal charges, a system of court-assigned attorneys was instituted in July 1940. A set of regulations for safeguarding personal freedom was promulgated in 1944.[4] It was most encouraging that a government at the time of national emergency should begin to take measures for the protection of individual freedom. Unfortunately, the political and military authorities did not always observe the provisions of these regulations.

The Examining Yuan

The work of the Examining *Yuan* was not greatly interrupted by the war. On September 24, 1942, the *Examination Law for Technical Personnel* was promulgated. The professional and technical personnel were required to pass the special examinations in order to receive certificates. With a view to convoking the second National Examination

[1] See also Ch. VI, Sec. 4, " Judicial Reforms."

[2] It was a scholastic society of a private nature. While the judicial officials showed a keen interest in its work, they had no intention to control it. The author was then elected as Secretary-General of the Society, when he held the same position at the Ministry of Information without any affiliation with the Judicial *Yuan*

[3] They were Hopei, Honan, Chekiang, Kiangsi, Anhwei, Kiangsu, Shantung, Shansi, and Kwangtung.

[4] For the English text of *Regulations for Safeguarding the Freedom of the Human Person* of July 15, 1944, see *China Handbook, 1937–1945**, pp. 265–266. These regulations became effective as of August 1, 1944.

and Personnel Registration Conference,[1] the Examining *Yuan* held in Chungking in March 1940, the National Personnel Administration Conference for making necessary preparations. Throughout the war period, it paid constant attention to the strengthening of the examination system. The number of people passing public examinations in wartime China was quite impressive.[2]

The Supervisory Yuan

The power of the Supervisory *Yuan* was enhanced to a certain extent at the time of war, because it was entrusted with some other functions in addition to its main responsibility of impeachment. The supervisory members and commissioners could, through appropriate channels, report a delinquent official to his superior, who had, however, the discretionary power as to what to do with the case. They could inspect government offices and propose necessary changes in the conduct of certain officials. Unlike impeachment, the other functions were only persuasive in nature. Thus their accusations, proposals, and inspection reports were not legally binding upon the government officials or agencies concerned.

In order to facilitate its supervisory work, the Supervisory *Yuan* made plans to divide the country into sixteen supervisory districts. Each district was to be headed by a Supervisory Commissioner. Despite the enormous difficulties during the war, it had, by March 1945, established ten districts.[3] In addition, two war area circuit supervisory parties were organized to supervise the activities of public functionaries and government agencies located therein.

7. THE PEOPLE'S POLITICAL COUNCIL

The origin of the Council

The National Emergency Conference called in April 1932 was the forerunner of a national representative body in Nationalist China. In December, the Central Executive Committee of the Nationalist Party

---

[1] The first conference was held in 1934.

[2] The following were some of the available figures: 657,475 successful candidates for public elective posts from June 1941 to March 1945; 42,418 successful candidates for government appointing posts from 1931 to March 1945; and 5,010 professional and technical personnel who had successfully passed the examinations from February 1942 to March 1945. For details, see *China Handbook, 1937–1945**, p. 104.

[3] They were Kiangsu; Anhwei and Kiangsi; Fukien and Chekiang; Hunan and Hupei; Honan and Shantung; Yunnan and Kweichow; Kansu, Ningsia and Chinghai; Kwantung and Kwangsi; Shansi and Shensi; and Sinkiang. The Hopei supervisory district was abolished after its occupation by the Japanese army at the beginning of the war.

adopted a resolution to establish a People's Political Council in the following year.[1] Four months later, the Party decided to call an Extraordinary Congress in July 1933, which would reconsider the problems of setting up the National Assembly and the People's Political Council. There was no Extraordinary Congress in 1933. At the Fifth National Congress in November 1935, it was decided to inaugurate the long-expected National Assembly in 1936. No mention was made of the People's Political Council at the Congress. The National Assembly was not convened at the appointed time. After the outbreak of the Sino-Japanese War, circumstances did not permit nation-wide elections. A National Defense Advisory Council was created instead to serve as a liaison between the Government and the leaders outside the National-ist Party. Yet that body was strictly advisory in nature and could not be considered as a representative organ.

It was not until the convocation of the Extraordinary National Congress of the Nationalist Party in March–April 1938 that a final decision was reached to establish the People's Political Council. During the period of its existence from July 1938 to March 1948, the Council served a useful purpose for national consolidation at the time of war and up to the eve of the inauguration of the National Assembly in accordance with the provisions of the 1946 Constitution. *The Organic Law of the People's Political Council* was revised many times.[2] Changes were made in the total number of membership, the selection of councillors, and its organization; but its functions underwent no major modifications.

The membership of the Council

The number of Council members or councillors was increased from 200 in 1938 to 362 in 1947, in order to include leaders from different groups and to give adequate representation to Taiwan and the North-eastern provinces. The councillors were divided into four categories: (1) the provinces and special municipalities, from 88 at the beginning and finally increased to 229; (2) Mongolia and Tibet, from 6 at the first two Councils and increased to 8 at the later two; (3) overseas Chinese, same as the second category; and (4) leading individuals in different

---

[1] See Ch. VI, Sec. 5, "the question of the early termination of political tutelage."
[2] The first one was promulgated on April 12, 1936, and the last amendment was made on March 1, 1947. For its English text, see *China Handbook, 1937-1943**, pp. 110-112.

professions, 100 in the first Council, 138 in the second, 60 in the third, 75–119 in the fourth.[1]

The term of office of the councillors was one year, but it was often extended. Most of them were either affiliated with the Nationalist Party or had indirect connections with it. Minor parties and other political groups were also represented even though their influence at the Council was comparatively insignificant. When the Nationalist relationship with the Communists turned from bad to worse, the latter gradually abstained from the Council meetings. In March 1941, the Communist attendance was only one or two at a time; and after 1945, none whatsoever. The councillors enjoyed freedom of speech and could make proposals if they were not in conflict with the efforts of the war and "The Three People's Principles." This stipulation automatically precluded the free action of other political parties and groups.

The organization of the Council

The People's Political Council had, at the beginning, a Speaker and a Deputy Speaker, whose function was to preside over the meetings.[2] Later the Speakership was replaced by a Presidium composed of at first five and then of seven members, who took turns in presiding over the Council meetings. The Council first had quarterly sessions; after April 1939, plenary sessions were held every six months. A majority of the councillors constituted a quorum and resolutions could be adopted by a majority vote of those present at the meetings according to the Council's organic law and rules of procedure. The routine administration was conducted by the Secretary-General and his staff of the Council's Secretariat.

The Council had five standing committees and also some special committees to deal with various matters. During the period of the recess of the Council, a Resident Committee was to exercise the power

[1] The councillors of the first category were elected by the provincial and municipal councils; but, at the first Council, they were selected by the Central Executive Committee of the Nationalist Party from the following: (1) twice the number of candidates nominated by the local party and government; and (2) twice the number of candidates nominated by the Supreme National Defense Council. Those of the second and third categories were selected by the Central Executive Committee of the Nationalist Party from twice the number of candidates nominated by the Mongolian and Tibetan Affairs Commission and the Overseas Chinese Affairs Commission respectively. Councillors under the fourth category were appointed by the Central Executive Committee from twice the number of candidates nominated by the Supreme National Defense Council. The gradual reduction of the councillors under the fourth category was in proportion to the increase of elective members of the first category.

[2] Wang Ching-wei was the first Speaker. When Wang left Chungking for Nanking to head the Japanese puppet regime, Chiang Kai-shek was elected to succeed him.

of the Council with the exception of the function of examining government policies and programs which had to be directly performed by the Council itself. The Resident Committee was composed of 25 at first and later 31 members, selected among the councillors at the last meeting of each session. It met once every two weeks and gradually gained respect from the government agencies through diligent performance of its duties.

The functions of the Council

In every respect, the People's Political Council was not of the same nature as a Parliament or Congress of the Western democracies. Throughout its decade of existence, it was more or less dominated by the Nationalist Party and Government. Nevertheless, it did have certain functions or powers generally exercised by a national representative body. Among these the following were most important.

(1) To deliberate on and decide the important national policies and programs before their execution by the National Government. However, the Council's resolutions could not become effective without the approval of the Supreme National Defense Council. Furthermore, the Chairman of this highest wartime organ could, when necessary, dispose of national affairs by decrees. Thus the People's Political Council in exercising this function was at most advisory in nature.

(2) To receive government reports and to put interpellations to the government. While the Council's comments and interpellations could not control the actions of the government, the public functionaries were bound to take these into serious consideration in the exercise of their duties.

(3) To make proposals to the government. The proposals made by the Council were not binding upon the government, which, in practice, took them seriously for fear of adverse public opinion.

(4) To establish committees of inquiry to investigate matters requested by the government. In this case, the government reserved the discretionary power as to how to act on the results of the Council's investigations.

(5) To examine the budget prepared by the government before it became final. Again, the government was not bound by the decisions of the Council on budgetary matters.[1]

The functions mentioned above under (4) and (5) were entrusted to the Council only later in the war. Independent observers doubted whether the Nationalist Party and Government ever expected the

[1] Arts. 6–10 of the *Organic Law of the People's Political Council*, September 16, 1944.

Council to be a responsible and representative organ of the nation. Admittedly, they did endeavor to use it as a convenient instrument for wartime purposes. It was, however, the sincere intention of the ruling party and government to maintain the Council as a respectable body and a symbol of national unity. As a matter of fact, the Supreme National Defense Council very seldom expressed flat disapproval of the Council's proposals or resolutions even though evasive and vague responses were not uncommon. Unfortunately, the Council became impotent when the Communist members started to abstain from its meetings after 1941; but, on the whole, it had fulfilled its mission under the existing circumstances.[1]

8. THE WARTIME LOCAL GOVERNMENT

The provincial and municipal government

During the period of the Sino-Japanese war, the Chinese local government system did not undergo major changes. As a large part of territory was under Japanese and Communist control, it would be impracticable to devise a completely new system with no possibility of universal enforcement. The wartime provincial government was based on its revised organic law of March 23, 1931; and the municipal government, on the organic law of May 20, 1930. However, minor modifications of their organizations and functions were made in different cases in order to be adaptable to the changing circumstances in a time of war.[2]

The office of administrative inspector

The Temporary Regulations governing the Office of Administrative Inspectors of 1936 were still in force during the war. In order to carry out administrative functions in areas occupied by the enemy, the National Government promulgated the Regulations to Unify Administration in the War Areas on May 31, 1938. According to these regulations, all party and political workers, local militia, and regular troops were all placed at the disposal of the administrative inspector in the area under his jurisdiction. In case his administrative area was occupied by the enemy, he was required to set up a provisional office at a suitable place and to carry on his entrusted duties.

[1] See Ch'ien Tuan-sheng, op. cit., pp. 280–295; also Chen Chih-mai, The Government of China, Vol. II, pp. 259–266; Pan Wei-Tung, The Chinese Constitution*, Ch. V.

[2] For a full description of the pre-war system of provincial and municipal governments see Ch. VI, Sec. 6.

The district government

Upon Chiang's recommendation in 1939, the National Government adopted the so-called "new district system" as provided for in the *Outline of the Organization of the Several Levels of the District (Hsien) Government* of September 19, 1939.[1] This *Outline* was to supersede the *Organic Law of Districts* of June 5, 1929. Chiefly as a wartime measure, the *Outline* placed more emphasis on economic development and local security than did the 1929 law which paid more attention to people's political training for their participation in government offices. Otherwise, there was no fundamental differences.

According to the new district system, the smallest unit of a district *(hsien)* was a *chia* which was composed of six to fifteen families. The chief of a *chia* was elected by the heads of its component families. *Pao* was the next higher unit, constituted by six to fifteen *chia*. The chief of *pao* was elected by its component *chia*. This *pao-chia* system, practiced in China during various periods, was purported to enforce mutual guarantee of good conduct of the family members residing therein. Chiang used the *pao-chia* organization against the Communists throughout his annihilation campaigns and for the collection of revenue and enlistment of soldiers during the war period.

Above the *pao* was the village *(hsiang)* in rural areas and township *(chen)* in the cities. Standing between the village or township and the district was the sub-district *(ch'ü)*. Whether or not this intermediate level *ch'ü* should be established was entirely at the option of the district concerned. The sizes of village, township, and sub-district varied in individual cases. At each level of these local units, there was a representative body of the people. This new district system served some useful purpose during the war in militia training and many local functions including the promotion of education, construction of roads, and assistance to health, relief, and security. Strictly speaking, the districts could perform the same functions equally well under the 1929 law.[2]

In order to carry out the regular functions of district governments in the war areas, the National Government enacted a series of regulations to meet the local emergency. If a district was cut off from the provincial government, the magistrate or head of the district could take orders from the office of the administrative inspector in that area. In case the district was entirely isolated from any of its superior offices,

---

[1] For its English text, see *China Handbook, 1937–1945**, pp. 122–126.

[2] *Cf.* the district government described in Ch. VI, Sec. 6.

the magistrate could exercise discretionary powers and might move the district government to a temporary site. Under such circumstances, the magistrate might reduce the regular organization and staff of the district. In any event, he had to keep close contact with the national troops operating in that area. The civilian administration of the district had to coordinate its efforts with military movements. Since a magistrate in the war area served concurrently as commander of district militia, peace preservation corps, and other self-defence units, he was required to engage in the following activities: guerilla warfare behind the enemy lines, collection of intelligence, training of the reserves, and participation in all sorts of wartime work. With manifold duties, the office of magistrate was most important in the local government system of China either in peace or at war.

9. THE LOCAL REPRESENTATIVE BODIES

The provisional provincial council

At its inaugural session in July 1938, the People's Political Council adopted resolutions urging the government to set up local representative bodies. On September 26, 1938, the National Government promulgated organic laws governing the provisional provincial council and the provisional municipal council in the special municipalities directly under the Executive *Yuan*. Both laws came into effect on November 1, 1938 and were revised on April 14, 1941.

A provincial council was composed of members from 20 to 80 in number, depending upon the population and importance of the province.[1] All persons of Chinese nationality of the age of twenty-five or more, with high school education or its equivalent, were eligible to be provincial councillors if they had either one of the following qualifications: (1) having been born in the province and having rendered distinguished services to government or private organizations for more than two years; or (2) having served well in important economic or cultural institutions in that province for more than two years. The provincial councillors were chosen on both geographical and occupational bases at a ratio of six to four. Those on a geographical basis were submitted to the provincial government by the district governments in consultation with the local Nationalist Party and the leading civic associations. In the case of those from occupational groups, the

[1] The provisional provincial councils in Chinghai, Ningsia, and Suiyuan had only 20 members each; while the Szechwan provincial council was composed of 80 members.

provincial government selected twice the number of candidates. Then the provincial government submitted the candidates of both groups, through the Executive *Yuan*, to the Supreme National Defense Council for final approval. The Supreme National Defense Council could select persons outside of the submitted lists, but the persons so selected could not exceed twenty percent of the total number of provincial councillors.

The term of provincial councillors was one year. It could be extended by the Executive *Yuan* when necessary. The councillors received no salaries. Their travelling expenses from home to the council meetings were paid by the government. The council had a Speaker and a Deputy Speaker. The duty of the Speaker was to preside over its meetings, which were held once every six months. Each session was to last two weeks and could be prolonged when necessary. The provincial government had the power to call special sessions and to extend the duration of the regular ones. Attendance of one-half of the members was required for a quorum, and decisions were made by a majority vote of those present.

The essential functions of the provincial council were as follows: (1) to deliberate on and decide all important provincial matters before putting them into effect; (2) to make proposals to the provincial government; (3) to receive reports from the provincial governments; and (4) to interpellate the provincial government. In order to cope with an emergency, the provincial government could secure the approval of the Executive *Yuan* of any necessary action taken during the council's recess and report these matters to its next session. The provincial government could ask the council to reconsider its resolutions, but should put them into effect if two-thirds of the councillors decided to uphold their original resolutions and the Executive *Yuan* did not act otherwise. During its recess, the council had a standing committee of five to nine councillors elected from among themselves. This standing committee was to carry out the routine functions of the council, listen to the reports from the provincial government, and check on the actual enforcement of the council resolutions.[1]

The provisional municipal council

The provisional municipal councils were similar to the provisional provincial councils in the following respects: membership qualifi-

[1] In March 1945, 19 provisional provincial councils were established in the following provinces: Anhwei, Chekiang, Chinghai, Fukien, Honan, Hunan, Hupei, Kansu, Kiangsi, Kwangtung, Kwangsi, Ningsia, Shantung, Shensi, Sikang, Suiyuan, Szechwan, Kweichow, and Yunnan.

cations, classifications, methods of selection, sessions and functions. Of course, the number of councillors in a municipality was smaller and fixed at only 25. The Supreme National Defense Council could only select ten percent of the total number of municipal councillors other than those submitted by the municipal government. Another difference was that the ratio of councillors selected on a geographical basis in comparison with those from occupational groups was seven to three.[1]

The district (hsien) council.

The district council was based on the *Provisional Organic Law of the District Council*, promulgated on August 9, 1941. It did not come into effect until May 5, 1943. All citizens in the district above twenty-five years of age were eligible to be district councillors provided they had passed the examinations for candidates for district councillors or were qualified through other conditions. However, students, soldiers, policemen, and other public functionaries were ineligible to be district councillors. The term of office of district councillors was two years. They were eligible for re-election and also were subject to recall.

The district council was composed of one delegate from each village or township in that district. Professional groups in the district could also elect delegates to the district council, but they could not exceed thirty percent of the total number of district councillors. The following professional groups were recognized by the government: farmers, laborers, merchants, teachers, fishermen, and free professionals.

The powers and functions of the district council were to decide on the budget, taxes, bonds, regulations, and various matters concerning local self-government and the disposal of district property. The district council had the right to suggest new projects to and interpellate the district government, which had to send periodical reports to the council. If there was any conflict between the district council and the government, they could appeal to the provincial government for instructions. The district council was to meet once every three months for a period of three to seven days which could be extended if necessary. Under no circumstances could the district council pass any resolution contradictory to the "Three People's Principles" or national policy. If so, the provincial government could, with the approval of the Executive *Yuan*, have the council dissolved and call for the election of a new one.[2]

---

[1] Chungking, China's wartime capital, was the only municipality which established the provisional municipal council under the existing regulations.

[2] By the end of April 1944, there were 906 district councils in 17 provinces.

The village or township council

According to the *Provisional Organic Regulations of Village or Township Council* of August 9, 1941, the village or township council was composed of two delegates from each component *pao*. Their qualifications were similar to those of the district councillors. The council met once every two months, with the powers and functions corresponding to those of the district council. It was to elect and recall its delegates to the district council and the chief officer of the village or township.[1]

The pao general council

The *pao* general council was composed of one delegate each from its component households. It met once every month, with the functions corresponding to those of the village council. As a basic unit of local self-government, the *pao* general council was to decide on drafting and recruiting its residents for labor service.[2]

The chia council

The *chia* council was composed of the heads of its component households and met once every month. Its chief functions were to elect and recall the chief officer of the *chia*, to enforce laws and orders, to report the census in its area, and to decide or suggest matters concerning sanitation, health, or other reforms. Since the *chia* was the lowest and smallest unit of local self-government, its residents could be easily called to meetings to decide on important matters whenever necessary.

[1] In 1944, such village or township councils were established in 371 districts (*hsien*).
[2] In 1944, *pao* general councils were established in 975 districts (*hsien*).

FROM THE MAINLAND TO TAIWAN (FORMOSA): POLITICAL INSTITUTIONS DURING THE POSTWAR PERIOD

I. PEACE NEGOTIATIONS THROUGH THE POLITICAL CONSULTATIVE CONFERENCE

Marshall's mission of American mediation

When the Nationalist and Communist hostilities intensified in October 1945, the United States became very much concerned with the situation in China which had just emerged as one of the Great Powers. After the resignation of Ambassador Patrick Hurley on November 27, 1945, President Truman appointed General George C. Marshall as his special envoy to China with ambassadorial rank. Marshall's mission of mediation between the two hostile parties was expressed in Truman's policy statement on China on December 15. Before the end of the year, seven Communist delegates arrived in Chungking to resume negotiations with the Government.[1] Upon the proposal of the Government, the Communists agreed to accept Marshall as a mediator of their differences. Necessary arrangements were made in early January of 1946 to hold a Political Consultative Conference for the negotiation of peace.

The party alignment at the Political Consultative Conference

The Political Consultative Conference was held in Chungking from January 10 to January 31, 1946. There were 29 delegates representing different political parties and groups at the Conference: the Nationalist Party, 8; the Communist Party, 7; the China Democratic League 2; the Chinese Youth Party, 5; the China Democratic Socialist Party, 2; the National Salvation Association of the Chinese People, 2; the Chinese Vocational Education Association, 1; the Liberation Committee of the

---

[1] They were Chou En-lai, Yeh Chien-ying, Tung Pi-wu, Ch'in Pang-hsien, Wang Jo-fei, Wu Yu-chang, and Teng Ying-ch'ao (Madame Chou).

Chinese People, 1; and the Chinese Rural Reconstruction Group, 1. Some of the above political parties and groups were also components of the China Democratic League. In addition to the party delegates, 9 independent leaders were invited to attend the Conference. The Nationalist delegation was composed of Sun Fo, Wu Te-chen, Wang Shih-chieh, Ch'en Li-fu, Chang Chun, Ch'en Pu-lei, Shao Li-tze, and Chang Li-sheng. Many important figures of other political affiliations attended the Conference, including Chou En-lai, Tung Pi-wu, Tseng Chi, Chen Chi-tien, Chang Lan, Carsun Chang, Huang Yen-pei, Chang Po-chun, and Liang Shu-min. Among the independents were Mo Teh-hui and Wang Yun-wu.[1]

The above quota was certainly not apportioned according to the relative strength of the different parties but rather was a result of hard bargains and compromises. The Government relied on the friendly attitude of the minor parties and the independents. The China Democratic League was not pleased with the comparatively large quota assigned to the Chinese Youth Party, then still one of its constituent parts. As it finally developed, the Chinese Youth Party and most of the independents were friendly to the Government and the others were allied with the Communists.[2] Neither side had an overwhelming majority. This party alignment compelled the Nationalists and the Communists to be more receptive to compromise proposals.

Resolutions adopted at the Political Consultative Conference

The most imminent problem facing the Conference was how to avert the civil war. Largely through the efforts of General Marshall, both parties agreed to set up a tripartite executive headquarters at Peiping for the enforcement of the cessation of hostilities, consisting of one member from each side and one mediator. By the time of its adjournment on January 31, the Conference adopted a number of important resolutions on the reorganization of the National Government and military forces, revision of the Draft Constitution of 1936, and various problems concerning the National Assembly to be convened in the near future. The delegates also worked out the Program of Peaceful National Reconstruction for the guidance of the reorganized government.[3]

[1] For the complete list of the delegates, see *China Handbook, 1937–1945**, pp. 741–742.

[2] For further comments on the party alignment at the Political Consultative Conference, see Ch'ien Tuan-sheng, *The Government and Politics of China**, pp. 375–379.

[3] For details of the resolutions, see *China Handbook, 1937–1945**, pp. 744–751; for Chiang Kai-shek's remarks on the resolutions, see Chiang Chung-cheng, *Soviet Russia in China**, pp. 155–160.

Negotiations continued after the Conference. On February 25, 1946, the representatives of the two major parties signed an Agreement for Military Reorganization and for the Integration of the Communist Forces into the National Army.[1] Unfortunately, this agreement was never carried out.

The resumption of civil war

On March 17, 1946, the Central Executive Committee of the Nationalist Party approved the agreements for cooperation with the Communists and the reorganization of the National Government. The government forces entered Mukden in March after the withdrawal of the Soviet troops. Meantime, the Communists established administrative machinery in their occupied areas in Manchuria. With two hostile armies moving toward the same objective, serious conflicts were inevitable. On April 15, Chou En-lai declared all-out hostilities in Manchuria. Three days later, Changchun was captured by the Communists.

General Marshall left for Washington on March 12 and returned to China on April 18. Through his efforts, a new truce in Central China was proclaimed on May 10; but intensive fighting was soon resumed in other parts of the nation, including Shantung, Hopei, and Jehol. The hope of peace was rapidly vanishing in June 1946, when Mao Tse-tung openly demanded the termination of American aid to the government and the withdrawal of all American forces from China.

Following the outbreak of full-scale hostilities, the Communists declared the establishment of a government in Manchuria. However, the Nationalist forces were still strong, and they conquered Kalgan on October 11. After this decisive victory, the National Government decided to convoke the Constituent National Assembly on November 15, 1946. Political observers doubted the advisability of enforcing constitutional rule during a period of civil war; also it could be expected that the Communists and the members of the China Democratic League would abstain from the Assembly. As a result of non-cooperation, each party took unilateral action. In December 1946, the Communists launched a drastic land reform policy in their occupied areas by enforcing the *Regulations on Compulsory Purchase of Excess Land from the Landlords*. Gloom prevailed in China.

---

[1] The Agreement was signed by Chang Chih-chung on behalf of the Government, Chou En-lai of the Communists and General Marshall in the capacity as mediator. For its English text, see *China Handbook, 1937–1945**, pp. 755–758.

Because General Marshall was preoccupied with the mediation efforts, he recommended to the United States Government the appointment of Dr. J. Leighton Stuart as American Ambassador to China. A devoted educator in China, Ambassador Stuart was well respected by the different Chinese parties. Despite American efforts for the restoration of peace, nothing could be accomplished under the prevailing circumstances. Admitting the failure of his mission, General Marshall returned to the United States on January 7, 1947. Chiang Kai-shek doubted strongly the chance of success for Marshall's mission from the very beginning, but wanted Marshall to discover this for himself.[1] The prolonged period of intermittent truce and war considerably affected the morale and fighting spirit of the Nationalist forces, which might have been able to control the situation with resolute action after the victory over Japan. According to some anti-Communist critics, the fall of China's Mainland to the Communists was partly attributed to Chiang's inability to achieve peace and lack of resolution to make war. Perhaps Chiang himself was also aware of this dangerous situation, but his position was complicated by other international and domestic considerations.

2. THE CONVOCATION OF THE NATIONAL ASSEMBLY AND THE CONSTITUTION OF 1946

The Constituent National Assembly in 1946

The convocation of a National Assembly as the representative organ of the people was especially emphasized by Dr. Sun Yat-sen in his last will and had long been delayed owing to internal and external circumstances. Among the important problems discussed at the Political Consultative Conference in January 1946 were the nature and composition of the National Assembly as well as the revision of the Draft Constitution of 1936. The Communist Party and the China Democratic League emphasized the restraint on presidential powers and the increase of the voice of the minor parties in the National Assembly. Of course, the government position on these points was the direct opposite. Since the overwhelming majority of the delegates to the National Assembly elected in 1936–1937 were affiliated with the Nationalist Party, the opposition parties at the Political Consultative Conference wanted to limit this coming Assembly to a Constituent or Constitution-Making Assembly. They hoped that a new National

[1] See Chiang Chung-cheng, *Soviet Russia in China**, pp. 155–156.

Assembly to be elected in accordance with the new Constitution might consist of more of their own members. As finally agreed, the nature and the function of the coming National Assembly was limited to Constitution-making.

The military situation in the fall of 1946 favored the Nationalist forces. With the support of the Chinese Youth Party, the China Democratic Socialist Party, and the independents participating in the Political Consultative Conference, the National Government decided to hold the Constituent National Assembly in Nanking on November 15, 1946. On the ground of the Nationalist failure to make a fair apportionment of the delegates to the National Assembly and to reorganize the National Government as agreed upon at the Political Consultative Conference, the Communist Party and the China Democratic League decided that their delegates would abstain from the Assembly.

The Constituent National Assembly held its opening ceremony on November 15, 1946. Out of the total of 1,744 delegates the actual attendance at the meetings ranged from 1,300 to 1,500. Some 1,200 delegates were selected under the organic law and the electoral law of the National Assembly promulgated on May 14, 1936. There were 150 delegates newly assigned to Taiwan, the Northeastern Provinces, and other areas. The additional delegates assigned to different parties and selected from independant leaders were appointed by the National Government as agreed upon at the Political Consultative Conference. In short, expediency and compromise were the prevailing practices.

The Constituent National Assembly adopted the *Constitution of the Republic of China* on December 25, 1946, which has been and still is the fundamental law of Nationalist China.[1] The Constitution as adopted was in accordance with the understandings reached at the Political Consultative Conference with the exception of the presidential powers, which were, however, enlarged to a certain extent. On the whole, it is a carefully prepared and well considered document, arguments to the contrary notwithstanding. The Constituent National Assembly also adopted the *Preparatory Procedures for the Enforcement of the Constitution.*

The Constitution of 1946

General provisions – *The Constitution of the Republic of China*, adopted at the Constituent National Assembly on December 25, 1946, came into effect on December 25, 1947. It has 175 articles, grouped into

[1] For its English text, see Appendix G.

fourteen chapters: (1) general provisions; (2) rights and duties of the people; (3) the National Assembly; (4) the President; (5) Administration; (6) Legislation; (7) Judiciary; (8) Examination; (9) Supervision; (10) powers of Central and local governments; (11) system of local government; (12) election, recall, initiative, and referendum; (13) fundamental national policies; and (14) enforcement and amendment of the Constitution. Dr. Sun Yat-sen's political theory is the guiding principle of this Constitution, especially "The Three People's Principles" and "The Five-Power Constitution." The fundamental national policies enumerated in this Constitution include national defense, foreign affairs, national economy, social security, education and culture, and nationalities.[1] The Constitution may be amended directly by the National Assembly or upon the proposal of the Legislative *Yuan* to the National Assembly.[2]

Freedoms and rights of the people – Persons of Chinese nationality are citizens of the Republic of China.[3] All citizens have the fundamental freedoms and rights as generally provided in the bill of rights in Western democracies. Such freedoms and rights are guaranteed under the Constitution unless they are detrimental to social order, public welfare, or the freedoms of other people.[4] All citizens twenty years of age have the right to vote and those of twenty-three years of age, the right to be elected. Elected functionaries are subject to recall by their constituencies. The exercise of the rights of initiative and referendum is to be prescribed by law.[5]

Political organs – The highest representative organ of the nation is the National Assembly, which exercises political powers on behalf of the whole body of citizens.[6] At the head of the State is the President of the Republic, under whom are the five *Yuan:* the Executive, the Legislative, the Judiciary, the Examining, and the Supervisory.[7] The

[1] Arts. 137–169.
[2] Art. 174.
[3] The first Chinese nationality law was promulgated by the Imperial Government on March 28, 1909. After the establishment of the Chinese Republic, the nationality law of 1909 was re-enacted and the new law was promulgated on November 18, 1912. The law of 1912 was later replaced by that of December 30, 1914, which was superseded by that promulgated on February 5, 1929. For the English text of the provisions of the nationality law of 1929 on the acquisition of Chinese nationality by birth and naturalization, see William L. Tung, *Cases and Other Readings on International Law** (Shanghai: Evans Book Co., 1940), pp. 139, 142, 143. The Chinese texts of all the nationality laws mentioned above can be found in *The Nationality Laws of China* (Chungking: Kuomin Press, 1943), by the same author.
[4] Arts. 22–23.
[5] Arts. 130, 133, 136.
[6] Art. 25.
[7] Arts. 35, 53–106.

functions of the five *Yuan* are similar to those under the National Government during the period of political tutelage. The local government system consists of two levels: the province or special municipality under the direct jurisdiction of the Executive *Yuan;* and the district *(hsien)*, which is below the province. Each province or district has its own government in charge of administration and a council (assembly) as a legislative body, both elected by the people.[1]

Division of powers between the Central and local governments – China is a unitary state. In order to prevent over-concentration of powers in the central government, all the Chinese constitutional documents in the past carefully prescribed the demarcation of powers between the Central and local governments. The Constitution of 1946 provides that the power of legislation and administration of the following matters belongs to the Central government: (1) foreign affairs; (2) national defense; (3) nationality, criminal, civil, and commercial laws; (4) judicial system; (5) aviation, national highways, state-owned railways, navigation, postal and telegraph administration; (6) Central government finance and national revenues; (7) demarcation of national, provincial, and district revenues; (9) currency system and state banks; (10) weights and measures; (11) foreign trade policies; (12) financial and economic matters affecting foreigners or foreign countries; and (13) other matters relating to the Central government as provided in the Constitution.[2] In many other matters, the Central government has the power of legislation and administration, but it may delegate the power of administration to the local governments.[3] These are enumerated in the Constitution, which also stipulates the demarcation of powers between the province and the district to be described later.

The enforcement of the Constitution

The Preparatory Procedures for the Enforcement of the Constitution,

---

[1] Arts. 113, 121, 124. The English terms "assembly" and "council" are sometimes used interchangeably to designate the Chinese representative or legislative bodies. In the English text of the Constitution of 1946, the representative bodies convened only for the enactment of self-government regulations are called provincial and district assemblies and those in charge of regular legislative functions are called provincial and district councils (Arts. 112, 113, 122, 124 of the Constitution). However, in various levels of the Chinese government, there are councils in charge of collective deliberation on administrative matters, such as the provincial council presided over by the Chairman of he provincial government. In order to avoid any possible confusion, the term "assembly" is generally used in this work to designate the representative or legislative bodies through popular election.

[2] Art. 107.

[3] Art. 108.

adopted at the Constituent National Assembly in 1946, contained five points:

(1) Pursuant to the promulgation of the Constitution, all existing laws and ordinances in conflict with the provisions of the Constitution were to be revised or repealed prior to the convocation of the First National Assembly.

(2) After the promulgation of the Constitution, the National Government was to enact and promulgate the laws on the following matters within a period of three months: (a) the organization of the National Assembly and the election and recall of the delegates to the National Assembly, (b) the election and recall of the President and Vice President of the Republic, (c) the election and recall of the Members of the Legislative *Yuan*, (d) the election and recall of the Members of the Supervisory *Yuan*, and (e) the organization of the five *Yuan*.

(3) The delegates to the First National Assembly and Members of the Legislative and Supervisory *Yuan*, as provided in the Constitution, were to be elected within six months after the promulgation of the pertinent electoral laws.

(4) The first National Assembly was to be convened by the President of the Republic; the first Legislative *Yuan* as provided in the Constitution was to function, seven days after the adjournment of the National Assembly; and the first Supervisory *Yuan* was to be called by the President of the Republic after the adjournment of the National Assembly.

(5) When the six-month period for the election had elapsed and two-thirds of the total membership of the National Assembly and the Legislative and Supervisory *Yuan* had been duly elected, these elected bodies would be lawfully convened.

In pursuance of the above enforcement procedures, the National Government promulgated the *Constitution of the Republic* on January 1, 1947, and took effective steps to execute these measures. As a result, the First National Assembly was convened in Nanking on March 29, 1947, and the other elected bodies duly performed their functions.

3. THE CENTRAL AND LOCAL GOVERNMENTS
UNDER THE CONSTITUTION OF 1946

The National Assembly

The National assembly is the highest representative organ of the nation, exercising political powers on behalf of the people. It is composed of delegates elected on geographical and occupational bases. Each district *(hsien)*, municipality, or area of its equivalent status is entitled to one delegate, and one additional delegate for each additional 50,000 population in case the population of that district exceeds 500,000. Delegates from Mongolia, Tibet, overseas Chinese, occupational groups, and women's organizations are prescribed by special laws. No incumbent official can be elected as delegate in the electoral area where he holds office. The term of office of the delegates is six years, terminating on the day of the convocation of the next National Assembly.

The functions of the National Assembly are twofold: (1) to elect and recall the President and Vice President of the Republic; and (2) to amend the Constitution or to vote on proposed constitutional amendments submitted by the Legislative *Yuan*. The exercise of the rights of initiative and referendum is to be prescribed by special laws and regulations. The National Assembly is to be convoked by the President to meet 90 days prior to the expiration date of each presidential term. Extraordinary sessions may be held under special circumstances.[1] The National Assembly elected in 1947 held its first session in 1948, the seond in 1954, and the third in 1960, each of which will be separately described later.

The President and Vice President

The Constitution of 1946 provides the President of the Republic with extensive powers: (1) to represent the Republic in foreign relations; (2) to command the armed forces of the country; (3) to promulgate laws and issue mandates with the countersignature of the President of the Executive *Yuan* or, when required, of both the President of the *Yuan* and the Minister concerned; (4) to negotiate for peace, declare war, and conclude treaties; (5) to grant amnesties, pardons, remission of sentences, and restitution of civil rights; (6) to appoint and remove civil and military officials; (7) to confer honors and decorations; (8) to settle disputes between two or more *Yuan;* (9) to convene the sessions of the National Assembly; and (10) to declare martial law and issue emergency orders, originally subject to certain limitations but later removed by the *Temporary Provisions Effective During the Period of Communist Rebellion* adopted by the first session of the First National Assembly in 1947.[2]

---

[1] See Arts. 25–30 of the Constitution of 1946.
[2] Arts. 29, 30, 35–44 of the Constitution.

In the exercise of his power of appointment, the consent of certain *Yuan* is required in some cases. Thus the President of the Republic is to nominate and appoint, with the consent of the Legislative *Yuan*, the President of the Executive *Yuan* and the Auditor General of the Supervisory *Yuan;* and he is to nominate and appoint, with the consent of the Supervisory *Yuan*, the President and Vice President of the Judicial *Yuan*, the Grand Justices, and the President, Vice President, and Members of the Examining *Yuan*. Taking all the constitutional provisions into consideration, the President of the Chinese Republic has more powers than the President of the United States. The Vice President of the Republic wields no actual power, but he is to act for the President in case the latter cannot attend to office for any reason. If the office of the President becomes vacant, the Vice President is to succeed until the expiration of the original presidential term.[1]

Any Chinese citizen forty years of age is eligible for the office of the President or Vice President. Their term of office is six years and they may be re-elected for a second term.[2] This two-term restriction has since been removed by an amendment of the *Temporary Provisions Effective During the Period of Communist Rebellion* adopted at the third session of the National Assembly in 1960. Chiang Kai-shek is now serving his third term as President of the Republic.

Under the Office of the President, there is an Advisory Council composed of an indefinite number of Grand Councillors. These Grand Councillors are appointed by the President to serve as his advisers. Also under the President, there are a National Policy Advisory Committee and a Military Strategy Advisory Committee in charge of specific functions. The Secretary General and his staff are in charge of the general administration of the Presidential Office. The President is also assisted by a number of military aides for the execution of his functions in the military field. In November 1954, the Planning Commission for the Recovery of the Mainland was created under the Office of the President, with Vice President Chen Cheng concurrently as its Chairman. This Commission, composed of approximately 1,800 members, has been occupied with the formulation of plans for the recovery of the Mainland.

[1] Art. 49.
[2] Arts. 47.

The Executive Yuan

The Executive *Yuan*, the highest administrative organ of the state, is composed of a President, a Vice President, heads of various Ministries and Commissions, and a certain number of Ministers without portfolio. The President of the Executive *Yuan* is nominated and appointed by the President of the Republic with the consent of the Legislative *Yuan*. The Vice President, Ministers, and Chairmen of the Commissions are appointed by the President of the Republic upon the recommendation of the President of the Executive *Yuan*.

The Executive *Yuan* is required to submit periodical reports on its policies to the Legislative *Yuan*, which may interpellate, or refuse to concur, or alter by resolution any important policy. With the consent of the President of the Republic, the Executive *Yuan* may request the Legislative *Yuan* to reconsider its resolution. If, after reconsideration, two-thirds of the Members of the Legislative *Yuan* present at the meeting uphold the original resolution, the President of the Executive *Yuan* must either abide by the resolution or resign from office.[1] Theoretically under no collective responsibility, the ministers do not have to resign with the President of the Executive *Yuan;* but a new President of the Executive *Yuan* has, in practice, the freedom to choose new ministers. The Legislative *Yuan* has no power to change the President of the Executive *Yuan* through a vote of non-confidence. Nor can the President of the Executive *Yuan* dissolve the Legislative *Yuan*. Thus the President of the Republic would be the only one to break any impasse under the present Constitution.

The President of the Executive *Yuan* is not all-powerful in the national administration. Many important matters under the jurisdiction of the Executive *Yuan* are to be deliberated on by the Council of the Executive *Yuan*, which is composed of the President, Vice President, Ministers, and Chairmen of the *Yuan*. The Council meets once a week. Special meetings may be held if necessary.

The Legislative Yuan

The Legislative *Yuan*, the highest legislative organ of the state. has the power to decide by resolution upon statutory or budgetary bills or bills concerning martial law, amnesty, declaration of war, conclusion of peace or treaties, and other important matters. It is composed of a President, a Vice President, and Members of the *Yuan*. The President and Vice President are elected by and from the Members. Through a

[1] Arts. 54, 57.

complicated procedure in accordance with the provisions of the Constitution as well as the organic law and electoral law of the Legislative *Yuan* of 1947, a nation-wide election was held in 1948. The Members, 760 in all, were proportionally distributed along the same manner as the delegates to the National Assembly. Members are not permitted to hold government offices concurrently. Their term of office is three years, but they are eligible for re-election.

The Legislative *Yuan* meets twice a year, presided over by its President: the first session from February to May and the second from September to December. The duration of the meetings may be extended if necessary. Extraordinary sessions may be held under special circumstances. A quorum requires one-fifth of the members, and resolutions are adopted by a majority of the members present and voting. Members are assigned to 12 committees and 4 special committees. The regular committees are: (1) interior affairs, (2) foreign affairs, (3) national defense, (4) economic affairs, (5) finance, (6) budget, (7) education, (8) communications, (9) border affairs, (10) overseas Chinese affairs, (11) laws and regulations, and (12) judicial affairs. The special committees are: (1) credentials, (2) maintenance of order, (3) rules, and (4) accounts. Other special committees may be set up whenever necessary.[1]

The Judicial Yuan

The Judicial *Yuan*, the highest judicial organ of the state, is in charge of civil, criminal, and administrative cases, and of cases covering disciplinary measures against public functionaries. It is also empowered by the Constitution to interpret the Constitution and to standardize the interpretation of laws and ordinances. The President, Vice President, and Grand Justices of the Judicial *Yuan* are nominated and appointed by the President of the Republic with the consent of the Supervisory *Yuan*. The organization of the Judicial *Yuan* and of the courts are prescribed by separate laws. The Judicial *Yuan* is now composed of the Supreme Court, the Administrative Court, the Committee on the Discipline of Public Functionaries, and the Council of Grand Justices. The district and high courts are under the direct supervision of the Ministry of Justice, which is still a component part of the Executive *Yuan* despite the opinions advocating its transfer back to the Judicial *Yuan*.[2]

[1] Arts. 63–69, 75–76.
[2] Arts. 78–82.

The Examining Yuan

The Examining *Yuan*, the highest examination organ of the state, is in charge of matters relating to examination, employment, registration, service rating, scale of salaries, promotion and transfer, security of tenure, commendation, pecuniary aid in case of death, retirement, old age pensions, and other related matters. The President, Vice President, and Members of the Examining *Yuan* are nominated and, with the consent of the Supervisory *Yuan*, appointed by the President of the Republic for a term of six years. The President, Vice President, and 19 Members of the Examining *Yuan* constitute the Council of the Examining *Yuan*, which decides on all important matters under its jurisdiction. The Examining *Yuan* is now composed of the Ministry of Examination and the Ministry of Personnel.[1]

The Supervisory Yuan

The Supervisory *Yuan*, the highest supervisory organ of the state, exercises the powers of consent, impeachment, censure, and auditing. The President and Vice President of the Supervisory *Yuan* are elected from and by the Supervisory Members. The Members of the Supervisory *Yuan* are elected by provincial and municipal councils, local councils of Mongolia and Tibet, and overseas Chinese in accordance with law. The vocational groups are not independently represented at the Supervisory *Yuan*. Members serve a term of six years and are eligible for re-election. No member of the Supervisory *Yuan* is permitted to hold public office concurrently or engage in any profession.

Impeachment of a public functionary is to be instituted upon the proposal of one or more members of the Supervisory *Yuan*, and a decision to impeach made by nine or more members. In the case of the impeachment of the President and Vice President, the proposal must be made by no less than one-fourth of the total members and the resolution by a majority before its presentation to the National Assembly. Besides impeachment, the Supervisory *Yuan* may set up committees to investigate the activities of public functionaries and propose corrective measures to the government agencies concerned. The function of auditing is performed by the Ministry of Auditing under the Supervisory *Yuan*. At the head of this Ministry is an Auditor General, who is nominated and, with the consent of the Legislative *Yuan*, appointed by the President of the Republic.[2]

[1] Arts. 83, 84.
[2] Arts. 90–104.

From December 1947 to April 1948, a total of 180 Supervisory Members were elected. The Supervisory *Yuan* began to function on June 5, 1948. For the convenience of performing its duties, the Supervisory *Yuan* set up thirteen regional supervisory offices headed by Supervisory Commissioners. After 1949 all of them were closed, but the Fukien-Taiwan office continued to carry out its duties until January 1951.

The local government system

The local government under the Constitution of 1946 follows the existing system of two-levels, the province and the district *(hsien)*. Each province may convoke a provincial assembly for the enactment of provincial self-government regulations within the limit of the constitutional provisions. Likewise, a district may convoke a district assembly for the enactment of its self-government regulations if they are not in conflict with the provisions of the Constitution and of the provincial self-government regulations. A provincial council is to be set up as the legislative organ of the province. The provincial government is to be headed by a governor, chosen through popular election in charge of the provincial administration. In a district, there is to be a district council as the legislative organ and a magistrate in charge of the administration of the district government, all selected through popular election. The people in a district are to exercise the rights of initiative and referendum in matters within the sphere of the district self-government and also the rights of election and recall of the district magistrate and other officials of the district self-government. With regard to the self-government of municipalities, Mongolia, and Tibet, these will be prescribed by separate laws.

The Constitution stipulates, in detail, the demarcation of powers between the province and the district. The province is to have the power of legislation and administration of the following matters: (1) provincial eduaction, public health, industries, and communications; (2) management and disposal of provincial property; (3) administration of municipalities under provincial jurisdiction; (4) province-operated enterprises; (5) provincial cooperative enterprises; (6) provincial agriculture, forestry, water conservation, fisheries, animal husbandry, and public works; (7) provincial finance and revenues; (8) provincial debts; (9) provincial banks; (10) provincial police administration; (11) provincial charitable and public welfare work; and (12) other matters delegated to the provinces in accordance with national laws. All matters of the above nature but within the scope of the district are under the jurisdiction of the district for legislation and administration.[1]

4. THE FIRST SESSION OF THE FIRST NATIONAL ASSEMBLY

The fulfillment of Constitutional requirements

In accordance with the provisions of the *Preparatory Procedures for the Enforcement of the Constitution,* the National Government promulgated, on March 31, 1947, the *Organic Law of the National Assembly,* the *Law governing the Election and Recall of the Delegates to the National Assembly,* the *Law governing the Election and Recall of the President and Vice President,* the *Law governing the Election and Recall of the Members of the Legislative Yuan,* and the *Law governing the Election and Recall of the Members of the Supervisory Yuan.* Nation-wide elections were held for the election of the National Assemblymen and the Legislative and Supervisory Members. The first Session of the First National Assembly was convened in Nanking on March 29–May 1, 1948. The total number of delegates as provided by law was 3,045, but only 2,961 were elected. The National Assembly was attended by 2,841 delegates.

Presidential elections

The most important function of the First Session of the First National Assembly was to elect the President and Vice President of the Republic. At the Presidential election meeting on April 19, a total number of 2,734 votes were cast. Chiang Kai-shek received 2,420 votes. Chü Chêng, another candidate of the Nationalist Party, received 269 votes. According to the *Law governing the Election and Recall of the President and Vice President,*[2] Chiang was formally elected as the President of the Republic with an overwhelming majority of votes.

In the election of the Vice President, there was an intense competition among the candidates of the Nationalist Party itself. It is the general practice in Western democracies that the Presidential candidate chooses his own running mate. For one reason or another, Chiang did not designate a candidate for the Vice Presidency at the beginning. Instead, he allowed the Nationalist leaders to engage in free competititon for the post. Yet he showed his preference at the final stage of the cam-

---

[1] Arts. 109–110, 112–120.
[2] Art. 4.

paign. Through persuasion or pressure, a number of candidates withdrew; but Li Tsung-jen and Sun Fo remained. While most of Chiang's followers supported Sun, Li was finally elected as Vice President of the Republic on the fourth ballot.[1]

The amendment of the Constituiton

When the civil war was in full swing, the Nationalist leaders deemed that the President should have all the emergency powers without being subject to the procedural restrictions as prescribed by the Constitution of 1946.[2] Two proposals for constitutional amendment were made at the First Session of the First National Assembly, which finally adopted the *Temporary Provisions Effective During the Period of Communist Rebellion* on April 18, 1948. The Constitution of 1946 provided that, upon the proposal of one-fifth of the total number of the delegates to the National Assembly and by a resolution of three-fourths of the delegates present at a meeting having a quorum of two-thirds of the entire Assembly, the Constitution could be amended.[3] As these Temporary Provisions were decided by a vote of 1,624 out of 2,045 cast, this amendment was technically in accordance with the prescribed procedures of the Constitution.

As a result of the amendment, the President may, during the period of "Communist Rebellion," by resolution of the Executive *Yuan* Council, take emergency measures to avert an imminent danger to the security of the State or of the people, or to cope with any serious financial or economic crisis, without being subject to the procedural restrictions by the Legislative *Yuan* as prescribed in Article 39 and Article 43 of the Constitution.[4] Even though the Legislative *Yuan* may

[1] It was an open secret that Chiang and Li had never been in friendly terms. As President and Vice President, neither could trust the other. During a short period of Chiang's temporary retirement in 1949, Li became Acting President. Later Li complained that he could not fully exercise his constitutional functions, because Chiang still kept all the powers in his own hands. This charge Chiang flatly denied.

[2] Arts. 39, 43.

[3] Art. 174, Sec. 1.

[4] Art. 39 provides: "The President may, in accordance with law, declare martial law with the approval of, or subject to the confirmation by, the Legislative *Yuan*. When the Legislative *Yuan* deems it necessary, it may adopt a resolution requesting the President to terminate martial law."

Art. 43 provides: ' In case of a natural calamity, an epidemic, or a national financial or economic crisis that calls for emergency measures, the President during the recess of the Legislative *Yuan* may, by resolution of the Executive *Yuan* Council, and in accordance with the Law on Emergency Decrees, issue emergency orders, proclaiming such measures as may be necessary to cope with the situation. Such orders shall, within one month after issuance, be presented to the Legislative *Yuan* for confirmation; in case the Legislative *Yuan* withholds confirmation, the said orders shall forthwith cease to be valid."

still modify or abrogate certain emergency measures in accordance with Paragraph 2 of Article 57 of the Constitution, the restrictions thus imposed upon the Presidential emergency powers are more apparent than real.[1]

It was not expected that these Temporary Provisions would continue in force for an indefinite time; on the contrary, one article of the Provisions imposed certain restrictions.[2] The President of the Republic was to convoke a special session of the National Assembly not later than December 25, 1950, to deliberate on the amendment of the Constitution. If the period of the "Communist Rebellion" had not yet been terminated by a Presidential declaration, the special session of the National Assembly would decide whether the Temporary Provisions should continue in force or be repealed.[3] Due to the prevailing circumstances, the special session of the National Assembly was not convened. The second session of the National Assembly in 1954 maintained these Temporary Provisions, but they were amended by its third session in 1960 for the removal of the two-term restriction of the Presidency.

5. THE NATIONALIST DEBACLE AND RETREAT TO TAIWAN

The Chinese civil war and the Soviet-American rivalry

The year 1947 was perhaps the turning point of the history of modern China, marking the beginning of the eventual victory of the Communists on the Mainland. The departure of General Marshall from China indicated the abandonment of the efforts of American mediation; the termination was officially declared by the State Department on January 29, 1947. After the peace negotiations ended, the National Government ordered, on February 11, Chou En-lai and other members of the Communist delegation to leave Nanking. Then both sides decided to resort to force. On March 19, the Nationalist forces made a victorious entry into Yenan, Mao's capital since 1936, and continued to occupy this historic stronghold until its recapture by the Communist troops on April 22 of the following year.

---

[1] Par. 2 of Art. 57 provides: "If the Legislative *Yuan* does not concur in any important policy of the Executive *Yuan*, it may, by resolution, request the Executive *Yuan* to alter such a policy. With respect to such resolution, the Executive *Yuan* may, with the approval of the President of the Republic, request the Legislative *Yuan* for reconsideration. If, after reconsideration, two thirds of the Members of the Legislative *Yuan* present at the meeting uphold the original resolution, the President of the Executive *Yuan* shall either abide by the same or resign from office."

[2] Art. 4.

[3] See Fo Chi-yu, *The Chinese Government*, pp. 132–133.

The loss of China to the Communists would not only be a death blow to the Nationalists, but also mean the tragic failure of American Far Eastern policy. Because of this basic reason, the United States could not afford to give up China completely. On July 22, 1947, President Truman sent Lt. General Albert C. Wedemeyer to China for a general survey of the situation; but his report did not yield any practical result.[1] The continued occupation of Dairen by Soviet Russia was a cause of anxiety for the United States, which made an official protest to the Soviet Government on August 21 about the arbitrary prevention of free access to the port by the ships of other nations. Largely as a consequence of Congressional sympathy to the Nationalist cause, American aid to China was resumed on a moderate scale by the conclusion of an *Economic Aid Agreement* on July 3, 1948, and was continued on this basis. However, the balance of power between the two hostile parties was materially shifted by the Soviet transfer to the Chinese Communists of the tremendous amount of military equipment and munitions captured from the Japanese army in Manchuria.

After a period of intensive training and regrouping and of consolidating the occupied areas in Manchuria and other parts of North China, the Communist army was ready to march southward in 1949. The National Government realized the futility of military resistance and attempted to secure a negotiated peace with its historical enemy. Chiang Kai-shek was compelled by circumstances to retire temporarily and Vice President Li Tsung-jen became Acting President. In the spring of 1949, Li sent a peace delegation to Peiping. Mao allowed the delegates to remain in Peiping but refused the peace. The terms put forward by the Communists were nothing but unconditional surrender of the Nationalists. The National Government even hoped for further foreign mediation but received little encouragement.

Then the Nationalist forces suffered one defeat after another, and all the important cities fell in rapid succession. Peiping and Tientsin were lost in January 1949. After the fall of Süchow in the previous month, Central China became almost defenseless. Nanking, Shanghai, Canton, and Chungking were all captured by the Communists in the same year.[2] At this desperate moment, the State Department issued, in August

[1] Wedemeyer's views were expressed in his *Wedemeyer Reports** (New York: Holt, 1958).

[2] The following is a list of important cities and the dates of their fall to the Communists: Chinchow (10/15/1948), Changchun (10/19/1948), Mukden (11/2/1948), Süchow (12/1/1948), Tientsin (1/15/1949), Peiping (1/31/1949), Nanking (4/23/1949), Hankow (5/16/1949), Shanghai (5/17/1949), Foochow (8/17/1949), Lanchow (8/26/1949), Canton (10/14/1949), Amoy (10/14/1949), Chungking (11/30/1949), Kweilin (12/22/1949), and Chengtu (12/27/1949). Hainan Island was occupied by the Communist troops in April 1950.

1949, a White Paper on Sino-American relations. This controversial document released at that particular time was to relieve the American government from any responsibility for the imminent fall of China's Mainland.

The National Government during this brief period moved first from Nanking to Canton, then to Chungking, and finally to Taiwan. In December 1949, the Government began to function in its temporary capital, Taipei. It should be recalled that, on October 2, Soviet Russia had already recognized the Communist government in Peking. As a reply to the Soviet action, the State Department issued a statement two days later, reaffirming American recognition of the National Government of China.

Factors contributing to the Nationalist defeat

In discussing the fundamental reasons for the Nationalist collapse on the Mainland, perhaps it is well to refer to the analysis made by no less an authority than Chiang Kai-shek, the central figure of this episode. In writing on Soviet aggression in China in 1956, Chiang frankly admitted some basic factors contributing to the tragic reverses of the Nationalists.

First, the Nationalist organization was not strict enough to prevent Communist infiltration and instill sufficient vigilance in meeting Communist tactics.

Second, Nationalist propaganda lacked initiative and was not militant enough in ideology to counter the political and psychological offensive of the Communist International.

Third, the National Government was diplomatically isolated through the maneuvering of the international Communists and found it difficult to win help and sympathy from the friendly powers, including the United States.

Fourth, the postwar financial and economic measures of the National Government failed to achieve their intended purposes and resulted in mounting inflation and eventual disaster for the national economy.

Fifth, the National Government was too confident of Soviet and Communist good intentions in its resumption of diplomatic relations with Soviet Russia and in its reorganization and integration of the Communist troops into the national army. These measures had practically facilitated Soviet assistance to the Chinese Communists and the build-up of Communist military strength.

Sixth, the National Government should have called off the take-over operations in Manchuria and submitted the Manchurian problem, including Soviet assistance to the Chinese Communists, to the United Nations. Chiang reasoned that, in this way, the Nationalist forces could have concentrated in North China for effective defense against the Communist southward invasion. In consequence of its failure to adopt this strategy, the National Government committed a military blunder of the most serious nature. Thus when Manchuria fell, North China became defenseless, and the whole situation was out of control.[1]

Chiang's reasoning was fairly frank and mainly correct. He was particularly disappointed with the result of the third factor. According to Chiang, pro-Communists in the United States utilized all the slanderous attacks instigated by Soviet Russia against the National Government and against him personally. "It was under this pressure," Chiang suggested, "that the United States evacuated her troops from China and also ceased her financial and military assistance to my country." [1] The sudden halt of an American loan of $500,000,000 to the National Government at the time of Marshall's mediation was deemed by Chiang as a death blow to the Sino-American economic cooperation and to the popular confidence in China's postwar reconstruction. While Chiang did not explicitly blame his own government for the diplomatic isolation and setbacks, such self-criticism might have been implied in his remarks.

Other important factors have been held to be responsible for the Nationalist collapse on the Mainland, but were not specifically mentioned by Chiang. These included the corruption and inefficiency in the government, poor strategy of the commanding generals, lack of will power to fight among the soldiers, and the loss of popular support due to no fault other than that of the government itself. It was these combined factors that contributed to the decline and fall of the Nationalist government on the Mainland. Soviet military assistance to the Chinese Communists was an important but not a determinant force of the change of power in China, because "the use of military force was but one of the numerous weapons used by the Chinese Communists in the final battle." [2] In analyzing the reasons for the success of the Communists, Chiang commented that "their effective use of propaganda, espionage and the deceptive tactics of contact, infiltration, organization, etc., and the fact that they could prepare

---

[1] See Chiang Chung-cheng, *Soviet Russia in China**, pp. 212–234.
[2] *Ibid.*, p. 223.
[3] *Ibid.*, p. 237.

war under the cover of their "anti-civil war" slogan, accounted for the Government's loss of control over the nation-wide situation." [1]

6. THE NATIONAL GOVERNMENT IN TAIWAN

Major Events in the domestic field

Since the National Government moved to Taiwan in 1949, the domestic situation has been fairly stable. The most important events in the past were perhaps the two sessions of the National Assembly and two presidential elections. While there are various opinions on certain constitutional issues, probably practical politics under the prevailing circumstances made it difficult to abide by all the technical requirements. For a clear understanding of these events, an analysis of the various phases of the Assembly sessions and presidential elections in 1954 and 1960 is necessary. The present status of the Five-*Yuan* system in Taiwan will be briefly described.

The National Assembly and its Presidential election in 1954

The Constitutional interpretation by the Council of Grand Justices – The first term of the President and Vice President of the Republic was to expire on May 20, 1954. According to the Constitution, the National Assembly had to be convened for the Presidential election 90 days prior to the expiration date of the term of the incumbent President.[2] A serious question arose as to whether this function of Presidential election should be performed by a new National Assembly or by the existing one. The Constitution provides that "delegates to the National Assembly shall be elected every six years." [3] Due to extraordinary circumstances, a nation-wide election was not possible. The term of the incumbent delegates elected to office in 1948 would expire in 1954, but no new delegates were elected to replace them. A possible solution was found in Article 28 of the Constitution, which prescribes the means for the continuous functioning of the National Assembly: "The term of office of the delegates to each National Assembly shall terminate on the day on which the next National Assembly convenes." [4] Since a new National Assembly could not be created without a nation-wide election, the present National Assembly

---

[1] *Loc. cit.*
[2] Art. 29.
[3] Art. 28, Par. 1.
[4] Art. 28, Par. 2.

had to be convened to hold its Second Session for the Presidential election.

Upon the request of the Secretariat of the National Assembly, the Council of Grand Justices of the Judicial *Yuan* interpreted, on July 10, 1953, that the convening date of the Second Session of the National Assembly should be February 19, 1954, exactly 90 days before the expiration date of the term of the incumbent President. The next problem was the attendance of a sufficient number of delegates in order to fulfill the requirement for a quorum. The Government then enacted laws and regulations governing the conditions for the maintenance of delegates' status and provisions for their replacement by alternate delegates or appointees. Notwithstanding these efforts, the attendance of the delegates to the Second Session of the National Assembly could not be expected to be more than one half of the total membership. According to the *Organic Law of the National Assembly*, a quorum of the Assembly meetings requires the attendance of more than one half of the total members of the National Assembly.[1] In order to avoid any risk of the lack of a quorum, the Legislative *Yuan* immediately amended this provision by reducing the quorum requirement from a majority to one-third of the total membership.

The election of the President and Vice President – The Second Session of the National Assembly met in Taipei on February 19–March 25, 1954, with an attendance of 1,578 delegates. Chiang Kai-shek was elected President on the second ballot on March 22 and Chen Cheng, as Vice President on the fourth ballot on March 24. At this Second Session, the total membership was based on the number provided by law, that is, 3,045. This formula of membership was the same as that followed by the First Session, even though the quorum requirement was reduced at the Second Session.[2] Some questioned the legality of this Presidential

---

[1] Art. 8.

[2] At the election meeting on March 20, a total number of 1,573 delegates cast their votes. Chiang received 1,387; Hsü Fu-lin of the China Democratic Socialist Party, 172; and 14 votes were declared invalid for various reasons. According to Art. 4 of the *Law governing the Election and Recall of the President and Vice President*, promulgated on March 31, 1947 and revised on March 13, 1954, the candidate receiving votes of more than half of the total membership of the National Assembly would be elected. As one half of the total membership of 3,045 votes should be 1,523, none of these two candidates was elected. The same article provides that, under the above circumstances, a second ballot would be cast and the candidate receiving the majority of votes cast would be elected. At the second election meeting on March 22, a total number of 1,576 delegates cast their votes. Chiang and Hsü received 1,507 and 48 votes respectively; 20 votes being declared invalid. Thus Chiang was formally elected as President. The third election meeting was held on March 23 for the election of the Vice President. Chen Cheng received 1,276 out of 1,572 votes cast; another candidate, Shih Tse-chien, received 231 votes; and 64 votes were declared invalid. None was elected. At the fourth election meeting on March 24, a total number of 1,570 votes was cast. Chen received 1,417 and Shih, 109. Thus Chen was formally elected as Vice President.

election by the existing National Assembly instead of a new one; while others maintained that, before the expiration date of its term, the National Assembly could definitely exercise its constitutional powers of Presidential election.

Other major decisions of the Second Session of the National Assembly – When Chiang was forced by circumstances to retire temporarily in the spring of 1949, Vice President Li Tsung-jen became Acting President. After his failure to negotiate with the Communists for a peaceful settlement of the domestic situation in China, Li left the country for the United States in November for medical treatment and remained there. Li's departure at a time of national emergency was criticized by many in party and government circles. As early as January 12, 1952, the Supervisory *Yuan* impeached Li on the ground of his dereliction of duty. It was then up to the Second Session of the National Assembly to decide on the issue. At its meeting on March 10, 1954, Li was recalled from the Vice Presidency by a vote of 1,403 to 40. Actually, a new Vice President would have been elected at the Second Session with or without Li's recall.

There was also discussion at the Second Session regarding the amendment of the Constitution, which requires the affirmative vote of two-thirds of the total membership of the National Assembly, that is, 2,030. As the Second Session was attended by only 1,578 delegates, it would have been unconstitutional to amend the Constitution. As to the *Temporary Provisions Effective During the Period of Communist Rebellion*, the Assembly decided to keep them in effect at its meeting on March 11.

The National Assembly and its Presidential election in 1960

The problem of Chiang's third term – The Third Session of the National Assembly was held in Taipei on February 20–March 25, 1960. There were a number of serious problems to be considered both before and during the meetings. The most important question was how to amend the two-term restriction in the Constitution so that Chiang could serve his third term as President of the Republic. The Constitution of 1946 stipulates that the term of office of the President and Vice President is six years and that they may be re-elected for a second term.[1] While Chiang's second term would expire on May 20, 1960, a change of leadership in Taiwan at that time was deemed inadvisable. Some suggested that Chiang might step down from the Presidency and remain in

[1] Art. 47.

power in his capacity as *Tsungtsai* or Leader of the Nationalist Party and possibly as President of the Executive *Yuan* at the same time. They reasoned that in the past Chiang had long led the country when he was not the Head of the State.

On the other hand, many leaders in Taiwan considered that it was extremely necessary to maintain the continuity of national policy by electing President Chiang to serve a third term. According to them, an amendment of Article 47 of the Constitution was inevitable. The next problem was how to assure a quorum at the Third Session for the purposes of constitutional amendment and presidential election. These puzzles were eventually solved through a series of ingenious devices.

The problem of total membership – The interpretation of membership at the Third Session was not as simple as that at the Second Session because of the necessity of constitutional amendment for the removal of the two-term restriction. Such amendment could be made through either one of two procedures: by the National Assembly directly or by the National Assembly upon the recommendation of the Legislative *Yuan*. The second procedure required a waiting period of at least six months and was, therefore, not feasible because of the imminent expiration of President Chiang's second term.[1] Under the circumstances, only the first procedure·could be followed:

Upon the proposal of one fifth of the total number of the delegates to the National Assembly and by a resolution of three fourths of the delegates present at a meeting having a quorum of two thirds of the entire Assembly, the Constitution may be amended.[2]

The total number of the membership was 3,045, two-thirds of which for a quorum would be 2,030. In view of the experience of the Second Session, the expected attendance to the Third Session would be much less than that figure. Thus the membership requirement would be a formidable obstacle to any constitutional amendment unless the Council of Grand Justices could interpret it in a more convenient manner. Upon the request of the Secretariat of the National Assembly, the Council, presided over by Hsieh Kuan-sheng, President of the Judicial *Yuan*, interpreted the constitutional provision on the total membership in the following way:

[1] The second procedure is contained in Art. 174, Par. 3 of the Constitution: "Upon the proposal of one fourth of the Members of the Legislative *Yuan* and by a resolution of three fourths of the Members present at a meeting having a quorum of three fourths of the Members of the *Yuan*, an amendment may be drawn up and submitted to the National Assembly by way of referendum. Such a proposed amendment to the Constitution shall be publicly published half a year before the National Assembly convenes."

[2] Art. 174, Par. 2.

The total membership of the National Assembly under the Constitution shall be counted on the basis, in the present situation, of the number of delegates who are duly elected according to law, and able to answer summons to attend the meeting of the Assembly.[1]

In making this unique interpretation, the Grand Justices relied on the doctrine of *rebus sic stantibus*, which would justify the revision or unenforceability of a legal provision owing to a vital change of circumstances. Thus the total membership was practically reduced from 3,045 to no more than 1,600, an estimate made by the Ministry of Interior.[2] Some critics pointed out that the vital change of circumstances occurred in China in 1949, but not between the Second Session in 1954 and the Third Session in 1960. As the total membership of the Second Session followed the same figure of the First Session, there seemed to be no justification for the drastic reduction at the Third Session.[3] It should be understood, however, that many measures taken by the government at a time of national emergency could probably be justified on the ground of practical necessity rather than legal technicality.

Revision of the Temporary Provisions – The Third Session of the National Assembly was attended by 1,454 delegates. The total membership according to the new interpretation was computed as 1,576, including those delegates who were free to but did not actually attend the meetings. Having solved the problem of a quorum requirement, the National Assembly concerned itself with the amendment of the two-term restriction. After due consideration, the delegates finally agreed that the Constitution itself should not be amended but that the Temporary Provisions should be revised. Evidently, they did not consider the latter as a part of the Constitution. On March 12, the National Assembly adopted, by a majority vote of 1,188 to 16, a resolution for the revision of the *Temporary Provisions Effective During the Period of Communist Rebellion*. The pertinent part of the revision, which made the election of President Chiang to a third term possible, is as follows:

During the Period of Communist Rebellion, the President and the Vice President may be re-elected without being subject to the two-term restriction prescribed in Article 47 of the Constitution.[4]

[1] Adopted by the Council on February 12, 1960.

[2] The Ministry of Interior announced that, up to February 12, 1960, the call had gone to a total of 1,576 National Assemblymen to attend the Third Session of the National Assembly.

[3] Among the articles and editorials on this subject, Chiang Yun-tien's "Comments on the Interpretation of the Constitution by the Grand Justices" was a representative one. See *The China Tribune* (a daily paper published in New York), April 7–8, 1960. Chiang Yun-tien, a leading member of the China Democratic Socialist Party, has held a government position as Adviser to President Chiang.

[4] These Temporary Provisions are affixed to Appendix G.

The election of the President and Vice President – After the removal of the two-term restriction by the National Assembly, the Central Executive Committee of the Nationalist Party nominated Chiang Kai-shek and Chen Cheng as candidates for the Presidency and Vice Presidency. Their nomination was officially announced by the Presidium of the National Assembly and countersigned by 1,430 and 1,428 delegates respectively. The Chinese Youth Party and the China Democratic Socialist Party did not nominate their own candidates but pledged their support to the Chiang-Chen ticket of the Nationalist Party. At its first election meeting on March 21, Chiang was elected President by an overwhelming majority of 1,481 votes. Chen Cheng was elected Vice President by 1,381 votes at the second election meeting on the next day. Chiang and Chen were unopposed in the elections.

The increasing importance of the National Assembly – The National Assemblymen had long complained about their treatment by the Government in comparison with that received by the members of the Legislative and Supervisory *Yuan*. In a recent interpretation, the Council of Grand Justices ruled that the National Assembly, together with the Legislative and Supervisory *Yuan*, is equivalent to the Parliament or Congress, of Western democracies. This principle of equal status and treatment was expressly recognized by the National Government.[1]

With respect to the rights of initiative and referendum,[2] the Constitution provides:

... the National Assembly shall make regulations pertaining thereto and put them into effect, after the above-mentioned two political rights shall have been exercised in one half of the *hsien* and municipalities of the whole country.[3]

Under the prevailing circumstances, the two political rights of initiative and referendum could not possibly be exercised in the near future in one half of the districts and municipalities of the entire country. The delegates at the Third Session of the National Assembly demanded the removal of the restrictions on the exercise of initiative and referendum in order to establish a sound system of division of power and accelerate the democratic rule of law. It was finally decided that the *Temporary Provisions Effective During the Period of Communist Rebellion* would be appended with a new provision as a major step

---

[1] See *The China Tribune*, March 22, 1960.
[2] Art. 17 of the Constitution stipulates that the people shall have the right of election, recall, initiative, and referendum.
[3] Art. 27, Par. 2.

toward the eventual exercise of the rights of initiative and referendum:

> An organ shall be established after the conclusion of the third plenary session of the National Assembly to study and draft proposals relating to the powers of initiative and referendum by the National Assembly. These, together with other proposals pertaining to constitutional amendment, shall be discussed by the National Assembly at an extraordinary session to be convoked by the President.[1]

Besides the election of the President and Vice President and the revisions of the Temporary Provisions, the Third Session of the National Assembly passed more than 400 bills concerning government administration and received reports from the government on administrative, military, financial, educational, and international affairs.

The legality of the revision of the Temporary Provisions – The revision of the Temporary Provisions at the Third Session followed the same procedure as that for the amendment of the Constitution, that is, upon the proposal of the one fifth of the total number of the delegates to the National Assembly and by a resolution of three fourths of the delegates present at a meeting having a quorum of two thirds of the Assembly.[2] In spite of all the legal technicalities, the revision of the Temporary Provisions materially changed the substance of the Constitution. In this case, the removal of the two-term restriction was, in effect, an amendment of the Constitution itself, because no law may alter a provision of the Constitution and any law in conflct with the Constitution shall become null and void. Even though the Temporary Provisions would only be effective during the period of "Communist Rebellion," their adoption by the National Assembly on April 18, 1948, in accordance with the same procedure as constitutional amendment was nothing else but an amendment of the Constitution.

Any Constitution is subject to amendment in order to adapt itself to changing time and circumstances. There is nothing wrong with the amendment if it conforms with the prescribed constitutional procedure. Fully realizing the advisability of Chiang's re-election as President in order to maintain political stability in Taiwan, students of constitutional law questioned the logic of Chiang's address at the closing ceremony of the Third Session of the National Assembly on March 25, in his particular emphasis on maintaining the nation's legal continuity by revising the Temporary Provisions instead of amending the Constitution.[3] The manifesto issued by the National Assembly held the same position

---

1 Appendix G.
2 Art. 174, Par. 2.
3 See *China Handbook, 1960–1961**, p. 157.

as Chiang. It did, however, frankly admit the reasons for the revision in the following words:

> The election of the President and Vice President is a sacred right vested in the National Assembly by the Constitution. During the current session, the Assembly carefully deliberated on the problem and came to the conclusion that the Constitution itself should not be amended, but the Temporary Provisions should be revised, so that, during the period of Communist Rebellion, the term of office of the President would not be subject to the restriction of Article 47 of the Constitution.[1]

Opinions of legal experts were by no means in unanimous agreement with the reasoning put forward by Chiang and other leaders that the revision of the Temporary Provisions was not an amendment of the Constitution. Nor they could support the interpretation of the total membership of the National Assembly by the Council of Grand Justices. On the other hand, they were not unaware of the necessity of the consideration of political expediency under the present conditions in China. The re-election of President Chiang had certainly reassured the political continuity and stability in Taiwan. One Western comment concluded that the course taken by the Third Session of the National Assembly was "a logical thing to do" for the following reasons:

> Whatever shortcomings may be charged against him, President Chiang is and remains the outstanding symbol of the hope for a free China. If that hope appears remote, it still keeps Taiwan going, engages the loyalties of the oversea Chinese and in conjunction with American aid provides the impetus for a remarkable economic and political transformation of Taiwan which at least demonstrates Chinese capacity for such achievements without the Communist blood toll.[2]

The Five Yuan of the National Government

When the National Government moved to Taiwan, the main structure of the five *Yuan* system was retained for the maintenance of constitutional sanctity. However, non-essential offices and personnel were considerably reduced, especially in the case of the Executive *Yuan*. Immediately after his inauguration on May 20, 1960, President Chiang appointed Vice President Chen Cheng as concurrently President of the Executive *Yuan*, a post the Vice President has held since 1958. The new Executive *Yuan* under Chen has 8 Ministries, 2 Commissions, 2 Offices or Bureaus, and 5 Ministers without Portfolio. The Ministries are: (1) interior, (2) foreign affairs, (3) national defense, (4) finance, (5) education, (6) justice, (7) economic affairs, and (8) communications. The Overseas Affairs Commission, Mongolian and Tibetan Affairs

[1] *Loc. cit.*
[2] *New York Times*, March 22, 1960, editorial.

Commission, Comptroller-General's Office, and Government Information Office are of the same rank as the Ministries but smaller in scope. Among the Ministers, two are Taiwanese.[1]

When the National Government moved to Taiwan, many members of the Legislative and Supervisory *Yuan* were left behind on the Mainland. Vacancies were later filled by alternate members. Since new elections cannot be held because of the prevailing situation, their term of office has had to be extended. Through an interpretation of the laws involved by the Council of Grand Justices, members of both *Yuan* will remain in Office until new members are duly elected and new *Yuan* duly convened. Free from controversial issues, the Examining *Yuan* performs its functions quietly in Taiwan.

The problem with the Judicial *Yuan* after its removal to Taiwan was the appointment of new Grand Justices to fill in the vacancies. According to the *Organic Law of the Judicial Yuan*,[2] the Council of Grand Justices is composed of seventeen Justices of high standing. Among the twelve appointed in 1948, only two went to Taiwan. The Council of Grand Justice is empowered to interpret the Constitution, laws, and ordinances for the adjustment of differences and uniformity of application. An interpretation of the Constitution can only be made with the concurrence of three-fourths or more of the members present, at a meeting where three-fourths of the total number of Grand Justices constitute a quorum. In March 1952, seven new members were appointed; but the term of the incumbent Justices expired in July 1958. The President appointed fifteen new Grand Justices in September of the same year.

Another problem of the Judicial *Yuan* is its jurisdiction over the courts. The Chinese judicial system consists of three grades of courts and three trials, namely, the Supreme Court, the high courts, and the district courts. The Supreme Court is directly under the Judicial *Yuan*. The other two courts are under the Ministry of Justice, which was originally a part of the Judicial *Yuan* but was transferred to the Executive *Yuan* in 1942. It has long been argued that the jurisdiction of the Executive *Yuan*, through the Ministry of Justice, over the nation's lower courts constituted interference in the independence of the judicial system by the executive branch of the government.

---

[1] They are Lien Chen-tung, Minister of Interior and Ts'ai Pei-huo, Minister without Portfolio. The new members of the Executive *Yuan* were appointed by the Presidential mandate of May 31, 1960. See the Chinese News Service (an information agency of the National Government in Taiwan), *Free China Weekly* (a news bulletin published in New York), June 1, 1960.

[2] Art. 3.

Recently, the Supervisory *Yuan* requested the Council of Grand Justices to determine whether or not the high courts and the district courts should remain under the jurisdiction of the Executive *Yuan*. In a resolution passed by an overwhelming majority, the Council of Grand Justices held that "they should be placed under the Judicial *Yuan*." [1] Since the decision of the Council of Grand Justices is final and binding, the Executive *Yuan* is expected to submit to the Legislative *Yuan* draft revisions of the *Organic Law of the Ministry of Justice* for the implementation of the Council's decision.

7. THE LOCAL GOVERNMENT SYSTEM IN TAIWAN

The administrative divisions

Taiwan (Formosa) was made a province by the Chinese government after its restoration to China in conformity with the wartime agreements among the Great Powers.[2] The population consists mainly of Taiwanese, who are Taiwan-born Chinese; the Mainlanders, who came to Taiwan at the time of the Communist control of the Mainland; and a small number of aborigines. Taiwan province is now administratively divided into sixteen districts *(hsien)* and five municipalities. All of them are under the jurisdiction of the provincial government.[3] Taipei and Taichung, two important municipalities, are the seats of the National Government and the provincial government respectively.

Each district is composed of a number of townships *(chen)* and villages *(hsiang)*, which are subdivided into precincts *(li)* and hamlets *(ts'un)* respectively. A *li* consists of 150 to 300 households and a *ts'un*, 100 to 200 households. A municipality is composed of a number of

---

[1] All fifteen Grand Justices took part in the deliberation, the vote being 14 to 1. The Grand Justices based their decision upon Art. 77 of the Constitution: "The Judicial *Yuan* shall be the highest judicial organ of the State and have charge of civil, criminal, and administrative cases, and over cases concerning disciplinary measures against public functionaries." Chinese News Service, *Free China Weekly*, September 7, 1960.

[2] For a historical analysis of the status of Taiwan, see Joseph W. Ballantine, *Formosa: United States Foreign Policy** (Washington: The Brookings Institution, 1952), pp. 1–95.

[3] The 16 districts are: Taipei, Taoyuan, Hsinchu, Miaoli, Taichung, Changhua, Nantou, Yunlin, Chiayi, Tainan, Kaohsiung, Pingtung, Yilan, Hualien, Taitung, and Penghu (Pescadores). The following are the municipalities: Keelung, Taipei, Taichung, Tainan, and Kaohsiung. There are a number of the Nationalist-held offshore islands, including Quemoy and Matsu. The Quemoy group comprises Big Quemoy, Little Quemoy, and twelve smaller islets, with a total area of 68 square miles. These islands may be used by the Nationalists to block the Communists' free use of Amoy harbor. The Matsu group consists of five islets: Nankan, Peikan, Kaoteng, Hsichuan, and Tungchuan, with an area of 10 square miles. This group of islets under the Nationalist command may deny the Communists' free use of the seaport of Foochow. Both Amoy and Foochow are important ports in Fukien province, which is separated from Taiwan by the Formosa Strait.

boroughs or sub-districts *(ch'ü)*, each of which is constituted by a number of *li*. Under the *li* and *ts'un* is the "neighborhood" *(lin)*, composed of 6 to 15 households.[1]

The provincial government

The provincial government of Taiwan is based upon the provisions of the 1946 Constitution and the *Revised Organic Law of the Provincial Government* of March 23, 1931, and is under the direct control of the National Government. At the head of the provincial government is the Chairman or Governor, who is appointed by the President of the Republic upon the recommendation of the President of the Executive *Yuan*. As a collective organ of deliberation on administrative matters, the provincial council is composed of 21 members. These members of the provincial government are nominated by the Chairman and appointed by the Executive *Yuan*, for the performance of provincial administrative functions.

For the purpose of discharging various administrative duties, the provincial government has a number of departments, including civil affairs, finance, education, reconstruction, and agriculture and forestry. The heads of the departments are commissioners, appointed from among the members of the provincial government. There are other organs, under the direction of the Chairman, in charge of police, communications, social affairs, health, personnel, accounting and statistics, information, food, and others. The secretary general and the staff of the Secretariat are responsible for the general adminis-tration of the provincial government. The organization and functions of the Taiwan provincial government are similar to those as provided in the *Revised Organic Law of the Provincial Government of 1931*.[2]

The provincial assembly

The origin – The representative body in Taiwan was first created on December 11, 1951, with the inauguration of the provisional provincial assembly. Its temporary nature and limited powers were the source of dissatisfaction often expressed by the assemblymen. In order to correct this undesirable situation, the provincial government ordered the change of the assembly's name from the fifth session of the third provisional provincial assembly to the first session of the first provincial

---

[1] There are in Taiwan today 77 *chen*, 235 *hsiang*, 3,489 *li*, 3,066 *ts'un*, and 82,290 *lin*. See *China Yearbook, 1953*, p. 643.
[2] See Ch. VI, Sec. 6, "The Provincial Government."

assembly in accordance with the provisions of the *Organic Law of the Provincial Assembly*, promulgated on August 26, 1959. The term of the first provincial assembly expired on June 1, 1960. An election was held on April 24 for the selection of 73 new members of the second provincial assembly which was inaugurated on June 2, 1960.

The membership – The members of the provincial assembly are elected directly by the citizens of the districts and municipalities, who are over twenty years of age and have lived in the election area for more than six months. All citizens over twenty three years of age are eligible to be elected as assemblymen provided they are not legally deprived of political rights. The following people are temporarily excluded from eligibility: students, policemen, military personnel in active service, and people in charge of the current election. Members of the assembly are subject to recall in accordance with stipulated procedures.

A minimum of one assemblyman is apportioned to each district or municipality in Taiwan, which has a population of 150,000 or less. There will be an additional member for every 150,000 if the population of that district or municipality exceeds 150,000, and one more if the remaining figure reaches 75,000. Special quotas are reserved for female citizens and Taiwan aborigines: in the case of the former, one female to every four members; and of the latter, two for the mountain aborigines and one for those living in the plains. There are seventy-three members of the second provincial assembly, who serve a term of three years and may be re-elected.

The organization – The provincial assembly has a speaker and a deputy speaker, elected from among the members.[1] The assembly meets every six months, two months each time, presided over by the speaker. Special sessions may be called by the Chairman of the provincial government or by one-third or more of the assemblymen. A majority of the total members constitutes a quorum, and resolutions may be adopted by a majority vote of the total members present at the meeting. Various committees are set up to conduct the affairs of the assembly when it is in session. They include a procedural committee, a disciplinary committee, and a committee for screening proposals. The functions of the assembly during its recess are exercised by a resident committee of nine members, elected from among the assemblymen.

The functions – The powers and functions of the provincial assembly

---

[1] Huang Choa-chin and Hsieh Tung-ming are speaker and deputy speaker of the second provincial assembly respectively.

have been enlarged to a certain extent by the promulgation of the *Organic Law of the Provincial Assembly* of 1959, and may be grouped as follows: (1) to deliberate on and enact rules and regulations concerning people's rights and obligations; (2) to examine and approve the provincial budget and audit reports; (3) to review proposals of the provincial government and to suggest reform measures for its adoption; (4) to decide on the disposal of public properties of the province; and (5) to receive the petitions from the people. When the provincial assembly is in recess, the provincial government may, with the approval of the Executive *Yuan*, take necessary actions and report them to the provincial assembly at its next session. If the provincial government disagrees with the resolutions of the provincial assembly, the government may request a reconsideration by the assembly and may even submit the disputes to the Executive *Yuan* for final decision in case the assembly upholds its original resolutions. Of course, no assembly resolution may become effective if it is in conflict with the Constitution and national laws.

The district and municipal governments

There are sixteen districts and five municipalities in Taiwan province, each headed by a magistrate or mayor as the case may be. Their term of office was originally three years, but has now been changed to four. They are eligible for a second term if re-elected. While the magistrates and mayors are responsible to the district and municipal assemblies, they can only be recalled by popular vote. The last election of the magistrates and mayors was held simultaneously with that of the assemblymen on April 24, 1960.

According to the *Revised Regulations for the Enforcement of Local Self-Government of Districts and Municipalities in Taiwan Province*, promulgated on November 2, 1954,[1] there are three major functions of the district and municipal governments. They are: (1) to carry out orders from the provincial government and other superior organs, (2) to take charge of all matters of local self-government, and (3) to direct and supervise the work of the villages and townships. Under the magistrate or mayor, there are a number of bureaus, including those in charge of civil affairs, finance, reconstruction, education, police, land, and public health.

The heads of the offices of the villages, townships, and other lower

---

[1] These Regulations came into force on November 5, 1954. The Taiwan provincial government had, however, discovered these inadequate to meet the actual needs and suggested further revisions to the Executive *Yuan* in October 1959.

units are all selected through popular election for a term of three years. However, the heads of villages and townships are eligible for a second term and those of lower units may serve indefinitely if re-elected. Their duties are to dispose of matters of self-government in their respective areas and to carry out orders from their superior offices.

The district and municipal assemblies

The district and municipal assemblies are the deliberative and representative bodies of the districts and municipalities. The assemblymen are directly elected by local voters for a term of three years and are eligible for re-election. The qualifications for voters and candidates are the same as those applied to the provincial assemblymen. Likewise, there are two reserved quotas: one female for every ten members, and a certain number of aborigines in proportion to their population. The latest election was held on April 24, 1960. Each assembly has a speaker and a deputy speaker, elected from among the members. The assembly meets every four months, presided over by the speaker. The functions of the district and municipal assemblies correspond to those of the provincial assembly.

There are also representative bodies in villages and townships. Their representatives are elected by the local voters for a term of three years and are eligible for re-election. The residents of lower local units have general meetings to discuss local matters within their respective areas.

Fair representation of local people

After the National Government moved to Taiwan, there were complaints about insufficient representation of the Taiwanese in the government. The general criticism is that politically Taiwan is dominated by the Mainlanders or those coming to the Island during the period of Communist victory on the Mainland. It is true that important figures in the National Government and armed forces before 1949 remain in power in Taiwan and that popular election has not yet been applied to the officials of the provincial government. Yet the provincial and other local assemblies as well as the magistrates and mayors are elected by the local people. With a few exceptions, the successful candidates are native-born Taiwanese. As far as local politics are concerned, it is safe to say that the Taiwanese are fairly represented.[1]

---

[1] For the election returns of the assemblymen, magistrates, and mayors in 1960, see *China Yearbook, 1960–1961**, pp. 213–218. The fact of fair representation of the Taiwanese was also

8. TAIWAN TODAY

The political situation

Taiwan, a Nationalist stronghold since 1950, has been fairly prosperous under a stable government. Technically the National Government is no longer under one-party dictatorship, but the Nationalist Party still has the controlling voice in Taiwan. The party itself underwent a thorough reorganization. Chiang remains the *Tsungtsai* or Leader, with Chen Cheng as his deputy. The Chinese Youth Party and China Democratic Socialist Party continue to cooperate with the government, which has always tried to include some members of the two minor parties in various offices and representative bodies. Actually neither of these two minor parties has a wide popular following or substantial political influence, because each of them has suffered from internal dissensions for years. Recent reports from Taiwan indicate that the different factions of each party has promised to unite. As to how far they can succeed, it remains to be seen.[1]

While sincerely hoping that internal harmony could be restored to the two minor parties, the government would not tolerate any political activity that might interfere with its task of preparing for the eventual invasion of the Mainland. Some foreign observers believe that "the government is particularly on guard against any activity that might lead to the emergence of a 'Taiwanese Party.'"[2]

observed by westerners. See Fred W. Riggs, *Formosa Under Nationalist Rule** (New York: Institute of Pacific Relations, 1952), p. 52.

[1] See *The China Tribune*, May 18 and June 20, 1962.

[2] *New York Times*, March 31, 1962. The Lei Chen case had agitated wide criticism in the United States. Lei, publisher of *Free China Fortnightly*, an independent periodical, had been active in organizing the Taiwanese to form a new opposition party. He was arrested and sentenced to ten-years in prison by the military tribunal of the Taiwan Garrison-General Headquarters, on the ground of sedition and Communist connection. Lei lost his appeal to the High Court of Review of the Ministry of National Defense, which, on November 23, 1960, handed down its verdict upholding the decision of the military tribunal. For adverse comments of this case, see the letters sent to the *New York Times* editor by Robert A. Scalapino, Professor of Political Science at the University of California on September 21, 1960 and by John King Fairbank, Professor of History at Harvard University on October 27, 1960. *New York Times*, September 27 and November 7, 1960.

On the other hand, the Chinese government deemed that Lei's sentence had nothing to do with his attempt to form an opposition party. In his letter to the *New York Times* editor on October 3, 1960, George K. C. Yeh, then Chinese Ambassador to the United States, defended the government action in the following manner:

"The Chinese Government's indictment against Lei Chen and two of his associates was published on September 26. They are now being tried on different charges, none of which has anything to do with their attempts to form an opposition party. Lei is being charged with sedition because as publisher of the *Free China Fortnightly* he had openly advocated "revolution" and "bloodshed" to overthrow the Chinese Government.

"Lei Chen and his associates are being tried by a military court in accordance with Article 10 of the Statute for the Punishment of Sedition adopted in 1949 by the legislative *Yuan*.

Economic prospects

The economic progress in Taiwan in recent years has been comparatively impressive. The increase in gross national product has ranged from 6.5 to 8% each year and that for per capita income from 3.5 to 5% annually.[1] The living standard on Taiwan is one of the highest among the nations in Asia.

Perhaps the most outstanding achievement in Taiwan is the land reform program which was initiated by the Taiwan provincial government under Chairman Chen Cheng with the enforcement of the farm rent-reduction regulations in 1949. By limiting rentals of farm-land to 37.5% of the annual yield according to a standard rate for each grade of farm land, almost 50% of the total farm families benefited. This rental limitation was followed in 1951 by the sale of public land to tenant farmers and in 1953 by the implementation of the land-to-the-tiller program. The sale price of public land was fixed at two and half times the value of the annual main-crop yield and is to be paid by the tenant purchasers in semi-annual instalments over a period of ten years. By the end of 1959, the government had collected on the average over 95% of the amount due. According to the *Land-to-the-Tiller Act* of 1953, the ultimate purpose of the program is the equalization of land ownership through government purchase of private-owned surplus farm-land and resale of the purchased land to tenant farmers. Following the land policy of Dr. Sun Yat-sen, the Government promulgated the *Equalization of Urban Land Rights Act* in August 1954. The essentials of the Act are: (1) assessment of land value, (2) government taxation on and purchase of the land according to its declared value, and (3) accrual of unearned increments of the land to the public. Such a farm reform program is vitally important in a country which is characterized by an agricultural economy.

In spite of the economic growth rate and the success of the land reform program, the Government has faced many difficult problems. First, Taiwan is short of investment capital. For encouragement of investment by foreign nationals and overseas Chinese, the Government promulgated a new statute on August 31, 1960, granting investors a

This article states specifically that persons charged with sedition in areas where martial law is in force shall be tried by a military court. The province of Taiwan was declared such an area some time ago and remains so today in view of the state of emergency arising from the Communist threat of attack which continues to exist." *New York Times*, October 5, 1960.

However, Yeh's view was not shared by many Nationalist sympathizers in the United States. See *The China Tribune* editorials, September 8–9, 1960.

[1] See *U.S. News and World Report*, January 1, 1962, p. 38. For details, see U.S. Department of State, *The Republic of China* (Far Eastern Series 81, released October 1959), pp. 21–41.

liberal tax incentive. Another problem is overpopulation, which is serious but not imminent. Perhaps what has hurt the Taiwan economy most is the high cost of government. Military expenditures constitute almost 80% of the national budget. The economic aid from the United States over the last decade amounts to more than one billion, a stabilizing factor of the economy of Taiwan. According to his statement of June 22, 1961, Roy E. James, Deputy Director of the Taiwan Mission of the United States International Cooperation Administration, frankly admitted his deep concern with Taiwan's economy. He asserted that the Chinese government "was too reliant on 'temporary and uncertain' United States economic assistance to cover its deficits." [1]

Perhaps the Government is aware of the fact that American aid can neither be increased nor last forever. By the promulgation of the *Regulations for the Collection of Provisional Special Defense Assessments* on May 1, 1962, the existing taxes and public utility rates were, in many cases, raised by additional assessments from 20 to 50%. These regulations are to be terminated on June 30, 1963. Within the 14-month period, the Government expected to collect $60 million dollars for national defense purposes. Whether or not this measure would accelerate inflation and sacrifice economic and industrial development remains to be ascertained. [2]

International status

The existence of two governments in China for more than a decade is not only a serious problem to the Chinese but also a matter of constant concern to the rest of the world. While each government declares that it is the only legal government of China, observers of international affairs have, from time to time, advocated a two-China policy. According to their theoretical formula, each government is to maintain its territorial sovereignty within the area under its present control and jurisdiction and to be recognized by other nations in such a way. As to membership in the United Nations, their idea is to keep the permanent membership of Nationalist China in the Security Council and to admit Communist China as a member of the General Assembly. Some have even gone so far as to suggest that China's occupation of Taiwan does not automatically entitle her to legal possession of

---

[1] For details of his statement, see *New York Times*, June 23, 1961.

[2] There are 14 kinds of taxes and utility rates affected under this statute, including individual income tax, import duty, merchandise tax, land value tax, slaughter tax, salt tax, and rates of electricity, telephone, railways and buses. See Chinese News Service, *Free China Weekly*, May 8, 1962.

the territory. Nothing is further from the truth. The restoration of Taiwan and Penghu (Pescadores) to China was clearly stated in the Cairo Declaration of December 1, 1943 and reassured by the Potsdam Declaration of July 25, 1945. While the Nationalists and Communists have been irrevocably antagonistic to each other, they do agree that Taiwan is an integral part of China and that there should never be two Chinas.

A small number of Westerners and Taiwanese residing abroad have been in favor of the establishment of an independent state of Taiwan by and for the Taiwanese. This equally unrealistic plan is based upon the current misconception in the West that the Taiwanese and the Mainlanders are of two different races. Actually the only native people in Taiwan are the aborigines living mostly in mountaneous areas. This tiny group has neither the capacity nor the ambition to form a new state even with the assistance of foreign adventurers. As to the Taiwanese, they were born in Taiwan but are of Chinese race and culture. Their ancestors came to Taiwan earlier than the so-called Mainlanders today. If any distinction must be made between the Taiwanese and the Mainlanders, it is the time of arrival and the place of birth. However, any democratic constitution provides that nationals of one country have the freedom of residence and of change of residence. Thus any discrimination against the Mainlanders domiciling in Taiwan and any scheme of creating a Taiwanese State are both unconstitutional and impractical.

Throughout the last decade, the National Government in Taiwan has endeavored to maintain diplomatic relations with as many nations as possible to strengthen its diplomatic front. Of course, the United States is the staunch ally of Nationalist China and has the treaty obligation to defend Taiwan and Penghu under the Sino-American Mutual Defense Treaty of December 2, 1954. As to whether or not the American defense applies to the offshore islands, including Quemoy and Matsu, it is subject to the interpretation by the contracting parties of the letter and spirit of the Treaty and its Exchange of Notes.[1] It seems that the Nationalist leaders in Taiwan are still determined to recover the Mainland with or without American assistance. According to the estimate of military experts in the West, the Nationalist army in Taiwan is too small to invade the Mainland but too large for defense

---

[1] For the United States policy toward Taiwan, see U.S. Department of State, *The Republic of China*, pp. 53–63; also President Kennedy's recent statement on the defense of Taiwan and the Communist threat, *New York Times*, June 28, 1962.

purposes. Again it is a matter of opinion. Under the prevailing circumstances and with its limited resources, the National Government can neither support a larger army nor reduce the armament for political and psychological considerations. The future of Taiwan depends much upon the external assistance and internal harmony. However, the disputes between the Nationalists and Communists can only be settled by the Chinese themselves.

CHAPTER X

THE COMMUNIST PARTY IN POWER:
MAO'S POLITICAL THOUGHT
AND THE PARTY ORGANIZATION

I. ON THE ROAD TO VICTORY

Mao's economic programs for popular support

When the civil war resumed after the breakdown of peace negotiations in 1947, the Communists intensified their efforts to win popular support for the eventual control of the country. On October 10, 1947, the "Chinese People's Liberation Army" issued a declaration, calling upon all the Chinese people to overthrow the National Government and build a new China on the basis of Communist programs. On the same day, a new land law 'was announced. It was to be enforced in the "liberated areas" for the re-distribution of land among the peasants.

Mao's economic programs were more systematically presented to the public as early as December 1945, when he made a report on "The Present Situation and Our Tasks" at a meeting of the Party's Central Committee in northern Shensi. Declaring that the "Chinese People's war of liberation has turned into an offensive on all fronts," he re-iterated the Communist economic policies as follows: (1) to confiscate the land of the feudal class and redistribute it among the peasants, (2) to confiscate all bureaucrat-capital and make it capital of the new democratic state, and (3) to protect all national industries and commerce. Mao severely criticized certain Party members in their excessive "left" policy toward middle and petty-bourgeois elements, who were considered as necessary to the national economy in the transitional stage. Evidently Mao attempted to gain support from different segments of the people during the transitional period.[1]

---

[1] For the English text of the Report, see *Selected Works of Mao Tse-tung* (Peking: Foreign Languages Press, 1961), Vol. IV, pp. 157–176. Its essentials are described in the following section.

Political expansion and military triumphs

On May 5, 1948, the Chinese Democratic League, the National Salvation Association of the Chinese People, and a number of newly organized political groups sent telegrams to the Communist Party urging the convocation of a new political consultative conference. Mass organizations were expanded at the same time. From August 1-22, the Sixth Congress of the All-China Federation of Labor met in Harbin, attended by 504 delegates from all over the country. It elected Ch'en Yun as Chairman and decided to restore the organization of the Federation of Labor Unions in China.

Following the military triumphs, independant regimes were established in strategic areas under Communist control. On August 19, a North China People's Government was created at Shih-chia-chung (Shihkiachwang), Hopei province. Before the end of the year, the Communist forces occupied one important city after another in Manchuria. After the conquest of Mukden, the Communist Party set up a Northeast Bureau of the Central Committee headed by Kao Kang and also a Northeast Administrative Council with Lin Feng as Chairman. With victory in sight, the Communists rushed to make necessary preparations for taking over the country.

The Second Plenary Session of the Seventh Central Committee met near Shih-chia-chung on March 16-23, 1949. It called on Party members to shift their emphasis from countryside to urban areas and to learn industrial, productive, and managerial technics. For the building of a "new democratic" China, the Party urged the cooperation of the working class with the peasantry and other revolutionary forces. On March 25, the headquarters of the Communist Party and the People's Liberation Army moved to Peiping which fell to the Communists at the end of January after the loss of Tientsin. On the next day, Mao declared that peace negotiations with the Nationalists would resume in Peiping on April 1.

In spite of all the military gains, the Communists never neglected the importance of the mass movement. In March 1949, the All-China Students' Federation was formed at a meeting of the All-China Students Congress in Peiping. The All-China Women's Congress met in Peiping on March 27, and resulted in the formation of the All-China Federation of Democratic Women. From April 11-18, the First Congress of the New Democratic Youth League was held in Peiping. Then, on May 11, the All-China Youth Congress decided to set up the All-China Federation of Democratic Youth, which was a united-front organization different from the Party-affiliated New Democratic Youth League. In July, the First All-China Conference of Writers and Artists formed the All-China Federation of Writers and Artists. Meanwhile, the Sino-Soviet Friendship Association was organized in Peiping with branches in other cities.

The Communist military victory was culminated in the capture of Nanking, Hankow, and Shanghai in April–May. With representatives from different political affiliations, the Preparatory Committee of the Chinese People's Political Consultative Conference met in Peiping on June 15–19. On July 1, Mao published his work, *On the People's Democratic Dictatorship*, in which he defined the People's Republic of China as a "people's democratic dictatorship led by the working class and with the alliance of workers and peasants as its foundation." [1] Foochow and Lanchow fell in the following month. In Manchuria, a Northeast People's Government was organized with Kao Kang as Chairman. The situation in China at that time was definitely in favor of the Communists, who could count on the sympathy and support of the Soviet Union. On the other hand, the Western powers adopted a wait and see policy and extended no substantial assistance to the Nationalists. [2]

The establishment of the Central People's Government

The Communist Party utilized the Chinese People's Political Consultative Conference as the constituent body for the establishment of a formal government. The Conference was convened in Peiping on September 21, 1949, attended by 510 regular, 77 alternate, and 75 invited delegates. They represented different political affiliations which were willing to accept Communist programs. Before its adjournment on September 30, the Conference adopted the *Organic Law of the Chinese People's Political Consultative Conference*, the *Organic Law of the Central People's Government of the People's Republic of China*, and also the *Common Program of the Chinese People's Political Consultative Conference*. [3]

This constituent Conference elected the Central People's Government Council of the Central People's Government with Mao Tse-tung

[1] For the English text of Mao's *On the People's Democratic Dictatorship*, see *Selected Works of Mao Tse-tung*, Vol. IV, pp. 411–424.

[2] When the Red Army crossed the Yangtze River, the British ship, *H. M. S. Amethyst*, was damaged by Communist guns in retaliation for her firing on the Communist units. Otherwise, there was no serious incident between the Communists and foreign nations.

[3] Unless otherwise indicated, all these and other fundamental laws of Communist China can be found in Albert P. Blaustein, *Fundamental Legal Documents of Communist China* (South Hackensack, N. J.: Fred B. Rothman Co., 1962).

as its Chairman. It also elected its First National Committee, which would exercise the functions of the Conference for the duration of the latter's recess. Peking, renamed from Peiping, was declared the Capital of the country. The national anthem and national flag were also adopted at the Conference.

On October 1, 1949, Mao Tse-tung formally proclaimed the establishment of the Central People's Government of the Republic of China. As its Chairman, Mao held the first meeting of the Central People's Government Council. The Vice-Chairmen were Chu Teh, Liu Shao-ch'i, Soong Ching-ling (Madame Sun Yat-sen), Li Chi-tsen, Chang Lan, and Kao Kang. Chou En-lai was appointed Premier of the State Administrative Council and concurrently Minister of Foreign Affairs. On the next day, Soviet Russia recognized the Peking regime as the legal government of China. General N. Roshin, former Soviet Ambassador to the Nationalist Government, was appointed as first Soviet Ambassador to Peking.[1] Recognition was soon granted by other nations.[2]

2. THE POLITICAL THOUGHT AND STRATEGY OF MAO TSE-TUNG

The question of the originality of Maoism

As leader of the ruling party, Mao Tse-tung has certainly established himself as the most important figure in Communist China today. Due to his increasing influence in the world, students of Communism and of Far Eastern Affairs have devoted considerable time to analyzing Mao's political thought and strategy, which have contributed to his rise to the present position and to the victory of the Communist Party. Some praised Mao as a theoretical innovator in the line of Marx, Engels, Lenin, and Stalin; while others considered him as only a faithful practitioner of the established socialist doctrines. In his research on Maoism, Professor Benjamin I. Schwartz stated his views on Mao in the following words:

On the basis of the documentation available to us, however, we cannot but conclude that Mao established his leadership within the Chinese Communist

---

[1] The Nationalist Government in Canton declared its severance of diplomatic relations with Soviet Russia on October 3, 1949.

[2] Other nations, which granted recognition to the Peking government before the end of 1950, are as follows: Bulgaria (10/4/49); Rumania (10/5/49); Hungary, Czechoslovakia, and North Korea (10/6/49); Poland (10/7/49); Outer Mongolia (10/16/49); East Germany (10/27/49); Albania (10/23/49); Great Britain (1/6/50); Ceylon and Norway (1/7/50); Israel (1/9/50); Afghanistan (1/12/50); North Vietnam (1/18/50); The Netherlands (3/27/50); India (4/1/50); Sweden (5/9/50); Denmark (5/11/50); Burma (6/8/50); Indonesia (6/9/50); Switzerland (9/14/50); Finland (10/28/50).

movement by dint of the real military, financial, and mass power which had been created by his own successful strategy that the gravitation of power into the hands of Mao Tse-tung and Chu Teh was the result of circumstances and power relations existing within the Chinese Communist movement rather than of any decision made in Moscow.[1]

The same writer observed that the Chinese Communist Party under Mao's leadership has been neither "the vanguard of the proletariat" nor a "peasant Party" in the Marxist-Leninist sense, "but an elite of professional revolutionaries which has risen to power by basing itself on the dynamic of peasant discontent.[2]" With the publication of his *On the New Democracy* in January 1940, Mao's status as a Marxist theoretician was further raised. According to some Western scholars, the peculiar and original feature of Mao's work represented "a genuinely new contribution to Marxist-Leninist theory – a contribution which had originated in China and which presumably placed its author, Mao Tse-tung, in the ranks of the great theoreticians of Marxism." [3]

On the other hand, Professir Karl A. Wittfogel contended that Mao's political thought completely follows that of Marx and Lenin and that there is nothing essentially new in Maoism.[4] After analyzing Mao's famous *Report on Investigation into the Peasant Movement in Hunan* and other important works, he went further to assert that Mao had neither outlined "a concept for a Communist-led peasant-supported revolution" in his *Report* nor presented himself "as an original top ranking Marxist-Leninist theoretician" in his *On the New Democracy*.[5] In the opinion of Progessor Wittfogel, Mao's *Report* contained not a word on the land question, the core of the agrarian revolution and "the two key features of the 'Maoist' strategy – Communist leadership and the appeal to the peasants by means of the agrarian revolution – were inserted by Mao only in 1951." [6] In dismissing Mao from the Politburo, the Enlarged Plenary Session of the Politburo of the Chinese Communist Party blamed Mao for his neglect of the agrarian revolution in the Autumn Harvest Uprising in Hunan in 1927.[7] In this connection, Professor Schwartz countered that the "principal cause of Mao's fall from grace was the fact that he had failed." [8]

[1] Benjamin I. Schwartz, *Chinese Communism and the Rise of Mao**, p. 187.
[2] *Ibid.*, p. 199.
[3] Conrad Brandt, et al., *A Documentary History of Chinese Communism**, p. 260.
[4] See Karl A. Wittfogel, "The Legend of Maoism," *The China Quarterly*, No. 1 (Jan.-Mar., 1960), pp. 75–77.
[5] *Ibid.*, No. 2 (April-June, 1960), p. 16.
[6] *Ibid.*, pp. 20, 29.
[7] See *Kuo-wen Chou-pao*, an independent Chinese weekly, 1928, No. 3, p. 7.
[8] Benjamin I. Schwartz, "The Legend of the 'Legend of Maoism,' " *The China Quarterly*, No. 2 (April-June, 1960), p. 41.

It is difficult to determine the political thought of a revolutionist from his writings designed for some specific purposes, because he has to consider the political impact of his publications on his career under the prevailing circumstances. The Hunan *Report* was made at the time of the first united front between the Communists and the Nationalists, when the former were not strong enough to launch an agrarian revolution with a reasonable possibility of success. Discussing Mao's *On the New Democracy* in particular and his revolutionary contribution in general, Professor John King Fairbank made the following comments:

> Thus in his New Democracy, Mao Tse-tung toward his non-Marxist audience blandly claimed to inherit the mantle of Sun Yat-sen as the democratic leader of the Chinese revolution and skillfully identified the May Fourth Movement with Communism. Meanwhile for Marxists he put himself on the level of Marx-Engels-Lenin-Stalin as an original contributor to Communist theory. In actual fact Mao's "innovations" had been in the realm of practice, not theory. All his dicta could be found in earlier literature. His real "contribution" had been the creation of a state within a state – a party, an army, and mass support in a territorial base.[1]

Essentials of Mao's works

The above observations made by the recognized authorities in their respective fields indicate divergent views of Mao's theoretical contributions. There is, however, no doubt that Mao's successful strategy has led the Communist Party to victory. For the benefit of the general public, perhaps it is advisable to describe briefly a few of his important works. The following writings are listed in the chronological order of their publication dates.[2]

Analysis of the Classes in Chinese Society, March 1926. Mao analyzed the five main social forces existing in China: (a) the landlord and comprador classes, (b) the bourgeoisie, (c) the middle peasants and the other sections of the petty-bourgeoisie, (d) the poor peasants and other semi-proletarians, and (e) the proletariat. He emphasized that the Chinese proletariat had in the peasantry its staunchest and most numerous ally. "As to the vacillating middle class," Mao pointed out, "its right wing may become our enemy and its left wing may become our friend, but we must be constantly on our guard toward the latter and not allow it to create confusion in our front."[3]

---

[1] John King Fairbank, *The United States and China**, p. 243.

[2] The English texts of Mao's writings to be described in this section can be found in *Mao Tse-tung: Selected Works* (New York: International Publishers, 5 vols., 1926–1949) and also *Selected Works of Mao Tse-tung* (Peking: Foreign Languages Press, 1961, Vol. IV. The English translation of the first three volumes is now under preparation.)

[3] *Mao Tse-tung: Selected Works*, Vol. I, p. 20.

Report on an Investigation into the Peasant Movement in Hunan, March 1927. This controversial Report as it is published today contains the following points: (a) the important role of peasants, especially the poor peasants, in the Chinese revolution; (b) the necessity of establishing a peasants' army in the rural areas; and (c) the increasing need for mass movement. This Report was made as a result of Mao's thirty-two days investigation into the revolutionary struggles in Hunan. In appraising the colossal movement of the peasants, Mao declared that "all revolutionary parties and all revolutionary comrades will stand before them to be tested, and to be accepted or rejected as they decide." [1]

Why Can China's Red Political Power Exist? October, 1928. This article, originally under the title, "Political Problems and the Tasks of the Party Organization in the Border Area," was part of a resolution adopted by the Second Party Conference of the Hunan-Kiangsi Border Area in 1928. Mao summarized the following main conditions as the reasons for the continued existence of the Red Regime: (a) China's localized agricultural economy, (b) the impact of imperialistic exploitations on the Chinese society, (c) the continued growth of revolutionary influence throughout the country, (d) the support of the Red Regime by the Red Army, and (e) the guidance of the Communist Party.

A Single Spark Can Start A Prairie Fire, January 1930. Mao wrote this letter to a Communist member, criticizing the pessimistic ideas then prevalent in the Communist Party. He considered the expansion of the Red Army as "the highest form of the peasant struggle under the leadership of the proletariat in semi-colonial China," [2] and advised the furtherance of the civil war and agrarian revolution for the build-up of a revolutionary regime.

Strategic Problems of China's Revolutionary War, December 1936. Originally delivered as lectures at the Red Army College in northern Shensi, this booklet expounded the correct strategy of the Red Army. Mao characterized the campaigns of "encirclement and annihilation" and counter-campaigns as the main forms of China's civil war and strongly advocated the importance of smashing the enemy's manpower by the tactics of mobile warfare. He distinguished the active defense and passive defense and pointed out that real defense is not passive but active.[3] The Chinese Communist Party regards this booklet

[1] *Ibid.*, p. 22.
[2] *Ibid.*, p. 117.
[3] *Ibid.*, p. 205.

as "one of the most brilliant Marxist works on military science in the world Communist movement." [1]

On Practice, July 1937. Originally delivered as a lecture at the Anti-Japanese Military and Political College in Yenan, this article was designed to expose doctrinaire subjectivism which belittles practice. According to Mao, this incorrect conception caused considerable setbacks to the Communist revolution in 1931–34. Declaring that Marxism is not a dogma but a guide to action, Mao explained the inter-relationship between knowledge and practice:

> To discover truth through practice, and through practice to verify and develop truth. To start from perceptual knowledge and actively develop it into rational knowledge, actively direct revolutionary practice so as to remold the subjective and objective world... Such is the whole of the dialectical materialist theory of the unity of knowing and doing.[2]

On Contradiction, August 1937. This companion piece to *On Practice* was a speech made at the Anti-Japanese Military and Political College in Yenan. Mao has since made certain additions, deletions, and revisions. Combatting the doctrinairism existing within the Communist Party at that time, Mao expounded the theory of the universality of contradiction, the basic law of nature and society. "All contradictory things are interconnected," Mao asserted, "and they do not only co-exist in an entity under certain conditions, but also transform themselves into each other under certain conditions." This is Mao's conception of the identity of contradictions. "Antagonism is a form of struggle within contradiction," according to Mao, "but not the universal form." In his application of this formula to China, Mao promised that "the old semi-colonial and semi-feudal society will change into a new, democratic society." [3]

On Protracted War, May–June 1938. This is a series of lectures delivered at the Association for the Study of the Anti-Japanese War in Yenan from May 26 to June 3, 1938. Mao stated that the war with Japan would be a protracted war through three stages: first, the strategic offensive of the enemy and China's strategic defensive; second, the strategic defensive of the enemy and China's preparation of strategic counter-offensive; and third, the enemy's retreat as a result of China's conter-offensive.[4] He discussed at length mobile warfare, guerrilla warfare, and positional warfare. This is perhaps the most

---

[1] Hu Chao-mu, *Thirty Years of the Communist Party of China**, p. 49.
[2] *Mao Tse-tung: Selected Works*, Vol. I, p. 297.
[3] *Ibid.*, Vol. II, pp. 39, 45, 49.
[4] See *ibid.*, pp. 183–184.

famous piece of Mao's works on military subjects, which include *Strategic Problems of China's Revolutionary War* (December 1936), *Strategic Problems in the Anti-Japanese Guerrilla War* (May 1938), and *Problems of War and Strategy* (November 1938). It is due to these writings and eventual victory in China's civil war that Mao has been claimed by his followers as one of the greatest military strategists in the world.

The Chinese Revolution and the Chinese Communist Party, December 1939. Prepared as a textbook for the party members and masses, this unfinished work is composed of three chapters: the first, on the "Chinese Society," originally drafted by one of his followers but revised by Mao; the second, on the "Chinese Revolution," written by Mao himself; and third, on the "Party Building," never completed. In the second chapter, Mao discussed the following classes in Chinese society: (a) the landlord class, (b) the bourgeoisie, (c) various types of the petty bourgeoisie other than the peasantry, (d) the peasantry, (e) the proletariat, and (f) the vagrants, unemployed people forced to resort to illegitimate means of making a living. He concluded that the characteristics of the Chinese revolution were two-fold, the bourgeois-democratic and proletarian-socialist at both the present and future stages.[1]

On the New Democracy, January 1940. In this work, Mao amplified his views on the Chinese revolution as put forth in his previous book, *The Chinese Revolution and the Chinese Communist Party*. Explaining the difference in character between the two steps of revolution, democratic and socialist, Mao emphatically stated that the type of democracy under discussion is a New Democracy. He warned that China "can only proceed from one revolution to the other, and that there is no such thing as accomplishing both at one stroke." His conception is that "only a government of democratic centralism can fully express the will of all the revolutionary people and most powerfully fight the enemies of the revolution." Like Dr. Sun Yat-sen's "principle of people's livelihood," Mao advocated the development of China's economy along the path of "control of capital" and "equalization of landownership." However, in the judgment of Mao, the Communists have a revolutionary thoroughness not shared by the bourgeoisie. Mao has the firm conviction that the state of New Democracy under the leadership of the proletariat class would lead ultimately to socialism.[2]

[1] See *ibid.*, Vol. III, p. 100.
[2] Mao's theory was well elaborated by Kuan Ta-tung in his book under the title of *The Socialism Transformation of Capitalist Industry and Commerce in China** (Peking: Foreign Languages Press, 1960).

With this final goal in mind, Mao urged the Communist Party to adopt political, economic, and cultural programs on the basis of the spirit of New Democracy, which is neither capitalist nor socialist.[1] The publication of this book helped unify the ideology and policy of the Communist Party at that time.

On Coalition Government, April 1945. A report made at the Seventh National Congress on April 24, 1945, this work first deals with the international and domestic situation as well as the relationship between the Communist and Nationalist Parties *vis-a-vis* the armed invasion of Japan and then analyzes the general and specific programs for the solution of China's problems. As a prerequisite for all necessary reforms, Mao proposed the abolition of the Nationalist one-party dictatorship and the adoption of the following two steps: "first, at the present stage, to form a provisional coalition government by common agreement of the representatives of all parties and people without party affiliation; secondly, at the next stage, through free and unrestricted elections, to convene a national assembly which will form a proper coalition government." [2]

The Present Situation and Our Tasks, December 1947. This report was presented by Mao to a Central Committee meeting of the Communist Party on December 25, 1947. It analyzed the military and economic problems and also various questions relating to the united front. Mao reiterated the importance of thorough reform of the land system and the protection of the middle and petty bourgeois elements. According to his analysis, the new democratic national economy consists of three parts: "(1) the state-owned economy, which is the leading sector; (2) the agricultural economy, developing step by step from individual to collective; and (3) the economy of small independent craftsmen and traders and the economy of small and middle private capital." [3] In this connection, Mao criticized the excessive "left" policy within the Party toward the third category of the economy.

On People's Democratic Dictatorship, July 1949. This article was written in commemoration of the twenty-eighth anniversary of the Chinese Communist Party on July 1, 1949, when the Communist victory was already in sight. Mao attempted to lay down some basic principles on which the Central People's Government would be based. He unequivocally advocated democratic dictatorship by the working

[1] *Mao Tse-tung: Selected Works*, Vol. III, pp. 109, 121, 122, 130, 133.
[2] *Ibid.*, Vol. IV, p. 285.
[3] *Selected Works of Mao Tse-tung*, Vol. IV, p. 169.

class in alliance with the peasantry and urban petty bourgeoisie. During the transitional stage, he deemed it necessary to allow the existence of national bourgeoisie and of capitalism under strict regulation.

In a state under democratic dictatorship, only the "people," not the reactionaries, have the right to speak. In Mao's opinion, the "people" are only limited to the above classes. Led by the working class and the Communist Party, they would unite to form their own state and elect their own government. With regard to his foreign policy, Mao held that China should lean to the side of socialism, opposite to that of capitalistic "imperialism." "In order to win victory and consolidate it," he declared, "we must lean to one side" because "sitting on the fence will not do, nor is there a third road." [1] Mao's domestic and foreign policies as stated above were officially adopted in the Common Program, which was, in effect, the provisional constitution of the People's Republic for the period 1949–1954.

Mao's creation of a Chinese form of Marxism

In addition to the works described above, Mao wrote many other articles concerning economy and finance, art and literature, party and politics, and the united front. While chiefly following the Marxist-Leninist principles, his political thought and strategy are specially adaptable to the changing circumstances in China. Perhaps some degree of flexibility is essential to the success of any revolutionary practitioner. It is only through a realistic approach to the existing situation that domestic and international problems can be solved. Among the various evaluations of Mao's political thought, Liu Shao-ch'i has probably made a most appropriate appraisal. Having known Mao so well, Liu stated: "Mao Tse-tung's great accomplishment has been to change Marxism from a European to an Asiatic form." A renowned Marxist theoretician in his own right, Liu elaborated his views in the following words:

Marx and Lenin were Europeans; they wrote in European languages about European histories and problems, seldom Asia or China. The basic principles of Marxism are undoubtedly adaptable to all countries, but to apply their general truth to concrete revolutionary practices in China is a difficult task. Mao Tse-tung is Chinese; he analyzes Chinese problems and guides the Chinese people in their struggle to victory. He uses Marxist-Leninist principles to explain Chinese history and the practical problems of China. He is the first that has succeeded in doing so.[2]

[1] *Ibid.*, pp. 415, 417, 421.
[2] Anna Louise Strong, "The Thought of Mao Tse-t ung," *Amerasia*, June 1947, pp. 161–162.

The above remarks were made by Liu to Anna Louise Strong in Yenan in 1947. After her article was written on the basis of her several all-day interviews with Yenan theoreticians, it was translated back into Chinese and corrected in great detail. Thus there should be no question about the authenticity and accuracy of Liu's statement. According to Liu, Mao Tse-tung made a number of "inventions and discoveries." Among these are the role of peasants and Red Army in the revolution, the strong organization and correct guidance of the Chinese Communist Party, the united front among classes, and the new military strategy and supply system. Emphasizing the special conditions in China, Liu made the following conclusive statement on Mao's contributions to the world Communist movement:

> On every kind of problem – the nation, the peasants, strategy, the construction of the party, literature and culture, military affairs, finance and economy, methods of work, philosophy – Mao has not only applied Marxism to new conditions but has given it a new development. He has created a Chinese or Asiatic form of Marxism.[1]

The views on Mao's political thought and strategy by Communist theoreticians or neutral scholars would probably not be shared by the Nationalists or other anti-Communist commentators. Like other political leaders, Mao is not immune from making mistakes. On account of his unsuccessful role in the Autumn Harvest Uprising in Hunan, he was condemned by the Politburo of the Communist Party in November 1927. Today Mao is acclaimed as one of the greatest leaders in the world because of the Communist victory and his predominance on the Mainland. In the political arena, nothing is more successful than success itself, the dislike of the opposition notwithstanding. Events in China will eventually prove whether Mao's political thought and strategy will withstand international and domestic storms.

3. THE CONSTITUTION OF THE CHINESE COMMUNIST PARTY AND ITS GUIDING PRINCIPLES

The rapid development of the Party and its Constitution of 1956

With the victory of the Red Army in 1949, the Communist Party of China has finally become the actual ruler on the Mainland. The guiding principles of the Party are Marxism, Leninism, and Maoism.

---

[1] *Ibid.*, p. 162. For a selected list of reference to the published works and statements attributed to Mao Tse-tung, consult *Mao Tse-tung: Published Works* (External Research Paper 138, April 1962), prepared by the External Research Division of the Department of State.

As the government at every level is controlled and operated by the party personnel, a study of the Party Constitution and organization is necessary in order to have a clear understanding of Chinese Communism in practice.

When the Sino-Japanese war broke out in 1937, the Communist Party had approximately 40,000 members. The party membership grew rapidly with the expansion of the Communist-controlled areas during the war. It reached 1,210,000 when the Party held the Seventh National Congress and adopted the Constitution on June 11, 1945. After taking over the Mainland, the Party carried out its recruitment program with such an intensity that it could claim a total membership of 10,734,000 in June 1956. As the position of the Communist Party turned from an opposition organization in 1945 to a ruling party in 1956, the 1945 Party Constitution was no longer adaptable. Hence its Eighth National Congress adopted a new constitution on September 26, 1956, which is still the fundamental law of the Communist Party of China today.[1]

The guiding principles of the Party Constitution

The Party Constitution declares that, as the vanguard of the Chinese working class and the highest form of its class organization, the Communist Party aims at the achievement of socialism and communism in China. Against all doctrinaire or empiricist deviations, the Party is to integrate Marxism-Leninism with the revolutionary experience in China. Strictly following the political thought and strategy dictated by Mao Tse-tung, the Party stresses the necessity of the gradual ownership into collective ownership by the working masses. At the same time, the Constitution provides that every step has to be taken to consolidate the system of democratic dictatorship as discussed in Mao's *On People's Democratic Dictatorship*.

Externally, the Party is in favor of world peace and temporary coexistence between countries with different systems.[2] Such Communist terminology is, of course, subject to different interpretations depending upon the circumstances. The Party definitely supports the struggle of world communism, as expressed in the slogan, "Proletar-

---

[1] Its English text can be found in Albert P. Blaustein, *op. cit.*, pp. 55–95; Peter S. H. Tang, *Communist China Today*, Vol. II, pp. 112–133. For the English text of the 1945 Constitution, see *ibid.*, pp. 70–88.

[2] For an analysis of China's attitude toward co-existence, see A. M. Halpern, "Communist China and Peaceful Co-existence," *The China Quarterly*, July-September, 1960, No. 3, pp. 16–31.

ians of all lands, unite!" The fundamental foreign policy of the Chinese Communist Party is generally to strengthen the friendship with all socialist countries.

The organizational principle of the Party is democratic centralism, which becomes the guiding rule of the state structure. Democratic centralism demands that every party organization and the members are to abide strictly by the principle of collective leadership coupled with individual responsibility and should be subject to party supervision from above and from below. The Constitution emphasizes that democracy within the Party is not to be separated from centralism and strong discipline is to be enforced on all its members.

In order to secure solidarity and unity within the Party, no action in violation of its political line or organizational principles is permissible. The Party forbids its members to carry on any activity or factional movement aimed at splitting the Party, to act independently of the Party, or to place the individual above the collective body of the Party. Recognizing that no political organization or individual person can be free from committing mistakes, the Party directs its members to practice criticism and self-criticism for the purpose of exposing and correcting shortcomings. It is imperative for the Party members to prevent and resist corrosion by bourgeois and petty-bourgeois ways of thinking and styles of work, and guard against any "rightist" or "leftist" opportunist deviation within the Party. Any member who persists in his mistakes will be subject to severe punishment, including expulsion from the Party,[1] which, in a Communist country, amounts to a political death sentence.

4. THE ORGANIZATION AND FUNCTIONS OF THE COMMUNIST PARTY

National party organizations

As stated before, the Communist Party of China is formed on the principle of democratic centralism, which means centralism on the basis of democracy and democracy under centralized guidance. The highest organ of the Party is the National Party Congress, and that of each local organization is the local party congress. The National Party Congress, elected for a term of five years, meets once a year under ordinary circumstances. The Central Committee of the Party, elected

[1] For further details, see the General Program of *The Constitution of the Communist Party of China*, 1956.

by the National Party Congress for the same term, directs the entire work of the Party when the Congress is not in session.

The Party Constitution lays down a most important provision governing the relationship between the Party and the Government: "The Central Committee guides the work of the central state organs and people's organizations of a national character through leading Party members' groups within them." [1] The Party exercises strict control over the Army, which has always been the pivotal force of Chinese politics. The Party organizations in the "Chinese People's Liberation Army" carry on their work in accordance with the instructions of the Central Committee.

The organization and actual functioning of the Party hierarchy is prescribed by the Constitution in the following manner. The Central Committee elects at its plenary session the Political Bureau, the Standing Committee of the Political Bureau, and the Secretariat, as well as the Chairman, Vice-Chairmen, and the Secretary-General of the Central Committee. The Plenary Session of the Central Committee is convened at least twice a year by the Political Bureau, which together with its Standing Committee exercise the powers and functions of the Central Committee when the latter is not in session. The Secretariat takes charge of the routine work of the Central Committee under the direction of the Political Bureau and its Standing Committee. The Chairman and Vice-Chairmen of the Central Committee are concurrently Chairman and Vice-Chairmen of the Political Bureau. The Constitution further provides that the Central Committee may, at its discretion, create an office of honorary Chairman.[2] No reason was given for this provision. It is speculated that the Party may wish to confer this honor upon and utilize the prestige of the present Chairman when he reaches the age of retirement.

Local party organizations

The local party congresses, convened once a year, elect their respective local party committees. The party congress or committee for an area above the district *(hsien* or county) level is elected for a term of three years; and that at lower levels, for a term of two years. The local party committee meets at least three or four times a year depending upon the area level. Party election units and procedures are prescribed in separate regulations. When a local party congress is not

---

[1] *The Constitution of the Communist Party of China*, 1956, Art. 34.
[2] Arts. 31-37.

in session, a higher party committee may transfer or appoint responsible members of a lower party organization.[1]

Primary party organizations

The basic unit of the Communist Party is the primary party organization, which is formed in factories, mines, and other enterprises, in villages *(hsiang)*, in townships *(chen)*, in agricultural producers' cooperatives, in offices, schools, and dwelling blocks, in companies of the "People's Liberation Army," and in other units where there are three or more full party members. The leading body of the primary party organization is its meeting of delegates or of the general membership meeting. When such a meeting is not in session, its elected committee is to perform its duties.

The primary party organizations have various functions, including the following: (1) to carry on propaganda and organizational work among the masses and put into practice party decisions; (2) to lead the masses to take an active part in the political life of the country and to report their sentiments and demands to higher party organizations; (3) to recruit new party members, to collect membership dues, to examine and appraise party members, and to maintain party discipline among them; and (4) to organize party members to study Marxism-Leninism as well as party policies and experience, and to promote criticism and self-criticism among themselves.

In public institutions and organizations, the primary units are to supervise ideologically and politically all party members, including those in leading administrative posts. The basic party units are obliged to take a constant interest in supervising the work in their respective units, strengthen labor discipline, combat bureaucracy, and report any shortcomings to the administrative chiefs of the given units and to higher party organizations. Primary party organizations in the enterprises, villages, schools, and army units are to guide and supervise the administrative bodies and mass organizations in their respective units in the fulfillment of the decisions of higher party organizations and state organs and in improving their work.[2]

Leading party members' groups

The leading party members' group is formed in the leading body of a state organ or non-party organization where there are three or more

---

[1] Arts. 38–46.
[2] Arts. 21, 48, 49.

party members holding responsible posts. Under the direction of the competent party committee, such a group performs the following functions: (1) to assume the responsibility of carrying out party policy and decisions, (2) to fortify unity with non-party cadres, (3) to cement the ties with the masses, (4) to strengthen party and state discipline, and (5) to combat bureaucracy.[1] It is evident that the Party carries out its activities anywhere and everywhere. Through the ceaseless efforts of these groups, the Party can be in the position to dominate and control all the state organs and non-party organizations.

Control organs of the party

The central and local committees of the Party are to elect, at their plenary sessions, central and local control commissions at their respective levels; but the election of local control commissions is subject to the approval of the higher party committees. Higher control commissions have the power to check up on the work of lower control commissions, and to approve or modify their decisions. Lower control commissions are required to report on their work to higher control commissions and present accurate reports on the violation of discipline by party members.

Under the direction of the party committees at corresponding levels, the central and local commissions perform the following functions: (1) to examine and deal with cases of violations of the Party Constitution, party discipline, Communist ethics, and state laws and decrees on the part of party members; (2) to decide on or cancel disciplinary measures against party members; and (3) to deal with appeals and complaints from party members.[2] It is noteworthy that the control commissions are not on an equal basis but subject to the direction of the party committees at the same levels.

5. THE COMMUNIST YOUTH LEAGUE

The relationship between the Party and the League

The Communist Youth League is the Party's subsidiary organization. It was formerly known as the "New Democratic Youth League," which decided to adopt the present name at its Representative Congress in May 1957.[3] A new League Constitution was adopted on May 24, on the

[1] Arts. 59, 60.

[2] Arts. 52–54.

[3] The New Democratic Youth League was originated in 1946 and carried out its activities in various " liberated areas." It was not, however, until the summer of 1949 that a national

basis of the revised Constitution of the New Democratic Youth League of 1953. Any person between fourteen and twenty-five may apply for membership in the League, while the minimum age required for Party membership is eighteen. Members of the League have to withdraw when they are admitted to full Party membership if they do not hold positions in the League.

The Central Committee of the Communist Youth League accepts the leadership of the Party's Central Committee. The League's local organizations are simultaneously under the leadership of the Party organizations at the corresponding levels and of higher League organizations. In their relations with the League organizations, the Party committees at all levels are to perform the following functions: (1) to encourage and assist the League's ideological and organizational work, (2) to guide the League in imbuing all its members with the Communist spirit and educating them in Marxist-Leninist theory, (3) to insure the League's close contact with the broad masses of young people, and (4) to pay constant attention to selecting members for the positions of leadership in the League.[1]

The functions of the League

The League has rendered effective assistance to the Party in publicizing and carrying out party policies and decisions, in promoting production, and in exposing and correcting shortcomings and mistakes in work.[2] In order to gain control of the minds of the youngsters between nine to fifteen years of age through various phases of training, the League set up "Pioneers" headquarters in schools, streets, and villages. Under the direct control and supervision of League organizations, the "Pioneers" are organized into teams, platoons, squadrons, and detachments. With these auxiliary organizations, the Communist Party is able to control not only the adults but also the children. This is characteristic of the thoroughness of the Communist organizational policy.

---

congress of the League was scheduled. Similar organizations as the Party's subsidiaries were formed in early years, for example, the Chinese Socialist Youth Corps in 1920–25 and the Chinese Communist Youth Corps in the following years. During the period of the Sino-Japanese war, a variety of organizations serving the same purpose existed.

[1] Arts. 55, 57, 58.
[2] Art. 56.

6. THE COMMUNIST RELATIONSHIP
WITH MINOR POLITICAL PARTIES AND MASS ORGANIZATIONS

The coexistence between the Communist and other political parties

During the period of transition, Mao Tse-tung repeatedly enunciated the necessity of Communist cooperation with non-Communist political parties, social groups, and democratic individuals. *The Constitution of the People's Republic of China* of 1954 declares that "in the course of the great struggle to establish the People's Republic of China, the people of our country forged a broad people's democratic united front, composed of all democratic classes, democratic parties and groups, and popular organizations, and led by the Communist Party of China." [1] The important point is that these parties and groups must be "democratic" and led by the Communist Party. The implied meaning of the word, "democratic," is too evident to be elaborated. This policy was re-affirmed by the Party Constitution of 1956 in the following words: "The Party must work in every way to fortify the fraternal alliance of workers and peasants, to consolidate the united front of all patriotic forces and to strengthen its lasting cooperation with the other demo-cratic parties as well as democrats without party affiliations." [2]

The minor parties are expected to help the Communists solicit the support of all segments of the society and build up a socialist state. Such a hope is clearly expressed in the Preamble of the 1954 Consti-tution: "This people's democratic united front will continue to play its part in mobilizing and rallying the whole people in common struggle to fulfill the fundamental task of the state during the transition and to oppose enemies within and without." [3] This united front with non-Communist parties and groups has suited the purpose of the Communist Party. They took an active part in the Chinese People's Political Consultative Conference (CPPCC) to create the Central People's Government and adopt the Common Program as provisional consti-tution for the period of 1949–1954. At the First National People's Congress in 1954, they again fulfilled their mission of legalizing the Communist state institutions by passing *The Constitution of the People's Republic of China* and other fundamental laws for "democratic dictator-ship."

The following is a list of the non-Communist parties, which were

---

[1] Preamble of the Constitution of 1954. See Liu Shao-ch'i, *Report of the Draft Constitution**, p. 70.

[2] General Program of the Party Constitution of 1956. See Albert P.Blaustein, *op.cit.*, p. 58.

[3] Liu Shao-ch'i, *op. cit.*, p. 70.

represented at the 1949 Plenary Session of the Chinese People's Political Consultative Conference, the constituent body of the People's Republic of China:

(1) The Revolutionary Committee of the Kuomintang, which was organized in 1948 by the Nationalist dissidents, with Li Chi-tsen as Chairman;

(2) China (or Chinese) Democratic League, which, as previously described,[1] had become a close ally of the Communists by the end of the Sino-Japanese war, with Shen Chun-ju as Chairman;[2]

(3) China Democratic National Construction Association, which was formed in 1945 by people in industrial, commercial, and educational fields, with Huang Yen-p'ei as Chairman;

(4) China Association for Promoting Democracy, which was founded in Shanghai in 1945 by people in cultural and publishing circles, with Ma Hsu-lun as Chairman;

(5) Peasants and Workers' Democratic Party, which, as mentioned before,[3] was known as the Liberation Action Committee of the Chinese People during the war and which adopted its present name in 1947, with Chang Pai-chun as Chairman;

(6) China Chih Kung Tang, which came into being in San Francisco in 1925 as a result of the reorganization of the Hung Men Chih Kung Tang;[4]

(7) Chiu San Society (September Third Society), which was organized in 1944 by a group of intellectuals in Chungking as the Democracy and Science Forum and adopted its present name in commemoration of V-J Day, September 3, 1945, with Hsü Teh-heng as Chairman;

(8) Taiwan Democratic Self-Government League, which was formed in 1947 by a group of Taiwanese on the Mainland, with Hsieh Hsueh-hung as Chairman.

While there have been changes of leadership in the above non-Communist parties due to natural death and internal shake-ups, they are still permitted to coexist with the Communist Party. They have not only availed themselves of the opportunity to display the broad basis of the present regime, but also have contributed in propagating Communist principles and policies among their members and partici-

---

[1] Ch. VIII, Sec. 3.
[2] Shen became Chairman after the death of his predecessor, Chang Lan.
[3] Ch. VIII, Sec. 3.
[4] This organization was established at the end of the Taiping Revolution during the middle of the nineteenth century for the purpose of overthrowing the Ch'ing and restoring the Ming dynasty.

pating in Communist programs for national reconstruction. Nevertheless, the political life of these parties still depends upon their constant and unreserved cooperation with the Communist Party. This condition was illustrated by the rectification campaign in 1957–1958. Due to their independant expression of views, many leaders of the minor parties were denounced and removed from their posts.[1]

On the other hand, the Communists have generously provided honorary high-ranking positions for the leaders of the minor parties who are willing to work whole-heartedly for the regime. The mere existence of minor parties with little independence can hardly demonstrate the true spirit of democracy according to Western standards. It is, however, a unique phenomenon in a Communist country to permit the activities of other political parties, the underlying motives of the Communist Party notwithstanding.

The Communist relationship with mass organizations

The mass is the life line of the Communist Party. The expansion of Communist power before 1949 was due to the rapid growth of mass organizations, which were created or directed by the Party. The close relationship between the Party and the mass is no less important today than before. Mao Tse-tung and other leaders have paid the greatest attention to the mass line in party work. The Party Constitution reaffirms the importance of this relationship in the most emphatic manner:

> Whether the Party is able to continue to give correct leadership depends on whether or not the Party will, through analysis and synthesis, systematically summarize the experience and opinions of the masses, turn the resulting ideas into the policy of the Party and then, as a result of the Party's propaganda and organizational work among the masses, transform it into the views and action of the masses themselves, testing the correctness of Party policy, and supplementing and revising it in the course of mass activity. It is the duty of the Party leadership to ensure that in the endless repetition of this process of "coming from the masses and going back to the masses" the Party members' level of understanding and that of the masses of the people are continually raised and the cause of the Party and the people is constantly advanced.[2]

Through the operation of the basic party units with the assistance of state organs, no mass organization is free from Communist penetration and no mass is not organized by the Communists. Workers, peasants, students, women, artists, and other people in various professions all belong to one organization or another. Indoctrination through organi-

---

[1] For further details, see Peter S. H. Tang, op. cit., Vol. I, pp. 177–183.
[2] General Program of the Party Constitution of 1956. See Albert P. Blaustein, op. cit., p. 59.

zation and organization for indoctrination are the characteristics of the Party's mass policy. As the future of the Communist regime depends much on the masses, the Party urges the members to "maintain close and extensive ties with the workers, peasants, intellectuals, and other patriots and strive constantly to make such ties ever stronger and more widespread."[2]

---

[1] *Loc. cit.*

FUNDAMENTAL LAWS OF THE PEOPLE'S REPUBLIC: FROM THE COMMON PROGRAM TO THE CONSTITUTION OF 1954

I. THE CHINESE PEOPLE'S POLITICAL CONSULTATIVE CONFERENCE (CPPCC)

The convocation of the CPPCC

The Chinese People's Political Consultative Conference (CPPCC), held in Peking from September 21 to 30, 1949, served as a constituent body of the People's Republic for the creation of the Central People's Government and the enactment of the Common Program. This Common Program and other fundamental laws adopted by the Conference constituted, in effect, a provisional constitution during the transitional period of 1949–1954. The CPPCC was claimed by the Communists to be "the organization of the democratic united front of the entire Chinese people," composed of "all democratic classes and all nationalities throughout China," for the establishment of "the unity of all democratic parties and groups and people's organizations."

The purpose of the Conference was to enable the Chinese people "to put forward their combined efforts in carrying out New Democracy, opposing imperialism, feudalism and bureaucratic capitalism, overthrowing the reactionary rule of the Kuomintang, eliminating open and secret remnant counter-revolutionary forces." [1] Theoretically the CPPCC was to be the supreme national organ of state authority prior to the convocation of the First National People's Congress, but actually it exercised only constituent and electoral powers.

The CPPCC was represented by delegates from all political parties, groups, and organizations which expressed their willingness to cooperate with the Communists. The First Plenary Session of the CPPCC had 585

---

[1] Art. 1 of the *Organic Law of the Chinese People's Political Consultative Conference*, September 29, 1949. Its English text can be found in Albert P. Blaustein, *Fundamental Legal Documents of Communist China*, pp. 96–103.

delegates and 77 alternates. The minor political parties and. groups were assigned 5 or 6 delegates each. Besides the party delegates, there were 206 from mass organizations, 60 from the armed forces, 102 from political and administrative organs, and 75 specially invited individuals. No matter how broad its nature of representation might be, the Conference was completely controlled by the Communist Party.

All the participating units and delegates were obligated to abide by and carry out all the resolutions passed by the plenary session of the Conference and also those of its National Committee adopted during the recess of the Conference. Once decisions were reached by a majority vote, the dissenting delegates would either reserve their opinions for further discussion at the next session or withdraw from the Conference. Otherwise, disciplinary measures could be taken by the Conference or its National Committee against the delegate or unit concerned in the form of a warning, replacing the delegate, or cancelling the right of representation of that unit. Theoretically the unit or delegate concerned could appeal to the next session in the event of any disagreement with the disciplinary measures, but it is doubtful whether such an appeal would have been effective.[1]

Functions of the Plenary Session and the National Committee of the CPPCC

According to the *Organic Law of the CPPCC*, the plenary session was to be convened once every three years by the National Committee of the CPPCC; but the first plenary session was summoned by the Preparatory Committee of the CPPCC. The powers and functions of the plenary sessions were the following:

(1) to enact or amend the Common Program and the Organic Law of the CPPCC;

(2) to perform the functions of the National People's Congress prior to its convocation, including the enactment or amendment of the Organic Law of the Central People's Government of the People's Republic and the election of the Central People's Government Council for the exercise of state authority;

(3) to submit proposals on fundamental policies and on important measures relating to national reconstruction work to the Central People's Government and to the National People's Congress whenever convened; and

(4) to elect members of the National Committee of the CPPCC.[2]

[1] See the *Organic Law of the CPPCC*, Arts. 4, 5.
[2] Arts. 6, 7.

The number of members and alternates of the National Committee was to be decided by each plenary session and their election would be held before the session's recess. Between plenary sessions, the National Committee was to exercise the following functions:

(1) to ensure the implementation of the resolutions of the plenary session and of the National Committee of the CPPCC;

(2) to discuss and submit proposals to the Central People's Government;

(3) to assist the Government in mobilizing the people to participate in the work of the revolution and reconstruction;

(4) to discuss and submit the list of candidates of units participating in the CPPCC for the election of representatives to the National People's Congress;

(5) to discuss and determine the units, number, and choice of delegates to the next plenary session of the CPPCC and to convene it; and

(6) to direct the work of local united fronts and deal with other matters concerning the internal cooperation of the CPPCC.[1]

The organization of the CPPCC

The Plenary Session – A quorum of the plenary session required the presence of a majority of the members and a resolution was to be adopted by a vote of more than one half of the members present and voting. Each plenary session was to elect a presidium and a secretary-general. Various committees might be organized at each session to dispose of specific matters. The rules of procedure of each session were to be worked out by the presidium. Mao Tse-tung, Liu Shao-ch'i, Chou En-lai, and other Communist leaders paid serious attention to the plenary session of the CPPCC and delivered detailed speeches and reports in person.

The National Committee – The National Committee was to meet once every six months, convened by its Standing Committee. For the disposal of routine matters, the National Committee had a secretariat with a secretary-general at its head. Elected from among the National Committee members, the Standing Committee consisted of a Chairman, and a number of Vice-Chairmen to conduct Committee affairs.

The local committees – Local committees of the CPPCC were to be set up in major cities, provincial capitals, and other important areas at the discretion of the National Committee and in accordance with their

---

[1] *Ibid.*, Arts. 13, 14.

organic regulations. Local committees served as organs for consultation and for ensuring the implementation of resolutions previously adopted.[1]

The change of role of the CPPCC

The first plenary session of the CPPCC elected its First National Committee, which, in turn, chose Mao Tse-tung as Chairman and Chou En-lai, Li Chi-tsen, Shen Chun-ju Kuo Mo-jo, and Ch'en Shu-tung as Vice Chairmen. This National Committee served as the temporary National People's Congress for almost five years. When the First National People's Congress was convened in September 1954, the nature of the CPPCC was changed from an organ of state power to a consultative body.

Before its dissolution, the First National Committee selected members of the Second CPPCC, which met on December 21–25, 1954. Represented by the leaders from different political affiliations, the Second National Committee elected Mao Honorary Chairman, Chou En-lai Chairman, and 16 Vice-Chairmen. The Vice-Chairmen, who were chosen from both Communist and non-Communist parties, included Soong Ching-ling, Tung Pi-wu, Li Chi-tsen, Kuo Mo-jo, Shen Chun-ju, and Li Sze-kuang. The Second National Committee adopted new regulations for the CPPCC, which laid down the following as its main tasks:

(1) to solve social problems among different classes through cooperation with the Government;

(2) to solve, by thorough consultation, problems affecting cooperation within the CPPCC or between any of the different parties, groups, and organizations affiliated to it;

(3) to exchange views on international problems, and on the nomination of candidates to the National People's Congress and local people's congresses, as well as of members of the CPPCC at all levels; and

(4) to make arrangements for members to study Marxism-Leninism and to remold outworn ways of thinking.

With its functions limited as above, the CPPCC continues to carry out its activities. As a liason office of the different political parties, groups, and organizations, the CPPCC has served a useful purpose for the Communist regime.

---

[1] For further details of the organization of the CPPCC, see Arts. 8–20.

2. THE COMMON PROGRAM OF 1949
IN THE NATURE OF A PROVISIONAL CONSTITUTION

Fundamental laws for the transitional period

Prior to the adoption of the *Constitution of the People's Republic of China* on September 20, 1954, the Communist regime in Peking was established and governed by three fundamental laws: the *Common Program of the CPPCC*, the *Organic Law of the CPPCC*, and the *Organic Law of the Central People's Government*.[1] These three laws, all adopted by the first plenary session of the CPPCC on September 29, 1949, laid down the legal foundation of the People's Republic. Jointly they served the purpose of a provisional constitution for the period of 1949–1954. The organization and functions of the CPPCC have already been described and those of the Central People's Government will be analyzed in the succeeding sections. The present analysis will concentrate on the Common Program.

Basic principles of the Common Program

The Common Program emphatically declared that the Chinese People's democratic dictatorship was to be the political foundation for national reconstruction. Such a democratic dictatorship was based on the state power of the people's democratic united front, composed of the working class, peasantry, petty bourgeoisie, national bourgeoisie, and "other patriotic democratic elements." Although this united front was an alliance of workers and peasants as well as other classes, the working class was destined to be the guiding spirit to lead the people "for independence, democracy, peace, unity, prosperity and strength of China." [2]

According to the Common Program, the ultimate aim of the state was to "transform the feudal and semi-feudal land ownership system into a peasant land ownership" and to "develop the people's economy of New Democracy" from an agricultural into an industrial one. During the transitional period, certain measures had to be taken, such as the confiscation of bureaucratic capital, protection of public property of the state and of the cooperatives, and safeguarding the economic interests and private property of workers, peasants, the petty bourgeoisie, and the national bourgeoisie.[3] The *Organic Law of the*

---

[1] Their English texts can be found in Albert P. Blaustein, *op. cit.*, pp. 34–53, 96–103, and 104–114 respectively.

[2] *The Common Program of the CPPCC*, Art. 1.

[3] *Ibid.*, Art. 3.

Central People's Government of 1949 had similar provisions in this respect.[1] It is evident that the economic system as provided in the Common Program was not strict socialism, because the Communists realized that a transitional period was necessary however short it might be.

Rights and duties of the people

The Common Program literally granted the people not only the freedom of thought, speech, publication, assembly, association, correspondence, person, domicile, change of domicile, and religious belief, but also the freedom to hold processions and demonstrations. Even though there was no provision concerning restrictions of such freedoms in accordance with law, later events confirmed that people's freedom could only be exercised within the limit of the Communist standard. Provisions concerning equal rights and duties were extended to women and national minorities. The right to elect and to be elected and to bring complaints against government organs or public functionaries was not universally applicable to all the people. Such a right could only be enjoyed by those approved by the Communist regime.[2]

In a state under "democratic dictatorship," only those who would cooperate with the Communists could be entitled to the above freedoms and rights. Thus feudal landlords, bureaucratic capitalists, and "reactionary elements in general" would be deprived of their political rights for a necessary period. These undesirable people would be given some means of livelihood, but would also be compelled to reform themselves through labor. If re-education and forced labor should produce no result, they would be severely punished. Here the term "reactionary elements in general" would probably include the former members of the Nationalist Party and any others who have not been friendly to the Communists.[3]

Under the provisions of the Common Program, every Chinese national had the duty "to defend the fatherland, to abide by the law, to observe labor discipline, to protect public property, to perform public and millitary service, and to pay taxes." [4] At the time of the drafting of the Common Program, private ownership was still permitted to a certain extent. For this reason, taxation was imposed on personal income and property. In addition to the above duties, people under

---

[1] Art. 1 of the *Organic Law of the Central People's Government.*
[2] See the *Common Program*, Arts. 3–6, 19.
[3] *Ibid.*, Art. 7.
[4] Art. 8.

"democratic dictatorship" were required to observe "a revolutionary working-style, embodying honesty, simplicity and service to the people." Thus any corruption, extravagance, and "the bureaucratic working-style" would be severely punished. By means of these requirements, Communist standards would be enforced on the people in every phase of life.[1] It was deemed necessary to abolish all the laws, decrees, and judicial systems of the Nationalist regime and replace them with new ones for the purpose of "protecting the people."

Economic policy

The Common Program paid special attention to economic policy and also devoted some space to the military, educational, cultural, and minority fields. The basic economic policy was to coordinate and regulate all economic activities so that they could, under the leadership of the state-owned economy, contribute in promoting the development of social economy as a whole. The following were to be under state coordination and regulation: state-owned economy, cooperative economy, the individual economy of peasants and handicraftsmen, private capitalist economy, and state capitalist economy. Emphasis was laid on their spheres of operations, supply of raw materials, marketing, labor conditions, technical equipment, policies of public and general finance. Only the state-owned economy could be considered socialist, and the cooperative economy was classified as semi-socialist.

All enterprises involving the economic life of the country and exercising a dominant influence over the people's livelihood were to be under the unified operation of the state, but the government was also to foster the development of cooperative economy by granting it preferential treatment. Supply and marketing, consumers', credit, producers', and transport cooperatives were to be organized in towns and villages; the consumers' cooperatives were to be first instituted in factories, institutions, and schools. Private economic enterprises beneficial to the national welfare and to the people's livelihood were to be encouraged. Private capital was to be directed toward state-owned enterprises and resources in the form of concessions. Thus the Common Program permitted the existence of an economy of a state-capitalist nature, jointly operated by state and private capital.

The Common Program deemed agrarian reform as the necessary condition for the development of nation's productive power and for its industrialization. In order to enforce such a reform, the "land-to-

[1] Art. 18.

the-tiller" policy had to be put into effect. As to the workers' participation in the management of production, it was only to be established in state-owned enterprises for the time being. In private-owned enterprises, collective contracts were to be signed by the trade unions, representing the workers and employees on one side and the employer on the other. Minimum wages, working hours, labor insurance, and protection of juvenile and women workers were to be prescribed. The Common Program recommended eight to ten working hours a day under the prevailing circumstances.

A general plan for economic rehabilitation was to be drawn up by the Government with special provisions concerning the division and coordination of labor between the central and local governments. Emphasis was on the development of agriculture, forestry, fisheries, and animal husbandry. Attention was also paid to the construction and repair of irrigation works for the prevention of floods and droughts.

With regard to the industrialization of the country, the Common Program considered that its central task was to be the planning, systematic rehabilitation, and development of heavy industry. Concerning the production of the textile industry and other light industries, it was to be restored and increased so as to meet the needs of the people's daily consumption. All means of communications were to be restored and improved. While all legitimate public and private trade would be protected, it was to be the responsibility of the state-owned trade organizations to adjust supply and demand, stabilize commodity prices, and assist the people's cooperatives.

Remittances from overseas Chinese, one of the important revenues of the country, was to be encouraged by all necessary means. Currency and banking were to be under the jurisdiction of the state. Any individual engaging in financial speculation and undermining the financial enterprises of the state would be severely punished. The Common Program stressed a sound and balanced budget and a simple and equitable tax system.[1]

Military policy

The national armed forces were to be under a unified command of the People's Revolutionary Military Council. An air force and a navy were to be built up in order to strengthen national defense, and a militia system was to be put into effect for the maintenance of local order. Conscription would be enforced at the appropriate time. A

[1] For details, see Arts. 26–40.

system of political training was to be set up for the purpose of educating the officers and rank and file of the armed forces. In peace time, the armed forces were to take part in agricultural and industrial production in order to facilitate national reconstruction work.[1] The participation of the soldiers in agricultural work had been practiced in China at different periods in her history. The wisdom of this system has been questioned by military experts in view of the full-time training required for a modern army.

Cultural and educational policy

The cultural and educational task was to train the people for national reconstruction work and to develop "the ideology of service to the people." With the ultimate purpose of unification of theory and practice, the Government was to reform the old educational system, subject matter, and teaching methods in a planned and systematic manner. "Revolutionary political education" was to "be accorded to both young and old-type intellectuals." Even though the freedom of press was, on principle, to be safeguarded, the Common Program stressed the importance of prohibiting the press from undermining "the interests of the state and the people." [2]

Policy toward national minorities

The Common Program emphasized equality, unity, and fraternity among the various nationalities in China.[3] Any act involving discrimination, oppression, and disunity of the national minorities would be prohibited. While equal treatment of all races was to be a cardinal principle, the national minorities were allowed to preserve their own customs, religious beliefs, dialects and languages. An appropriate number of representatives in the local political organs would be apportioned to the national minorities living in scattered places. In areas where national minorities were concentrated, regional autonomy would be exercised.[4] In the following years, the Communist Government did establish several regional autonomous areas.

Foreign policy

The Common Program declared that the Central People's Government would maintain diplomatic and commercial relations with

---

[1] Arts. 20–24.

[2] Arts. 41–49.

[3] For the number and names of the national minorities in China and their geographical distribution, see Ch. VII, Sec. 4, on self-determination of national minorities.

[4] Arts. 50–53.

friendly nations on the basis of equality and mutual benefit. The Government would re-examine all the existing treaties concluded by the Nationalist Government and foreign countries, and would recognize, abrogate, and revise them according to their contents. The Government would protect law-abiding aliens in China and the proper rights and interests of Chinese nationals residing abroad. Like the Communist Constitution of 1931, the Common Program had a special provision granting the right of asylum to foreign political refugees.[1] While this practice is in accordance with the rules of international law, the People's Republic gave it a special significance in the interest of the personal safety of international Communists for the furtherance of world revolution.

Organs of state power

The Common Program provided that the people's congresses and the people's governments on all levels were to be the organs for the exercise of state power by the people. The people's congresses, created through universal suffrage, were to elect the people's governments on the same levels, exercising the state power during the recess of the congresses. On the national level, the supreme organ of state power would be the National People's Congress and, when it was not in session, the Central People's Government. Pending the convocation of the National People's Congress, the plenary session of the CPPCC would exercise the powers and functions of the Congress, enact the organic law of the Central People's Government, and elect the Central People's Government Council. All these were acted upon as described before. The CPPCC has become a consultative body after the convocation of the National People's Congress, still reserving the right to submit proposals on fundamental policies to the Congress or to the Government.

In newly occupied areas, all-circles [2] representative conferences were to be convened to exercise the powers and functions of the local people's congresses pending the latter's establishment. The people's government of a lower level was to be under the jurisdiction of that of the upper level. While the Central People's Government was to be the highest government organ, the demarcation of power between the central and local governments was to be defined in the spirit of national unity and local expediency.

[1] Arts. 54–60.
[2] This is an official translation of the term for the local conference composed of representatives from all occupations.

The Common Program established a new judicial system, the People's Revolutionary Military Council, and the people's supervisory organs of district and municipal levels. The supervisory organs were empowered to watch the performance of the government organs and public functionaries, and to recommend disciplinary action against them in case of their violation of law or negligence of duty.[1]

3. THE CENTRAL GOVERNMENT SYSTEM, 1949–1954 [2]

Organs of the Central People's Government

According to the *Organic Law of the Central People's Government* of 1949, the People's Republic was a state of the people's democratic dictatorship and the Central People's Government was a government of the people's congress system based on the principle of democratic centralism. The highest organ of the state was the Central People's Government Council, elected by the first plenary session of the CPPCC. Under the Central People's Government Council, there were the Government Administration Council as the highest body of government administration, the People's Revolutionary Military Council as the supreme military organ, and the Supreme People's Court and the People's Procurator-General's Office as the highest judicial and supervisory bodies of the state.[3]

The power of amendment of this important Organic Law was vested in the plenary session of the CPPCC or, when it was not in session, in the Central People's Government Council. As to the interpretation of its fundamental law, it came under the jurisdiction of the Central People's Government Council.[4] The basic spirit of this Organic Law was the centralization of power in the government councils, even though the National People's Congress nominally represented the people in general in the exercise of state authority. In his work, *On Coalition Government*, Mao Tse-tung described democratic centralism as "centralized on the basis of democracy and democratic under centralized guidance." This has been and still is the characteristic of the government system in Communist China.

---

[1] Arts. 12–20.

[2] The following is an institutional description of the state organs of the Central People's Government. For the chronological development of Communist control over the Mainland during the period of 1949–1954, see Richard L. Walker, *China under Communism**, pp. 1–24.

[3] *The Organic Law of the Central People's Government* of 1949, Arts. 1–5.

[4] *Ibid.*, Art. 31.

The Central People's Government Council

The Central People's Government Council was composed of a Chairman, six Vice-Chairmen, and fifty-six Council Members, all elected by the plenary session of the CPPCC. As mentioned before, Mao Tse-tung was elected Chairman, who, as head of the state, represented Communist China in international relations. He was to preside over the Council meetings and, with the assistance of the Vice-Chairmen and a Secretary-General, to direct the work of the Council. The Secretary-General, elected by and from among the Council Members, was in charge of the Secretariat of the Council. In general, the sessions of the Council were held once every two months.[1] Resolutions were adopted by a majority vote of the members present and a quorum required more than one half of the Council members.[2]

The powers and functions of the Central People's Government Council were as follows: (1) to enact, interpret, and promulgate laws and decrees; (2) to decide on the administrative policies of the state; (3) to revise or repeal the decisions of the subordinate organs when necessary; (4) to ratify, abrogate, and revise treaties and agreements with foreign countries; (5) to deal with the vital questions of war and peace; (6) to approve and revise the state budget and financial statement; (7) to grant general amnesties and pardons; (8) to institute and award orders, medals, and titles of honor; (9) to appoint and remove high-ranking government officials; and (10) to prepare for and convene the National People's Congress.[3]

The Government Administration Council

The highest administrative organ of the state, the Government Administration Council was composed of a Premier, Vice-Premiers, a Secretary-General, and Council Members, all appointed by the Central People's Government Council. The Government Administration Council was under the direction and supervision of the Central People's Government Council and, if that body was not in session, of the Chairman of the Republic. With the assistance of the Vice-Premiers and the Secretary-General, the Premier was to direct the Council work and preside over its weekly meetings. The number of Council members required to constitute a quorum or to adopt a resolution was the same

---

[1] The schedule of the Council meetings was flexible. During the five-year period of its existence, the Council held one meeting approximately every fifty-two days.

[2] *The Organic Law of the Central People's Government*, Arts. 6, 8, 9, 10, 11.

[3] *Ibid.*, Art. 7.

as in the case of the Central People's Government Council.[1]

The Government Administration Council was to exercise the following powers and functions in accordance with the Common Program and the laws and decrees promulgated by the Central People's Government Council: (1) to enforce the execution of the provisions of the Common Program and the prevailing laws and decrees; (2) to annul or revise the decisions and orders of the subordinate organs; (3) to submit bills to the Central People's Government Council; (4) to direct and supervise the work of the subordinate organs and of the local people's governments throughout the country; and (5) to appoint or remove such Central and local government officials as prescribed by law. The decisions and orders of the Government Administration Council would come into effect when they were signed by the Premier alone or by the Premier and countersigned by the heads of the ministries or other organs of the Council as the case might be.[2]

Under the Premiership of Chou En-lai, the Government Administration Council established a large number of ministries, commissions, and other organs. Between the ministries and the Council there were, at the beginning, a number of intermediary committees. Each committee was responsible to the Government Administration Council to direct and supervise several ministries or corresponding organs of the Council. These committees were as follows:

(1) The Committee of Political and Legal Affairs, headed by Tung Pi-wu, which supervised: (a) the ministry of interior, (b) the ministry of public security, (c) the ministry of justice, (d) the commission of legislative affairs, and (e) the commission of nationalities affairs.

(2) The Committee of Financial and Economic Affairs, headed by Ch'en Yun, which supervised: (a) the ministry of finance, (b) the ministry of trade, (c) the ministry of heavy industry, (d) the ministry of textile industry, (e) the ministry of food industry, (f) the ministry of light industry, (g) the ministry of railways, (h) the ministry of posts and telecommunications, (i) the ministry of communications, (j) the ministry of agriculture, (k) the ministry of forestry and land reclamation, (l) the ministry of water conservancy, (m) the ministry of labor, (n) the people's bank, and (o) the customs administration.

(3) The Committee of Cultural and Educational Affairs, headed by Kuo Mo-jo, which supervised: (a) the ministry of cultural affairs, (b) the ministry of education, (c) the ministry of public health, (d) the

[1] Arts. 13, 14, 16, 17.
[2] Arts. 15, 17.

academy of sciences, (e) the press administration, and (f) the publications administration.

(4) The Committee of People's Control, headed by T'an P'ing-shan: different from the other committees, this committee was to supervise the execution of duties by the various government organs and public functionaries.[1]

The Members of the Government Administration Council could hold concurrently posts as heads of the committees and ministries. All of the above-mentioned organs were subject to re-organization whenever necessary and were guided by their respective organic laws and regulations.[2] In the following years, there were many changes in the organization of committees and ministries.[3] By the end of this transitional period, the intermediary committees were abolished. Thus the ministries and other organs of the corresponding rank were put under the direct control and supervision of the Premier.

The People's Revolutionary Military Council

All armed forces were put under the unified control and command of the People's Revolutionary Military Council, which was composed of a Chairman, Vice-Chairmen, and Council Members.[4] Mao Tse-tung concurrently held the position of the Chairman of the Military Council. Other important leaders appointed to the Council were Chu Teh, Chou En-lai, Liu Shao-ch'i, Kao Kang, P'eng Teh-huai, Lin Piao, and Ch'eng Ch'ien.[5]

The supreme People's Court and the People's Procurator-General's Office

The Supreme People's Court, the highest judicial body of the country, was to direct and supervise the judicial organs of all levels. It was composed of a President, Vice-Presidents, and Committee Members. As the supreme supervisory authority, the People's Procurator-General's Office was to ensure the strict observance of law by all government organs and public functionaries as well as the people in general. The Office was headed by a Procurator-General, under whom there were Deputy Procurators-General and Committee Members. The organic laws of these two bodies were enacted by the Central Govern-

---

[1] Art. 18.
[2] Arts. 13, 21, 22.
[3] See S. B. Thomas, *Government and Administration in Communist China**, p. 32.
[4] Arts. 23–25.
[5] Ch'eng, a former Nationalist general, went over to the Communists in 1949.

ment Council.[1] Shen Chun-ju and Lo Jung-huan were appointed as President of the Court and Procurator-General respectively.

The chief difficulty in the enforcement of law in Communist China was the lack of a complete legal system. After the abrogation of all the legal codes enacted by the Nationalist Government, the Central People's Government did not hasten to replace them with new ones. It took a few years before the following laws and regulations were promulgated: *Agrarian Reform Law* of 1950,[2] *Trade Union Law* of 1950, *Marriage Law* of 1950, *Labor-Capital Consultative Councils in Private Enterprise* of 1950, *Statute on Punishment for Counter-Revolutionary Activity* of 1951, *Provisional Statute on Penalties for Undermining the State Monetary System* of 1951, *Temporary Regulations of the Surveillance of Counter-Revolutionary Elements* of 1952, *Statute on Penalties for Corruption* of 1952, and several others in later years.[3] Yet there were still no complete legal codes. Thus the judges and law enforcement officials had to rely on the previous judicial practices of the Communist Party in its occupied areas and also those of Soviet Russia.

The court system during the transitional period was based on the *Provisional Regulations governing the Organization of Courts in the People's Republic of China* of 1951. According to these Regulations, a three-level court system was adopted: (1) the district *(hsien)* people's courts, (2) the provincial people's courts, and (3) the Supreme People's Court. On principle, Communist China adopted a two-trial system: the district court as first trial and the provincial court as the second. However, the provincial court might conduct the first trial in important cases and the Supreme Court the second trial. In cases designated by the Central People's Government, the Supreme Court would conduct the first and also the final trial. However, the trial procedures in Communist China were not always in accordance with the normal standard. During the period of land reform and the campaign for the "suppression of counter-revolutionaries," the Government resorted to many extraordinary measures, mass denunciations for example.

[1] Arts. 26–30.

[2] The English texts of the *Agrarian Reform Law* and other relevant documents can be found in a booklet under the title, *The Agrarian Reform Law of the People's Republic of China* (Peking: Foreign Languages Press, 1959).

[3] Most of these laws and regulations were printed in separate pamphlets. Their English texts can be found in Albert P. Blaustein, *op. cit.* (1962).

4. THE LOCAL GOVERNMENT SYSTEM, 1949–1954

The six regional committees

Following the military conquest of the Mainland in 1949, the Communist Government divided the country into six administrative areas under the direction of six military and administrative committees or commissions. Considering the uncertainty of the local situation in various parts of the country and the insufficiency of transportation and communication facilities, Mao Tse-tung declared that "only with the establishment of these strong regional organizations could things be done properly in a big country like China." [1]

These Greater Administrative Areas and the headquarters of the Committees were as follows: (1) the Northeast Committee at Mukden, having jurisdiction over Manchuria and Jehol; (2) the North China Committee at Peking, over Hopei, Shansi, Suiyuan, and other adjacent territories; (3) the East China Committee at Shanghai, over Shantung, Chekiang, Fukien, Kiangsu, and Anhwei; (4) the Central-South China Committee at Wuhan, over Honan, Hupei, Hunan, Kiangsi, Kwangtung, and Kwangsi; (5) the Northwest China Committee at Sian, over Shensi, Kansu, Ninghsia, Sinkiang, and Chinghai; and (6) the Southwest Committee at Chungking, over Sikang, Kweichow, Yunnan, and Szechwan. [2]

According to the *Organic Law of the New Regional Government Committees* (Councils), promulgated by the Government Administration Council on December 16, 1949, [3] the six military-administrative committees were the agent of the Central People's Government to supervise and direct the work of the provincial, municipal, and district governments in their respective areas. They were temporary in nature. When the military action in the country was concluded and popular elections were held, these committees were transformed from military-administrative to purely administrative committees, in accordance with the decree of Nobember 15, 1952, issued by the Central People's Government Council. [4] Each administrative committee was headed by a leading Communist whose growing influence in the particular area under his jurisdiction could not be overlooked by the Central Government.

[1] *China Digest* (Hongkong), December 14, 1949, p. 28.
[2] As early as the middle of 1948, a people's government was set up in the "liberated areas" of North China. On August 27, 1949, another people's government was formed in the Northeast. Thus these two areas had already set up regional governments even before the inauguration of the Central People's Government on October 1, 1949.
[3] Its text can be found in *Current Background* (Hongkong), No. 170. April 8, 1952.
[4] *New China News Agency* (Peking), November 17, 1952.

The six regional committees in the Greater Administrative Areas were finally abolished in June 1954.

From the time of the abolition of the above-mentioned regional system, there has not been any intermediary organization between the Central and provincial governments. The administrative divisions on and below the provincial level will be described in the following chapter.

All-circles representative conference

After the Communist victory on the Mainland in 1949, the all-circles representative conferences of the local levels were created side by side with the military control committees and local people's governments. "Pending the convocation of the local people's congresses elected by the universal franchise," the Common Program prescribed that "the local all-circles representative conferences shall gradually assume the functions and powers of the local people's congresses." [1] The delegates to the all-circles representative conferences were not all elected by the people. Many of them were appointed by the local military control committees and some were selected by the local organizations through a process of consultation. The strict control over the local conferences and governments by the corresponding organs at higher levels is the characteristic practice of democratic centralism, which has been the guiding principle of all the local laws and regulations. Among these were the *General Regulations for Provincial All-Circles Representative Conferences*, adopted by the Central People's Government Council on December 2, 1949, and the *General Regulations for the Organization of the Provincial People's Governments, District People's Governments, and Municipal People's Governments*, promulgated by the Government Administration Council on January 6, 1950.[2]

In the local elections, the electoral procedure was quite different from that of the Western democracies. Open balloting, usually through a show of hands, was the common practice of the voters to signify final approval of the single lists of candidates. In his speech at a Peking people's representative conference, Liu Shao-ch'i commended the democratic nature of this system and repudiated the "universal, equal, direct, and secret-balloting" as unsuitable to the prevailing circumstances in Communist China.[3]

---

[1] Art. 14 of the Common Program.

[2] The English texts can be found in the *Research Project on the Chinese Communist Party Line* (Russia-Research Center, Harvard University, Cambridge, Mass.), Docs. 1 and 4*.

[3] *China Monthly Review* (Shanghai), December 1950, p. 118. For further details, see S. B. Thomas, *op. cit.*, pp. 86–94.

The all-circles representative conferences were gradually established in various provinces, districts, and municipalities. They elected the people's government councils of the same levels. With the completion of military operations and the enforcement of agrarian reforms, popular elections were held in different localities for the establishment of local people's congresses as prescribed in the Common Program. After the promulgation of the *Constitution of the People's Republic of China* in 1954, a new local system of people's congresses and people's councils was installed.

Local people's government councils

The basic regulations governing local people's government councils prior to the promulgation of the Constitution of 1954 were issued by the Government Administration Council on January 6, 1950. According to these regulations, all local people's government councils in provinces, districts and municipalities were elected by the local all-circles representative conferences of the same levels, subject to the approval of the Central People's Government Council. During the early transitional period, local people's government councils were appointed by the higher people's government councils or military authorities. The head of the local government council was the governor in a province, magistrate in a district *(hsien* or county), and a mayor in a municipality. They were all assisted by their deputies, council members, and secretarial staff.

Under each government council, there were various administrative units in charge of civil administration, public security, finance, reconstruction, culture and education, labor, and other matters. The heads and their deputies of these administrative units were all appointed by the Central People's Government in accordance with its decree of November 5, 1951, on the appointment and removal of administrative personnel. In addition to the administrative units, each local people's government council was to set up a people's court, a people's supervisory committee, and a people's procuratorate.

Self-government organs of national autonomous areas

As previously mentioned, the Chinese population is composed of approximately 94% Han and 6% of other national minorities. Among the latter are Tibetan, Mongolian, Chuang, Uighur, Hui, Yi, Miao, Puyi, T'ung, Yao, T'ai, and Korean. Ranging from one-half to six million in population, they live mainly in the northwest, southwest, and northeast of China; but a small number of them reside in scattered areas.[1] Over 85% of the national minorities are engaged in agriculture and the remainder in animal husbandry and forestry.

The protection of national minorities was particularly emphasized in the Common Program. Appropriate representation was granted to the minorities living in scattered locations, and those in compact areas had the right of regional autonomy.[2] The dimension of the minority problem in China is not as serious as that in Soviet Russia and other countries. The Communist device of self-government for national minorities is motivated by two purposes: first, as a precautionary measure for preventing secession movements; and, second, as an effective means of keeping close contact and supervision.

Following the principles laid down by the Common Program, the Central People's Government took various steps to promote the self-government of national minorities. On February 22, 1952, the Government Administration Council adopted the *Regulations on the Protection of the Right of All Scattered National Minority People to National Equality* and the *Regulations on Measures for the Establishment of Local Democratic-Coalition Governments of Nationalities* which prescribed the areas where such governments were to be established as well as the number and the choice of deputies to the people's representative conferences and to the people's government councils. The Common Program stressed the principle of national equality among the minorities, who could use their own languages and preserve or change their religious beliefs as well as national customs and habits.

With the promulgation of the *General Program of the People's Republic of China for the Implementation of Regional Autonomy for Nationalities* by the Central People's Government Council on August 9, 1952, legal provisions concerning national minorities became more complete. This General Program stipulated the basis for the establishment of autonomous regions, functions of autonomous organs, inter-relationship among the different nationalities within an autonomous region, and the duty of the people's government of higher levels to respect and assist the development of autonomous regions. Except for areas where regional autonomy had already been practiced, preparations for regional autonomy were to be made wherever national minorities were concentrated.

---

[1] See Ch. VII, Sec. 4, on self-determination.
[2] Arts. 50–53 of the Common Program.

5. THE ADOPTION OF THE CONSTITUTION
BY THE NATIONAL PEOPLE'S CONGRESS

The drafting of the constitution

The CPPCC, as a constituent body, adopted the Common Program and two organic laws, which served as a provisional constitution for the period of 1949–1954. The drafting of the constitution was, however, entrusted to another organ, the Committee for Drafting the Constitution of the People's Republic of China. This Committee, formed by the Central People's Government Council on January 13, 1953, was headed by Mao Tse-tung himself, but actually it did not prepare the first draft. It was the Central Committee of the Communist Party which proposed a draft of the constitution and submitted it to the constitution-drafting Committee in March of the following year. Using this draft as a basis, the Committee conducted discussions throughout the country. According to the report of Liu Shao-ch'i to the First National People's Congress, "more than 8,000 persons, representative of the various democratic parties and groups, people's organizations and people of all sections of the society, took part for more than two months." [1]

The revised draft was made public on June 14, 1954. In the following two months, the Committee made further revisions on the basis of various new proposals. The Central People's Government Council passed the final draft at its 34th meeting on September 9, 1954, and submitted it to the First National People's Congress for its formal adoption. In concluding his report, Liu stated that the Drafting Committee "referred to all the constitutions, past and present, of the Soviet Union as well as to the constitutions of the People's Democracies." [2] This 1954 Constitution, as finally adopted by the National People's Congress, is similar to the constitutions of other socialist countries.

The convocation of the First National People's Congress

As an initial step in the implementation of a constitutional government, the Central People's Government Council promulgated, on March 1, 1953, the *Electoral Law of the People's Republic of China for the National People's Congress and Local People's Congresses of All Levels*.[3]

---

[1] Liu Shao-ch'i, *Report on the Draft Constitution of the People's Republic of China**, p. 3.
[2] *Ibid.*, p. 19.
[3] The English text of this Law together with an explanation was issued in a pamphlet form by the Foreign Languages Press, Peking 1953. The term, "National People's Congress," is sometimes translated as "The All-China People's Congress."

According to the provisions of this Electoral Law, the National People's Congress was to be composed of the following deputies: (1) one for every 800,000 persons from a province; (2) one for every 100,000 persons from a municipality directly under the Central People's Government and from an industrial municipality with a population of more than 500,000 directly under a provincial government; (3) 150 from the national minorities; (4) 60 from the armed forces; and (5) 30 from the overseas Chinese.[1]

The favoring of urban workers was clearly demonstrated in the method of apportioning representatives. Popular elections were held in May 1954, and in September, the deputies assembled in Peking to attend the constitution-making Congress. The first session of the First National People's Congress was convoked on September 15–28, 1954. There were altogether 1,226 deputies, including 147 women and 177 from national minorities.

The adoption of the Constitution and other fundamental laws

Mao Tse-tung presided over the opening session of the Congress. The report on the draft constitution was made by Liu Shao-ch'i on behalf of the Drafting Committee. After three days of discussion, on September 20, the deputies unanimously adopted it as the *Constitution of the People's Republic of China*. Other important laws adopted by the same session were: (1) the *Organic Law of the National People's Congress of the People's Republic of China*, (2) the *Organic Law of the State Council of the People's Republic of China*, (3) the *Organic Law of the People's Courts of the People's Republic of China*, (4) the *Organic Law of the People's Procuratorates of the People's Republic of China*, and (5) the *Organic Law of the Local People's Congresses and Local People's Councils of the People's Republic of China*.[2]

The election and approval of leading government personnel

After the adoption of the Constitution and other fundamental laws, the first session of the National People's Congress heard the government report from Premier Chou En-lai on September 23. Then followed the election and approval of leading government personnel as provided

[1] Arts. 3, 20–23, 25. The procedures for the election of deputies under categories (4) and (5) were left to the discretion of the Government.

[2] All the Laws were adopted on September 21, 1954, with the exception of number (1) which was passed one day earlier. The laws under (2) and (5) were amended at the second session of the National People's Congress on July 30, 1955. For their English texts, see Albert P. Blaustein, *op. cit.*, pp. 104–171.

in the Constitution. On September 27, the Congress unanimously elected Mao Tse-tung as Chairman and Chu Teh as Vice-Chairman of the People's Republic of China. Other leading posts elected or approved by the Congress included Chou En-lai as Premier of the State Council, Tung Pi-wu as President of the Supreme People's Court, Chang Ting-cheng as Procurator-General, as well as Vice-Premiers, Ministers, and Chairmen of Commissions under the State Council. The Congress also approved the appointment of the Vice-Chairmen and Members of the Council of National Defense upon the recommendation of Mao Tse-tung, concurrently Chairman of the Council.

The organization of the National People's Congress provided a Standing Committee, which was to exercise the functions and powers of the Congress during the period of its recess.[1] Liu Shao-ch'i was elected Chairman of this all powerful Committee; its Vice-Chairmen were selected from various political parties and groups. The nomination and election of other personnel of the various committees of the National People's Congress took place at its closing session on September 28.

6. GENERAL PRINCIPLES OF THE CONSTITUTION OF 1954 [2]

General provisions of the Constitution

The Constitution of the People's Republic of China represents the ideas and programs of the victorious Communist Party, although its preamble states that "it reflects the basic needs of the state in the period of transition, as well as the general desire of the people as a whole to build a socialist society." On the basis of the Common Program adopted by the CPPCC in 1949, this Constitution consists of a preamble and 106 articles in 4 chapters:

Preamble
Ch. I.   General Principles (Arts. 1–20)
     II.   The State Structure (Arts. 21–84)
          Sec. 1.   The National People's Congress (Arts. 21–38)
               2.   The Chairman of the People's Republic of China (Arts. 39–46)
               3.   The State Council (Arts. 47–52)

---

[1] The organization and functions of the National People's Congress to be described in Ch. XII.

[2] The text of the Constitution is available in pamphlet form, published by the People's Press, Peking, 1954; for its English translation, see Appendix H. The English text of the Constitution and Liu Shao-ch'i's report are published in a booklet by the Foreign Languages Press, Peking, 1954.

4. The Local People's Congresses and Local People's Councils (Arts. 53–66)
5. The Organs of Self-Government of National Autonomous Areas (Arts. 67–72)
6. The People's Courts and the People's Procuratorate (Arts. 73–84).

III. Fundamental Rights and Duties of Citizens (Arts. 85–103)
IV. National Flag, National Emblem, Capital (Arts. 104–106).

Apart from the provisions of substance to be discussed separately, this Constitution has two distinct features: one is the simple procedure for amendment, only requiring a two-thirds majority of the deputies to the National People's Congress; and the other is the lack of territorial specifications, probably for the sake of flexibility. The present discussion of the provisions of this Constitution will be limited to the nature of the state, basic programs, as well as fundamental rights and duties of people; the organization and functions of the state organs will be analyzed in the following chapter.

The nature of the state

The Constitution emphatically declares that the People's Republic is "a people's democratic state" under the leadership of the alliance of workers and peasants and that it is "a single multi-national state." All nationalities are equal before the law. While regional self-governments are to be granted to "compact communities" of national minorities, all autonomous areas "are inalienable parts of the People's Republic of China." [1] With the ultimate authority vested in the people, the National People's Congress and the local people's congresses are to exercise state powers under the principle of democratic centralism.

Programs for the socialist economy

The building of a socialist society is to be a gradual process in accordance with the provisions of the Constitution. The elimination of the exploitation system and the construction of a socialist society is to be accomplished by "the organs of state and the social forces" through the process of socialist industrialization and transformation. The Constitution explicitly recognizes that the following forms of ownership and means of production are to exist in the People's Re-

---

[1] Arts. 1, 3.

public: state ownership by the whole people; cooperative ownership by the working masses collectively; individual ownership by the working class; and capitalist ownership, permissible in the transitional period.

The development of state ownership takes priority, because this ownership is to be the leading force in the national economy for socialist transformation. The cooperative economy is either socialist or semi-socialist, depending upon the degree of collective ownership by the working masses. Private collective ownership is a transitional form of the advance of the working people toward collective ownership. State encouragement and assistance in the development of cooperatives is guaranteed. Producers' cooperatives are deemed to be the chief means of transforming individual farming and handicrafts.

During the transitional period, the Constitution guarantees the right of peasants to own land and other means of production. The state gives necessary assistance to the peasants in increasing their own production and encourages the organization of producers', supply and marketing, and credit cooperatives. The rich-peasant economy is to be restricted and gradually eliminated. The same assistance and encouragement are to be extended to the handicraftmen. The Government implemented these constitutional provisions with special regulations in the following years, including *Model Regulations for An Agricultural Producers' Cooperative* and *Model Regulations for Advanced Agricultural Producers' Cooperatives* of 1956.

The restriction and gradual abolition of capitalists and protection of private property are specially provided in the Constitution. According to article 10, capitalists also have the right to own means of production and capital in accordance with law. The state is to use the positive side of capitalism to benefit "the national welfare and the people's livelihood," and restrict its negative side. Capitalist ownership is to be gradually replaced with state ownership through its administrative organs and under the workers' supervision. Capitalists are, however, forbidden to work against the public interest, "disrupt the social-economic order, or undermine the economic plan of the state." The state guarantees "the rights of citizens to their lawfully-earned incomes, savings, houses and other means of life," as well as their right to inherit property. Whenever public interest demands, the state may buy, requisition, or nationalize land and other means of production according to law. In any event, the use of private property "to the detriment of the public interest" is prohibited. The Constitution stresses the role of the state in its direction of the growth and transformation of the economy.[1]

Fundamental rights and duties of citizens

The Constitution emphasizes the equality of citizens "before the law," equal status of women, as well as sanctity of marriage and family. Citizens eighteen years of age or more have the right to vote and stand for election, with the exception of those who are insane or deprived "by law" of such right. The latter include feudal landlords and bureaucrat-capitalists, but they are allowed to reform through work for the eventual restitution of their political rights. This constitutional provision was implemented by separate laws, such as the *Regulations on Labor-Reformation* of September 7, 1954.

According to the Constitution, citizens are entitled to such freedoms as speech, press, assembly, correspondance, association, domicile, religion, procession, and demonstration, as well as cultural endeavors. They may not be arrested without the decision of the courts or the sanction of "a people's procuratorate." However, these rights and freedoms do not apply when the suppression of counter-revolutionary activities and measures for national security by the armed forces are involved. To Western observers, the suspension of civil rights under these special circumstances went far beyond the literary provisions of the Constitution.

The state is to guarantee the right of the citizens to work and to encourage them to seek employment. Measures for increasing employment and improving working conditions, wages, old age pensions, and medical assistance are provided in the Constitution. A series of beneficial regulations were issued after the promulgation of the Constitution, including *Regulations on Factory Safety and Sanitation* of 1956, *Regulations governing Safe Working Conditions in Building Construction and Installation Projects* of 1956, *Provisional Regulations of the State Council concerning the Retirement of Workers and Staff Members* of 1958, and *Provisional Regulations of the State Council concerning the Granting of Home Leave to Workers and Staff Members and Wages to Them on Such Leave* of 1958. Some regulations of this category were enacted before the promulgation of the Constitution, for example, the *Trade Union Law* of 1950, the *Labor Insurance Regulations* of 1953, and *Provisional Regulations on Awards for Inventions, Technical Improvements and Rational-*

---

[1] See Arts. 4–15 of the Constitution.

ization Proposals concerning Production of 1954.[1] There is no doubt that the Communist regime has paid special attention to labor legislation for the eventual benefit to the working class. Nevertheless, the living conditions of the workers today are far below the Western standard.

The Constitution deals with other phases of citizens' rights and state protection. Educational and cultural facilities are to be provided for the citizens. Public functionaries are obligated to serve and keep close contact with the people, who may bring complaints against them and receive compensation for losses suffered. The Constitution not only guarantees the protection of Chinese nationals abroad but also extends asylum in China to "persecuted" foreign nationals. The granting of asylum to political criminals is the consistent policy of the Communist regime, as the same was provided in the Communist Constitution of 1931 and in the Common Program of 1949.

With regard to the fundamental duties of citizens, the Constitution requires them to abide by the law, respect discipline at work, maintain public order, observe social ethics, protect public property, pay taxes, perform military services, and defend the homeland. It can be seen that the provisions of the Constitution on people's duties are simple but comprehensive in comparison with those on their rights. However, all the rights and duties of citizens as enumerated in this fundamental law are general in nature and subject to restrictions and modifications by special legislation in conformity with the practical need of the state.[2] According to the analysis of the experts on Communist affairs, reports from the Mainland have confirmed that this is actually the case.

---

[1] The English texts of these labor laws and regulations can be found in *Important Labor Laws and Regulations of the People's Republic of China* (Peking: Foreign Languages Press, enlarged ed., 1961).

[2] For constitutional provisions on people's rights and duties as discussed above, see Arts. 16–20, 85–103.

THE GOVERNMENT OF "DEMOCRATIC CENTRALISM": POLITICAL INSTITUTIONS UNDER THE CONSTITUTION OF 1954

I. THE PRESENT SYSTEM OF GOVERNMENT

The change of state organs in 1954

"Democratic centralism" is the characteristic of the government system of all socialist countries, which practice centralism on the basis of democracy, and democracy under central guidance. The people's authority is vested in the people's congresses, which elect and supervise the people's councils on the same levels for the execution and administration of the policies and programs decided by the congresses. In Communist China, the plenary session of the CPPCC functioned as the temporary National People's Congress during the transitional period of 1949–1954. On the local level, the all-circles representative conferences exercised certain powers and functions of the local people's congresses. With the promulgation of the *Constitution of the People's Republic of China* in 1954, the people's congresses became the supreme authority on both national and local levels.

In the Central Government, the executive and administrative organs had changed either their names or functions or both from those established under the *Common Program* and the *Organic Law of the Central People's Government* of 1949. The Central People's Government Council was abolished and its powers were taken over by the National People's Congress and the Chairman of the People's Republic. With the exception of the Supreme People's Court, other state organs underwent changes in names and, to a certain extent, powers and functions. The State Council, the National Defense Council, and the Supreme People's Procuratorate replaced the former Government Administration Council, People's Revolutionary Military Council, and the Procurator-General's Office respectively. In local government, all-circles conferences were replaced by local people's congresses, which assumed the function of directing the work of the local government councils on the same levels. Other variations are evidenced in the powers, functions, and inter-relationship of different government organs.

The legal foundation of the present government system is based on the Constitution and various organic laws of the state organs as previously mentioned. Many administrative decisions have the same effect as laws. *The Electoral Law for the National People's Congress and Local People's Congresses of All Levels* of 1953 is an important source for the study of the representative system of Communist China. However, legal provision is one thing and the actual application is another. Only time and facts will prove how much power the people can actually exercise and how democratically the government will actually operate; but there is no question that the present government system on the Mainland is highly centralized.

The administrative divisions

The administrative divisions of China under the People's Republic are not essentially different from those under the Nationalist Government. The Constitution of 1954 divides the country into provinces, autonomous regions, and municipalities directly under the central authority;[1] all on the same level and under the direct control of the Central People's Government. The provinces have undergone many changes through division, consolidation and delimitation of boundaries.[2] The municipalities under the direct control of the Central People's Government have been reduced to three only: Peking, Shanghai, and Tientsin. The autonomous regions have been extended to wider areas, including Inner Mongolia, Sinkiang Uighur, and also Tibet which is still at the preparatory stage.

Provinces and autonomous regions have again been divided into autonomous prefectures *(chou)*, districts *(hsien* or counties), autonomous districts, and municipalities not directly under the central authority.[3] Districts and municipalities generally constitute the second level of the Chinese local government system; but, in the case of the prefecture, it stands between the provinces and the districts or municipalities. As an intermediary division, each prefecture may cover a number of

[1] Art. 53, Par. 1.
[2] The following is a list of the provinces on the Mainland in 1957: Anhwei, Chekiang, Chinghai, Fukien, Heilungkiang, Honan, Hopei, Hunan, Hupei, Kansu, Kiangsi, Kiangsu, Kirin, Kwangsi, Kwangtung, Kweichow, Liaoning, Shansi, Shantung, Shensi, Szechwan, and Yunnan. *Handbook on People's China* (Peking: Foreign Languages Press, 1957), p. 77.
[3] Art. 53, Par. 2 of the *Constitution* of 1954.

districts, autonomous districts, and municipalities. In effect, the present system corresponds to the three-level pattern of the local government during the early Republican period.[1] However, the present system of prefectures is only applied to areas where national minorities are concentrated, approximately thirty in all.

The administrative divisions below the district *(hsien)* level are villages *(hsiang)* nationality villages, and townships *(chen)*. Municipalities directly under the central authority and other large municipalities are divided into sub-districts or boroughs *(ch'ü)*.[2] These are the administrative divisions in Communist China today.[3] The *pao-chia* system adopted by the Nationalist Government as an effective system to prevent the spread of Communist activities in Central China was abolished. Instead, the Communist Government makes use of all kinds of mass organizations for the furtherance of indoctrination among the people and the maintenance of security in the local community.

2. THE NATIONAL PEOPLE'S CONGRESS

The organization of the National People's Congress

The National People's Congress is an integral part of the central government system; due to its unique nature and importance, it is treated first among the organs of the Central People's Government. According to the Constitution of 1954, the National People's Congress is the "highest organ of state authority" and the "only legislative authority" in the People's Rupublic.[4] The number of deputies to the

---

[1] *Cf.* the local administration described in Ch. II, Sec. 9 and Ch. III, Sec. 4.

[2] Art. 53, Par. 3 of the *Constitution* of 1954.

[3] In the English text of the Constitution of 1954 and also in other English sources, the terms of different administrative divisions vary slightly from those used in the present work. The following list is prepared for the convenient reference of the reader in order to avoid confusion arising out of the differences.

Proper Chinese terms	English terms used in the present work	English terms used in the Constitution	English terms used in other sources
chou	prefecture	*chou*	prefecture or county
hsien	district	county	district or county
hsiang	village	*hsiang*	village, town, or township
chen	township	town	township or town
ch'ü	sub-district or borough	district	district or borough
ts'un	hamlet	(not mentioned)	village
li	precinct	,, ,,	*li*
lin	neighborhood	,, ,,	*lin*
pao	*pao*	,, ,,	*pao* or *po*
chia	*chia*	,, ,,	*chia*

[4] Arts. 21, 22, of the *Constitution*.

Congress from the provinces, autonomous regions, municipalities directly under the central authority, the armed forces, and overseas Chinese are prescribed by the *Electoral Law of the People's Republic of China for the National People's Congress and Local People's Congresses of All Levels*, promulgated on March 1, 1953.[1]

The term of office of the deputies is four years, which may be extended in case the election of deputies to a new Congress is not completed.[2] When a deputy is unable to perform his duties, his electoral unit will hold a by-election to fill the vacancy. The new deputy so elected is to serve the remainder of the unexpired term.[3] The deputies are not subject to arrest or trial without the consent of the Congress or its Standing Committee when the Congress is in recess. They are, however, under the supervision of the units they represent and may be replaced in accordance with law.[4] The deputies may attend the meetings of the people's congresses of their own local units.[5]

The National People's Congress has a Standing Committee as well as other committees. The annual session of the Congress is to be convened by the Standing Committee, which may also call special sessions upon the proposal of one-fifth of the deputies.[6] The meetings of the Congress are presided over by an Executive Chairman of the Presidium, elected by the deputies at the beginning of the session. For each session, the Congress sets up a Secretariat, which, under the direction of a Secretary-General, conducts the routine business of the Congress.[7]

Functions of the National People's Congress

The National People's Congress has the following powers and functions: (1) to supervise the enforcement of the Constitution and amend it; (2) to enact laws; (3) to elect the Chairman and Vice-Chairman of the People's Republic of China, the President of the Supreme People's Court, and the Procurator-General; (4) to decide on the choice of the Premier of the State Council and the Vice-Chairmen and Members of the Council of National Defense upon recommendation by the Chairman of the People's Republic, and of the component Members of the State Council upon recommendation by the Premier; (5) to remove from office the officials elected or appointed by the

[1] Arts. 19–23 of the *Electoral Law*.
[2] Art. 24 of the *Constitution*.
[3] Art. 38 of the *Organic Law of the National People's Congress* of 1954.
[4] Arts. 37 and 38 of the *Constitution*.
[5] Art. 33 of the *Organic Law of the National People's Congress*.
[6] Art. 25 of the *Constitution*.
[7] Arts. 4–6 of the *Organic Law of the National People's Congress*; Art. 26 of the *Constitution*.

Congress; (6) to examine and approve the state budget and the financial report; (7) to interpellate the responsible officials of the State Council or of its ministries and commissions; (8) to decide on national economic plans, general amnesties, and questions of war and peace; (9) to ratify the status and boundaries of provinces, autonomous regions, and municipalities directly under the central autority; and (10) to exercise such other functions and powers as the Congress may consider necessary.[1] As the highest state authority, the power of the National People's Congress would be almost unlimited; yet, in fact, it is dominated by the Communist Party which actually wields the ultimate authority of the state.

The Standing Committee of the National People's Congress

The Standing Committee is a permanent body of the National People's Congress to which it is responsible and reports. It is composed of a Chairman and a number of Vice-Chairmen and Members, as well as a Secretary-General. They are elected by the Congress to perform its functions until the election of a new Committee by the succeeding Congress or their recall by the existing Congress.[2] The Chairman presides over the meetings of the Standing Committee. Resolutions may be adopted by a vote of a simple majority.[3] The Standing Committee, elected by the First National People's Congress on September 27, 1954, was composed of a Chairman, 13 Vice-Chairmen, and 65 members. Liu Shao-ch'i was elected Chairman. Political leaders of different parties and groups were well represented at the Committee.

The Standing Committee exercises the following powers and functions: (1) to conduct the election of deputies to the National People's Congress; (2) to convene the next National People's Congress; (3) to interpret laws and issue decrees; (4) to supervise the work of the State Council, the Supreme People's Court, and the Supreme People's Procuratorate; (5) to annul decisions and orders of the State Council which are in conflict with the Constitution, laws or decrees; (6) to revise or annul inappropriate decisions of the government authorities of provinces, autonomous regions, and municipalities directly under the central authority; (7) to decide on the appointment or removal of the Vice-Premiers, Ministers, Heads of Commissions, or the Secretary-General of the State Council when the Congress is not

---

[1] Arts. 27, 28, and 36 of the *Constitution.*
[2] *Ibid.,* Arts. 30, 32, 33.
[3] Arts. 18, 23 of the *Organic Law of the National People's Congress.*

in session; (8) to appoint or remove the Vice-Presidents, Judges, Deputy Procurators-general, Procurators, and other Members of the Judicial Committee of the Supreme People's Court and the Procuratorial Committee of the Supreme People's Procuratorate; (9) to decide on the appointment or recall of diplomatic representatives to foreign states; (11) to institute military, diplomatic, and other special titles and ranks; (12) to institute and decide on the award of state orders, medals, and titles of honor; (13) to decide on the granting of pardons; (14) to decide, when the National People's Congress is in recess, on the proclamation of a state of war in the event of foreign invasion or due to treaty obligations for collective defense; (15) to decide on general or partial mobilization or the enforcement of martial law; and (16) to exercise such other functions and powers authorized by the National People's Congress.[1]

Other Committees and Commissions of Inquiry

In addition to the Standing Committee, the National People's Congress has a Nationalities Committee, a Bills Committee, a Budget Committee, a Credentials Committee, and other necessary committees. Commissions of inquiry for the investigation of specific matters may be instituted by the National People's Congress, or, if not in session, by the Standing Committee. All state organs, people's organizations, and citizens concerned are required to supply necessary information to these commissions if requested. When the National People's Congress is not in session, the Nationalities Committee and the Bills Committee are under the direction of the Standing Committee.[2] Each committee is composed of a chairman and a certain number of vice-chairmen and members. The chairman directs the work and presides over the meetings of the committee.[3]

While the nature of the committees on bills, budgets, and credentials are self-explanatory,[4] the work of the Nationalities Committee requires further elaboration. The functions of the Committee are as follows: (1) to examine provisions of the bills concerning the affairs of nationalities referred to it by the Congress or its Standing Committee; (2) to examine laws and regulations concerning the exercise of autonomy submitted by different autonomous units for approval by the Standing Committee; (3) to submit bills and proposals concerning the affairs of

---

[1] Art. 31 of the *Constitution*.
[2] *Ibid.*, Arts. 33–35.
[3] Art. 25 of the *Organic Law of the National Peoples' Congress*.
[4] *Ibid.*, Arts. 27–29.

nationalities to the National People's Congress or its Standing Committee; and (4) to study matters concerning the affairs of the nationalities.[1] Instead of creating a second chamber of the legislature representing various nationalities as practiced in the Soviet Union; the People's Republic simply set up a committee in charge of the affairs of national minorities. Perhaps this arrangement suits the Chinese situation with a small number of national minorities.

3. THE HEAD OF THE STATE

The Chairman and Vice-Chairman of the People's Republic

As Head of the state, the Chairman of the People's Republic is elected by the National People's Congress for a term of four years. The Vice-Chairman is to assist the Chairman in the performance of functions assigned to him by the Chairman. Any Chinese citizen, who is qualified to vote and stand for election at the age of thirty-five or more may be elected as Chairman or Vice-Chairman of the People's Republic. Both are to continue in office until the inauguration of their successors. Since there is no restriction in the Constitution on their re-election, they may be re-elected for an indefinite number of terms. In the event that the Chairman, for reason of health, is unable to perform his functions for a long period, the Vice-Chairman is to exercise the functions of the Chairman. The Vice-Chairman is to succeed to the office of the Chairman if it becomes vacant.[2]

Powers and functions of the Chairman

The Chairman is to represent the state, receive foreign envoys, appoint or recall diplomatic representatives to other nations, and ratify treaties concluded with foreign countries. He is also empowered by the Constitution to promulgate laws and decrees; to appoint or remove the Premier, Vice-Premiers, Ministers, Heads of Commissions, the Secretary-General of the State Council, Vice-Chairmen and Members of the Council of National Defense; to confer state orders, medals, and titles of honor; to grant general amnesties and pardons; to proclaim martial law or a state of war; and to order mobilization.[3]

Another important power of the Chairman is that he commands the armed forces of the country and is concurrently Chairman of the

[1] *Ibid.*, Art. 26.
[2] Arts. 39, 44–46 of the *Constitution*.
[3] *Ibid.*, Arts. 40, 41.

Council of National Defense.[1] This Council is different from the Ministry of Defense under the State Council which has the direct responsibility for military administration. Composed of a Chairman, 15 Vice-Chairmen, and 81 members, the Council of National Defense acts as a brain trust of top military strategists.[2] It is important to note that the appointment and removal of the Council's Vice-Chairmen and Members are solely within the jurisdiction of the National People's Congress and not of its Standing Committee.

Furthermore, the Chairman of the People's Republic may convene and preside over a Supreme State Conference to discuss important affairs of state. The participating members of the Conference are the Vice-Chairman of the People's Republic, the Chairman of the Standing Committee of the National People's Congress, the Premier of the State Council, and other persons concerned. The Chairman of the People's Republic is to present the views of the Conference for consideration and discussion to the National People's Congress, its Standing Committee, the State Council, and other interested organs.[3] In effect, this Supreme State Conference acts as a liason center of the complicated state apparatus for the exchange of opinions and settling disputes among different state organs through the prestige and power of the Chairman. It is not likely that the state organs concerned would act contrary to the wishes of the Chairman, especially when Mao Tse-tung held that office.

It must be emphasized in this connection that the actual source of state power rests in the Communist Party, however important the office of the Head of the State may be. It is for this reason that, after his resignation as Chairman of the People's Republic in order to relieve himself of routine administration, Mao remains the most influential man on the Mainland in his capacity as leader of the ruling party. As the incumbent Chairman of the People's Republic, Liu Shao-ch'i is still next to Mao in importance. Moreover, the Chairman and Vice-Chairman of the People's Republic may be recalled by the National People's Congress which is definitely controlled by the Communist Party through its deputies to the Congress.

---

[1] *Ibid.*, Art. 42.

[2] There is some resemblance of the military set-up of Communist China with that of the Nationalist Government. The Ministry of Defense under the State Council corresponds to the same organ under the Executive *Yuan*, and the National Defense Council corresponds to the National Military Commission. At present in Taiwan, there is a Military Strategy Advisory Committee under the President of the Republic.

[3] Art. 42 of the *Constitution*.

4. THE STATE COUNCIL

The organization of the State Council

The State Council is "the executive organ of the highest state authority" and also "the highest administrative organ of state." [1] Under the direction of the Chairman of the People's Republic, the Council is to execute and administer the affairs of state. It is also responsible to the National People's Congress and reports to it, or to the Standing Committee if the Congress is not in session. The Council is composed of a Premier, Vice-Premiers, Ministers, Heads of Commissions, and a Secretary-General. With the assistance of Vice-Premiers and the Secretary-General, the Premier is to direct the work of the State Council and preside over its meetings. The Ministers and Heads of Commissions are under the direction and supervision of the Premier to carry out the work of their respective organs. They may issue orders and directions within their jurisdiction in accordance with law. [2]

In order to insure flexibility, the organization of the State Council is not prescribed in the Constitution but governed by the *Organic Law of the State Council of the People's Republic of China* of 1954. According to this law, the State Council consists of the following ministries and commissions:

(1) Ministries: interior affairs, foreign affairs, defense, public security, justice, supervision, finance, food, commerce, foreign trade, heavy industry, fuel industries, geology, building, textile industry, light industry, local industry, railways, communications, posts and telecommunications, agriculture, forestry, water conservation, labor, culture, higher education, education, public health, and the first and second ministries of machine building.

(2) Commissions: state planning, national construction, physical culture and sports, nationalities affairs, and overseas Chinese affairs.

The Premier may recommend any addition, abolition, or consolidation of the ministries and commissions to the National People's Congress for decision or to its Standing Committee if the Congress is not in session. [3] On July 30, 1955, the *Organic Law of the State Council* was amended, abolishing the ministries of coal industry, electric power industry, petroleum industry, ministry for the purchase of agricultural produce, and a third ministry of machine building. The State Council

---

[1] *Ibid.*, 47.
[2] *Ibid.*, Arts. 48, 50–52.
[3] Art. 2 of the *Organic Law of the State Council of 1954.*

has a Secretariat under the direction of a Secretary-General and a number of deputies. Other administrative organs may be established to assist the Premier in the conduct of Council affairs. Each Ministry has a Minister, Vice-Ministers, and a number of assistants to the Minister if necessary. Each Commission is composed of a Head, Deputy Heads, and members.[1]

While the general organization of the State Council is similar to that of the former Government Administration Council, there are certain differences between the two organs. The intermediary committees between the Premier and the ministers were abolished. Nor is there a provision for Council members without portfolio. Variations can also be found in the number of Vice-Premiers and ministries and commissions. The State Council resembles the Soviet Council of the People's Commissars in some respects, but the Chinese Communist Government chooses to retain the traditional pattern of ministries and commissions.

Although the Premier directs the work of the State Council, any resolution has to be deliberated and adopted at the Council's plenary or executive meetings. Plenary meetings are generally held once a month, attended by the Premier, Vice-Premiers, the Secretary-General, Ministers, and Heads of Commissions. The members attending the executive meetings are limited to the Premier, Vice-Premiers, and the Secretary-General, who constitute a so-called "inner cabinet." Chou En-lai has been the Premier since 1949. With his power and prestige in the Communist hierarchy, it is not likely that any resolution may be adopted against his wishes. Probably both the plenary and executive meetings act as a channel of collective deliberation and responsibility within the scope and in a manner directed by the Premier.

Powers and functions of the State Council

The powers and functions of the State Council are as follows: (1) to adopt administrative measures, and to issue and enforce decisions and orders: (2) to submit bills to the National People's Congress or its Standing Committee; (3) to coordinate and direct the work of the ministries and commissions under the Council and also of the local administrative organs throughout the country; (4) to revise or annul inappropriate orders and directions issued by the ministries, commissions, as well as the local administrative organs; (5) to enforce the national economic plans and provisions of the state budget; (6) to direct the conduct of external affairs as well as foreign and domestic

[1] *Ibid.*, Arts. 3, 6–8.

trade; (7) to direct cultural, educational, and public health work, as well as the affairs concerning national minorities and overseas Chinese; (8) to protect the interests of the state, maintain order, and safeguard the rights of citizens; (9) to strengthen the national defense forces; (10) to ratify the status and boundaries of autonomous prefectures *(chou)*, districts *(hsien)*, autonomous districts, and municipalities; (11) to appoint or remove administrative personnel according to provisions of law; and (12) to exercise such other functions and powers as are vested in the State Council by the National People's Congress or its Standing Committee.[1]

According to the *Organic Law of the State Council* of 1954, the State Council has the power to appoint and remove the administrative personnel under the following groupings: (1) Deputy Secretaries-General of the State Council, Vice-Ministers and Assistants to the Ministers, Deputy Heads and Members of Commissions, Heads and Deputy Heads of Departments, and Directors and Deputy Directors of Bureaus under the Ministries and Commissions; (2) Heads and Deputy Heads of Boards, Directors and Deputy Directors of Bureaus under the People's Councils of provinces and municipalities directly subject to the central authority; (3) Commissioners of Special Administrative Offices;[2] (4) officials in autonomous regions with the rank corresponding to those listed under categories (2) and (3); (5) Counsellors of diplomatic missions and Consuls-General; (6) Presidents and Vice-Presidents of national universities and colleges; and (7) other officials corresponding to the above ranks.[3] Although the State Council has the vast power of appointment and removal of officials, those on local levels are practically decided upon by the local government councils, which submit them to the State Council for confirmation as a matter of procedural requirement.

5. THE PEOPLE'S COURTS AND PROCURATORATES

The People's Courts

With the promulgation of the Constitution and the *Organic Law of the People's Courts* in September 1954,[4] the organization and functions

---

[1] *Ibid.*, Art. 49.

[2] Commissioners of Special Administrative Offices correspond to the administrative inspectors under the Nationalist Government, who are to supervise and direct the work of several districts *(hsien)* under their jurisdiction.

[3] Art. 9 of the *Organic Law of the State Council* of 1954.

[4] This Organic Law was adopted by the First Session of the National People's Congress on September 21, 1954.

of the People's Courts set up during the transitional period of 1949–1954 have undergone further changes. The Constitution provides that in the People's Republic of China judicial authority is exercised by the Supreme People's Court, local people's courts, and special people's courts.[1] Local people's courts are divided into three grades: basic people's courts, intermediate people's courts, and higher people's courts. The basic people's courts are established in districts *(hsien* or counties), autonomous districts, and boroughs *(ch'ü);* intermediate people's courts, in various areas of a province or autonomous region, large municipalities, and autonomous prefectures *(chou);* and higher people's courts, in provinces, autonomous regions, and municipalities directly under the central authority. Special people's courts are military courts, railway-transport courts, and water-transport courts.[2]

The Supreme People's Court is responsible and reports to the National People's Congress or to its Standing Committee when the Congress is not in session; and local people's courts, to the people's congresses at corresponding levels. The judicial work of the lower people's courts is subject to the supervision of the higher people's courts; the Supreme People's Court is the highest judicial organ of the state. While the judicial administrative work of the people's courts at all levels is directed by the judicial administrative organs, the people's courts are independent in administering justice and are subject only to the law.[3]

The functions of the people's courts are to try criminal and civil cases, punish criminals, and settle disputes. There is, however, a very important mission which the courts are required to fulfill, that is, "to educate citizens in loyalty to their country" and "to ensure the successful carrying out of social construction and socialist transformation in the country." [4] Cases are heard in public and the accused has the right to defense; yet these provisions may be restricted by law "in order to safeguard the people's democratic system." [5]

In the administration of justice, the people's courts carry out the system of the court of second instance as the court of last instance. A judgment or order of a local people's court as a court of first instance becomes legally effective if, within the period of appeal, no party to the case has appealed nor has the people's procuratorate protested.

---

[1] Art. 73 of the *Constitution.*
[2] Arts. 1, 15, 20, and 26 of the *Organic Law of the People's Courts* of 1954.
[3] *Ibid.*, Art. 14; Arts. 78–80 of the *Constitution.*
[4] Art. 3 of the *Organic Law of the People's Court* of 1954.
[5] *Loc. cit.*; Art. 76 of the *Constitution.*

The following are deemed judgments or orders in the last instance and become legally effective: judgments or orders of intermediate people's courts, higher people's courts or the Supreme People's Court as courts of second instance; and those of the Supreme People's Court as a court of first instance.[1] The judicial proceeding in the people's courts include a system of people's assessors, laymen selected for consultations by judges in hearing trials.[2] The value of the assessor system depends upon whether or not they may perform their functions independent of any direct or indirect interference from the state.

Each of the people's courts is composed of a president, vice-presidents, chief judges of divisions, associate judges of divisions, and judges. The presidents are elected by the people's congresses at the corresponding levels for a term of four years, and may be removed by the same congresses. The vice-presidents and judges of the Supreme People's Court are appointed or removed by the Standing Committee of the National People's Congress; and those of the local people's courts, by the local people's councils at corresponding levels. Chinese citizens over twenty-three years of age, who have the right to vote and stand for election, are eligible for such posts.[3]

It must be noted that the "people's tribunals" were not within the regular judicial system. They were established during the period of 1950–1951, for the enforcement of agrarian reform and the suppression of "counter-revolutionaries." These tribunals did not follow judicial proceedings in their trials of the alleged offenders. The large-scale persecution of landlords and "counter-revolutionaries" in the past was in conformity with the provisions in the Constitution and laws, but was necessitated by the Communist aid to strengthen the regime of "democratic dictatorship." Furthermore, the present status of Communist laws is still inadequate for a sound judicial system. This undesirable situation has caused a deep concern to no less a person than Tung Pi-wu, former President of the Supreme People's Court.[4]

The People's Procuratorates

For the enforcement of laws as provided in the Constitution of 1954, the People's Republic establishes the Supreme People's Procuratorate, local people's procuratorates, and special people's procuratorates. The

[1] Art. 11 of the *Organic Law of the People's Courts*, 1954.
[2] Art. 75 of the *Constitution*.
[3] Arts. 31–33 of the *Organic Law of the People's Courts*, 1954.
[4] In his report to the National People's Congress on September 19, 1956, Tung frankly admitted that the incomplete system of laws would create a serious problem.

Supreme People's Procuratorate exercises the procuratorial authority over all organs under the State Council, all local organs of state, public functionaries, and individual citizens. Local and special people's procuratorates work under the coordinating direction of the Supreme People's Procuratorate and the people's procuratorates at higher levels in their execution of procuratorial authority. They are not subject to interference by local organs of state. The Supreme People's Procuratorate is responsible and reports to the National People's Congress or its Standing Committee if the Congress is not in session.[1]

According to the *Organic Law of the People's Procuratorates of the People's Republic of China* of 1954,[2] a people's procuratorate on any level is composed of a procurator-general, a number of deputy procurators-general, and a procuratorial committee. The Procurator-General of the Supreme People's Procuratorate is elected by the National People's Congress for a term of four years. His deputies, procurators, and other members are appointed and removed by the Standing Committee of the Congress. The officials of the people's procuratorates above the district level (*hsien* or county) level are appointed and removed by the Supreme People's Procuratorate with the approval of the Standing Committee of the Congress; and those of the people's procuratorates at or below the district level or of the branch offices of procuratorates, by the people's procuratorates of a higher level with the approval of the Supreme People's Procuratorate.[3]

The people's procuratorates supervise the activities of organs in charge of reform through labor. In exercising this function, the procuratorates have the right to correct the errors committed by the organs concerned.[4] The Central People's Government enacted a *Statute on Labor Reeducation* on the basis of Article 7 of the *Common Program* of the CPPCC and also the *Regulations for the Surveillance and Punishment of Counter-revolutionary Activities* in 1951.[5] The term "counter-revolutionary" is so broad and vague that it may "include all persons or groups who by action or attitude fail to obey the laws or to support the regime."[6] Used synonymously with the term "reactionary," "the list of counter-revolutionary enemies is a long one," described by one

---

[1] Arts. 81, 83, 84 of the *Constitution*.

[2] Adopted by the First Session of the First National People's Congress on September 21, 1954.

[3] Arts. 2, 20, 21 of the *Organic Law of the People's Procuratorates* of 1954.

[4] *Ibid.*, Art. 18.

[5] For the English texts, see Albert P. Blaustein, *Fundamental Legal Documents of Communist China*, pp. 215–226, 240–265.

[6] Peter S. H. Tang, *Communist China Today*, Vol. I, p. 269.

observer of Communist affairs, "including among others spies, traitors, saboteurs, rumor-mongers, bandits, foreign agents, despots, 'bad' landlords, and especially former Nationalist officials who withhold active support from the Peking regime." [1]

The use of all instruments to suppress "hostile classes" is in accordance with the theory in Mao Tse-tung's *On People's Democratic Dictatorship*. The institution of labor camps has had tremendous significance in Communist China both politically and economically. From the Communist point of view, the Government is most lenient in giving the counter-revolutionary enemies a chance of reform, instead of putting them to death. However, "they shall be compelled to reform themselves through labor so as to become new men." [2] This is merely one instance to show that the legal conception and standard of the Communist regime is quite different from those of Western democracies. In exercising such functions as reform through labor and suppression of "counter-revolutionary" activities, the people's procuratorates are extremely powerful in Communist China.

6. LOCAL PEOPLE'S CONGRESSES AND COUNCILS

The local government authority and executive organ

The Constitution of the People's Republic of 1954 provides that people's congresses and people's councils are established in provinces, municipalities directly under the central authority, districts *(hsien* or county), municipalities, boroughs *(ch'ü* or sub-districts), villages *(hsiang)*, nationality villages, and townships *(chen)*. Organs of self-government are established in autonomous regions, autonomous prefectures *(chou)*, and autonomous districts *(hsien)*.[3] Local people's congresses at all levels are organs of government authority in their respective localities; local people's councils are executive organs of local people's congresses at corresponding levels, in charge of government administration in their respective localities.[4]

All Chinese citizens eighteen years of age or more have the right to vote and to be candidates for office, with the exception of the following persons: (1) landlords whose status has not yet been changed according to law: (2) counter-revolutionaries and others who have been deprived

---

[1] *Loc. cit.*
[2] Art. 7 of the *Common Program*.
[3] Art. 54 of the *Constitution*.
[4] *Ibid.*, Arts. 55, 62.

of political rights according to law; and (3) insane persons.[1] The exclusion of people under the first two categories again follows the line of "democratic dictatorship." On the other hand, the law forbids any discrimination in both national and local elections against race, sex, occupation, social origin, religion, education, property status, or residence. Evidently, the suspension of political rights of landlords and other undesirable persons from the Communist standard is not construed as discrimination according to the legal code of the People's Republic.

Local People's Congresses

As organs of government authority and representative body, all local people's congresses are elected by the people for a term of four years in the provincial level and two years in others.[2] Deputies to the people's congresses of provinces, municipalities directly under the central authority, districts *(hsien* or county), and municipalities divided into sub-districts or boroughs *(ch'ü)* are elected by the people's congresses of next lower levels. Deputies to all local people's congresses other than those stated above are directly elected by the voters. The electoral units and electorates which elect the deputies to the local people's congresses have the power to recall their deputies at any time in accordance with law.[3] If deputies to the local people's congresses are unable to perform their duties for any reason, the electoral units and electorates which elect them will hold by-elections to fill the vacancies.[4] The number of deputies to local people's congresses and the manner of their election are prescribed by the Electoral Law of 1953.

From the following list which indicates the general distribution of deputies at different levels,[5] it can be seen that urban areas are apportioned more deputies than rural ones. The *Electoral Law* of 1953 explicitly stipulates that "the number of persons represented by one deputy from a municipal suburban district shall be greater than the number of persons represented by one deputy from a municipal urban district." [6] As "the People's Republic of China is a people's democratic

---

[1] Arts. 4 and 5 of the *Electoral Law of the People's Republic of China for the National People's Congress and Local People's Congresses of All Levels*, March 1, 1953.

[2] Art. 57 of the *Constitution*.

[3] *Ibid.*, Arts. 56, 61.

[4] Art. 22 of the *Organic Law of the Local People's Congresses and Local People's Councils of the People's Republic of China*, September 21, 1954.

[5] The figures on this list are based on Arts. 9–18 of the Electoral Law of 1953.

[6] Art. 16 of the *Electoral Law* of 1953.

LOCAL PEOPLE'S CONGRESSES AND DEPUTIES

Units of Local Congresses	Deputies of Lower Units	Minimum	Maximum
village *(hsiang)* or township *(chen)*		7	50
district *(hsien* or county		30	450
	village *(hsiang)*	1	3
	township *(chen)* or important industrial or mining area	1	(one more for every 1,000 of population)
	armed forces	1	5
province		50	600
	district *(hsien)*	1	5
	municipality or important industrial or mining area	1	(one more for every 20,000 of population)
	armed forces	3	15
municipality		50	800
	armed forces	2	10
	borough *(ch'ü)*	35	200

state led by the working class," [1] it is only logical to emphasize the urban areas where the working class is concentrated.

Deputies to local people's congresses are entitled to special protection. They may not be arrested or placed on trial without permission of the presidium during the period of their attendance at the sessions. If they are apprehended while actually committing criminal acts, the government organ detaining them must immediately report the matter to the presidium of the local people's congress for approval of the arrest.[2]

The local people's congresses at or above the district *(hsien* or county) level exercise in their respective areas of jurisdiction the following functions and powers: (1) to ensure the observance and

---

[1] Art. 1 of the Constitution.

[2] Art. 18 of the *Organic Law of the Local People's Congresses and Local People's Councils,* 1954.

execution of laws and decrees, and of decisions of the people's congresses at higher levels; (2) to adopt and issue decisions within the limits of their jurisdiction; (3) to formulate plans for economic and cultural development, public works, relief, welfare of the dependents of revolutionists sacrificed for the Communist cause; (4) to examine and approve budgets and financial reports; (5) to elect or recall members of the people's councils at corresponding levels and deputies to the people's congresses at the next higher level; (6) to elect or recall presidents of the people's courts at corresponding levels, and also presidents of the intermediate people's courts by the people's congresses of provinces and municipalities directly under the central authority; (7) to hear and examine reports on the work of the people's councils and people's courts at corresponding levels; (8) to revise or annul inappropriate decisions and orders of the people's councils at corresponding levels and of the people's councils at the next lower level, and also inappropriate decisions of the people's congresses at the next lower level; and (9) to protect public property, maintain public order, and safeguard the rights of citizens as well as the equality of national minorities.[1]

The people's congresses below the district (hsien or county) level exercise in their respective areas similar powers and functions as stated above, except that those concerning the people's courts as well as supervision over the lower level councils and congresses are not applicable. On the other hand, people's congresses below the district level are to pay special attention to the formulation of plans for the production, mutual aid, and cooperation in agriculture and handicrafts, and for other economic activities.[2]

Local people's congresses are convened by the people's councils at corresponding levels. Local congresses below the district level meet once every three months and others twice a year. People's congresses of provinces where communication is difficult may meet once a year. In all cases, special sessions may be held whenever the people's councils at corresponding levels deem it necessary or one-fifth of the deputies so propose. The local people's congress in session elects a presidium and sets up necessary committees on credentials, bills, and other matters. Secretarial staffs are also provided to conduct business. Proposals may be submitted to the congress by the deputies and the people's councils

---

[1] *Ibid.*, Arts. 6, 8; Art. 61 of the *Constitution*.
[2] Art. 7 of the *Organic Law of the Local People's Congresses and Local People's Councils*, 1954.

at the corresponding level. The adoption of decisions requires a simple majority vote of all the deputies to the congress.[1]

The manner or procedure of election is noteworthy. Local people's congresses at or above district levels elect members of the people's councils and presidents of the people's courts at corresponding levels by secret ballot; while those of lower levels elect members of the people's councils at corresponding levels by a show of hands.[2] This practice evidences the increasing importance the Communist leaders place on the use of the secret ballot.

Local People's Councils

As executive organs of local people's congresses in charge of local administration, local people's councils are responsible to the people's congresses at corresponding levels and to the administrative organs of state at the next higher level, and report to them. On the basis of the principle of democratic centralism, local people's councils throughout the country are subordinate to and under the coordinating direction of the State Council. The term of office of a local people's council is the same as that of the people's congress at corresponding level.[3]

The people's councils at or above the district *(hsien* or county) level meet once a month, and others twice a month. Special sessions may be convened whenever necessary. The council meetings are presided over and conducted by its administrative chief, who is governor in a province, mayor in a municipality, magistrate in a district, and head in a borough, village *(hsiang)*, or township *(chen)*. Each administrative chief is assisted by a number of deputies and council members. The number of council members varies at different levels: 25 to 55 in provinces; 9 to 45 in municipalities; 9 to 31 in districts; 9 to 21 in boroughs; and 3 to 13 in villages, nationality villages, or townships. If members of the local people's councils are unable to perform their duties for any reason, the people's congresses at corresponding levels will hold by-elections to fill the vacancies.[4]

The organization of the local people's councils is not basically different from that of the local governments during the Nationalist period, but there are certain variations at different levels: the lower the level, the simpler the organization. The administrative units of

[1] *Ibid.*, Arts. 9–14.
[2] *Ibid.*, Art. 15.
[3] Arts. 63 and 66 of the *Constitution.*
[4] *Ibid.*, Art. 63; Arts. 25, 29, 30 of the *Organic Law of the Local People's Congresses and Local People's Councils*, 1954.

the local people's councils differ in names and scope at various levels: boards, bureaus, divisions, committees, or commissions in provinces and municipalities directly under the central authority; sections or bureaus in districts *(hsien* or county) and other municipalities; sections in boroughs *(ch'ü* or sub-districts); and working committees in villages

ADMINISTRATIVE UNITS OF LOCAL PEOPLE'S COUNCILS AT DIFFERENT LEVELS

(The sign " × " indicates that this unit is provided for in the council, which is represented by the following initials designating different levels: P (province); M (municipalities directly under the central authority or divided into boroughs); O-M (other municipalities); D (districts); B (boroughs); V-T (villages or townships). One administrative unit in charge of both matters is indicated by the sign ")" joining two " × .")

Administrative Units	P	M	O-M	D	B	V-T
civil affairs	×	×	×	×	×	×
public security	×	×	×	×		×
justice	×	×				
supervision	×	×				
planning	×	×				
finance	×	×	×	×		×)
food	×	×	×	×		×)
taxation		×	×	×	×	
industry	×	×	×)	×)	×)	
commerce	×	×	×)	×)	×)	
communications	×			×		
agriculture and forestry	×			×		
water conservation	×					
labor	×	×	×		×	
culture	×	×	×)	×)	×)	×)
education	×	×	×)	×)	×)	×)
public health	×	×	×	×	×	
physical education and sports	×	×				
nationalities	×	×				
Chinese from abroad	×	×				
general offices	×	×	×	×	×	
sub-provincial administrative offices	×					
sub-district offices				×		
street offices			×		×	
construction		×	×			
public services		×				
producers' cooperatives					×	×
arbitration						×
armed forces						×

Note: (1) The bureaus in charge of public security and taxation under the people's councils of municipalities may set up sub-bureaus in boroughs.
(2) The general offices, sub-provincial administrative offices, sub-district offices, street offices, and organs for nationalities and Chinese from abroad may be established when necessary.

(hsiang) and townships *(chen)*. The above is a list of administrative units of local people's councils at different levels.

The administrative units are composed of officials with different ranks. The boards, bureaus, divisions, sections, and sub-sections may have board directors, bureau directors, division chiefs, section or sub-section chiefs respectively. There are also heads of commissions or committees. These officials may have assistants if necessary. General offices may have directors and, when required, deputy directors. People's councils of villages and townships may have a clerk for each council and may also draw members of their working committees from the people's congresses at corresponding levels. People's councils of large townships may set up administrative organs if required. Local people's councils of higher levels may have a secretary-general and a number of his deputies for each council.

Any addition to, and amalgamation or abolition of the administrative organs of local people's councils are required to report the matter to the people's councils at the next higher level for approval. All administrative organs are subject to the coordinating direction of the people's councils concerned, and under the direction of the corresponding organs of the people's councils at the next higher level. The Ministries and Commissions of the State Council are the highest administrative organs in charge of the same kind of matters within the sphere of the various administrative units of local people's councils. Thus the State Council can concentrate the administrative powers of the state by means of direct and indirect control and supervision of its subordinate organs throughout the country.[1]

The people's councils at or above the district level exercise the following functions and powers in their respective areas: (1) to formulate administrative measures, issue orders, and verify their execution; (2) to conduct the election of deputies to the people's congresses at higher levels; (3) to convene and submit proposals to the people's congresses at corresponding levels; (4) to direct the work of subordinate units and of the people's councils at lower levels; (5) to revise or annul inappropriate orders and directions issued by their subordinate units and those issued by the people's councils at lower levels; (6) to appoint or remove government workers in accordance with law; (7) to put into effect economic plans and the provisions of budgets; (8) to control the market and such state-owned industrial and commercial enterprises as

[1] See Arts. 31–42 of the *Organic Law of the Local People's Congresses and Local People's Councils*, 1954.

are under the local authority, and to guide the socialist transformation of capitalist industry and commerce; (9) to direct the production of and cooperation in agriculture and handicrafts; (10) to direct the collection of taxes, public health, educational and cultural work, the care of the dependents of the revolutionists sacrificed for the Communist cause, as well as relief and welfare services; (11) to administer affairs concerning military service, communications, and public works; (12) to protect public property, maintain public order, and safeguard the rights of citizens as well as the equality of national minorities; (13) to assist in and supervise the work of organs of state, state-owned enterprises, and joint state-private enterprises which are located in their respective administrative areas but are not under their direct jurisdiction; and (14) to fulfill other tasks assigned by the administrative organs of state at higher levels.[1]

The people's councils below the district level exercise the corresponding functions as stated above with the exception of those under the categories from (4) to (8).[2] The control of rural areas through the village and organizations of peasant masses has been and still is the most effective means to indoctrinate the majority of the population of China. With the promulgation of the *Regulations on the Organization of Municipal Street Offices* and *Regulations on the Organization of City Residents' Committees* in 1954, the bonds between the Communist Government and city residents have been tightened. The urban areas today are subject to the strict surveillance of the party workers.

7. SELF-GOVERNMENT ORGANS
OF NATIONAL AUTONOMOUS AREAS

Legal provisions

The general principles and measures concerning the autonomy of national minorities as enforced during the period of 1949–1954 were reaffirmed by the Constitution of the People's Republic.[3] For the exercise of the functions and powers of local organs of state, organs of self-government of all autonomous regions, autonomous prefectures *(chou)*, and autonomous districts *(hsien* or counties) have been formed. An autonomous region corresponds to a province; an autonomous district has the same status as a district in the general system of local

---

[1] *Ibid.*, Arts. 27, 41.
[2] *Ibid.*, Art. 28.
[3] See Ch. XI, Sec. 4, "self-government organs of national autonomous areas."

government; a prefecture as an intermediate division stands between a region and a district, and is generally composed of a number of districts and municipalities. In an autonomous district *(hsien* or county), there are nationality villages *(hsiang)* and townships *(chen)*. Regional autonomy is exercised in areas where national minorities live in compact communities. In autonomous areas where a number of nationalities live together, each nationality is entitled to appropriate representation on the organs of self-government.

Apart from the regular functions and powers of the local state organs, the self-government organs of autonomous areas administer their own local finances, organize their own public security forces in accordance with law, adopt special laws and regulations suitable to their political, economic, and cultural characteristics upon the approval of the Standing Committee of the National People's Congress. The autonomous organs are permitted to use the languages of national minorities in performing functions within their areas.[1]

Autonomous areas

There are two autonomous regions in Communist China today. Founded in 1949 and occupying approximately one-ninth of the area of the country, the Inner.Mongolian Autonomous Region is composed of Mongolian, Manchu, Han, Hui, Tahur, Olunchun, and Solon peoples, totaling more than 7.4 million. The Sinkiang Uighur Autonomous Region, established in 1955, comprises one-sixth of China's total area. Almost three-quarters of the five million population in this region are Uighur. The other national minorities in addition to Uighur are Hui, Han, Mongolian, Tartar, Tadjik, Uzbek, Kazakh, Khalkha, Sibo, and Russian. Besides the above two autonomous regions, there is a Preparatory Committee for the Autonomous Region of Tibet where 3 million Tibetan people are located.

Below the regional level, there are approximately 30 autonomous prefectures *(chou)* and 50 autonomous districts *(hsien* or counties). Of these, the Chuang autonomous prefecture, created in 1952 in western Kwangsi province, is the most populous. Two-thirds of the 8 million people are Chuang, and the other one-third includes Han, Miao, Yao, T'ung, and Hui. The least populous area is the Olunchun autonomous area in the northeast of Inner Mongolia, with the status corresponding to a district and a population of only 2,000 Olunchun.[2]

---

[1] Arts. 53–54, 67–72 of the *Constitution*.
[2] See *Handbook on People's China* (1957), pp. 80–83.

In all autonomous areas, the organs of state should· be in the form of self-government; but, in practice, the principle of "democratic centralism" has been intensely enforced. The central authority, especially through its State Council, is supreme throughout the land whether or not the areas are populated by national minorities. The conformity to Communist ideology and standards has been gradually achieved by means of training the students from national minority groups in special nationality institutes and colleges, as well as the unceasing indoctrination of the people through mass organizations. The large-scale migration of the Han people to the compact regions of national minorities in the recent years could possibly have strengthened Communist control in such areas, but might also have caused concern and suspicion of the minority groups concerned.

8. THE COMMUNIST GOVERNMENT IN ACTION

Political developments

The Communist Party in China, with its well-known iron discipline and its control of the state organs and mass organizations throughout the country, should constitute an effective instrument for the enforcement of socialist programs. However, the power to overthrow an old regime does not automatically ensure the success of a new one. Certain weaknesses of the Communist Party and Government exposed thus far are the products of the system itself. Bureaucracy is the necessary evil of a huge organization with strict regimentation. As Marxism-Leninism is considered by the Communists as universal truth, ideological rigidity is the natural inclination prevalent among the leaders. Sectarianism is also an inevitable development in a party which emphasizes class struggle and organizational strength. Once a government falls under monolithic rule by a single party with no opposition, other corollary defects will grow if not checked in time.

It was because of these shortcomings that Mao Tse-tung directed the party to carry out the "Three-Anti" campaign in 1951. The three evils were: (1) corruption, (2) waste, and (3) bureaucracy among the party and government organs and public functionaries. Although high-ranking leaders were not affected by this campaign, many government officials both within and without the Communist Party were convicted and removed from office. While no reliable figures are available, the effect was nation-wide.[1]

[1] See Theodore H. E. and Wen-hui C. Chen, "The 'Three-Anti' and 'Five-Anti' Movements in Communist China," *Pacific Affairs*, Vol. 26, No. 1 (March 1953), pp. 3–23.

As the Communist government system is founded on "democratic dictatorship," the first move toward the direction of proletarian rule would be the liquidation of the national bourgeoisie. This task was accomplished by the "Five-Anti" campaign in 1952 against the so-called "five poisons": (1) bribery, (2) tax evasion, (3) fraud, (4) illegal use of public property, and (5) stealing of economic secrets. The main targets of this drive were the industrialists and businessmen, few of whom were not convicted for one reason or another during the campaign. The Communist Government had not only succeeded in whipping the national bourgeoisie into line for the socialist order but also profited considerably through the confiscation of private property. The nation's industries suffered to no small extent because the confiscation halted or interrupted production.

Although the leading members of the Communist Party of China were fully aware of the importance of internal solidarity, there were evidences of intra-party struggles for power. The purge of Kao-Jao in the spring of 1954 was the most notable case. A joint plot against the present leadership was to be engineered by Kao Kang, party leader in Manchuria, and Jao Shu-shih, Chairman of the East China Military and Political Committee. As a result of the party's early discovery, both of them were arrested and imprisoned. Kao managed to commit suicide. In view of the Kao-Jao incident and the untrustworthiness of other members, Mao Tse-tung launched the Party Reform Movement. The purpose of this campaign was to get rid of the dissident elements and ensure absolute loyalty and support of the party members to the present leadership.

In 1956 and 1957 there was the so-called "Blooming and Contending" campaign. In his address to the Supreme State Conference on May 2, 1956, Mao initiated the movement of the blooming of flowers and contending of thought. This movement was dramatized by the well-known slogan, "Let a hundred flowers bloom and a hundred schools of thought contend." The first part was originally applied by Mao in 1955 to encourage creative literature and drama. He spoke of the second phrase in 1956 as an analogy to the first with the hope that the other political parties and independent individuals would fully express their opinions on government policies and programs. This ideological maneuver reached its climax in April 1957, but was suddenly abandoned in June of the same year.[1] The abrupt halting of this campaign was due

[1] A result of the "thought contending" movement was the Hanyang student uprising in June 1957. Many party and government offices were wrecked by approximately one thousand

to the intensive nature and wide scope of criticism of the Communist regime far beyond its expectations. In order to suppress potential threats, the outspoken leaders of the minor political parties were condemned as rightist elements, including Chang Pai-chun and Lo Lung-chi.[1] Many intellectuals and public functionaries were accused of affiliation with the "Chang-Lo Alliance." These rightist elements were not only removed from their posts but were compelled to go through a process of re-education. This was the end of the "thought contending" movement.

After these campaigns, the Communist grip on personal activities, political thought, and economic life has become tighter than ever. On the other hand, the minor political parties and groups are still permitted to exist and carry out limited functions. Late in April 1962, these parties held a series of meetings for the coordination of their work with the goals of the Communist Party.[2] Although campaigns of reform and purges are not uncommon in socialist countries, such revolutionary upheavels indicate that Communist China today is still in the process of internal consolidation.

Economic measures

Following the example of Soviet Russia, the Communists in China were anxious to industrialize the nation after a brief period of economic rehabilitation. In 1953, the Central People's Government launched the First Five-Year Plan (1953–1957). Although the general goals and annual targets of the Plan were made known to the public from time to time, its formal adoption by the First National People's Congress was not made until July 30, 1955.[3] The primary purpose of the First Five-Year Plan was to develop heavy industry for the socialist transformation of agriculture, handicrafts, private industry, and commerce.

students taking part in the riot. Effective measures to prevent the recurrence of criticism and riot were adopted by the Central Committee of the Communist Party in September 1957. For further reference of the Communist thought control and suppression of religion, see Paul K. T. Sih, *Decision of China: Communism or Christianity,** pp. 103–114, 137–157.

[1] Chang was Chairman of the Chinese Peasants and Workers Democratic Party and Minister of Communications. Lo was Vice-Chairman of the China Democratic League and Minister of Timber Industry.

[2] See *Survey of China Mainland Press* (Hongkong: American Consulate General), No. 2736 (May 11, 1962). For personal observations of the Communist attitude toward minor political parties, see Chou Ching-wen, *Ten Years of Storm**, pp. 46–49. Formerly a leading member of the China Democratic League and a high-ranking official of the Communist Government in Peking, Chou managed to escape from the Mainland. This book is a record of his personal experience in Communist China.

[3] It was published in August 1955, under the title, *The First Five Year Plan for National Economic Development of the Chinese People's Republic.*

Another important objective was the strengthening of military power as a consequence of economic development. Judging from sources available, reasonable progress was made in various phases of national reconstruction even though the Plan's original targets were too ambitious to be fully achieved.

Encouraged by the success of the First Five-Year Plan in many respects, the State Council adopted, on February 7, 1957, a Second Five-Year Plan (1958–1962). Based largely upon the proposals passed by the Eighth National Congress of the Chinese Communist Party on September 27, 1956, the Second Five-Year Plan laid down the following as its principal tasks: (1) to continue the construction of heavy industry, (2) to build a solid foundation for socialist transformation, (3) to strengthen the national defense on the basis of industrial and agricultural production, and (4) to raise the standard of the people's material and cultural life. However, this draft Plan did not go through the normal procedure for formal approval by the National People's Congress at the time when the First Five-Year Plan expired in March 1958. As a replacement, "The Great Leap Forward" project (1958–1961) became the official economic plan of Communist China.

Under the leadership of the Soviet Union, the Communist countries agreed in 1957 to launch an intensive economic competition with the capitalist West. In May 1958, the Central Committee of the Chinese Communist Party adopted a large-scale economic program with the purpose of surpassing the total production of Great Britain. Known as "The Great Leap Forward," this program represented a most ambitious project in the fields of steel production, light industries, communications, and grain production. It was under this project that the people were ordered to collect scrap iron and install native blast furnaces for the increase of steel production. However, China was not economically prepared for the "great leap" program, which has now been slowed down owing to famine; as a consequence, emphasis has temporarily shifted from industry to agriculture.

The success of the agrarian reforms encouraged the Chinese Communists to start the program of collectivization,[1] which was enforced through a comparatively gradual and slow process: first, temporary arrangements of mutual aid among the peasants; second, the organization of agricultural producers' cooperatives, through which the peasants pooled their labor, tools, and land as investment; and third,

[1] For land redistribution and its implications, see Yuan-li Wu, *An Economic Survey of Communist China**, pp. 113–153.

the formation of collective farms, in which land was to be held under collective ownership. One step further from the collective farms was to be the state farms, with the state as owner of the land. For the purpose of promoting agricultural producers' cooperatives, the Central People's Government promulgated the *Model Regulations for an Agricultural Producers' Cooperative* on March 17, 1956 and the *Model Regulations for Advanced Agricultural Producers' Cooperatives* on June 30, 1956.[1] At the beginning, the Communist Government had great expectations of the agricultural producers' cooperatives as an effective means for socialist transformation;[2] but, because of organizational defects and the peasants' apathy, the results were less than satisfactory.

In order to improve the efficiency of the cooperatives and to fully utilize human resources, the Communist Party decided in March 1958 to combine the agricultural cooperatives into large units, later known as the communes. The model commune, Weihsing (Sputnik), was set up in Honan province in April 1958, as a result of the merger of 27 agricultural producers' cooperatives. This model commune was composed of 9,300 households with 43,000 people. The *Tentative Regulations of Weihsing People's Commune* of August 7, 1958 prescribed, among other things, the ownership of the means of production, the system of distribution, organization, and management, as well as the political, economic, military, and cultural tasks of the commune.[3]

According to these Regulations, agricultural producers' cooperatives are to turn over all their collectively-owned property, as well as privately-owned land, houses, livestock, and other means of production to the communes. To increase working efficiency, the villages are to merge with the communes. All residents sixteen years of age or over are to be full members of the communes. Pending the restoration of their political rights, former landlords, rich peasants, and counter-revolutionaries may be accepted as unofficial members. The communes are to set up community canteens, nurseries, and sewing teams to free women from household work. With the poor and lower-middle peasants as the core, the communes are required to strengthen political eduction in Communist ideas. For the institution of a system of citizen soldiery, the young and middle-aged men as well as demobilized servicemen are

[1] For their texts, see Albert P. Blaustein, *op. cit.*, pp. 362–441.
[2] See Mao Tse-tung's speech, *On the Question of Agricultural Cooperation* of July 31, 1955. Its text was reproduced in the *People's Daily* of October 17, 1955.
[3] For the English text of the *Regulations*, see Albert P. Blaustein, *op. cit.*, pp. 450–469.

to be organized into militia units to receive military training and to undertake tasks assigned by the state.[1]

The highest organ of management in a commune is the congress, which is composed of representatives of all production brigades and all groups of people, such as the women, youth, old people, cultural and educational workers, medical workers, scientific and technical workers, the personnel of industrial enterprises, traders, and national minorities. The congress is to elect a management committee, consisting of a head, his deputies, and committee members. Under their direction are the departments and commissions in charge of agriculture, water conservation, forestry, animal husbandry, industry and communications, finance and food supply, trade, cultural and educational work, armed defense, as well as planning and research. A supervisory committee is to be elected by the congress. Composed of a chairman, vice-chairmen, and committee members, this committee is to supervise the commune's affairs and is responsible to the state supervisory organs. The personnel of the commune's congress, management committee, and supervisory committee are to hold a term of two years.[2]

On August 29, 1958, the Central Committee of the Communist Party adopted a resolution on the establishment of people's communes. This resolution laid down the standards concerning the organization of communes on the basis of the size of the area, topographical conditions, the number of residents, and the need for the development of production. The communes could be classified under the following categories: (1) one commune to a village, comprising approximately 2,000 peasant households; (2) several communes in a village of a vast area and sparse population, each with less than 2,000 households; (3) one commune comprising several villages, with approximately 6,000 to 7,000 households; and (4) one commune with more than 10,000 households whenever advisable. As the communes grow, they may form a federation with the district (hsien or county) as a unit.[3] With the adoption of the above resolution, the people's communes have passed from the experimental stage to a nation-wide system.

Unlike the Soviet collective farms, the Chinese communes pay attention to both industrial and agricultural production and also to militia work.[4] The distribution system of the Chinese communes follows

[1] Ibid., Arts. 3, 5, 10, 11, 16, 17.
[2] Ibid., Art. 12.
[3] For further details, see the text of the resolution as contained in Albert. P. Blaustein, op. cit., pp. 442–449.
[4] See Geoffrey Hudson, et al., The Chinese Communes*, p. 9.

the cardinal principle of "from each according to his ability and to each according to his work." The communes generally provide daily necessities for the members with supplemental wages. Due to the difference in nature of the urban communes, the communization of cities and townships has not been as vigorously enforced as that in the villages. The urban communes are generally organized in the following units: (1) state-owned factories, mines, and other enterprises; (2) schools and offices; and (3) dwelling blocks.

It will take considerable time for the Chinese people to adapt to the abrupt transition from traditional family life to a new system of collective living without any individual privacy and personal ownership.[1] The commune system itself is still at a stage of trial and error, and many changes have been made concerning management-production relationships, forms of collective living, as well as the distribution and wage system. Rigid regimentation, long working hours, and poor living conditions are among the causes of dissatisfaction. After analyzing various aspects of the people's communes on the basis of his personal observation in Communist China, Chou Ching-wen wrote in December 1961 that this system has proved a complete failure. Commenting on the Communist blame for the setbacks "on natural calamities, 'bad elements' and the cadres," he pointed out that "none of these accusations and measures will produce any fundamental effect upon the effort of saving the failure from becoming a catastrophic disaster." In conclusion, he said that the "passive go-slow strike constitutes indeed one of the most effective ways of resistance against the Communist regime with regard to the commune system."[2]

While opinion in the West claimed that the current shortage of food in Communist China was the result of the mismanagement of the commune system, the Communist regime praised the system as the best possible instrument for combating natural calamities. In this connection, one commentator observed that in the experience of the Chinese Communists "the ability to marshal vast labor forces to fight the floods and famines of the 1960–1961 growing season has proven extremely beneficial."[3] The expectation is that the system of people's communes will probably continue to exist in China, but that its

[1] For the Communist Revolution and the Chinese family, see C. K. Yang, *The Chinese Family in the Communist Revolution**, pp. 3–21.

[2] Chow Ching-wen, *Criticism on People's Communes**, pp. 22, 42. Divergent views on the Chinese communes have been expressed by other writers. See Anna Louise Strong, *The Rise of the Chinese Communes**, Peter S. H. Tang, *The Commune System in Mainland China**, and Gerald Clark, *Impatient Giant: Red China Today**, pp. 79–92.

[3] Peter S. H. Tang, *Communist China Today*,* Vol. I, p. 484.

organizational and operational details will be subject to constant changes.

Perhaps no regime in existence more than a decade is merely incidental and no government purposely carries out programs detrimental to the interests of the people. Yet the justification of a revolution and the evaluation of the relative merits of policies depend upon the actual benefit bestowed on the public. Popular confidence in a government cannot long be maintained through high-sounding slogans and vague promises only to be fulfilled in the remote future. In spite of the arguments for and against Communism, the present status of the economic situation on the Mainland is far from satisfactory. Whatever the causes for the current calamities and however promising the future may be, the supply of basic necessities to the people for a decent living is the responsibility of any government in power, Communist or otherwise.

International relations

In the field of international relations, the Central People's Government has generally adhered to the principles contained in the Common Program and to Mao Tse-tung's lean-to-one-side policy. The tactics for the propagation of Communism may change, but the basic theory of world revolution remains the same. Since the foundation of the Sino-Soviet alliance was established by the treaty of February 14, 1950, a series of agreements on trade, economic and technical aid have been concluded. In spite of the much-discussed differences on the conception of coexistence and the decrease in aid and trade volume between the two countries,[1] there will be no armed conflict for the simple reason that neither China nor Soviet Russia can afford to fight against the other under the prevailing international circumstances.

The difference between the two Communist giants toward the policy of coexistence with the West is more apparent than real. The excessive exercise of the veto power in the Security Council, the collapse of the summit meeting in Paris, the problem of the unification of Germany, and the deadlock at the Geneva conference on disarmament are sufficient to show that Soviet Russia has not had any real intention to coexist peaceably with Western democracies. Dormant disagreements might have long been in existence, but the solidarity between Communist China and Soviet Russia in the face of serious international

[1] *New York Times*, March 30, August 9, 1962.

issues has been repeatedly tested. There are ample instances of their cooperation: the Korean war; the Indochina war and the Geneva conference in 1954; the Hungarian revolution in 1956; the problems of Taiwan and the United Nations representation; and the recent development in Laos. However, friction between the two great powers is unavoidable not only due to ideological quarrels and personality clashes but also because of the conflict of national interests and the struggle for leadership in the international Communist movement.[1]

At various international conferences, the Chinese Communists proclaimed to the Asian nations that their victory would be the model for all colonial and less developed countries. In her agreement with India on April 29, 1954, Communist China expressed her willingness to abide by the five principles as the guiding spirit of her foreign relations: (1) respect for territorial integrity and sovereignty, (2) non-aggression, (3) non-interference in domestic affairs, (4) equality among nations, and (5) mutual benefit and peaceful coexistence. At the Bandung Conference of Asian and African nations in April 1955, Chou En-lai reasserted these principles. To follow up this friendly attitude, Communist China concluded with Indonesia a treaty for the settlement of disputes arising out of the dual nationality of the Chinese in Indonesia.

In spite of her careful cultivation of cordial relations with neighboring countries, Communist China would not make any concessions when her vital interests are involved.[2] In the case of the Communist control of Tibet in 1954, India was compelled to recognize the *fait accompli* and gracefully withdraw her special interests and concessions originally obtained by Great Britain in Tibet. While the re-demarcation of the boundaries between China and Burma was amicably settled by means of a bilateral treaty, the Sino-Indian territorial dispute over 15,000 square miles of the border area in Ladakh has become more serious.[3] This issue can only be settled on the basis of mutual concessions. Communist China would not tolerate any non-Communist power dominating her border areas. Her intervention in Korea and Indochina was condemned by the West as aggression; but, to the Chinese Communists, their military actions were motivated by self-defense. Probably Peking's "Great Leap Forward"

[1] See Howard L. Boorman, *et al.*, *Moscow-Peking Axis**, pp. 1–49; Charles B. McLane, *Soviet Policy and the Chinese Communists, 1931–1946**, pp. 194–260; Zbigniew K. Brzezinski, *The Soviet Bloc: Unity and Conflict**, pp. 269–332.

[2] For an individual analysis of China's relations with different Asiatic nations, see A. Doak Barnett, *Communist China and Asia**, pp. 291–336.

[3] See *The New York Times*, 7/24, 7/26, 7/27, 8/7, 8/14, 8/15, 1962. The Chinese Communists have occupied approximately 12,000 square miles of the disputed territory.

policy could be applied to foreign relations too. In the continents of Africa and Latin America, the influence of the Chinese Communists will be felt more than before.

The ideological differences between Communist China and Western democracies make it difficult to reach any sincere and substantial cooperation. Sino-British relations are less than cordial even though Great Britain granted recognition to the Central People's Government at an early moment. The Communist resentment against the United States was deepened by the American commitment to defend Taiwan and other areas in Asia. Such political issues as a result of conflicting interests between the two antagonistic countries cannot be fundamentally settled under the prevailing circumstances, multitudinous ambassadorial talks nothwithstanding.[1] Nor can Communist China be easily appeased by mere recognition or admission to the United Nations. Western statesmen and experts have over-emphasized these secondary issues. To the Chinese Communists, a government in existence is a government in fact with or without recognition.[2] To the United States, it is beyond comprehension to consider any step in conflict with her treaty obligations. This awkward situation will probably remain unchanged in the foreseeable future.

---

[1] This is in reference to the intermitent discussions in Warsaw between the diplomatic representatives of the United States and Communist China. The meetings, originally held in Geneva, have now exceeded one hundred in number.

[2] For divergent views on the problem of recognition, see "Conlon Associates' Report on Communist China and Taiwan," *Congressional Record*, Proceedings and Debates of the 86th Congress, 2nd Sess.; Stanley K. Hornbeck, *A Brief Study of Some Facts and Many Not Facts Regarding "China" and United States "China Policy"**; William F. Knowland, "The United States Should Not Recognize Communist China," *Journal of International Affairs*, Vol. XI, No. 2 (1957), pp. 160–170. One of the most exhaustive studies on the subject of the recognition of Communist China is Robert P. Newman's *Recognition of Communist China?** For a brief review of the international position of Communist China, see Arthur Steiner, "Communist China in the World Society," *International Conciliation*, No. 533 (May 1961), pp. 389–454.

PRINCIPLES OF CONSTITUTION (HSIEN-FA TA-KANG)

September 22, 1908 [1]

The Powers of the Sovereign

1. The Emperor of the Grand Ch'ing Dynasty [Ta Ch'ing] shall rule supreme over the Grand Ch'ing Empire for ten thousand generations in succession and be honored forever.

2. The sacred majesty of the sovereign may not be offended against.

3. The sovereign enacts and promulgates laws and determines what may be assigned to others for deliberation. (Laws passed by parliament shall not become effective without the approval and promulgation by the sovereign.)

4. The sovereign has the power to convoke, to open and close, to suspend or extend the time of, and to dissolve parliament. (On the dissolution of the parliament, the people shall be called upon to elect new members of parliament. The members of the old parliament shall be classed with the common people. If any of them raises objection, he shall be punished by the appropriate law according to circumstances.)

5. The sovereign has power to appoint and dismiss all officials and to fix their salaries. (The power of appointment rests with the sovereign upon the advice of his grand ministers. The parliament may not interfere with this power.)

6. The sovereign has supreme command over the army and navy, and the power to make all regulations concerning them. (The sovereign has the absolute power to dispatch armies and to fix the number of troops. Parliament may not interfere in military affairs.)

7. The sovereign has the power to declare war and make peace, to conclude treaties, and to appoint and receive diplomatic envoys. (National foreign relations shall be controlled by the sovereign only, without the advice of the parliament.)

8. The sovereign has the power to declare martial law and, in time of emergency, to restrict the personal liberty of the subjects.

9. The sovereign has the power to confer distinctions and to grant pardons. (Mercy is from above. Officials, below, may not arrogate it to themselves.)

10. The sovereign has supreme power over the administration of the laws and the appointment of judges, but he shall act in accordance with the imperially sanctioned laws and shall not alter them by decrees. (Power to administer the law rests with the sovereign. Judges are appointed by the sovereign to act

---

[1] Promulgated by the Manchu Government. Translation based on U.S. Department of State, *Papers Relating to the Foreign Relations of the United States*, 1908 (Washington, 1912), pp. 194–195, with modifications by the author. The date according to Chinese traditional calendar was August 27, 1908.

for him in the administration of the laws. Changes shall not be made by imperial decrees and the imperially sanctioned laws must be treated as final in order to avoid confusion, because the interests at stake in judicial cases are important.)

11. The sovereign has the power to issue imperial decrees or to cause them to be issued; but he shall not change or abrogate laws which have already received imperial sanction, without first obtaining the advice of parliament. (Statutes proceed from his judicial power and imperial decrees from his executive power. As the two powers should be separate, imperial decrees must not be used to abrogate statutes.)

12. When parliament is not in session, the sovereign may, in case of urgent necessity, issue imperial decrees with the same effect as laws and raise the necessary funds. But he shall refer these matters to the parliament when it meets next year.

13. The expenses of the Imperial Household shall be fixed by the sovereign and drawn from the national treasury. Parliament shall not interfere with this power.

14. The grand ceremonies of the Imperial Household shall be decided by the sovereign with the assistance of the members of the royal family and his specially appointed ministers. Parliament shall not interfere with this power.

Rights and Duties of the Subjects

(Details shall be stipulated at the time of drafting the constitution.)

1. All subjects, who have the qualifications prescribed by law, are eligible for appointment as civil and military officials and members of parliament.

2. All subjects shall have freedom of speech, press and assembly within the scope of law.

3. Subjects shall not be liable to arrest, imprisonment or punishment except as prescribed by law.

4. Subjects may ask the judicial officials to judge their cases.

5. Subjects can be tried only by the courts specified by law.

6. The property and dwellings of subjects shall not be disturbed without cause.

7. Subjects shall have the obligation to pay taxes and render military service in accordance with the law.

8. Subjects shall continue to pay taxes at the present rate unless and until it is changed by law.

9. Subjects shall have the obligation to abide by the law of the land.

THE NINETEEN ARTICLES (SHIH-CHIU HSIN-T'IAO)

November 3, 1911 [1]

Art. 1. The Grand Ch'ing Dynasty shall reign forever.

Art. 2. The person of the Emperor shall be inviolable.

Art. 3. The power of the Emperor shall be limited by the Constitution.

Art. 4. The order of succession shall be prescribed in the Constitution.

Art. 5. The Constitution shall be drawn up and adopted by the National Legislative Council *(Tse-cheng Yuan)* and promulgated by the Emperor.

Art. 6. The power of amending the Constitution shall belong to the National Assembly.

Art. 7. The members of the Upper House shall be elected by the people from among those eligible for the position.

Art. 8. The National Assembly shall elect the Premier, whom the Emperor will then appoint. The other Cabinet ministers shall be recommended by the Premier and appointed by the Emperor. Members of the Imperial Family shall be ineligible to serve as Premier, Cabinet ministers and administrative heads of the provinces.

Art. 9. If the Premier, on being impeached by the National Assembly, does not dissolve the National Assembly, he shall resign; but one Cabinet shall not be allowed to dissolve the National Assembly more than once.

Art. 10. The Emperor shall assume direct control of the army and navy; but, when this power is used with regard to internal affairs, he must observe special conditions to be prescribed by the National Assembly.

Art. 11. Imperial decrees shall not be made to replace law; except in the event of emergency, decrees shall be issued only for the execution of law and under the authorization of law.

Art. 12. International treaties shall not be concluded without the consent of the National Assembly; but, when the National Assembly is not in session, the declaration of war and conclusion of peace may be made by the Emperor and approved by it afterwards.

Art. 13. Ordinances in connection with government administration shall be prescribed by law.

Art. 14. In case the Budget fails to receive the approval of the National Assembly, the Government shall not act upon the previous year's Budget nor may items of expenditures not provided for in the Budget be appended to it. The Government shall not be allowed to adopt extraordinary financial measures outside the Budget.

---

[1] Promulgated by the Manchu Government. Translation based on *The China Year Book*, 1912, xxiii-xxiv, with modifications by the author.

Art. 15. The National Assembly shall fix the expenses of the Imperial Household and any increase or decrease therein.

Art. 16. The grand ceremonies of the Imperial Family shall not be in conflict with the Constitution.

Art. 17. The agency for the adjudication of state affairs shall be established by the two houses.

Art. 18. The Emperor shall promulgate the decisions of the National Assembly.

Art. 19. The National Legislative Council shall act upon Articles 8, 9, 10, 12, 13, 14, 15, and 18 until the opening of the National Assembly.

PROVISIONAL CONSTITUTION OF THE REPUBLIC OF CHINA (CHUNG-HUA MIN-KUO LIN-SHIH YÜEH-FA)

March 11, 1912 [1]

CHAPTER I. *General Provisions*

Art. 1. The Republic of China is composed of the Chinese people.

Art. 2. The sovereignty of the Chinese Republic is vested in the people.

Art. 3. The territory of the Chinese Republic consists of 22 Provinces, Inner and Outer Mongolia, Tibet and Chinghai.

Art. 4. The sovereignty of the Chinese Republic is exercised by the Legislative Assembly, the Provisional President, the Cabinet and the Judiciary.

CHAPTER II. *Citizens*

Art. 5. Citizens of the Chinese Republic are all equal and there shall be no racial, class, or religious distinctions.

Art. 6. Citizens shall enjoy the following rights:

(1) The person of the citizens shall not be arrested, imprisoned, tried or punished except in accordance with law.

(2) The residences of citizens shall not be entered or searched except in accordance with law.

(3) Citizens shall enjoy the right of the security of their property and the freedom of trade.

(4) Citizens shall have the freedom of speech, of writing, of publication, of assembly and of association.

(5) Citizens shall have the right of the secrecy of their correspondence.

(6) Citizens shall have the liberty of residence and freedom of movement.

(7) Citizens shall have the freedom of religion.

Art. 7. Citizens shall have the right to petition the Legislative Assembly.

Art. 8. Citizens shall have the right of petitioning the administrative offices.

Art. 9. Citizens shall have the right to institute proceedings before the judiciary and to receive its trial and judgments.

Art. 10. Citizens shall have the right of suing officials in the administrative courts for violation of law or against their rights.

Art. 11. Citizens shall have the right of participating in civil examinations.

Art. 12. Citizens shall have the right to vote and to be voted for.

Art. 13. Citizens shall have the duty to pay taxes according to law.

---

[1] Promulgated by the Provisional Government of the Republic of China. Translation based on *American Journal of International Law, Supp.*, 6 (1912), pp. 149–154, with modifications by the author.

Art. 14. Citizens shall have the duty to serve as soldiers according to law.

Art. 15. The rights of citizens as provided in the present chapter shall be limited or modified by laws, provided such limitation or modification shall be deemed necessary for the promotion of public welfare, for the maintenance of public order or on account of extraordinary emergency.

CHAPTER III. *The Legislative Assembly*

Art. 16. The legislative power of the Chinese Republic is exercised by the Legislative Assembly.

Art. 17. The Legislative Assembly shall be composed of members elected by the several districts as provided in Article 18.

Art. 18. The Provinces, Inner and Outer Mongolia, and Tibet shall each elect and depute five members to the Legislative Assembly, and Chinghai shall elect one member.

The election districts and methods of election shall be decided by the localities concerned.

During the meeting of the Legislative Assembly each member shall have one vote.

Art. 19. The Legislative Assembly shall have the following powers:

(1) To pass all bills.

(2) To pass the budget of the Provisional Government.

(3) To pass laws of taxation, of currency and of weights and measures for the whole country.

(4) To pass measures for the raising of public loans and to conclude contracts affecting the national treasury.

(5) To give consent to matters provided in Articles 34, 35, and 40.

(6) To reply to inquiries from the Provisional Government.

(7) To receive and consider petitions of citizens.

(8) To make suggestions to the Government on legal or other matters.

(9) To introduce interpellations of members of the Cabinet and to insist on their being present in the Assembly in making replies thereto.

(10) To insist on the Government investigating into any alleged bribery and infringement of laws by officials.

(11) To impeach the Provisional President for high treason by a majority vote of three fourths of the quorum consisting of more than four fifths of the total number of the members.

(12) To impeach members of the Cabinet for failure to perform their official duties or for violation of the law, by majority votes of two thirds of the quorum consisting of over three fourths of the total number of the members.

Art. 20. The Legislative Assembly shall itself convoke, open and adjourn its own meetings.

Art. 21. The meetings of the Legislative Assembly shall be conducted publicly, but secret meetings may be held at the instigation of members of the Cabinet or by the majority vote of its quorum.

Art. 22. Matters passed by the Legislative Assembly shall be communicated to the Provisional President for promulgation and execution.

Art. 23. If the Provisional President should veto matters passed by the Legislative Assembly, he shall, within ten days after he received such resolutions, return the same with stated reasons to the Assembly for reconsideration.

If the same matter should again be passed by a two thirds vote of the quorum of the Assembly, it shall be dealt with in accordance with Article 22.

Art. 24. The President of the Legislative Assembly shall be elected by ballots signed by the voting members and the nominee who receives more than one half of the total number of the votes cast shall be elected.

Art. 25. Members of the Legislative Assembly shall not, outside of the Assembly hall, be responsible for their opinions expressed and votes cast in the Assembly.

Art. 26. Members of the Assembly shall not be arrested without the permission of the President of the Assembly except for crimes committed at the time of arrest and for crimes pertaining to civil and international warfare.

Art. 27. Procedures of the Legislative Assembly shall be decided by its own members.

Art. 28. The Legislative Assembly shall be dissolved on the day of the convocation of the Parliament and its powers shall be exercised by the latter.

CHAPTER IV. *The Provisional President and Vice President*

Art. 29. The Provisional President and Vice President shall be elected by the Legislative Assembly and the person who receives two thirds of the total amount of votes cast by a sitting of the Assembly consisting of over three fourths of the total number of members shall be elected.

Art. 30. The Provisional President represents the Provisional Government, exercises all executive powers, and promulgates all laws.

Art. 31. The Provisional President may issue or cause to be issued orders for the execution of laws and of powers delegated to him by the laws.

Art. 32. The Provisional President shall be Commander-in-Chief of the army and navy of the whole country.

Art. 33. The Provisional President shall ordain and establish the administrative system and official regulations, but he must first submit them to the Legislative Assembly for its approval.

Art. 34. The Provisional President shall appoint and remove civil and military officials, but in the appointment of members of the Cabinet, ambassadors and ministers he must have the concurrence of the Legislative Assembly.

Art. 35. The Provisional President shall have power, with the concurrence of the Legislative Assembly, to declare war, negotiate for peace, and conclude treaties.

Art. 36. The Provisional President may, in accordance with law, declare a state of siege.

Art. 37. The Provisional President shall, on behalf of the country, receive ambassadors and ministers of foreign nations.

Art. 38. The Provisional President may introduce bills into the Legislative Assembly.

Art. 39. The Provisional President may confer decorations and other insignia of honor.

Art. 40. The Provisional President may declare general amnesty, grant special pardons, commute a punishment and restore rights; but, in the case of a general amnesty, he must have the concurrence of the Legislative Assembly.

Art. 41. In case the Provisional President is impeached by the Legislative Assembly, he shall be tried by a special court consisting of nine judges, elected among the justices of the Supreme Court of the realm.

Art. 42. In case the Provisional President vacates his office for various reasons or is unable to discharge the powers and duties of the said office, the Provisional Vice President shall take charge of his powers and duties.

CHAPTER V. *Members of the Cabinet*

Art. 43. The Premier and the Ministers of the Government Departments shall be called Members of the Cabinet.

Art. 44. Members of the Cabinet shall assist the Provisional President in assuming responsibilities.

Art. 45. Members of the Cabinet shall countersign all bills introduced by the Provisional President and all laws and orders issued by him.

Art. 46. Members of the Cabinet and their deputies may be present and speak in the Legislative Assembly.

Art. 47. After members of the Cabinet have been impeached by the Legislative Assembly, the Provisional President shall remove them from office, but he may request the Legislative Assembly to reconsider their cases.

CHAPTER VI. *The Judiciary*

Art. 48. The Judiciary shall be composed of those judges appointed by the Provisional President, and the Minister of the Department of Justice.

The organization of the courts and the qualifications of judges shall be determined by law.

Art. 49. The Judiciary shall try civil and criminal cases, but cases involving administrative affairs or arising from other particular causes shall be dealt with according to special laws.

Art. 50. The trial of cases in the law courts shall be conducted publicly, but those affecting public safety and order may be in camera.

Art. 51. Judges shall be independent and their judgments shall not be subject to the interference of higher offices.

Art. 52. Judges during their continuance in office shall not have their emoluments decreased and shall not be transferred to other offices, nor shall they be removed from office except when they are convicted of crimes or of offences punishable according to law by removal from office. Regulations for the punishment of judges shall be determined by law.

CHAPTER VII. *Supplementary Articles*

Art. 53. Within ten months after the promulgation of this Provisional Constitution the Provisional President shall convene a Parliament, the organization of which and the laws for the election of whose members shall be decided by the Legislative Assembly.

Art. 54. The Constitution of the Republic of China shall be adopted by the Parliament, but before the promulgation of the Constitution the Provisional Constitution shall be as effective as the Constitution itself.

Art. 55. The Provisional Constitution may be amended by the assent of two thirds of the members of the Legislative Assembly or upon the application of the Provisional President and being passed by over three fourths of the quorum of the Assembly consisting of over four fifths of the total number of it members.

Art. 56. The present Provisional Constitution shall take effect on the date of its promulgation and the Organic Law of the Provisional Government shall cease to be effective on the same date.

CONSTITUTIONAL COMPACT
(CHUNG-HUA MIN-KUO YÜEH-FA)

May 1, 1914 [1]

CHAPTER I. *The Nation*

Art. 1. The Chinese Republic is composed of the people of China.

Art. 2. The sovereignty of the Chinese Republic resides in the whole body of the people.

Art. 3. The territory of the Chinese Republic remains the same as that of the former Empire.

CHAPTER II. *The Citizens*

Art. 4. Citizens of the Chinese Republic shall be equal before the law, irrespective of race, rank or religion.

Art. 5. Citizens shall enjoy the following rights:

(1) No citizens shall be arrested, imprisoned, tried or punished, except in accordance with law.

(2) The habitation of any citizen shall not be forcibly entered into or searched, except in accordance with law.

(3) Within the limits of the law, citizens shall have the right to own and enjoy property and to trade freely.

(4) Within the limits of the law, citizens shall have the rights of freedom of speech, of writing and publication, and of assembly and association.

(5) Within the limits of the law, citizens shall have the right of secrecy of correspondence.

(6) Within the limits of the law, citizens shall have the right of abode and of changing the same.

(7) Within the limits of the law, citizens shall have the right of religious belief.

Art. 6. In accordance with the provisions of the law, citizens shall have the right of petitioning the Legislative *Yuan*

Art. 7. In accordance with the provisions of the law, citizens shall have the right to institute proceedings in the courts of law.

Art. 8. In accordance with the provisions of the law, citizens shall have the right of petitioning administrative offices and of lodging complaints with the Administrative Court.

Art. 9. In accordance with the provisions of law, citizens shall have the right

---

[1] Promulgated by President Yüan Shih-k'ai. Translation based on U.S. Department of State, *Papers Relating to the Foreign Relations of the United States*, 1914 (Washington D.C., 1922), pp. 56–60, with modification by the author.

to attend the examinations for the appointment of officers and to enter the public service.

Art. 10. In accordance with the provisions of law, citizens shall have the right to vote and to be elected.

Art. 11. In accordance with the provisions of law, citizens are subject to the duty of paying taxes.

Art. 12. In accordance with the provisions of law, citizens are subject to the duty of performing military service.

Art. 13. The provisions made in this chapter that are not in conflict with the law, ordinances and discipline of the Army and Navy shall be applicable to persons belonging to said services.

CHAPTER III. *The President*

Art. 14. The President is the head of the Nation and combines in himself all powers of government.

Art. 15. The President shall represent the Chinese Republic.

Art. 16. The President shall be responsible to the whole Nation.

Art. 17. The President shall convoke the Legislative *Yuan* and open, prorogue and adjourn its sessions. The President, with the concurrence of the Consultative *Yuan,* may dissolve the Legislative *Yuan;* in the case of dissolution, new members must be elected and the Legislative *Yuan* convoked within six months from the date of dissolution.

Art. 18. The President may initiate legislation and shall submit the budget to the Legislative *Yuan.*

Art. 19. For the promotion of public welfare, for the execution of the law or in pursuance of authority granted by law, the President may issue or cause to be issued ordinances; but no ordinance shall alter any law.

Art. 20. In order to maintain peace and order or to avert extraordinary calamities at a time of urgent necessity when the Legislative *Yuan* can not be convoked, the President, with the Concurrence of the Consultative *Yuan,* may issue emergency ordinances having the force of law; but such ordinances shall be submitted to the Legislative *Yuan* for ratification at the beginning of its next session. Should the said emergency ordinances be rejected by the Legislative *Yuan,* they shall thereafter be null and void.

Art. 21. The President shall prescribe the administrative system and official regulations.

The President shall appoint and dismiss civil and military officers.

Art. 22. The President shall declare war and conclude peace.

Art. 23. The President is the Commander-in-chief of the Army and Navy and controls the land and sea forces of the Nation.

The President shall determine the organization and the strength of the Army and Navy.

Art. 24. The President shall receive foreign ambassadors and ministers.

Art. 25. The President makes treaties; but, should articles therein provide for any change of territory or increase the burdens of the citizens, the concurrence of the Legislative *Yuan* shall be required.

Art. 26. The President may, in accordance with the provisions of law, declare a state of siege.

Art. 27. The President may confer titles of nobility, rank, orders and other marks of honor.

Art. 28. The President may grant general amnesties, special pardons, commutations of punishment and restoration of rights. In the case of general amnesties, the concurrence of the Legislative *Yuan* shall be required.

Art. 29. When the President, for any cause, vacates his office or is unable to exercise the powers and functions connected therewith, the Vice President shall act in his stead.

CHAPTER IV. *The Legislative* Yuan

Art. 30. Laws shall be enacted by the Legislative *Yuan* composed of members elected by the people.

The organization of the Legislative *Yuan* and the method of the election of its members shall be prescribed and determined by the Constitutional Compact Conference.

Art. 31. The functions of the Legislative *Yuan* shall be as follows:
(1) To discuss and pass bills.
(2) To discuss and pass the budget.
(3) To discuss and pass or approve measures relating to the assumption of public debts and to the contracting of other liabilities to the charge of the National Treasury.
(4) To reply to inquiries addressed to it by the President.
(5) To receive petitions from the people.
(6) To initiate legislation.
(7) To submit to the President suggestions and opinions relating to legislation and other matters.
(8) To raise questions in regard to administration over which doubts have arisen and to request the President to reply thereon. But the President may refuse to reply should he deem it necessary for the matter to be kept secret.
(9) Should the President make an attempt against the State, the Legislative *Yuan* may institute impeachment proceedings against him in the Supreme Court of Justice, if approved by a majority of three fourths or over of a quorum of four fifths or over of the total number of members of the Legislative *Yuan*.

The exercise of the powers mentioned in (1)–(8) of this article and articles 20, 25, 28, 55 and 57 shall require the concurrence of a majority of the members present in the Legislative *Yuan*.

Art. 32. The annual session of the Legislative *Yuan* shall not exceed four months in duration, but may be prolonged should the President consider it necessary. The President may call an extraordinary session during the recess.

Art. 33. The deliberations of the Legislative *Yuan* shall be public, but the members may sit in secret session at the request of the President or as a result of the decision of a majority of the members present.

Art. 34. Bills which have passed the Legislative *Yuan* shall be promulgated and enforced by the President.

But if the President shall disapprove a bill duly passed in the Legislative *Yuan*, he may return the bill to the Legislative *Yuan* for reconsideration, with a statement of the reasons for his disapproval. In case the former decision of the Legislative *Yuan* is supported by a majority of two thirds or over of the members present, if the President still maintains that the bill would greatly endanger or harm either the internal administration of the State or its foreign relations or that there are great and important obstacles in the way of its execution, in such a case the President may, with the concurrence of the Consultative *Yuan*, withhold promulgation.

Art. 35. The Speaker and the Deputy Speaker of the Legislative *Yuan* shall be elected from and among the members by a majority of the votes cast.

Art. 36. Members of the Legislative *Yuan* shall not be held responsible, outside of Parliament, for their speeches, debates or for votes cast in the hall.

Art. 37. Except when discovered in the commission of a crime or when involved in crimes connected with internal or external security of the state, no member of the Legislative *Yuan* shall be arrested during the session without its permission.

Art. 38. The Legislative *Yuan* shall prescribe its own rules of procedure.

CHAPTER V. *The Administration*

Art. 39. The President is chief of the Administration and shall be assisted by one Secretary of State.

Art. 40. The affairs of the Administration shall be separately conducted by the Departments of Foreign Affairs, Interior, Finance, War, Navy, Justice, Education, Agriculture and Commerce, and Communications.

Art. 41. The Ministers of the Departments shall manage the administration of their respective departments in accordance with laws and ordinances.

Art. 42. The Secretary of State, the Ministers of the Departments and Special Delegates representing the President, shall be entitled to sit and speak in the Legislative *Yuan*.

Art. 43. The Secretary of State and the Ministers of the Departments may be impeached by the Censors and judged by the Administrative Court, should they violate the law.

CHAPTER VI. *The Judiciary*

Art. 44. The Judiciary shall be composed of the judges appointed by the President.

The organization of the courts and the qualification of the judges shall be determined by law.

Art. 45. The courts of law, in accordance with the provisions of law, shall try and judge all civil and criminal cases. But administrative and other special proceedings shall be tried and judged according to their respective laws.

Art. 46. The procedure of impeachment cases in the Supreme Court of Justice, as provided for under clause 9 of article 31, shall be determined separately by law.

Art. 47. In the courts of law, trials shall be conducted and judgment shall be rendered publicly. When, however, it is considered that publicity may be prejudicial to peace and order or to the maintenance of public morality, secrecy may be observed.

Art. 48. During his term of office, the salary of a judge shall not be reduced nor shall he be transferred to another office nor deprived of his office except as a consequence of punishment according to law or of disciplinary measures entailing dismissal.

CHAPTER VII. *The Consultative* Yuan

Art. 49. The Consultative *Yuan*, when advised by the President, shall deliberate upon important matters of state.

The organization of the Consultative *Yuan* shall be determined by the Constitutional Compact Conference.

CHAPTER VIII. *Finance*

Art. 50. The imposition of new taxes and modification of rates of the existing taxes shall be made by law.

The taxes levied at present shall, unless changed by law, be collected as in the past.

Art. 51. Annual revenue and expenditures of the State shall be dealt with in accordance with the provisions of the budget passed by the Legislative *Yuan*.

Art. 52. In order to meet special requirements, there may be included in the budget appropriations to continue for a certain number of years as a Continuing Expenditure Fund.

Art. 53. In order to supply deficiencies in the budget or to meet requirements not provided for in the same, a Reserve Fund shall be provided for in the budget.

Art. 54. Estimates for the objects of expenditure specified below shall not be rejected or reduced except with the concurrence of the President:

(1) Those appertaining to the legal obligations of the State.

(2) Such necessary expenditures as prescribed by law.

(3) Expenditures necessary to carry out treaty provisions.

(4) Expenditures necessary for the organization of the army and navy.

Art. 55. In case of international warfare or internal disturbance, or under extraordinary circumstances, when the Legislative *Yuan* cannot be convoked, the President, with the concurrence of the Consultative *Yuan*, may make urgent financial appropriations. But he shall request the Legislative *Yuan* for ratification at the beginning of its next session.

Art. 56. If the new budget has not been acted upon, the appropriations of the previous year shall continue in force. The same procedure shall be observed, should the adoption of the budget be delayed after the fiscal year has already begun.

Art. 57. The fiscal accounts of the revenue and expenditures of the State shall be audited every year by the Board of Audit and shall be reported by the President to the Legislative *Yuan* for approval.

Art. 58. The organization of the Board of Audit shall be determined by the Constitutional Compact Conference.

CHAPTER IX. *The Procedure for Drafting the Constitution*

Art. 59. The Constitution of the Chinese Republic shall be drafted by a Committee established for this purpose.

Members of this Committee shall be composed of ten persons elected by the Consultative *Yuan*.

Art. 60. The Draft of the Constitution of the Chinese Republic shall be examined and passed by the Consultative *Yuan*.

Art. 61. After the Constitution of the Chinese Republic has been examined by the Consultative *Yuan*, it shall be submitted by the President to the National Convention for final adoption.

The organization of the National Convention shall be determined by the Constitutional Compact Conference.

Art. 62. The National Convention shall be convoked and dissolved by the President.

Art. 63. The Constitution of the Chinese Republic shall be promulgated by the President.

CHAPTER X. *Supplementary Articles*

Art. 64. The Constitutional Compact shall have the same effect as the constitution before the promulgation and enforcement of the Constitution of the Chinese Republic.

Laws and ordinances in force before the enforcement of the Constitutional Compact, so far as they do not come into conflict with the same, shall continue to be valid.

Art. 65. The Articles proclaimed on the twelfth day of the second month of the first year of the Chinese Republic, regarding the favorable treatment of the Ta Ch'ing Emperor after his abdication of the Throne, and the special treatment of the Ch'ing Imperial Clan, as well as the special treatment of the Manchus, Mongols, Mohammedans and Tibetans, shall never be modified.

The statute on the treatment of the Mongols, which is correlated with the foregoing Articles, shall continue to be effective unless changed by law.

Art. 66. On the proposal of a majority of two thirds or over of the members of the Legislative *Yuan*, or on the proposal of the President, in either case if approved by a majority of three fourths or over of a quorum of four fifths or over of the total number of members of the Legislative *Yuan*, the President shall convoke the Constitutional Compact Conference to amend the Constitutional Compact.

Art. 67. Before the Legislative *Yuan* shall have been established, its powers and functions shall be assumed and discharged by the Consultative *Yuan*.

Art. 68. The Constitutional Compact shall take effect as of the date of promulgation, on which day the Provisional Constitution, proclaimed on the eleventh day of the third month of the first year of the Republic, shall become null and void.

THE CONSTITUTION OF THE REPUBLIC OF CHINA
(CHUNG-HUA MIN-KUO HSIEN-FA)

October 10, 1923 [1]

[PREAMBLE]

We, the Constitutional Conference of the Republic of China, in order to make manifest and foster the national dignity, stabilize the national boundaries, promote the general welfare and defend the principle of humanity, do make this Constitution and proclaim it to the whole country, to be observed by all and forever.

CHAPTER I. *Form of Government*

Art. 1. The Republic of China shall be a unified Republic forever.

CHAPTER II. *Sovereignty*

Art. 2. The sovereignty of the Republic of China is vested in the people as a whole.

CHAPTER III. *Territory*

Art. 3. The territory which originally belonged to the Republic shall be the territory of the Republic of China.

The territory and the division of it into areas shall not be altered except by law.

CHAPTER IV. *Citizens*

Art. 4. All persons who, according to law, possess Chinese nationality, are citizens of the Republic of China.

Art. 5. Citizens of the Republic of China shall be equal before the law. without distinction of race, class or religion.

[1] Promulgated by the Constitutional Conference of Parliament, under the government of President Ts'ao K'un. Translation based on The China Commission on Extraterritoriality, *Constitution and Supplementary Laws and Documents of the Republic of China* (Peking, 1924), pp. 15–48, with modifications by the author.

Art. 6. Citizens of the Republic of China shall not be arrested, imprisoned, tried or punished except in accordance with law.

Any citizen under arrest may, in accordance with law, apply to the court for a "Petition for Protection" to have his person delivered before the court and the cause tried.

Art. 7. The residences of citizens of the Republic of China shall not be entered or searched except in accordance with law.

Art. 8. The secrecy of letters and correspondence of citizens of the Republic of China shall not be violated except in accordance with law.

Art. 9. A citizen of the Republic of China shall be free to choose his residence and occupation; such freedom shall not be restricted except in accordance with law.

Art. 10. A citizen of the Republic of China shall be free to assemble and to form associations; such freedom shall not be restricted except in accordance with law.

Art. 11. A citizen of the Republic of China shall have freedom of speech, writing and publication; such freedom shall not be restricted except in accordance with law.

Art. 12. A citizen of the Republic of China shall be free to honor Confucius and to profess any religion; such freedom shall not be restricted except in accordance with law.

Art. 13. The right of ownership of a citizen of the Republic of China shall be inviolable; but any necessary disposition of his property for the public benefit may be made in accordance with law.

Art. 14. Liberties of the citizens of the Republic of China other than those provided for in this Chapter are recognized; provided that such liberties are not contrary to the principles of constitutional government.

Art. 15. A citizen of the Republic of China shall have the right to institute and carry on legal proceedings in a court of justice in accordance with law.

Art. 16. A citizen of the Republic of China shall have the right to make petitions and complaints in accordance with law.

Art. 17. A citizen of the Republic of China shall have the right to vote and to be a candidate for election in accordance with law.

Art. 18. A citizen of the Republic of China shall have the right to hold public office in accordance with law.

Art. 19. A citizen of the Republic of China shall have the duty to pay taxes in accordance with law.

Art. 20. A citizen of the Republic of China shall have the duty to undertake military service in accordance with law.

Art. 21. A citizen of the Republic of China shall have the duty to receive elementary education in accordance with law.

CHAPTER V. *Public Powers*

Art. 22. Of the public powers of the Republic of China, those relating to national affairs shall be exercised in accordance with the provisions of this Constitution; and those relating to local affairs, in accordance with the provisions of this Constitution and the self-government laws of the Province.

Art. 23. The following matters shall be legislated upon and executed by the Republic:

(1) Foreign relations;

(2) National defense;

(3) Nationality law;
(4) Criminal, civil and commercial laws;
(5) Prison system;
(6) Weights and measures;
(7) Currency and national banks;
(8) Customs duty, salt tax, stamp tax, tobacco and wine taxes, and other consumption taxes, and such other taxes the rates of which shall be uniform throughout the country;
(9) Postal system, telegraph system, and aviation;
(10) National railways and highways;
(11) National property;
(12) National debts;
(13) Monopolies and licenses;
(14) Examination, appointment, investigation and protection of the civil and military officials of the country;
(15) Other matters which, according to the provisions of this Constitution, relate to the Republic

Art. 24. The following matters shall be legislated upon and executed by the Republic or, under its order, executed by the local government:
(1) Agriculture, industry, mining, and forestry;
(2) The educational system;
(3) The banking and exchange system;
(4) Navigation and coast fisheries;
(5) Irrigation and conservation concerned with two or more provinces, and waterways extending to two or more Provinces;
(6) General regulations relating to municipalities;
(7) Eminent domain;
(8) The national census and statistics;
(9) Immigration, emigration, reclamation and migration;
(10) The police system;
(11) Public sanitation;
(12) Relief work and administration of unemployed persons;
(13) Preservation of such ancient books, objects, and remains as are of historic, cultural or scientific interest.

A Province may enact local laws relating to the above clauses, provided that they shall not be contrary to the national laws.

A Province may, pending legislation by the Republic, legislate upon the matters specified in clauses 1, 4, 10, 12 and 13.

Art. 25. The following matters shall be legislated upon and executed by the Province or, under its order, executed by the District [*Hsien*]:
(1) Provincial education, industry and communications;
(2) Management and disposal of Provincial properties;
(3) Municipal affairs of the Province;
(4) Provincial irrigation, conservation and engineering works;
(5) The land tax, title-deed tax, and other Provincial taxes;
(6) Provincial debts;
(7) Provincial banks;
(8) Provincial police and matters relating to public safety;
(9) Provincial philanthropic work and work for the public welfare;
(10) Self-government of the lower grades;
(11) Other matters assigned by national laws.

Where any of the matters above referred to concerns two or more Provinces it may be undertaken by them jointly, unless it is otherwise provided by law.

When the funds are insufficient, the deficit may, with the approval of Parliament, be subsidized by the national treasury.

Art. 26. When any matter not specified in Articles 23, 24, and 25 arises, it shall be a matter of the Republic if by its nature it concerns the Republic, and of a Province if by its nature it concerns the Province. Any controversy arising in this connection shall be decided by the Supreme Court of Justice.

Art. 27. The Republic may, in order to obviate the following abuses, or when necessary for the promotion of public welfare, restrict by law any Provincial tax and its method of collection:

(1) Impairment of the national revenue or commerce;

(2) Double taxes;

(3) Excessive fees or fees detrimental to communications, charged for the use of public roads or other means of communication;

(4) Taxes imposed by the Provinces or other local areas for the purpose of protecting their local products but detrimental to goods imported therein;

(5) Duties imposed by the Provinces or other local areas for the transit of goods.

Art. 28. A Provincial law conflicting with a national law shall be void. When doubt arises as to whether a Provincial law conflicts with a national law, interpretation shall lie with the Supreme Court of Justice.

The foregoing provision in the matter of interpretation shall apply when a Provincial self-government law conflicts with a national law.

Art. 29. In case of a deficit in the national budget or financial emergency, the Provinces may, with the approval of Parliament, be required to share the burden at rates increasing progressively with their annual revenues.

Art. 30. In the event of financial deficiency or extraordinary calamity, the locality concerned may, with the approval of Parliament, be subsidized by the national treasury.

Art. 31. Controversies between Provinces shall be decided by the Senate.

Art. 32. The organization of the national army shall be based upon a system of compulsory citizen service.

The Provinces shall, in general, have no military duty other than that of the execution of matters provided by the law of military service.

Citizens liable for military service shall be drafted and trained for different periods in recruiting areas of the whole country; but the stationing of standing armies shall be restricted to the areas required for national defense.

The military expenses of the Republic shall not exceed one quarter of the national annual expenditure; but this provision shall not apply in case of war with any foreign country.

The strength of the national army shall be determined by Parliament.

Art. 33. No province shall enter into any political alliance.

No Province shall take any action detrimental to the interests of another Province or any other local area.

Art. 34. No province shall keep any standing army or establish any military academy or arsenal.

Art. 35. If any Province fail to perform its duty as provided by a national law and refuse to obey after a warning by the Republic, the Republic may, with the national power, compel performance.

The aforesaid measure shall be stopped when it is disapproved by Parliament.

Art. 36. In the event of an invasion with military force by one Province of another, the National Government may intervene in accordance with the provisions of the last preceding article.

Art. 37. In the event of a change of the form of government or the destruction of the fundamental organization under the Constitution, the Provinces shall, until the original condition is restored, adopt and carry out joint measures to maintain the organization provided by the Constitution.

Art. 38. The provisions of this Chapter relating to Provinces shall apply to localities where Districts, but not Provinces, have been established.

CHAPTER VI. *The Parliament*

Art. 39. The legislative power of the Republic of China shall be exercised by Parliament.

Art. 40. The Parliament shall be composed of the Senate and the House of Representatives.

Art. 41. The Senate shall be composed of members elected by the highest local assemblies and other legally constituted electoral bodies.

Art. 42. The House of Representatives shall be composed of members elected by the electoral districts, the number of members elected in a district being proportional to its population.

Art. 43. The election of members of both houses shall be regulated by law.

Art. 44. No person shall be a member of both houses simultaneously.

Art. 45. No member of either house shall concurrently hold office as a civil or military official.

Art. 46. Each house may examine the qualifications of its own members.

Art. 47. The term of office of a member of the Senate shall be six years. One third of the members shall be elected every two years.

Art. 48. The term of office for a member of the House of Representatives shall be three years.

Art. 49. Members referred to in Articles 47 and 48 shall, after the completion of a new election, not be relieved of their duties until the day before the opening of the session in accordance with law.

Art. 50. Each house shall have a Speaker and a Deputy Speaker who shall be elected from among its own members.

Art. 51. Each house shall itself convene, open, and close its session; but extraordinary sessions shall be called under any of the following circumstances: *(1)* Upon the joint notice of one third or more of the members of each house; *(2)* At the summons of the President.

Art. 52. The ordinary session of Parliament shall be opened on the first day of August in each year.

Art. 53. The period of the ordinary session shall be four months; such period may be extended, provided that the extension shall not exceed the period of an ordinary session.

Art. 54. The opening and closing of sessions shall take place simultaneously in both houses.

When one house is suspended, the other house shall simultaneously adjourn.

When the House of Representatives is dissolved, the Senate shall simultaneously adjourn.

Art. 55. Deliberations shall take place in the two houses separately.

No bill shall be introduced simultaneously in both houses.

Art. 56. No deliberation shall commence in either house unless more than half of its members are present.

Art. 57. Deliberations in either house shall be decided by the vote of more than half of the members present. In the event of a tie, the Speaker shall have a casting vote.

Art. 58. An identical decision of both houses shall be the decision of Parliament.

Art. 59. The sittings of the two houses shall be open to the public; but they may, at the request of the Government or by decision of the house, be closed to the public.

Art. 60. When the House of Representatives considers that the President or Vice President is guilty of any treasonable act, he may be impeached by the votes of two thirds of the members present; provided that two thirds of all the members shall be present.

Art. 61. When the House of Representatives considers that a Cabinet Minister is guilty of any act contrary to law, he may be impeached by the votes of two thirds of the members present; provided that two thirds of all the members shall be present.

Art. 62. The House of Representatives may pass a vote of non-confidence against a Cabinet Minister.

Art. 63. An impeached President, Vice President, or Cabinet Minister shall be tried by the Senate.

The decision that the person tried under the provisions of the above paragraph is guilty of a crime or has violated the law shall not be pronounced without the concurrence of two thirds of the members present.

When the President or Vice President is adjudged guilty of a crime, he shall be removed from his office; but the punishment to be inflicted shall be determined by the Supreme Court of Justice.

When a Cabinet Minister is adjuged to have violated the law, he shall be removed from his office and may also be deprived of public rights. If he is guilty of a crime, he shall be delivered to a court of justice to be tried.

Art. 64. Each house may request the Government to institute an investigation in the matter of the conduct of an official acting contrary to law or duty.

Art. 65. Each house may make proposals to the Government.

Art. 66. Each house may receive petitions of citizens.

Art. 67. Members of either house may address an interpellation to a Cabinet Minister or ask him to appear in the house to answer an interpellation.

Art. 68. Members of either house shall not be held responsible outside of the house for opinions expressed or for votes cast in the house.

Art. 69. A member of either house shall not, during the session, be arrested or kept under surveillance without the permission of the house except where taken *in flagrante delicto.*

When a member of either house is arrested *in flagrante delicto*, the Government shall at once report the cause to the house; but the house may, by its decision, ask for a suspension of judicial proceedings during the session and the surrender of the arrested member to the house.

Art. 70. The annual allowances of the members of both houses and their other expenses shall be determined by law.

CHAPTER VII. *The President*

Art. 71. The executive power of the Republic of China shall be exercised by the President with the assistance of the Cabinet Ministers.

Art. 72. Any citizen of th Republic of China forty or more years old, in full enjoyment of civil rights, and resident in the country for ten years or more, shall be eligible as President.

Art. 73. The President shall be elected by a Presidential Electoral College composed of all the members of Parliament.

The election above referred to shall be held by secret ballot, and two thirds of the electors shall be present. The person who obtains three fourths of the total votes shall be elected. In the event of no one being elected after a second vote, a further vote shall be taken upon the two persons obtaining the highest numbers of votes in the second vote, and the one who obtains a majority vote shall be elected.

Art. 74. The term of office of the President shall be five years. In case of relection, he may hold office for a second term.

Three months prior to the expiration of the term of office of the President, the members of Parliament shall themselves convene and organize a Presidential Electoral College for the election of a President for the following term.

Art. 75. When the President assumes office, he shall take oath as follows:

I hereby solemnly swear that I will most faithfully observe the Constitution and perform the duties of the President.

Art. 76. In the event of the office of the President becoming vacant, the Vice President shall succeed until the expiration of the term of office of the President.

In the event of the President being unable for any reason to perform his duties, the Vice President shall act in his place.

If the office of the Vice President is also vacant, the Cabinet shall act for the President. In such event, the members of Parliament shall themselves within three months convene and organize a Presidential Electoral College to elect the next President.

Art. 77. The President shall be relieved of his office at the expiration of his term of office. If at the time a new President has not yet been elected, or has been elected but has not assumed his office, and the new Vice President is also unable to act as President, the Cabinet shall act for him.

Art. 78. The election of the Vice President shall be held in accordance with the provisions relating to the election of the President and shall take place at the same time. In the event of the Vice Presidency becoming vacant, a new Vice President shall be elected.

Art. 79. The President shall promulgate laws and supervise and secure their execution.

Art. 80. The President may issue mandates for the execution of laws or in pursuance of the authority delegated to him by law.

Art. 81. The President shall appoint and dismiss civil and military officials; but this provision shall not apply where this Constitution or the law otherwise provides.

Art. 82. The President shall be the Commander-in-Chief of the army and navy of the Republic and shall be in command thereof.

The organization of the army and navy shall be prescribed by law.

Art. 83. The President shall be the representative of the Republic with regard to foreign powers.

Art. 84. The President may, with the concurrence of Parliament, declare war; but in the matter of defense against foreign invasion, he may request the approval of Parliament after the declaration of war.

Art. 85. The President may conclude treaties; but treaties of peace and those relating to legislative matters shall not be valid without the approval of Parliament.

Art. 86. The President may proclaim martial law in accordance with law; but, if Parliament considers that there is no such necessity, he shall forthwith proclaim the withdrawal of martial law.

Art. 87. The President may, with the approval of the Supreme Court of Justice, remit or reduce punishments and restore civil rights; but in an impeachment case, no restoration of civil rights shall be declared without the approval of the Senate.

Art. 88. The President may suspend the session of the House of Representatives or the Senate; provided that no session shall be suspended more than twice and no suspension shall exceed ten days.

Art. 89. When a vote of non-confidence has been passed against a Cabinet Minister, the President shall either remove the Cabinet Minister from office or dissolve the House of Representatives; but the House of Representatives shall not be dissolved without the consent of the Senate.

During the tenure of office of the same Cabinet Minister or during the same session, no dissolution shall take place a second time.

When the President dissolves the House of Representatives, he shall forthwith order a new election and fix a date, within five months, for the convocation of the House to continue the session.

Art. 90. The President shall not, for any offense other than treason, be liable to criminal proceedings before he has vacated his office.

Art. 91. The annual salaries of the President and the Vice President shall be fixed by law.

CHAPTER VIII. *The Cabinet*

Art. 92. The Cabinet shall be composed of Cabinet Ministers.

Art. 93. The Premier and the Ministers of the various Ministries shall be Cabinet Ministers.

Art. 94. The Premier shall be appointed with the approval of the House of Representatives.

In the event of the Premiership becoming vacant when Parliament is not in session, the President may appoint an acting Premier; provided that the nomination of the next Premier shall, within seven days after the opening of the next session of Parliament, be submitted to the House of Representatives for approval.

Art. 95. The Cabinet Ministers shall assist the President and are responsible to the House of Representatives.

The mandates of the President and other documents concerning state affairs shall not be valid without the countersignature of a Cabinet Minister; but this provision shall not apply to the appointment and dismissal of a Premier.

Art. 96. A Cabinet Minister may appear and speak in both houses; but he may, for the purpose of making explanations of bills introduced by the Government, depute delegates to act for him.

CHAPTER IX. *The Judiciary*

Art. 97. The Judicial power of the Republic of China shall be exercised by courts of justice.

Art. 98. The organization of the judiciary and the qualifications for judicial officials shall be prescribed by law.

The President of the Supreme Court of Justice shall be appointed with the approval of the Senate.

Art. 99. Courts of justice shall, in accordance with law, accept and deal with civil, criminal, administrative and all other cases; but this provision shall not apply where this Constitution or the law provides otherwise.

Art. 100. Trials in a court of justice shall be conducted in public; but they may be held in camera when it is considered necessary for public peace or public morals.

Art. 101. A judicial official shall try and decide cases independently; no person whatsoever shall interfere.

Art. 102. A judicial official shall not, during his tenure of office, be subjected to a reduction of salary, suspension from office or transference to another office otherwise than in accordance with law.

A judicial official shall not, during his tenure of office, be removed from his office unless he has been convicted of a crime or subjected to disciplinary punishment, provided that these provisions shall not apply in a case of an alteration in the organization of the judiciary or of the qualifications for entry thereto.

The disciplinary punishment of judicial officials shall be prescribed by law.

CHAPTER X. *Law*

Art. 103. Members of the two houses and the Government may introduce bills; but if a bill is rejected by either house, it shall not be reintroduced during the same session.

Art. 104. A bill passed by Parliament shall be promulgated by the President within fifteen days after its transmission to him.

Art. 105. If the President disapproves a bill passed by Parliament, he may, within the period for promulgation, state the reasons and request Parliament to reconsider. If the two houses adhere to their original decision, the bill shall be promulgated forthwith.

If a bill has not been submitted for reconsideration and the period for promulgation has expired, it shall forthwith become law; provided that this provision shall not apply when the session of Parliament is closed or the House of Representatives is dissolved before the expiration of the period for promulgation.

Art. 106. A law shall not be altered or repealed otherwise than by law.

Art. 107. When a resolution passed by Parliament is submitted for reconsideration, the provisions relating to bills shall apply.

Art. 108. A law in conflict with this Constitution shall be void.

CHAPTER XI. *Finance*

Art. 109. The imposition of new taxes and alterations in the rates shall be made by law.

Art. 110. The approval of Parliament shall be obtained for the floating of national loans and the conclusion of agreements increasing the burdens of the national treasury.

Art. 111. The House of Representatives shall have the right to deliberate first on a financial bill directly affecting the burdens of the citizens.

Art. 112. A budget shall be made by the Government of the annual expenditures and revenues of the Republic. The budget shall be submitted first to the House of Representatives within fifteen days after the opening of the session of Parliament.

If the Senate amends or rejects a budget passed by the House of Representatives, the concurrence of the House of Representatives shall be obtained; if no such concurrence is obtained, the bill as originally passed shall forthwith become the budget.

Art. 113. The Government may, for special undertakings, provide in the budget continuing expenditure funds for a previously fixed number of years.

Art. 114. The Government may provide a reserve fund to supply deficiencies in the budget or requirements unprovided for in the same.

Any defrayment made out of the reserve fund shall be submitted during the next session to the House of Representatives for subsequent approbation.

Art. 115. The following items of expenditure shall not be stricken off or reduced by Parliament without the concurrence of the Government:

(1) Expenditures legally due from the Government as obligations;

(2) Expenditures necessary to carry out treaties;

(3) Expenditures made necessary by provisions of law;

(4) Continuing expenditure funds.

Art. 116. Parliament shall not increase the expenditures in the budget.

Art. 117. After the commencement of a fiscal year and before the passing of the budget, the monthly expenditures of the Government shall be one twelfth of the amount allowed in the budget for the previous year.

Art. 118. The Government may adopt financial emergency measures on account of a war of defense against a foreign power, suppression of internal disturbances, or relief for an extraordinary calamity when the urgency of the situation makes it impossible to summon Parliament; provided that such measures shall be submitted to Parliament for subsequent approval within seven days after the opening of the next session.

Art. 119. An order for payment of an annual expenditure of the Republic shall first be referred to the Board of Audit for approval.

Art. 120. The final account of the annual expenditures and revenues of the Republic shall be verified and confirmed each year by the Board of Audit and reported by the Government to Parliament.

If the House of Representatives rejects such final account or a bill for subsequent approbation, the Cabinet Minister concerned shall be responsible.

Art. 121. The organization of the Board of Audit and the qualifications of auditors shall be determined by law.

An auditor shall not, during his tenure of office, be subjected to a reduction of salary, a suspension of his functions or a transference of office except in accordance with law.

The disciplinary punishment of auditors shall be prescribed by law.

Art. 122. The President of the Board of Audit shall be elected by the Senate.

The President of the Board of Audit may, in any matter relating to the report of the final account, appear and speak in the two houses.

Art. 123. A budget or a bill requiring subsequent approval by Parliament shall, when it has been passed by Parliament, be promulgated by the President after its transmission to him.

CHAPTER XII. *The Local System*

Art. 124. Local areas are of two grades, the Province and the District.

Art. 125. A Province may, in accordance with the provisions of Article 22 of Chapter V of this Constitution, make provincial self-government laws; provided that such laws shall not conflict with the Constitution and the national laws.

Art. 126. The provincial self-government laws shall be made by the Provincial

Self-Government Laws Conference composed of delegates elected by the provincial assembly, district assemblies and legally constituted professional associations of the Province.

Each District shall elect one delegate. The number of delegates elected by the provincial assembly as those elected by the legally constituted professional associations shall not exceed one half of the total number of delegates elected by district assemblies; but the candidates for election by provincial assemblies and district assemblies shall not be limited to members of the respective assemblies. The election shall be regulated by provincial law.

Art. 127. The following provisions shall apply to all provinces:

(1) A Province shall have a provincial assembly which shall be a unicameral representative body. The members of such assembly shall be elected by direct election.

(2) A Province shall have a provincial administrative council which shall administer all matters of provincial self-government. Such council shall be composed of from five to nine councilmen directly elected by the citizens of the province. Their term of office shall be four years. Before a direct election is possible, an electoral college may be organized in accordance with the provisions of the last preceding article to elect such members; provided that a person in military service shall not be eligible unless he has been relieved of office for at least one year.

(3) A provincial administrative council shall have a chairman who shall be elected from among the councilmen.

(4) The nationals of the Republic of China who have resided in the Province for one year or more shall be equal before the law of the Province and be in full enjoyment of civil rights.

Art. 128. The following provisions shall apply to all Districts:

(1) A District shall have a district assembly which shall have legislative power over all matters of self-government in the District.

(2) A District shall have a magistrate who shall be directly elected by the citizens of the District, and shall, with the assistance of the district council, administer all matters of district self-government; but this provision shall not apply before the judiciary shall have become independent and the system of self-government of the lower grades shall have become complete.

(3) A District shall have the right to retain a portion of the provincial taxes raised in the District; provided that such portion shall not exceed forty per cent of the whole amount.

(4) The Provincial Government shall not dispose of the property of the Districts or their self-government funds.

(5) A District may, in case of a natural or any other calamity, or on account of shortage of funds for self-government, apply to the provincial assembly, receive subsidies from the provincial treasury.

(6) A District shall have the duty to enforce the national and provincial laws and ordinances.

Art. 129. The separation of the provincial and district taxes shall be determined by the provincial assembly.

Art. 130. A Province shall not enforce special laws against one or more Districts; but this provision shall not apply to laws concerning the general interests of the whole province.

Art. 131. A District shall have full power to execute matters of self-government. The Province shall not interfere except in matters of disciplinary punishment prescribed by provincial laws.

Art. 132. National administrative matters in a Province or a District may, as well as being executed by officials appointed by the Republic, be entrusted to the self-government organs of the Province or District.

Art. 133. If a self-government organ of a District or Province in the execution of any administrative matter of the Republic violates the law or ordinance, the Republic may, in accordance with law, inflict a disciplinary punishment upon it.

Art. 134. The provisions of this Constitution shall apply to areas where Districts, but not Provinces, have been established.

Art. 135. Inner and Outer Mongolia, Tibet and Chinghai may, in compliance with the common wish of the people of the area, be divided into two grades, the Province and the Districts, and be governed by the provisions of this Chapter; provided that, pending the establishment of the Province and Districts, their administrative systems shall be prescribed by law.

CHAPTER XIII. *The Amendment, Interpretation and Validity of the Constitution*

Art. 136. Parliament may make proposals for an amendment to the Constitution.

Such proposals shall not be made without the concurrence of two thirds or more of the members present in each house.

The members of either house shall not make a motion for a proposal to amend the Constitution unless such motion is signed by one fourth of all the members of the house.

Art. 137. The amendment to the Constitution shall be made by the Constitutional Conference.

Art. 138. The form of government shall not be the subject of amendment.

Art. 139. If there is any doubt about the meaning of the Constitution, interpretation shall be made by the Constitutional Conference.

Art. 140. The Constitutional Conference shall be composed of the members of Parliament.

The aforesaid Conference shall not commence to deliberate without the presence of two thirds of all the members, and shall not make any decision without the concurrence of three fourths of the members present; provided that in matters of interpretation, decisions may be made with the concurrence of two thirds of the members present.

Art. 141. The Constitution shall, under no circumstances, lose its validity otherwise than in accordance with the procedure of the amendment prescribed by this Chapter.

PROVISIONAL CONSTITUTION OF THE REPUBLIC OF CHINA FOR THE PERIOD OF POLITICAL TUTELAGE (CHUNG-HUA MIN-KUO HSUN-CHENG SHIH-CHI YÜEH-FA)

June 1, 1931 [1]

PREAMBLE

The National Government, in order to reconstruct the Republic of China on the basis of *The Three People's Principles* and *The Five-Power Constitution*, which form the fundamental principles of the Revolution, having now brought the Revolution from the military to the political tutelage period, deems it necessary to promulgate a Provisional Constitution for general observance, so that the realization of constitutional government may be accelerated and political power restored to a popularly-elected Government and, further, in pursuance of the Last Will of the late *Tsung-li* of the Nationalist Party, has called at the national capital the National People's Convention (Kuo-min Hui-i). The said Convention hereby enacts and ordains the following *Provisional Constitution of the Republic of China for the Period of Political Tutelage:*

CHAPTER I. *General Principles*

Art. 1. The territory of the Republic of China consists of the various Provinces and Mongolia and Tibet.

Art. 2. The sovereignty of the Republic of China is vested in the people as a whole.

All persons who, according to law, enjoy the nationality of the Republic of China shall be citizens of the Republic of China.

Art. 3. The Republic of China shall be a unified Republic forever.

Art. 4. The national flag of the Republic of China shall have a red background with a blue sky and white sun in the upper left corner

Art. 5. Nanking shall be the national capital of the Republic of China.

CHAPTER II. *Rights and Duties of the People*

Art. 6. All citizens of the Republic of China shall be equal before the law, irrespective of sex, race, religion or caste.

Art. 7. Citizens of the Republic of China shall, according to Article 8 of *The Outline of National Reconstruction*, enjoy in all completely autonomous

---

[1] Promulgated by the National Government of the Republic of China. Translation based on *The China Year Book, 1935* (Shanghai, 1935), pp. 63–66, with modifications by the author.

districts *(hsien)* the rights of election, initiative, recall and referendum as provided by Article 9 of *The Outline of National Reconstruction.*

Art. 8. Except in accordance with law, no person shall be arrested, detained, tried, or punished.

When a person is arrested or detained on a criminal charge, the organ responsible for his arrest or detention shall send him to the competent court for trial not later than twenty four hours. The party concerned may himself petition, or some other person may petition on his behalf, that he be brought before the court for trial within twenty four hours.

Art. 9. Except in accordance with law, no person other than those in active military service shall be subject to trial by a military court.

Art. 10. Except in accordance with law, no private houses of the people shall be subject to forcible entry, search, or sealing.

Art. 11. All persons shall have liberty of conscience.

Art. 12. All persons shall be free to choose and change their residence; such freedom shall not be denied or restricted except in accordance with law.

Art. 13. All persons shall have the right to the privacy of correspondence and telegraphic communications; such freedom shall not be denied or restricted except in accordance with law.

Art. 14. All persons shall have the freedom of assembly and formation of associations; such freedom shall not be denied or restricted except in accordance with law.

Art. 15. All persons shall have the liberty of speech and publication; such liberty shall not be denied or restricted except in accordance with law.

Art. 16. Except in accordance with law, no private property shall be sealed or confiscated.

Art. 17. The exercise of the right of ownership by any private owner of property, insofar as it does not conflict with the public interest, shall be protected by law.

Art. 18. Where public interest necessitates, the property of the people may be expropriated in accordance with law.

Art. 19. All persons shall have the right to inherit property in accordance with law.

Art. 20. All persons shall have the right of petition [to the government].

Art. 21. All persons shall have the right to institute judicial proceedings in the courts of justice, in accordance with law.

Art. 22. All persons shall have the right to submit petitions and institute administrative proceedings [in the Administrative Court] in accordance with law [for the redress of wrongs done by Government organs].

Art. 23. All persons shall have the right to compete in civil service examinations in accordance with law.

Art. 24. All persons may, according to law, hold public posts.

Art. 25. All persons shall have the duty of paying taxes in accordance with law.

Art. 26. All persons shall have the duty of performing military service and compulsory labor [for the State] in accordance with law.

Art. 27. All persons shall have the duty to obey the measures adopted by Government organs in performance of their duties according to law.

CHAPTER III. *Essentials of Political Tutelage*

Art. 28. The political principles and programs during the period of political tutelage shall be in accordance with *The Outline of National Reconstruction.*

Art. 29. The local self-government shall be enforced in accordance with the provisions of *The Outline of National Reconstruction* and the *Methods of Applying Local Self-Government*.

Art. 30. During the period of political tutelage, the National Congress of the Nationalist Party shall exercise the governing powers of the Central Government on behalf of the National Assembly *(Kuo-min Ta-hui)*. During the adjournment of the National Congress of the Party, the Central Executive Committee shall exercise the said powers.

Art. 31. The National Government shall train and guide [the citizens] in the exercise of the four political rights of election, initiative, recall, and referendum.

Art. 32. The National Government shall exercise the five governing powers, namely, executive, legislative, judicial, examining, and supervisory.

CHAPTER IV. *People's Livelihood*

Art. 33. In order to develop the people's economic welfare, the State shall afford every encouragement and protection to the productive enterprises of the people.

Art. 34. In order to develop rural economy, to improve the living conditions of farmers and to promote the well-being of peasants, the State shall take active steps for the carrying out of the following measures:

(1) Reclamation of all waste land in the country and development of farm irrigation;

(2) Establishment of agricultural banks and encouragement of cooperative enterprises in the rural communities;

(3) Enforcement of the [public] granary system for the prevention of famine and other calamities and replenishment of the people's food supplies;

(4) Development of agricultural education with special emphasis on scientific experiments, extensive development of agricultural enterprises and increase of agricultural produce;

(5) Encouragement of road-building in the rural villages to facilitate the transportation of agricultural products.

Art. 35. The State shall open and develop all coal, gold and iron mines; and shall also encourage and protect private mining enterprises.

Art. 36. The State shall undertake and inaugurate State shipping enterprises; and shall also encourage and protect private shipping enterprises.

Art. 37. All persons shall be free to choose their profession or occupation. But when it is contrary to the public interest, the State may, by law, restrict or deny such freedom.

Art. 38. All persons shall be free to make contracts; such freedoms, insofar as it is not in conflict with the public interest or with good morals, shall be protected by law.

Art. 39. In order to better the economic well-being and to promote closer cooperation between capital and labor, the people may form occupational organizations in accordance with law.

Art. 40. Both capital and labor shall develop productive enterprises in accordance with the principle of cooperation and mutual benefit.

Art. 41. In order to improve the living conditions of labor, the State shall put into effect various laws for the protection of labor.

Special protection shall be given to women and children workers in respect of their age and health.

Art. 42. In order to safeguard and relieve peasants as well as workers, who are unable to work on account of accidents, sickness, disability or old age, the State shall put into effect a labor insurance system.

Art. 43. In order to promote the economic interests of the people, the State shall encourage and promote various cooperative enterprises.

Art. 44. The State may control or regulate the production or sale as well as the market price of daily necessities of the people.

Art. 45. Laws shall be enacted for the prohibition of usury and exorbitant rents for the use of immovable properties.

Art. 46. The State shall give appropriate relief to those members of the armed forces who are disabled in the course of active service.

CHAPTER V. *Education of the Citizens*

Art. 47. *The Three People's Principles* shall be the basic principles of education in the Republic of China.

Art. 48. Both sexes shall have equal opportunity for education.

Art. 49. All public and private educational institutions in the country shall be subject to the supervision of the State and shall also be responsible for the carrying out of the educational policies adopted by the State.

Art. 50. All children of school age shall receive free education. Details shall be separately provided by law.

Art. 51. Those who have not had free education [in their youth] shall receive special adult education. Details shall be separately provided by law.

Art. 52. The Central and local governments shall provide adequate funds for necessary educational expenses and shall also safeguard the security of funds which are by law specially set apart [for educational purposes].

Art. 53. The State shall give encouragement or grants to private educational institutions which have achieved particularly satisfactory results.

Art. 54. Encouragement and grants shall be given for the education of overseas Chinese

Art. 55. The State shall encourage and safeguard members of the administrative or teaching staffs of schools who hold satisfactory records and have been long in service.

Art. 56. All public and private educational institutions in the country shall establish scholarships and prizes for the encouragement of deserving, but needy students.

Art. 57. The State shall encourage and protect research and discoveries in science and arts.

Art. 58. The State shall protect and preserve historic remains and ancient relics which have historical, cultural, or artistic value.

CHAPTER VI. *Division of Power between the Central and Local Governments*

Art. 59. The principle of equilibrium shall be adopted in the division of power between the Central and local governments, as stipulated in Article 17 of *The Outline of National Reconstruction.*

Art. 60. The various local governments may, within their respective spheres of authority, enact and ordain local laws and regulations. Where such laws and regulations are in conflict with those promulgated by the Central Government, they shall be null and void.

Art. 61. The demarcation between Central and local revenues shall be separately determined by law.

Art. 62. The Central Government may by law restrict any local tax, when –

(1) It is contrary to public interest;

(2) It encroaches upon the source of Central revenue;

(3) It constitutes overlapping taxation;

(4) It is detrimental to communications;

(5) It is unjustifiably imposed upon goods imported from other localities for the sole benefit of the locality concerned;

(6) It is in the nature of a transit duty on commodities in circulation among various localities.

Art. 63. The power of granting patents and monopolies is vested in the Central Government.

Art. 64. When one of the Provinces reaches the period of constitutionalism, the division of power between the Central and the local governments shall be defined in detail by law in accordance with *The Outline of National Reconstruction.*

CHAPTER VII. *Organization of the Governments*

Section 1. The Central Government

Art. 65. The National Government shall exercise all the governing powers of the Republic of China.

Art. 66. The National Government shall have supreme command over the land, naval, and air forces.

Art. 67. The National Government shall have the power to declare war, to negotiate peace, and to conclude treaties.

Art. 68. The National Government shall exercise the power of granting amnesties, pardons, reprieves, and restitutions of civil rights.

Art. 69. The National Government shall exercise the power of conferring medals and decorations of honor.

Art. 70. The National Government shall compile and publish a budget and financial statement of the national revenues and expenditures for each fiscal year.

Art. 71. The National Government shall be composed of the five *Yuan:* the Executive *Yuan*, the Legislative *Yuan*, the Judicial *Yuan*, the Examining *Yuan*, and the Supervisory *Yuan*, as well as various Ministries and Commissions.

Art. 72. The National Government shall have a President and an appropriate number of State Councilors, who shall be selected and appointed by the Central Executive Committee of the Nationalist Party. The number of State Councilors shall be separately determined by law.

Art. 73. The President of the National Government shall represent the nation both internally and internationally.

Art. 74. The Presidents of the five *Yuan* and the heads of the various Ministries and Commissions shall be appointed or dismissed in accordance with law by the National Government at the instance of the President of the National Government.

Art. 75. All laws shall be promulgated and mandates issued upon the signature of the President of the National Government according to law.

Art. 76. The various *Yuan*, Ministries or Commissions shall, according to law, issue orders.

Art. 77. The organization of the National Government and of the various *Yuan*, Ministries and Commissions shall be separately determined by law.

Section 2. The Local Governments

Art. 78. In each Province, a Provincial Government shall be established in charge of the administration of provincial affairs under the direction of the National Government. Its organization shall be separately determined by law.

Art. 79. When, as stipulated in Article 16 of *The Outline of National Reconstruction*, a Province reaches the period of constitutional government, the People's Representative Assembly [of the Province] may elect a Provincial Governor.

Art. 80. The system of local government in Mongolia and Tibet shall be determined separately by law in the light of the local conditions.

Art. 81. In each district *(hsien)*, a district government shall be established in charge of the administration of district affairs under the direction of the Provincial Government. Its organization shall be separately determined by law.

Art. 82. In each of the districts, a District Autonomy Preparatory Committee shall be organized to carry out the preparations as provided in Article 8 of *The Outline of National Reconstruction*. Its organization shall be separately determined by law.

Art. 83. Municipalities may be established in localities where industry and commerce, population or other special conditions warrant. The organization of such municipalities shall be separately determined by law.

CHAPTER VIII. *Annex*

Art. 84. All laws which are in conflict with this Provisional Constitution shall be null and void.

Art. 85. The power of interpreting this Provisional Constitution shall be exercised by the Central Executive Committee of the Nationalist Party.

Art. 86. A draft of the Permanent Constitution *(Hsien-fa)* shall be prepared by the Legislative *Yuan* on the basis of *The Outline of National Reconstruction* as well as the achievements during the periods of political tutelage and constitutional government. The said draft shall be duly made known to the people at large in preparation for its adoption and enforcement at the opportune moment.

Art. 87. When a majority of the Provinces in the country reach the period of constitutional government, that is, when district autonomy has been completely instituted throughout each of such Provinces, then the National Government shall immediately summon a National Assembly to decide upon the adoption and promulgation of the Permanent Constitution.

Art. 88. The present Provisional Constitution shall be enacted by the National People's Convention and forwarded to the National Government for promulgation.

Art. 89. The present Provisional Constitution shall come into force from the date of promulgation.

THE CONSTITUTION OF THE REPUBLIC OF CHINA (CHUNG-HUA MIN-KUO HSIEN-FA)

December 25, 1946 [1]

The National Assembly of the Republic of China, by virtue of the mandate received from the whole body of citizens, in accordance with the teachings bequeathed by Dr. Sun Yat-sen in founding the Republic of China, and in order to consolidate the authority of the State, safeguard the rights of the people, ensure social tranquility, and promote the welfare of the people, do hereby adopt this Constitution, to be promulgated throughout the country for faithful and perpetual observance by all.

CHAPTER I. *General Provisions*

Art. 1. The Republic of China, founded on the *Three People's Principles*, shall be a democratic republic of the people, to be governed by the people and for the people.

Art. 2. The sovereignty of the Republic of China shall reside in the whole body of citizens.

Art. 3. Persons possessing the nationality of the Republic of China shall be citizens of the Republic of China.

Art. 4. The territory of the Republic of China according to its existing national boundaries shall not be altered except by resolution of the National Assembly.

Art. 5. There shall be equality among the various nationalities in the Republic of China.

Art. 6. The National flag of the Republic of China shall be of red ground with a blue sky and a white sun in the upper left corner.

CHAPTER II. *Rights and Duties of the People*

Art. 7. All citizens of the Republic of China, irrespective of sex, religion, race, class, or party affiliation, shall be equal before the law.

Art. 8. Personal freedom shall be guaranteed to the people. Except in case of *flagrante delicto* as provided by law, no person shall be arrested or detained otherwise than by a judicial or a police organ in accordance with the procedure prescribed by law. No person shall be tried or punished otherwise than by a

---

[1] Adopted by the National Assembly on December 25, 1946, promulgated by the National Government on January 1, 1947 and effective from December 25, 1947. Translation based on The *China Yearbook, 1960–61* (Taipei: China Publishing Co.), pp. 878–900, with modifications by the author.

law court in accordance with the procedure prescribed by law. Any arrest, detention, trial, or punishment which is not in accordance with the procedure prescribed by law may be resisted.

When a person is arrested or detained on suspicion of having committed a crime, the organ making the arrest or detention shall, in writing, inform the said person, and his designated relative or friend, of the grounds for his arrest or detention, and shall, within 24 hours, turn him over to a competent court for trial. The said person, or any other person, may petition the competent court that a writ be served within 24 hours on the organ making the arrest for the surrender of the said person for trial.

The court shall not reject the petition mentioned in the preceding paragraph, nor shall it order the organ concerned to make an investigation and report first. The organ concerned shall not refuse to execute, or delay in executing, the writ of the court for the surrender of the said person for trial.

When a person is unlawfully arrested or detained by any organ, he or any other person may petition the court for an investigation. The court shall not reject such a petition, and shall, within 24 hours, investigate the action of the organ concerned and deal with the matter in accordance with law.

Art. 9. Except those in active military service, no person shall be subject to trial by a military tribunal.

Art. 10. The people shall have freedom of residence and of change of residence.

Art. 11. The people shall have freedom of speech, teaching, writing, and publication.

Art. 12. The people shall have freedom of privacy of correspondence.

Art. 13. The people shall have freedom of religious belief.

Art. 14. The people shall have freedom of assembly and of association.

Art. 15. The right of existence, the right of work, and the right of property shall be guaranteed to the people.

Art. 16. The people shall have the right of presenting petitions, lodging administrative appeals, or instituting legal proceedings.

Art. 17. The people shall have the right of election, recall, initiative, and referendum.

Art. 18. The people shall have the right of taking public examinations and of holding public offices.

Art. 19. The people shall have the duty of paying taxes in accordance with law.

Art. 20. The people shall have the duty of performing military service in accordance with law.

Art. 21. The people shall have the right and the duty of receiving citizens' education.

Art. 22. All other freedoms and rights of the people that are not detrimental to social order or public welfare shall be guaranteed under the Constitution.

Art. 23. All the freedoms and rights enumerated in the preceding Articles shall not be restricted by law except by such as may be necessary to prevent infringement upon the freedom of other persons, to avert an imminent crisis, to maintain social order, or to advance public interest.

Art. 24. Any public functionary who, in violation of law, infringes upon the freedom or right of any person shall, in addition to being subject to disciplinary measures in accordance with law, be held responsible under criminal and civil laws. The injured person may, in accordance with law, claim compensation from the State for damage sustained.

CHAPTER III. *The National Assembly*

Art. 25. The National Assembly shall, in accordance with the provisions of this Constitution, exercise political powers on behalf of the whole body of citizens.

Art. 26. The National Assembly shall be composed of the following delegates:

(1) One delegate shall be elected from each *hsien* [district], municipality, or area of equivalent status. In case its population exceeds 500,000, one additional delegate shall be elected for each additional 500,000. Areas equivalent to *hsien* or municipalities shall be prescribed by law.

(2) Delegates to represent Mongolia shall be elected on the basis of four for each League and one for each Special Banner.[1]

(3) The number of delegates to be elected from Tibet shall be prescribed by law.

(4) The number of delegates to be elected by various nationalities in frontier regions shall be prescribed by law.

(5) The number of delegates to be elected by Chinese citizens residing abroad shall be prescribed by law.

(6) The number of delegates to be elected by occupational groups shall be prescribed by law.

(7) The number of delegates to be elected by women's organizations shall be prescribed by law.

Art. 27. The functions of the National Assembly shall be as follows:

(1) To elect the President and the Vice President;

(2) To recall the President or the Vice President;

(3) To amend the Constitution;

(4) To vote on proposed Constitutional amendments submitted by the Legislative *Yuan* by way of referendum.

With respect to the rights of initiative and referendum, except as is provided in Items (3) and (4) of the preceding paragraph, the National Assembly shall make regulations pertaining thereto and put them into effect, after the above-mentioned two political rights shall have been exercised in one half of the *hsien* and municipalities of the whole country.

Art. 28. Delegates to the National Assembly shall be elected every six years.

The term of office of the delegates to each National Assembly shall terminate on the day on which the next National Assembly convenes.

No incumbent Government official shall, in the electoral area where he holds office, be elected delegate to the National Assembly.

Art. 29. The National Assembly shall be convoked by the President to meet 90 days prior to the date of expiration of each presidential term.

Art. 30. An extraordinary session of the National Assembly shall be convoked in any of the following circumstances:

(1) When, in accordance with the provisions of Article 49 of this Constitution, a new President and a new Vice President are to be elected;

(2) When, by resolution of the Supervisory *Yuan*, an impeachment of the President or the Vice President is instituted;

(3) When, by resolution of the Legislative *Yuan*, an amendment to the Constitution is proposed;

(4) When a meeting is requested by not less than two fifths of the delegates to the National Assembly.

When an extraordinary session is to be convoked in accordance with Item (1) or Item (2) of the preceding paragraph, the President of the Legislative *Yuan* shall issue the notice of convocation; when it is to be convoked in accordance

---

[1] The Banner is a local unit in Mongolia, designated by a special flag or banner.

with Item (3) of Item (4), it shall be convoked by the President of the Republic.

Art. 31. The National Assembly shall meet at the seat of the Central Government.

Art. 32. No delegate to the National Assembly shall be held responsible outside the Assembly for opinions expressed or votes cast at meetings of the Assembly.

Art. 33. While the Assembly is in session, no delegate to the National Assembly shall, except in case of *flagrante delicto*, be arrested or detained without the permission of the National Assembly.

Art. 34. The organization of the National Assembly, the election and recall of delegates to the National Assembly, and the procedure whereby the National Assembly is to carry out its functions, shall be prescribed by law.

CHAPTER IV. *The President*

Art. 35. The President shall be the head of the State and shall represent the Republic of China in foreign relations.

Art. 36. The President shall have supreme command of the land, sea, and air forces of the whole country.

Art. 37. The President shall, in accordance with law, promulgate laws and issue mandates with the countersignature of the President of the Executive *Yuan* or with the countersignatures of both the President of the Executive *Yuan* and the head of the Ministry or Commission concerned.

Art. 38. The President shall, in accordance with the provisions of this Constitution, exercise the power of concluding treaties, declaring war, and negotiating peace.

Art. 39. The President may, in accordance with law, declare martial law with the approval of, or subject to the confirmation by, the Legislative *Yuan*. When the Legislative *Yuan* deems it necessary, it may adopt a resolution requesting the President to terminate martial law.

Art. 40. The President shall, in accordance with law, exercise the power of granting amnesties, pardons, remission of sentences, and restitution of civil rights.

Art. 41. The President shall, in accordance with law, appoint and remove civil and military officials.

Art. 42. The President may, in accordance with law, confer honors and decorations.

Art. 43. In case of a natural calamity, an epidemic, or a national financial or economic crisis that calls for emergency measures, the President during the recess of the Legislative *Yuan* may, by resolution of the Executive *Yuan* Council, and in accordance with the Law on Emergency Decrees, issue emergency orders, proclaiming such measures as may be necessary to cope with the situation. Such orders shall, within one month after issuance, be presented to the Legislative *Yuan* for confirmation; in case the Legislative *Yuan* withholds confirmation, the said orders shall forthwith cease to be valid.

Art. 44. In case of disputes between two or more *Yuan* other than those provided for in this Constitution, the President may call a meeting of the Presidents of the *Yuan* concerned for consultation and settlement.

Art. 45. Any citizen of the Republic of China having attained the age of forty years is eligible for the office of President or Vice President.

Art. 46. The election of the President and the Vice President shall be prescribed by law.

Art. 47. The term of office of the President and the Vice President shall be six years. They may be re-elected for a second term.

Art. 48. The President shall, at the time of assuming office, take the following oath:

"I do solemnly and sincerely swear before the people of the whole country that I shall abide by the Constitution, faithfully perform my duties, promote the welfare of the people, safeguard the security of the State, and will in no way betray the people's trust. Should I break my oath, I shall be willing to submit myself to severe punishment by the State. This is my solemn oath."

Art. 49. In case the office of the President should become vacant, the Vice President shall succeed until the expiration of the original presidential term. In case the office of both the President and the Vice President should become vacant, the President of the Executive *Yuan* shall act for the President; and, in accordance with the provisions of Article 30 of this Constitution, an extraordinary session of the National Assembly shall be convoked for the election of a new President and a new Vice President, who shall hold office until the completion of the term left unfinished by the preceding President. In case the President should be unable to attend to office due to any cause, the Vice President shall act for the President. In case both the President and the Vice President should be unable to attend to office, the President of the Executive *Yuan* shall act for the President.

Art. 50. The President shall be relieved of his functions on the day his term expires. If by that time the succeeding President has not yet been elected, or if the President-elect and the Vice President-elect have not yet assumed office, the President of the Executive *Yuan* shall act for the President.

Art. 51. The period during which the President of the Executive *Yuan* may act for the President shall not exceed three months.

Art. 52. The President shall not, without having been recalled, or having been relieved of his functions, be liable to criminal prosecution unless he is charged with having committed an act of rebellion or treason.

CHAPTER V. *Administration*

Art. 53. The Executive *Yuan* shall be the highest administrative organ of the State.

Art. 54. The Executive *Yuan* shall have a President, a Vice President, heads of various Ministries and Commissions, and a certain number of Ministers without Portfolio.

Art. 55. The President of the Executive *Yuan* shall be nominated and, with the consent of the Legislative *Yuan*, appointed by the President of the Republic.

If, during the recess of the Legislative *Yuan*, the President of the Executive *Yuan* should resign or if his office should become vacant, his functions shall be exercised by the Vice President of the *Yuan*, acting on his behalf; but the President of the Republic shall, within 40 days, request a meeting of the Legislative *Yuan* to confirm his nominee for the vacancy. Pending such confirmation, the Vice President of the Executive *Yuan* shall temporarily exercise the functions of the President of the said *Yuan*.

Art. 56. The Vice President of the Executive *Yuan*, heads of various Ministries and Commissions, and Ministers without Portfolio shall be appointed by the President of the Republic upon the recommendation of the President of the Executive *Yuan*.

Art. 57. The Executive *Yuan* shall be responsible to the Legislative *Yuan* in accordance with the following provisions:

(1) The Executive *Yuan* shall have the responsibility of presenting to the Legislative *Yuan* administrative policies and reports. While the Legislative *Yuan* is in session, Members of the Legislative *Yuan* shall have the right to interpellate the President and the heads of various Ministries and Commissions of the Executive *Yuan.*

(2) If the Legislative *Yuan* does not concur in any important policy of the Executive *Yuan,* it may, by resolution, request the Executive *Yuan* to alter such a policy. With respect to such resolution, the Executive *Yuan* may, with the approval of the President of the Republic, request the Legislative *Yuan* for reconsideration. If, after reconsideration, two thirds of the Members of the Legislative *Yuan* present at the meeting uphold the original resolution, the President of the Executive *Yuan* shall either abide by the same or resign from office.

(3) If the Executive *Yuan* deems a resolution on a statute, budget, or treaty passed by the Legislative *Yuan* difficult of execution, it may, with the approval of the President of the Republic and within ten days after its transmission to the Executive *Yuan,* request the Legislative *Yuan* to reconsider the said resolution. If, after reconsideration. two thirds of the Members of the Legislative *Yuan* present at the meeting uphold the original resolution, thePresident of the Executive *Yuan* shall either abide by the same or resign from office.

Art. 58. The Executive *Yuan* shall have an Executive *Yuan* Council, to be composed of its President, Vice President, various Ministers and Chairmen of Commissions, and Ministers without Portfolio, with its President as Chairman.

Statutory or budgetary bills or bills concerning martial law, amnesty, declaration of war, conclusion of peace or treaties, and other important affairs, all of which are to be submitted to the Legislative *Yuan,* as well as matters that are of common concern to the various Ministries and Commissions, shall be presented by the President and various Ministers and Chairmen of Commissions of the Executive *Yuan* to the Executive *Yuan* Council for decision.

Art. 59. The Executive *Yuan* shall, three months before the beginning of each fiscal year, present to the Legislative *Yuan* the budgetary bill for the following fiscal year.

Art. 60. The Executive *Yuan* shall, within four months after the end of each fiscal year, present final accounts of revenues and expenditures to the Supervisory *Yuan.*

Art. 61. The organization of the Executive *Yuan* shall be prescribed by law.

CHAPTER VI. *Legislation*

Art. 62. The Legislative *Yuan* shall be the highest legislative organ of the State, to be constituted of Members elected by the people. It shall exercise legislative power on behalf of the people.

Art. 63. The Legislative *Yuan* shall have the power to decide by resolution upon statutory or budgetary bills or bills concerning martial law, amnesty, declaration of war, conclusion of peace or treaties, and other important affairs of the State.

Art. 64. Members of the Legislative *Yuan* shall be elected in accordance with the following provisions:

(1) Those to be elected from the provinces and by the municipalities under the

direct jurisdiction of the Executive *Yuan* shall be five for each province or municipality with a population of not more than 3,000,000; where the population exceeds 3,000,000, one additional Member shall be elected for each additional 1,000,000;

(2) Those to be elected from Mongolian Leagues and Banners;
(3) Those to be elected from Tibet;
(4) Those to be elected by various nationalities in frontier regions;
(5) Those to be elected by Chinese citizens residing abroad;
(6) Those to be elected by occupational groups.

The election of Members of the Legislative *Yuan* and the number of those to be elected in accordance with Items (2) to (6) of the preceding paragraph shall be prescribed by law. The number of women to be elected under the various items enumerated in the first paragraph shall be prescribed by law.

Art. 65. Members of the Legislative *Yuan* shall serve a term of three years, and shall be re-eligible. The election of Members of the Legislative *Yuan* shall be completed within three months prior to the expiration of each term.

Art. 66. The Legislative *Yuan* shall have a President and a Vice President. who shall be elected by and from among its Members.

Art. 67. The Legislative *Yuan* may set up various committees.

Such committees may invite government officials and private persons concerned to be present at their meetings to answer questions.

Art. 68. The Legislative *Yuan* shall hold two sessions each year, and shall convene of its own accord. The first session shall last from February to the end of May, and the second session from September to the end of December. Whenever necessary, a session may be prolonged.

Art. 69. In any of the following circumstances, the Legislative *Yuan* may hold an extraordinary session.

(1) At the request of the President of the Republic;
(2) Upon the request of not less than one fourth of its Members.

Art. 70. The Legislative *Yuan* shall not make proposals for an increase in the expenditures listed in the budgetary bill presented by the Executive *Yuan*.

Art. 71. At the meetings of the Legislative *Yuan*, the Presidents of the various *Yuan* concerned and the various Ministers and Chairmen of Commissions concerned may be present to give their views.

Art. 72. Statutory bills passed by the Legislative *Yuan* shall be transmitted to the President of the Republic and to the Executive *Yuan*. The President shall, within ten days after receipt thereof, promulgate them; or he may deal with them in accordance with the provisions of Article 57 of this Constitution.

Art. 73. No Member of the Legislative *Yuan* shall be held responsible outside the *Yuan* for opinions expressed or votes cast in the *Yuan*.

Art. 74. No Member of the Legislative *Yuan* shall, except in case of *flagrante delicto*, be arrested or detained without the permission of the Legislative *Yuan*.

Art. 75. No Member of the Legislative *Yuan* shall concurrently hold a government post.

Art. 76. The organization of the Legislative *Yuan* shall be prescribed by law.

CHAPTER VII. *Judiciary*

Art. 77. The Judicial *Yuan* shall be the highest judicial organ of the State and shall have charge of civil, criminal, and administrative cases, and over cases concerning disciplinary measures against public functionaries.

Art. 78. The Judicial *Yuan* shall interpret the Constitution and shall have the power to standardize the interpretation of laws and ordinances.

Art. 79. The Judicial *Yuan* shall have a President and a Vice President, who shall be nominated and, with the consent of the Supervisory *Yuan*, appointed by the President of the Republic.

The Judicial *Yuan* shall have a certain number of Grand Justices to take charge of matters specified in Article 78 of this Constitution, who shall be nominated and, with the consent of the Supervisory *Yuan*, appointed by the President of the Republic.

Art. 80. Judges shall be above partisanship and shall, in accordance with law, hold trials independently, free from any interference.

Art. 81. Judges shall hold office for life. No judge shall be removed from office unless he has been found guilty of a criminal offense or subjected to disciplinary measures, or declared to be under interdiction. No judge shall, except in accordance with law, be suspended or transferred or have his salary reduced.

Art. 82. The organization of the Judicial *Yuan* and of the law courts of various grades shall be prescribed by law.

CHAPTER VIII. *Examination*

Art. 83. The Examination *Yuan* shall be the highest examination organ of the State and shall have charge of matters relating to examination, employment, registration, service rating, scale of salaries, promotion and transfer, security of tenure, commendation, pecuniary aid in case of death, retirement, old age pensions, and other related matters.

Art. 84. The Examination *Yuan* shall have a President and a Vice President and a certain number of Members, all of whom shall be nominated and, with the consent of the Supervisory *Yuan*, appointed by the President of the Republic.

Art. 85. In the selection of public functionaries, a system of open competitive examination shall be put into operation, and examinations shall be held in different areas, with prescribed numbers of persons to be selected according to various provinces and areas. No person shall be appointed to a public office unless he is qualified through examination.

Art. 86. The following qualifications shall be determined and registered through examination by the Examination *Yuan* in accordance with Law:

(1) Qualifications for appointment as public functionaries;

(2) Qualifications for practice in specialized professions or as technicians.

Art. 87. The Examination *Yuan* may, with respect to matters under its charge, present statutory bills to the Legislative *Yuan*.

Art. 88. Members of the Examination *Yuan* shall be above partisanship and shall independently exercise their functions in accordance with law.

Art. 89. The organization of the Examination *Yuan* shall be prescribed by law.

CHAPTER IX. *Supervision*

Art. 90. The Supervisory *Yuan* shall be the highest supervisory organ of the State and shall exercise powers of consent, impeachment, censure, and auditing.

Art. 91. The Supervisory *Yuan* sall be composed of Members who shall be elected by provincial and municipal councils, and local councils of Mongolia and

Tibet, and Chinese citizens residing abroad. Their numbers shall be determined in accordance with the following provisions:

(1) Five Members from each province;

(2) Two members from each municipality under the direct jurisdiction of the Executive *Yuan;*

(3) Eight Members from Mongolian Leagues and Banners;

(4) Eight Members from Tibet;

(5) Eight Members from Chinese citizens residing abroad.

Art. 92. The Supervisory *Yuan* shall have a President and a Vice President, who shall be elected by and from among its Members.

Art. 93. Members of the Supervisory *Yuan* shall serve a term of six years and shall be re-eligible.

Art. 94. When the Supervisory *Yuan* exercises the power of consent in accordance with this Constitution, it shall do so by resolution of a majority of the Members present at the meeting.

Art. 95. The Supervisory *Yuan* may, in the exercise of its powers of control, request the Executive *Yuan* and its Ministries and Commissions to submit to it for perusal the supervisory orders issued by them and all other relevant documents.

Art. 96. The Supervisory *Yuan* may, taking into account the work of the Executive *Yuan* and its various Ministries and Commissions, set up a certain number of committees to investigate their activities with a view to ascertaining whether or not they have been guilty of violation of law or neglect of duty.

Art. 97. The Supervisory *Yuan* may, on the basis of the investigations and resolutions of its committees, propose corrective measures and forward them to the Executive *Yuan* and the Ministries and Commissions concerned, directing their attention to effecting improvements.

When the Supervisory *Yuan* deems a public functionary in the Central Government or in a local government guilty of neglect of duty or violation of law, it may propose corrective measures or institute an impeachment. If it involves a criminal offense, the case shall be turned over to a law court.

Art. 98. Impeachment by the Supervisory *Yuan* of a public functionary in the Central Government or in a local government shall be instituted upon the proposal of one or more than one Member of the Supervisory *Yuan* and the decision, after due consideration, by nine or more Members.

Art. 99. In case of impeachment by the Supervisory *Yuan* of the personnel of the Judicial *Yuan* or of the Examination *Yuan* for neglect of duty or violation of law, the provisions of Articles 95, 97, and 98 of this Constitution shall be applicable.

Art. 100. Impeachment by the Supervisory *Yuan* of the President or the Vice President of the Republic shall be instituted upon the proposal of not less than one fourth of the whole body of Members of the Supervisory *Yuan*, and the resolution, after due consideration, by the majority of the whole body of Members of the Supervisory *Yuan*, and the same shall be presented to the National Assembly.

Art. 101. No Member of the Supervisory *Yuan* shall be held responsible outside the *Yuan* for opinions expressed or votes cast in the *Yuan*.

Art. 102. No Member of the Supervisory *Yuan* shall, except in case of *flagrante delicto*, be arrested or detained without the permission of the Supervisory *Yuan*.

Art. 103. No Member of the Supervisory *Yuan* shall concurrently hold a public office or engage in any profession.

Art. 104. In the Supervisory *Yuan*, there shall be an Auditor General, who shall be nominated and, with the consent of the Legislative *Yuan,* appointed by the President of the Republic.

Art. 105. The Auditor General shall within three months after presentation by the Executive *Yuan* of the final accounts of revenues and expenditures, complete the auditing thereof in accordance with law, and submit an auditing report to the Legislative *Yuan.*

Art. 106. The organization of the Supervisory *Yuan* shall be prescribed by law.

CHAPTER X. *Powers of the Central and Local Governments*

Art. 107. In the following matters, the Central Government shall have the power of legislation and administration:
(1) Foreign affairs;
(2) National defense and military affairs concerning national defense;
(3) Nationality law and criminal, civil, and commercial law;
(4) Judicial system;
(5) Aviation, national highways, State-owned railways, navigation, postal and telegraph administration;
(6) Central Government finance and national revenues;
(7) Demarcation of national, provincial and *hsien* revenues;
(8) State-operated economic enterprises;
(9) Currency system and State banks;
(10) Weights and measures;
(11 Foreign trade policies;
(12) Financial and economic matters affecting foreigners or foreign countries;
(13) Other matters relating to the Central Government as provided by this Constitution.

Art. 108. In the following matters, the Central Government shall have the power of legislation and administration, but the Central Government may delegate the power of administration to the provincial and *hsien* governments:
(1) General principles of provincial and *hsien* selfg-overnment;
(2) Division of administrative areas;
(3) Forestry, industry, mining, and commerce;
(4) Educational system;
(5) Banking and exchange system;
(6) Shipping and deep-sea fishery;
(7) Public utilities;
(8) Cooperative enterprises;
(9) Water and land communication and transportation covering two or more provinces;
(10) Water conservancy, waterways, agriculture, and pastoral enterprise covering two or more provinces;
(11) Registration, employment, supervision, and security of tenure of officials in the Central and local governments;
(12) Land legislation;
(13) Labor legislation and other social legislation;
(14) Eminent domain;
(15) Census-taking and compilation of population statistics for the whole country;
(16) Immigration and land reclamation;
(17) Police system;

(18) Public health;
(19) Relief, pecuniary aid in case of death, and aid in case of unemployment;
(20) Preservation of ancient books and articles and sites of cultural value.

With respect to the various items enmuerated in the preceding paragraph, the provinces may enact separate rules and regulations, provided these are not in conflict with national laws.

Art. 109. In the following matters, the provinces shall have the power of legislation and administration, but the provinces may delegate the power of administration to the *hsien:*

(1) Provincial education, public health, industries, and communications;
(2) Management and disposal of provincial property;
(3) Administration of municipalities under provincial jurisdiction;
(4) Province-operated enterprises;
(5) Provincial cooperative enterprises;
(6) Provincial agriculture, forestry, water conservancy, fishery, animal husbandry, and public works;
(7) Provincial finance and revenues;
(8) Provincial debts;
(9) Provincial banks;
(10) Provincial police administration;
(11) Provincial charitable and public welfare work;
(12) Other matters delegated to the provinces in accordance with national laws.

Except as otherwise provided by law, any of the matters enumerated in the various items of the preceding paragraph, in so far as it covers two or more provinces, may be undertaken jointly by the provinces concerned.

When any province, in undertaking matters listed in any of the items of the first paragraph, finds its funds insufficient, it may, by resolution of the Legislative *Yuan*, obtain subsidies from the National Treasury.

Art. 110. In the following matters, the *hsien* shall have the power of legislation and administration:

(1) *Hsien* education, public health, industries, and communications;
(2) Management and disposal of *hsien* property;
(3) *Hsien*-operated enterprises;
(4) *Hsien* cooperative enterprises;
(5) *Hsien* agriculture and forestry, water conservancy, fishery, animal husbandry, and public works;
(6) *Hsien* finance and revenues;
(7) *Hsien* debts;
(8) *Hsien* banks;
(9) Administration of *hsien* police and defense;
(10) *Hsien* charitable and public welfare work;
(11) Other matters delegated to the *hsien* in accordance with national laws and provincial self-government regulations.

Except as otherwise provided by law, any of the matters enumerated in the various items of the preceding paragraph, in so far as it covers two or more *hsien*, may be undertaken jointly by the *hsien* concerned.

Art. 111. Any matter not enumerated in Articles 107, 108, 109, and 110 shall fall within the jurisdiction of the Central Government, if it is national in nature; of the province, if it is provincial in nature; and of the *hsien*, if it is *hsien* in nature. In case of dispute, it shall be settled by the Legislative *Yuan*.

CHAPTER XI. *System of Local Government*

Section 1. The Province

Art. 112. The province may convoke a Provincial Assembly to enact, in accordance with the *General Principles of Provincial and Hsien Self-Government,* provincial self-government regulations, provided the said regulations are not in conflict with the Constitution.

The organization of the Provincial Assembly and the election of the Delegates shall be prescribed by law.

Art. 113. The provincial self-government regulations shall include the following provisions:

(1) In the province, there shall be a Provincial Council. Members of the Provincial Council shall be elected by the people of the province.

(2) In the province, there shall be a Provincial Government with a Provincial Governor who shall be elected by the people of the province.

(3) Relationship between the province and the *hsien.*

The legislative power of the province shall be exercised by the Provincial Council.

Art. 114. The provincial self-government regulations shall, after enactment, be forthwith submitted to the Judicial *Yuan.* The Judicial *Yuan,* if it deems any part thereof unconstitutional, shall declare null and void the articles repugnant to the Constitution.

Art. 115. If, during the enforcement of the provincial self-government regulations, there should arise any serious obstacle in the application of any of the articles contained therein, the Judicial *Yuan* shall first summon the various parties concerned to present their views; and thereupon the Presidents of the Executive *Yuan,* Legislative *Yuan,* Judicial *Yuan,* Examination *Yuan,* and Supervisory *Yuan* shall form a committee, with the President of the Judicial *Yuan* as Chairman, to propose a formula for solution.

Art. 116. Provincial rules and regulations that are in conflict with national laws shall be null and void.

Art. 117. When doubt arises as to whether or not there is a conflict between provincial rules or regulations and national laws, interpretation thereon shall be made by the Judicial *Yuan.*

Art. 118. The self-government of municipalities under the direct jurisdiction of the Executive *Yuan* shall be prescribed by law.

Art. 119. The local self-government system of the Mongolian Leagues and Banners shall be prescribed by law.

Art. 120. The self-government system of Tibet shall be safeguarded.

Section 2. The *Hsien*

Art. 121. The *hsien* shall enforce *hsien* self-government.

Art. 122. A *hsien* may convoke a *Hsien* Assembly to enact, in accordance with the *General Principles of Provincial and Hsien Self-Government, hsien* self-government regulations, provided the said regulations are not in conflict with the Constitution or with provincial self-government regulations.

Art. 123. The people of the *hsien* shall, in accordance with law, exercise the rights of initiative and referendum in matters within the sphere of *hsien* self-government, and shall, in accordance with law, exercise the rights of election and recall of the *Hsien* Magistrate and other *hsien* self-government officials.

Art. 124. In the *hsien*, there shall be a *Hsien* Council. Members of the *Hsien* Council shall be elected by the people of the *hsien*.

The legislative power of the *hsien* shall be exercised by the *Hsien* Council.

Art. 125. *Hsien* rules and regulations that are in conflict with national laws, or with provincial rules and regulations, shall be null and void.

Art. 126. In the *hsien*, there shall be a *Hsien* Government with a *Hsien* Magistrate who shall be elected by the people of the *hsien*.

Art. 127. The *Hsien* Magistrate shall have charge of *hsien* self-government and shall administer matters delegated to the *hsien* by the Central or provincial government.

Art. 128. The provisions governing the *hsien* shall apply *mutatis mutandis* to the municipality.

CHAPTER XII. *Election, Recall, Initiative, and Referendum*

Art. 129. The various kinds of elections prescribed in this Constitution, except as otherwise provided by this Constitution, shall be by universal, equal, and direct suffrage and by secret ballot.

Art. 130. Citizens of the Republic of China having attained the age of twenty years shall have the right to vote in accordance with law. Except as otherwise provided by this Constitution or by law, citizens having attained the age of twenty-three years shall have the right of being elected to office in accordance with law.

Art. 131. The candidates in the various kinds of elections prescribed in this Constitution shall openly campaign for their election.

Art. 132. Intimidation or inducement shall be strictly forbidden in elections. Suits arising in connection with elections shall be tried by the court.

Art. 133. A person elected may, in accordance with law, be recalled by his constituency.

Art. 134. In the various kinds of elections, the number of women to be elected shall be fixed, and measures pertaining thereto shall be prescribed by law.

Art. 135. The number of delegates to the National Assembly and the manner of their election by people in interior areas, where they have their own conditions of living and habits, shall be prescribed by law.

Art. 136. The exercise of the rights of initiative and referendum shall be prescribed by law.

CHAPTER XIII. *Fundamental National Policies*

Section 1. National Defense

Art. 137. The national defense of the Republic of China shall have as its objective the safeguarding of national security and the preservation of world peace.

The organization of national defense shall be prescribed by law.

Art. 138. The land, sea, and air forces of the whole country shall be above personal, regional, or party affiliations, shall be loyal to the State, and shall protect the people.

Art. 139. No political party and no indivicual shall make use of armed force as an instrument in a struggle for political power.

Art. 140. No military man in active service may concurrently hold a civil office.

Section 2. Foreign Policy

Art. 141. The foreign policy of the Republic of China shall, in a spirit of independence and initiative and on the basis of the principles of equality and reciprocity, cultivate friendly relations with other nations and respect treaties and the Charter of the United Nations, in order to protect the rights and interests of Chinese citizens residing abroad, promote international cooperation, advance international justice, and ensure world peace.

Section 3. National Economy

Art. 142. The National economy shall be based on the "Principle of Livelihood" and shall seek to effect equalization of landownership and restriction of private capital in order to attain a well-balanced development of national economy and people's livelihood.

Art. 143. All land within the territory of the Republic of China shall belong to the whole body of citizens. Private ownership of land, acquired by the people in accordance with law, shall be protected and restricted by law. Privately-owned land shall be liable to taxation according to its value, and the Government may buy such land according to its value.

Mineral deposits which are embedded in the land, and natural power which may, for economic purposes, be utilized for the public benefit shall belong to the State, regardless of the fact that private individuals may have acquired ownership over such land.

If the value of a piece of land has increased, not through the exertion of labor or the employment of capital, the State shall levy thereon an increment tax, the proceeds of which shall be enjoyed by the people in common.

In the distribution and readjustment of land, the State shall in principle assist self-farming landowners and persons who make use of the land by themselves, and shall also regulate their appropriate areas of operation.

Art. 144. Public utilities and other enterprises of a monopolistic nature shall, in principle, be under public operation. In cases permitted by law, they may be operated by private citizens.

Art. 145. With respect to private wealth and privately-operated enterprises, the State shall restrict them by law if they are deemed detrimental to a balanced development of national economy and people's livelihood.

Cooperative enterprises shall receive encouragement and assistance from the State.

Private productive enterprises and foreign trade shall receive encouragement, guidance, and protection from the State.

Art. 146. The State shall, by the use of scientific techniques, develop water conservancy, increase the productivity of land, improve agricultural conditions, plan for the utilization of land, develop agricultural resources, and hasten the industrialization of agriculture.

Art. 147. The Central Government, in order to attain a balanced economic development among the provinces, shall give appropriate aid to poor or unproductive provinces.

The provinces, in order to attain a balanced economic development among the *hsien*, shall give appropriate aid to poor or unproductive *hsien*.

Art. 148. Within the territory of the Republic of China, all goods shall be permitted to move freely from place to place.

Art. 149. Financial institutions shall, in accordance with law, be subject to State control.

Art. 150. The State shall extensively establish financial institutions for the common people, with a view to relieving unemployment.

Art. 151. With respect to Chinese citizens residing abroad, the State shall foster and protect the development of their economic enterprises.

Section 4. Social Security

Art. 152. The State shall provide suitable opportunity for work to all persons who are able to work.

Art. 153. The State, in order to improve the livelihood of laborers and farmers and to improve their productive skill, shall enact laws and carry out policies for their protection.

Women and children engaged in labor shall, according to their age and physical condition, be accorded special protection.

Art. 154. Capital and labor shall, in accordance with the principle of harmony and cooperation, promote productive enterprises. Conciliation and arbitration of disputes between capital and labor shall be prescribed by law.

Art. 155. The State, in order to promote social welfare, shall establish a social insurance system. To the aged and the infirm who are unable to earn a living, and to victims of unusual calamities, the State shall give appropriate assistance and relief.

Art. 156. The State, in order to consolidate the foundation of national existence and development, shall protect motherhood and carry out the policy of promoting the welfare of women and children.

Art. 157. The State, in order to improve national health, shall establish extensive services for sanitation and health protection, and a system of public medical service.

Section 5. Education and Culture

Art. 158. Education and culture shall aim at the development among the citizens of the national spirit, the spirit of self-government, national morality, good physique, scientific knowledge, and the ability to earn a living.

Art. 159. All citizens shall have equal opportunity to receive an education.

Art. 160. All children of school age from six to twelve years shall receive free primary education. Those from poor families shall be supplied with books by the Government.

All citizens above school age who have not received primary education shall receive supplementary education free of charge and shall also be supplied with books by the Government.

Art. 161. The national, provincial, and local governments shall extensively establish scholarships to assist students of good scholastic standing and exemplary conduct who lack the means to continue their school education.

Art. 162. All public and private educational and cultural institutions in the country shall, in accordance with law, be subject to State supervision.

Art. 163. The State shall pay due attention to the balanced development of education in different regions, and shall promote social education in order to raise the cultural standard of the citizens in general. Grants from the National Treasury shall be made to frontier regions and economically poor areas to help them meet their educational and cultural expenses. The Central Government may either itself undertake the more important educational and cultural enterprises in such regions or give them financial assistance.

Art. 164. Expenditures for educational programs, scientific studies, and cultural services shall not be, in respect of the Central Government, less than 15 percent of the total national budget; in respect of each province, less than 25 percent of the total provincial budget; and in respect of each municipality or *hsien*, less than 35 percent of the total municipal or *hsien* budget. Educational and cultural foundations established in accordance with law shall, together with their property, be protected.

Art. 165. The State shall safeguard the livelihood of those who work in the fields of education, sciences, and arts, and shall, in accordance with the development of national economy, increase their renumeration from time to time.

Art. 166. The State shall encourage scientific discoveries and inventions, and shall protect ancient landmarks and relics of historical, cultural or artistic value.

Art. 167. The State shall give encouragement or subsidies to the following enterprises or individuals:

(1) Educational enterprises in the country which have been operated with good record by private individuals;

(2) Educational enterprises which have been operated with good record by Chinese citizens residing abroad;

(3) Persons who have made discoveries or inventions in the fields of learning and technology;

(4) Persons who have rendered long and meritorious services in the field of education.

Section 6. Frontier Regions

Art. 168. The State shall accord to the various nationalities in the frontier regions legal protection of their status and shall give them special assistance in their local self-government undertakings.

Art. 169. The State shall, in a positive manner, undertake and foster the development of education, culture, communications, water conservancy, public health, and other economic and social enterprises of the various nationalities in the frontier regions. With respect to the utilization of land, the State shall, after taking into account the climatic conditions, the nature of the soil, and the life and habits of the people, adopt measures to protect the land and to assist in its development.

CHAPTER XIV. *Enforcement and Amendment of the Constitution*

Art. 170. The term "law," as used in this Constitution, shall denote any legislative bill that shall have been passed by the Legislative *Yuan* and promulgated by the President of the Republic.

Art. 171. Laws that are in conflict with the Constitution shall be null and void.

When doubt arises as to whether or not a law is in conflict with the Constitution, interpretation thereon shall be made by the Judicial *Yuan*.

Art. 172. Ordinances that are in conflict with the Constitution or with laws shall be null and void.

Art. 173. The Constitution shall be interpreted by the Judicial *Yuan*.

Art. 174. Amendments to the Constitution shall be made in accordance with one of the following procedures:

(1) Upon the proposal of one fifth of the total number of the delegates to the National Assembly and by a resolution of three fourths of the delegates

present at a meeting having a quorum of two thirds of the entire Assembly, the Constitution may be amended.

(2) Upon the proposal of one fourth of the Members of the Legislative *Yuan* and by a resolution of three fourths of the Members present at a meeting having a quorum of three fourths of the members of the *Yuan*, an amendment may be drawn up and submitted to the National Assembly by way of referendum. Such a proposed amendment to the Constitution shall be publicly published half a year before the National Assembly convenes.

Art. 175. Whenever necessary, enforcement procedures in regard to any matter prescribed in this Constitution shall be separately provided by law.

The preparatory procedures for the enforcement of this Constitution shall be decided upon by the Constitution-Making National Assembly.

TEMPORARY PROVISIONS EFFECTIVE DURING THE PERIOD OF COMMUNIST REBELLION [1]

In accordance with the procedure prescribed in Paragraph 1 of Article 174 of the Constitution, the following Temporary Provisions to be effective during the Period of Communist Rebellion are hereby enacted:

The President during the Period of Communist Rebellion may, by resolution of the Executive *Yuan* Council, take emergency measures to avert an imminent danger to the security of the State or of the people, or to cope with any serious financial or economic crisis, without being subject to the procedural restrictions prescribed in Article 39 or Article 43 of the Constitution.

The emergency measures mentioned in the preceding paragraph may be modified or abrogated by the Legislative *Yuan* in accordance with Paragraph 2 of Article 57 of the Constitution.

During the Period of Communist Rebellion, the President and the Vice President may be re-elected without being subject to the two-term restriction prescribed in Article 47 of the Constitution.

An organ shall be established after the conclusion of the third plenary session of the National Assembly to study and draft proposals relating to the powers of initiative and referendum by the National Assembly. These, together with other proposals pertaining to constitutional amendment, shall be discussed by the National Assembly at an extraordinary session to be convoked by the President.

The extraordinary session of the National Assembly shall be convoked by the third President elected under this Constitution, at an appropriate time during his time of office.

The termination of the Period of Communist Rebellion shall be declared by the President.

Amendment or abrogation of the Temporary Provisions shall be resolved by the National Assembly.

---

[1] Adopted by the National Assembly on April 18, 1948. Promulgated by the National Government on May 10, 1948, and amended by the National Assembly on March 11, 1960. Translation from *China Yearbook, 1960–61*, pp. 900–901.

THE CONSTITUTION OF THE PEOPLE'S REPUBLIC OF CHINA (CHUNG-HUA JEN-MIN KUNG-HO-KUO HSIEN-FA)

September 20, 1954 [1]

PREAMBLE

In the year 1949, after more than a century of heroic struggle, the Chinese people, led by the Communist Party of China, finally achieved their great victory in the people's revolution against imperialism, feudalism, and bureaucrat-capitalism; and so brought to an end a long history of oppression and enslavement and founded the People's Republic of China, a people's democratic dictatorship. The system of people's democracy – new democracy – of the People's Republic of China guarantees that China can in a peaceful way banish exploitation and poverty and build a prosperous and happy socialist society.

From the founding of the People's Republic of China to the attainment of a socialist society is a period of transition. During the transition the fundamental task of the state is, step by step, to accomplish the socialist transformation of agriculture, handicrafts and capitalist industry and commerce. In the last few years our people have successfully carried out a series of large-scale struggles: the reform of the agrarian system, resistance to American aggression and aid to Korea, the suppression of counter-revolutionaries and the rehabilitation of the national economy. As a result, the necessary conditions have been created for planned economic construction and gradual transition to socialism.

The First National People's Congress of the People's Republic of China, at its first session held in Peking, the capital, solemnly adopted the Constitution of the People's Republic of China on September 20, 1954. This Constitution is based on the Common Program of the Chinese People's Political Consultative Conference of 1949, and is an advance on it. It consolidates the gains of the Chinese people's revolution and the political and economic victories won since the founding of the People's Republic of China; and, moreover, it reflects the basic needs of the state in the period of transition, as well as the general desire of the people as a whole to build a socialist society.

In the course of the great struggle to establish the People's Republic of China, the people of our country forged a broad people's democratic united front, composed of all democratic classes, democratic parties and groups, and popular organizations, and led by the Communist Party of China. This people's democratic united front will continue to play its part in mobilizing and rallying the whole people in common struggle to fulfil the fundamental task of the state during the transition and to oppose enemies within and without.

---

[1] Adopted by the First National People's Congress of the People's Republic of China at its first session on September 20, 1954. Translation based on the English text published by the Foreign Languages Press (Peking, 1954), with modifications by the author.

All nationalities of our country are united in one great family of free and equal nations. This unity of China's nationalities will continue to gain in strength, founded as it is on ever-growing friendship and mutual aid among themselves, and on the struggle against imperialism, against public enemies of the people within the nationalities, and against both dominant-nation chauvinism and local nationalism. In the course of economic and cultural development, the state will concern itself with the needs of the different nationalities, and, in the matter of socialist transformation, pay full attention to the special characteristics in the development of each.

China has already built an indestructible friendship with the great Union of Soviet Socialist Republics and the People's Democracies; and the friendship between our people and peace-loving people in all other countries is growing day by day. Such friendship will be constantly strengthened and broadened. China's policy of establishing and extending diplomatic relations with all countries on the principle of equality, mutual benefit and mutual respect for each other's sovereignty and territorial integrity, which has already yielded success, will continue to be carried out. In international affairs our firm and consistent policy is to strive for the noble cause of world peace and the progress of humanity.

CHAPTER I. *General Principles*

Art. 1. The People's Republic of China is a people's democratic state led by the working class and based on the alliance of workers and peasants.

Art. 2. All power in the People's Republic of China belongs to the people. The organs through which the people exercise power are the National People's Congress and the local people's congresses.

The National People's Congress, the local people's congresses and other organs of state practice democratic centralism.

Art. 3. The People's Republic of China is a unitary multi-national state.

All the nationalities are equal. Discrimination against, or oppression of, any nationality, and acts which undermine the unity of the nationalities are prohibited.

All the nationalities have freedom to use and foster the growth of their spoken and written languages, and to preserve or reform their own customs or ways.

Regional autonomy applies in areas where people of national minorities live in compact communities. National autonomous areas are inalienable parts of the People's Republic of China.

Art. 4. The People's Republic of China, by relying on the organs of state and the social forces, and by means of socialist industrialization and socialist transformation, ensures the gradual abolition of systems of exploitation and the building of a socialist society.

Art. 5. At present, the following basic forms of ownership of means of production exist in the People's Republic of China: state ownership, that is, ownership by the whole people; co-operative ownership, that is, collective ownership by the working masses; ownership by individual working people; and capitalist ownership.

Art. 6. The state sector of the economy is a socialist sector, owned by the whole people. It is the leading force in the national economy and the material basis on which the state carries out socialist transformation. The state ensures priority for the development of the state sector of the economy.

All mineral resources and waters, as well as forests, undeveloped land and other resources which the state owns by law, are the property of the whole people.

Art. 7. The co-operative sector of the economy is either socialist, when collectively owned by the working masses, or semi-socialist, when in part collectively owned by the working masses. Partial collective ownership by the working masses is a transitional form by means of which individual peasants, handicraftsmen and other working people organize themselves in their advance toward collective ownership by the working masses.

The state protects the property of the co-operatives, encourages, guides and helps the development of the co-operative sector of the economy. It regards the promotion of producers' co-operatives as the chief means for the transformation of individual farming and individual handicrafts.

Art. 8. The state protects the right of peasants to own land and other means of production according to law.

The state guides and helps individual peasants to increase production and encourages them to organize producers', supply and marketing, and credit co-operatives voluntarily.

The policy of the state toward rich-peasant economy is to restrict and gradually eliminate it.

Art. 9. The state protects the right of handicraftsmen and other non-agricultural individual working people to own means of production according to law.

The state guides and helps individual handicraftsmen and other non-agricultural individual working people to improve their enterprise and encourages them to organize producers', and supply and marketing co-operatives voluntarily.

Art. 10. The state protects the right of capitalists to own means of production and other capital according to law.

The policy of the state toward capitalist industry and commerce is to use, restrict and transform them. The state makes use of the positive sides of capitalist industry and commerce which are beneficial to national welfare and the people's livelihood, restricts their negative sides which are not beneficial to national welfare and the people's livelihood, encourages and guides their transformation into various forms of state-capitalist economy, gradually replacing capitalist ownership with ownership by the whole people; and this it does by means of control exercised by administrative organs of state, the leadership given by the state sector of the economy, and supervision by the workers.

The state forbids capitalists to engage in unlawful activities which injure the public interest, disrupt the social-economic order, or undermine the economic plan of the state.

Art. 11. The state protects the right of citizens to own lawfully earned incomes, savings, houses and other means of life.

Art. 12. The state protects the right of citizens to inherit private property according to law.

Art. 13. The state may, in the public interest, buy, requisition or nationalize land and other means of production both in cities and country-side according to provisions of law.

Art. 14. The state forbids any person to use his private property to the detriment of the public interest.

Art. 15. By economic planning, the state directs the growth and transformation of the national economy to bring about the constant increase of productive forces, in this way enriching the material and cultural life of the people and consolidating the independence and security of the country.

Art. 16. Work is a matter of honor for every citizen of the People's Republic of China who is able to work. The state encourages citizens to take an active and creative part in their work.

Art. 17. All organs of state must rely on the masses of the people, constantly maintain close contact with them, heed their opinions and accept their super-vision.

Art. 18. All public functionaries of the state must be loyal to the people's democratic system, observe the Constitution and the law and strive to serve the people.

Art. 19. The People's Republic of China safeguards the people's democratic system, suppresses all treasonable and counter-revolutionary activities and punishes all traitors and counter-revolutionaries.

The state deprives feudal landlords and bureaucrat-capitalists of political rights for a specific period of time according to law; at the same time it provides them with a way to earn-a living, in order to enable them to reform through work and become citizens who earn their livelihood by their own labor.

Art. 20. The armed forces of the People's Republic of China belong to the people; their duty is to safeguard the gains of the people's revolution and the achievements of national construction, and to defend the sovereignty, territorial integrity and security of the country.

CHAPTER II. *The State Structure*

Section 1. The National People's Congress

Art. 21. The National People's Congress is the highest organ of state authority in the People's Republic of China.

Art. 22. The National People's Congress is the only legislative authority in the country.

Art. 23. The National People's Congress is composed of deputies elected by provinces, autonomous regions, municipalities directly under the central authority, the armed forces and Chinese resident abroad.

The number of deputies to the National People's Congress, including those representing national minorities, and the manner of their election, are prescribed by electoral law.

Art. 24. The National People's Congress is elected for a term of four years.

Two months before the term of office of the National People's Congress expires, its Standing Committee must complete the election of deputies to the succeeding National People's Congress. Should exceptional circumstances arise preventing such an election, the term of office of the sitting National People's Congress may be prolonged until the first session of the succeeding National People's Congress.

Art. 25. The National People's Congress meets once a year, convened by its Standing Committee. It may also be convened whenever its Standing Committee deems this necessary or one-fifth of the deputies so propose.

Art. 26. When the National People's Congress meets, it elects a presidium to conduct its session.

Art. 27. The National People's Congress exercises the following functions and powers:

(1) To amend the Constitution;
(2) To enact laws;
(3) To supervise the enforcement of the Constitution;
(4) To elect the Chairman and the Vice-Chairman of the People's Republic of China;
(5) To decide on the choice of the Premier of the State Council upon recom-mendation by the Chairman of the People's Republic of China, and of the

component members of the State Council upon recommendation by the Premier;

(6) To decide on the choice of the Vice-Chairmen and members of the Council of National Defense upon recommendation by the Chairman of the People's Republic of China;

(7) To elect the President of the Supreme People's Court;

(8) To elect the Chief Procurator of the Supreme People's Procuratorate;

(9) To decide on the national economic plans;

(10) To examine and approve the state budget and the financial report;

(11) To ratify the status and boundaries of provinces, autonomous regions, and municipalities directly under the central authority;

(12) To decide on general amnesties;

(13) To decide on questions of war and peace; and

(14) To exercise such other functions and powers as the National People's Congress considers necessary.

Art. 28. The National People's Congress has power to remove from office:

(1) The Chairman and the Vice-Chairman of the People's Republic of China;

(2) The Premier and Vice-Premiers, Ministers, Heads of Commissions and Secretary-General of the State Council;

(3) The Vice-Chairmen and other members of the Council of National Defense;

(4) The President of the Supreme People's Court; and

(5) The Chief Procurator of the Supreme People's Procuratorate.

Art. 29. Amendments to the Constitution require a two-thirds majority vote of all the deputies to the National People's Congress.

Laws and other bills require a simple majority vote of all the deputies to the National People's Congress.

Art. 30. The Standing Committee of the National People's Congress is a permanently acting body of the National People's Congress.

The Standing Committee is composed of the following members, elected by the National People's Congress:

the Chairman;
the Vice-Chairmen;
the Secretary-General; and
other members.

Art. 31. The Standing Committee of the National People's Congress exercises the following functions and powers:

(1) To conduct the election of deputies to the National People's Congress;

(2) To convene the National People's Congress;

(3) To interpret the laws;

(4) To adopt decrees;

(5) To supervise the work of the State Council, the Supreme People's Court and the Supreme People's Procuratorate;

(6) To annul decisons and orders of the State Council which contravene the Constitution, laws or decrees;

(7) To revise or annul inappropriate decisions of the government authorities of provinces, autonomous regions, and municipalities directly under the central authority;

(8) To decide on the appointment or removal of any Vice-Premier, Minister, Head of Commission or the Secretary-General of the State Council when the National People's Congress is not in session;

(9) To appoint or remove the Vice-Presidents, judges, and members of the Judicial Committee of the Supreme People's Court;

(10) To appoint or remove the the Deputy Chief Procurators, procurators, and members of the Procuratorial Committee of the Supreme People's Procuratorate;

(11) To decide on the appointment or recall of plenipotentiary representatives to foreign states;

(12) To decide on the ratification or abrogation of treaties concluded with foreign states;

(13) To institute military, diplomatic and other special titles and ranks;

(14) To institute and decide on the award of state orders, medals, and titles of honor;

(15) To decide on the granting of pardons;

(16) To decide, when the National People's Congress is not in session, on the proclamation of a state of war in the event of armed attack on the country or in fulfilment of international obligations concerning common defense against aggression;

(17) To decide on general or partial mobilization;

(18) To decide on the enforcement of martial law throughout the country or in certain areas; and

(19) To exercise such other functions and powers as are vested in it by the National People's Congress.

Art. 32. The Standing Committee of the National People's Congress exercises its functions and powers until a new Standing Committee is elected by the succeeding National People's Congress.

Art. 33. The Standing Committee of the National People's Congress is responsible to the National People's Congress and reports to it.

The National People's Congress has power to recall members of its Standing Committee.

Art. 34. The National People's Congress establishes a Nationalities Committee, a Bills Committee, a Budget Committee, a Credentials Committee and other necessary committees.

The Nationalities Committee and the Bills Committee are under the direction of the Standing Committee of the National People's Congress when the National People's Congress is not in session.

Art. 35. The National People's Congress, or its Standing Committee if the National People's Congress is not in session, may, if necessary, appoint commissions of inquiry for the investigation of specific questions.

All organs of state, people's organizations and citizens concerned are obliged to supply necessary information to these commissions when they conduct investigations.

Art. 36. Deputies to the National People's Congress have the right to address questions to the State Council, or to the ministries and Commissions of the State Council, which are under obligation to answer.

Art. 37. No deputy to the National People's Congress may be arrested or placed on trial without the consent of the National People's Congress or, when the National People's Congress is not in session, of its Standing Committee.

Art. 38. Deputies to the National People's Congress are subject to the supervision of the units which elect them. These electoral units have power to replace at any time the deputies they elect, according to the procedure prescribed by law.

Section 2. The Chairman of the People's Republic of China

Art. 39. The Chairman of the People's Republic of China is elected by the National People's Congress. Any citizen of the People's Republic of China who has the right to vote and stand for election and has reached the age of thirty-five is eligible for election as Chairman of the People's Republic of China.

The term of office of the Chairman of the People's Republic of China is four years.

Art. 40. The Chairman of the People's Republic of China, in pursuance of decisions of the National People's Congress or the Standing Committee of the National People's Congress, promulgates laws and decrees; appoints or removes the Premier, Vice-Premiers, Ministers, Heads of Commissions and the Secretary-General of the State Council; appoints or removes the Vice-Chairmen and members of the Council of National Defense; confers state orders, medals and titles of honor; proclaims general amnesties and grants pardons; proclaims martial law; proclaims a state of war; and orders mobilization.

Art. 41. The Chairman of the People's Republic of China represents the People's Republic of China in its relations with foreign states, receives foreign diplomatic representatives and, in pursuance of decisions of the Standing Committee of the National People's Congress, appoints or recalls plenipotentiary representatives to foreign states and ratifies treaties concluded with foreign states.

Art. 42. The Chairman of the People's Republic of China commands the armed forces of the country, and is Chairman of the Council of National Defense.

Art. 43. The Chairman of the People's Republic of China, whenever necessary, convenes a Supreme State Conference and acts as its chairman.

The Vice-Chairman of the People's Republic of China, the Chairman of the Standing Committee of the National People's Congress, the Premier of the State Council and other persons concerned take part in the Supreme State Conference.

The Chairman of the People's Republic of China submits the views of the Supreme State Conference on important affairs of state to the National People's Congress, its Standing Committee, the State Council, or other bodies concerned for their consideration and decision.

Art. 44. The Vice-Chairman of the People's Republic of China assists the Chairman in his work. The Vice-Chairman may exercise such part of the functions and powers of the Chairman as the Chairman may entrust to him.

The provisions of Article 39 of the Constitution governing the election and term of office of the Chairman of the People's Republic of China apply also to the election and term of office of the Vice-Chairman of the People's Republic of China.

Art. 45. The Chairman and the Vice-Chairman of the People's Republic of China exercise their functions and powers until the new Chairman and Vice-Chairman elected by the succeeding National People's Congress take office.

Art. 46. Should the Chairman of the People's Republic of China be incapacitated for a prolonged period by reason of health, the functions of Chairman shall be exercised by the Vice-Chairman.

Should the office of Chairman of the People's Republic of China fall vacant, the Vice-Chairman succeeds to the office of Chairman.

Section 3. The State Council

Art. 47. The State Council of the People's Republic of China, that is, the Central People's Government, is the executive organ of the highest state authority; it is the highest administrative organ of the state.

Art. 48. The State Council is composed of the following members:

> the Premier;
> the Vice-Premiers;
> the Ministers;
> the Heads of Commissions; and
> the Secretary-General.

The organization of the State Council is determined by law.

Art. 49. The State Council exercises the following functions and powers:

(1) To formulate administrative measures, issue decisions and orders and verify their execution, in accordance with the Constitution, laws and decrees;

(2) To submit bills to the National People's Congress or its Standing Committee;

(3) To co-ordinate and lead the work of Ministries and Commissions;

(4) To co-ordinate and lead the work of local administrative organs of state throughout the country;

(5) To revise or annul inappropriate orders and directives issued by Ministers or by Heads of Commissions;

(6) To revise or annul inappropriate decisions and orders issued by local administrative organs of state;

(7) To put into effect the national economic plans and provisions of the state budget;

(8) To control foreign and domestic trade;

(9) To direct cultural, educational and public health work;

(10) To administer affairs concerning the nationalities;

(11) To administer affairs concerning Chinese resident abroad;

(12) To protect the interest of the state, to maintain public order and to safeguard the rights of citizens;

(13) To direct the conduct of external affairs;

(14) To guide the building up of the defense forces;

(15) To ratify the status and boundaries of autonomous *chou*, counties [*hsien* or districts], autonomous counties, and municipalities;

(16) To appoint or remove administrative personnel according to provisions of law; and

(17) To exercise such other functions and powers as are vested in it by the National People's Congress or its Standing Committee.

Art. 50. The Premier directs the work of the State Council and presides over its meetings.

The Vice-Premiers assist the Premier in his work.

Art. 51. The Ministers and Heads of Commissions direct the work of their respective departments. They may issue orders and directives within the jurisdiction of their respective departments and in accordance with laws and decrees, and decisions and orders of the State Council.

Art. 52. The State Council is responsible to the National People's Congress and reports to it; or, when the National People's Congress is not in session, to its Standing Committee.

Section 4. The Local People's Congresses and Local People's Councils

Art. 53. The administrative division of the People's Republic of China is as follows:

(1) The country is divided into provinces, autonomous regions, and municipalities directly under the central authority;

(2) Provinces and autonomous regions are divided into autonomous *Chou*, counties, autonomous counties, and municipalities; and

(3) Counties and autonomous counties are divided into *hsiang*, nationality *hsiang*, and towns [*chen*].

Municipalities directly under the central authority and other large municipalities are divided into sub-districts [*ch'ü*]. Autonomous *chou* are divided into counties, autonomous counties and municipalities.

Autonomous regions, autonomous *chou* and autonomous counties are all national autonomous areas.

Art. 54. People's congresses and people's councils are established in provinces, municipalities directly under the central authority, counties, municipalities, municipal sub-districts, *hsiang*, nationality *hsiang*, and towns.

Organs of self-government are established in autonomous regions, autonomous *chou* and autonomous counties. The organization and work of organs of self-government are specified in Section 5 of Chapter II of the Constitution.

Art. 55. Local people's congresses at all levels are the organs of government authority in their respective localities.

Art. 56. Deputies to the people's congresses of provinces, municipalities directly under the central authority, counties, and municipalities divided into sub-districts are elected by the people's congresses of the next lower level; deputies to the people's congresses of municipalities not divided into sub-districts, municipal sub-districts, *hsiang*, nationality *hsiang*, and towns are directly elected by the voters.

The number of deputies to local people's congresses and the manner of their election are prescribed by electoral law.

Art. 57. The term of office of the provincial people's congresses is four years. The term of office of the people's congresses of municipalities directly under the central authority, counties, municipalities, municipal sub-districts, *hsiang*, nationality *hsiang*, and towns is two years.

Art. 58. The local people's congresses at every level ensure the observance and execution of laws and decrees in their respective administrative areas; draw up plans for local economic and cultural development and for public works; examine and approve local budgets and financial reports; protect public property; maintain public order; safeguard the rights of citizens and the equal rights of national minorities.

Art. 59. The local people's congresses elect, and have power to recall, members of the people's councils at corresponding levels.

The people's congresses at county level and above elect, and have power to recall, the presidents of people's courts at corresponding levels.

Art. 60. The local people's congresses adopt and issue decisions within the limits of the authority prescribed by law.

The people's congresses of nationality *hsiang* may, within the limits of the authority prescribed by law, take specific measures appropriate to the characteristics of the nationalities concerned.

The local people's congresses have power to revise or annul inappropriate decisions and orders of people's councils at corresponding levels.

The people's congresses at county level and above have power to revise or annul inappropriate decisions issued by people's congresses at the next lower level as well as inappropriate decisions and orders of people's councils at the next lower level.

Art. 61. Deputies to the people's congresses of provinces, municipalities directly under the central authority, counties, and municipalities divided into sub-districts are subject to supervision by the units which elect them; deputies to the people's congresses of municipalities not divided into sub-districts, municipal sub-districts, *hsiang*, nationality *hsiang*, and towns are subject to supervision by their electorates. The electoral units and electorates which elect the deputies to the local people's congresses have power at any time to recall their deputies according to the procedure prescribed by law.

Art. 62. Local people's councils, that is, local people's governments, are the executive organs of local people's congresses at corresponding levels, and are the administrative organs of state in their respective localities.

Art. 63. A local people's council is composed, according to its level, of the provincial governor and deputy provincial governors; or the mayor and deputy mayors; or the county head [magistrate] and deputy county heads; or the subdistrict head and deputy sub-district heads; or the *hsiang* head and deputy *hsiang* heads; or the town head and deputy town heads, as the case may be; together with council members.

The term of office of a local people's council is the same as that of the people's congress at corresponding level.

The organization of local people's councils is determined by law.

Art. 64. The local people's councils administer their respective areas within the limits of the authority prescribed by law.

The local people's councils carry out the decisions of people's congresses at corresponding levels and decisions and orders of administrative organs of state at higher levels.

The local people's councils issue decisions and orders within the limits of the authority prescribed by law.

Art. 65. The people's councils at county level and above direct the work of all their subordinate departments and of people's councils at lower levels, as well as appoint or remove personnel of organs of state according to provisions of law.

The people's councils at county level and above have power to suspend the carrying out of inappropriate decisions of people's congresses at the next lower level; and to revise or annul inappropriate orders and directives issued by their subordinate departments, and inappropriate decisions and orders issued by people's councils at lower levels.

Art. 66. The local people's councils are responsible to the people's congresses at corresponding levels and to the administrative organs of state at the next higher level, and report to them.

The local people's councils throughout the country are administrative organs of state, and are subordinate to and under the co-ordinating direction of the State Council.

Section 5. The Organs of Self-Government of National Autonomous Areas

Art. 67. The organs of self-government of all autonomous regions, autonomous *chou* and autonomous counties are formed in accordance with the basic principles governing the organization of local organs of state as specified in Section 4 of Chapter II of the Constitution. The form of each organ of self-government may be determined in accordance with the wishes of the majority of the people of the nationality or nationalities enjoying regional autonomy in a given area.

Art. 68. In all autonomous regions, autonomous *chou* and autonomous counties where a number of nationalities live together, each nationality is entitled to appropriate representation on the organs of self-government.

Art. 69. The organs of self-government of all autonomous regions, autonomous *chou* and autonomous counties exercise the functions and powers of local organs of state as specified in Section 4 of Chapter II of the Constitution.

Art. 70. The organs of self-government of all autonomous regions, autonomous *chou* and autonomous counties exercise autonomy within the limits of the authority prescribed by the Constitution and law.

The organs of self-government of all autonomous regions, autonomous *chou* and autonomous counties administer their own local finances within the limits of the authority prescribed by law.

The organs of self-government of all autonomous regions, autonomous *chou* and autonomous counties organize their local public security forces in accordance with the military system of the state.

The organs of self-government of all autonomous regions, autonomous *chou* and autonomous counties may draw up statutes governing the exercise of autonomy or separate regulations suited to the political, economic and cultural characteristics of the nationality or nationalities in a given area. Such statutes and regulations are subject to endorsement by the Standing Committee of the National People's Congress.

Art. 71. In performing their duties, organs of self-government of all autonomous regions, autonomous *chou* and autonomous counties employ the spoken and written language or languages commonly used in the locality.

Art. 72. The higher organs of state should fully safeguard the right of organs of self-government of all autonomous regions, autonomous *chou* and autonomous counties to exercise autonomy, and should assist the various national minorities in their political, economic and cultural development.

Section 6. The People's Courts and the People's Procuratorate

Art. 73. In the People's Republic of China judicial authority is exercised by the Supreme People's Court, local people's courts and special people's courts.

Art. 74. The term of office of the President of the Supreme People's Court and presidents of local people's courts is four years.

The organization of people's courts is determined by law.

Art. 75. The system of people's assessors applies, in accordance with law, to judicial proceedings in the people's courts.

Art. 76. Cases in the people's courts are heard in public unless otherwise provided for by law. The accused has the right to defense.

Art. 77. Citizens of all nationalities have the right to use their own spoken and written languages in court proceedings. The people's courts are to provide interpretation for any party unacquainted with the spoken or written language commonly used in the locality.

In an area where people of national minorities live in compact communities or where a number of nationalities live together, hearings in people's courts are conducted in the language commonly used in the locality, and judgments, notices and all other documents of the people's courts are made public in such language.

Art. 78. In administering justice the people's courts are independent, subject only to the law.

Art. 79. The Supreme People's Court is the highest judicial organ.

The Supreme People's Court supervises the judicial work of local people's courts and special people's courts; people's courts at higher levels supervise the judicial work of people's courts at lower levels.

Art. 80. The Supreme People's Court is responsible to the National People's Congress and reports to it; or, when the National People's Congress is not in session, to its Standing Committee. Local people's courts are responsible to the local people's congresses at corresponding levels and report to them.

Art. 81. The Supreme People's Procuratorate of the People's Republic of China exercises procuratorial authority over all departments of the State Council, all local organs of state, persons working in organs of state, and citizens, to ensure observance of the law. Local organs of the people's procuratorate and special people's procuratorates exercise procuratorial authority within the limits prescribed by law.

Local organs of the people's procuratorate and the special people's procuratorates work under the leadership of the people's procuratorates at higher levels, and all work under the co-ordinating direction of the Supreme People's Procuratorate.

Art. 82. The term of office of the Chief Procurator of the Supreme People's Procuratorate is four years.

The organization of people's procuratorates is determined by law.

Art. 83. In the exercise of their authority local organs of the people's procuratorate are independent and are not subject to interference by local organs of state.

Art. 84. The Supreme People's Procuratorate is responsible to the National People's Congress and report to it; or, when the National People's Congress is not in session, to its Standing Committee.

CHAPTER III. *Fundamental Rights and Duties of Citizens*

Art. 85. Citizens of the People's Republic of China are equal before the law.

Art. 86. Citizens of the People's Republic of China who have reached the age of eighteen have the right to vote and stand for election whatever their nationality, race, sex, occupation, social origin, religious belief, education, property status, or length of residence, except insane persons and persons deprived by law of the right to vote and stand for election.

Women have equal rights with men to vote and stand for election.

Art. 87. Citizens of the People's Republic of China enjoy freedom of speech, freedom of the press, freedom of assembly, freedom of association, freedom of procession and freedom of demonstration. The state guarantee to citizens enjoyment of these freedoms by providing the necessary material facilities.

Art. 88. Citizens of the People's Republic of China enjoy freedom of religious belief.

Art. 89. Freedom of the person of citizens of the People's Republic of China is inviolable. No citizen may be arrested except by decision of a people's court or with the sanction of a people's procuratorate.

Art. 90. The homes of citizens of the People's Republic of China are inviolable, and privacy of correspondence is protected by law.

Citizens of the People's Republic of China have freedom of residence and freedom to change their residence

Art. 91. Citizens of the People's Republic of China have the right to work. To guarantee enjoyment of this right, the state, by planned development of the national economy, gradually creates more employment, and better working conditions and wages.

Art. 92. Working people in the People's Republic of China have the right to rest and leisure. To guarantee enjoyment of this right, the state prescribes working hours and holidays for workers and office employees; at the same time it gradually expands material facilities to enable working people to rest and build up their health.

Art. 93. Working people in the People's Republic of China have the right to material assistance in old age, and in case of illness or disability. To guarantee enjoyment of this right, the state provides social insurance, social assistance and public health services and gradually expands these facilities.

Art. 94. Citizens of the People's Republic of China have the right to education. To guarantee enjoyment of this right, the state establishes and gradually extends the various types of schools and other cultural and educational institutions.

The state pays special attention to the physical and mental development of young people.

Art. 95. The People's Republic of China safeguards the freedom of citizens to engage in scientific research, literary and artistic creation and other cultural pursuits. The state encourages and assists creative work in science, education, literature, art and other cultural pursuits.

Art. 96. Women in the People's Republic of China enjoy equal rights with men in all spheres of political, economic, cultural, social and domestic life.

The state protects marriage, the family, and the mother and child.

Art. 97. Citizens of the People's Republic of China have the right to bring complaints against public functionaries for transgression of law or neglect of duty by making a written or verbal statement to any organ of state at any level. People suffering loss by reason of infringement by public functionaries of their rights as citizens have the right to compensation.

Art. 98. The People's Republic of China protects the proper rights and interests of Chinese resident abroad.

Art. 99. The People's Republic of China grants the right of asylum to any foreign national persecuted for supporting a just cause, for taking part in the peace movement or for engaging in scientific activity.

Art. 100. Citizens of the People's Republic of China must abide by the Constitution and the law, uphold discipline at work, keep public order and respect social ethics.

Art. 101. The public property of the People's Republic of China is sacred and inviolable.

It is the duty of every citizen to respect and protect public property.

Art. 102. It is the duty of citizens of the People's Republic of China to pay taxes according to law.

Art. 103. It is the sacred duty of every citizen of the People's Republic of China to defend the homeland.

It is an honorable duty of citizens of the People's Republic of China to perform military service according to law.

CHAPTER IV. *National Flag, National Emblem, Capital*

Art. 104. The national flag of the People's Republic of China is a red flag with five stars.

Art. 105. The national emblem of the People's Republic of China is: in the center, Tien An Men under the light of five stars, framed with ears of grain, and with a cogwheel at the base.

Art. 106. The capital of the People's Republic of China is Peking.

BIBLIOGRAPHY

I. OFFICIAL DOCUMENTS

Systematic studies on the political institutions of modern China are comparatively few in number. Several books dealing with this subject are limited to certain phases or to some particular time, and none covers the entire period from the beginning of the twentieth century to the present date. Because of such limitations, this work relies chiefly on official documents for reference. Of these documents referred to in the present research, the most important ones are listed in this bibliography in chronological order under the following categories: (A) constitutions and constitutional drafts; (B) laws and regulations dealing with the national government; (C) laws and regulations dealing with the local government; and (D) other documents. As their sources have already been indicated in the footnotes, no further notation is needed in the bibliography. These documents can be found in the government gazettes and party publications. Almost all of them are included in the collections of documents, China yearbooks, and appendices of other books, which are marked with the sign (d) at the end of each listing for the convenience of reference. The date after each document designates that of its promulgation and not of its revision. In many laws, the dates of promulgation and coming into force are different.

A. Constitutions and Constitutional Drafts

Principles of Constitution, September 22, 1908.
The Nineteen Articles, November 3, 1911.
Provisional Constitution of the Republic of China, March 11, 1912.
Draft Constitution of the Republic of China, October 13, 1913.
The Constitutional Compact, May 1, 1914.
The Draft Constitution of the Republic of China, August 12, 1919.
The Constitution of the Republic of China, October 10, 1923.
The Draft Constitution of the Republic of China, December 12, 1925.
The Draft Provisional Constitution of the Republic of China, October 27, 1930.
Provisional Constitution of the Republic of China for the Period of Political Tutelage, June 1, 1931.
The Constitution of the Communist Government, November 7, 1931.
The Draft Constitution of the Republic of China, May 5, 1936.
The Constitution of the Republic of China, December 25, 1946. (Temporary Provisions Effective During the Period of Communist Rebellion was adopted on April 18, 1948 and amended on March 11, 1960.)
The Constitution of the People's Republic of China, September 20, 1954.

B. Laws and Regulations dealing with the National Government

The List of Annual Preparatory Work Prior to the Convening of Parliament,
   September 22, 1908.
Outlines of Electoral Law, September 22, 1908.
Outlines of Parliamentary Procedures, September 22, 1908.
Organic Law of the National Legislative Council (Tse-cheng Yuan), September 20,
   1909.
Electoral Law of the National Legislative Council, October 26, 1909.
Organic Law of the Provisional Government of the Republic of China, December 3,
   1911, revised January 2, 1912.
Draft of the Organic Law of the Provisional Government of the Republic of China,
   submitted by the Provisional President to the Legislative Assembly in
   January, 1912.
Rules of Procedure of the Legislative Assembly, April 1, 1912.
Statute of the Cabinet, June 26, 1912.
General Regulations of the Various Ministries, July 18, 1912.
Electoral Law of the House of Representatives, August 10, 1912.
Electoral Law of the Senate, August 10, 1912.
Organic Law of Parliament, August 10, 1912.
Rules of Procedure of the Parliament, September 27, 1913.
Presidential Election Law, October 5, 1913.
Organic Law of the Constitutional Compact Conference, January 26, 1914.
*Presidential Order on the Organization of the Board of Political Affairs of the
   Presidential Office,* May 3, 1914.
Organic Law of the Consultative Yuan, May 24, 1914.
Electoral Law of the Legislative Yuan, October 27, 1914.
Organic Law of the Legislative Yuan, October 27, 1914.
Revised Presidential Election Law, December 29, 1914.
Organic Law of the National Convention of People's Representatives, October 8,
   1915.
Organic Law of the Military Council, May 1916.
Revised Electoral Law of the House of Representatives, February 17, 1917.
Revised Electoral Law of the Senate, February 17, 1918.
Revised Organic Law of Parliament, February 17, 1918.
Organic Law of the Emergency Session of Parliament, August 29, 1917.
Organic Law of the Military Government of the Republic of China, August 30, 1917.
Revised Organic Law of the Military Government, May 10, 1918.
Organic Law of the Government of the Republic of China, April 7, 1921.
Organic Law of the Provisional Government of the Republic of China, November 24,
   1924, revised December 26, 1924.
Regulations governing the Reorganization Conference, December 23, 1924.
Regulations governing the Financial Reorganization Commission, April 24, 1925.
Regulations governing the Military Reorganization Commission, April 24, 1925.
Regulations governing the People's Convention, April 24, 1925.
Regulations governing the Provisional Political Council, May 1, 1925.
Organic Law of the National Government, first promulgated on July 1, 1925 and
   revised many times.
Organic Law of the Military Government, June 18, 1927.
Electoral Rules of the National People's Convention, January 1, 1931.
Organic Law of the National People's Convention, April 24, 1931, revised May 4, 1931.
Rules governing the Organization of the National Emergency Conference, March 17,
   1932.

Organic Law of the Judiciary, July 1, 1935.
Organic Law of the People's Political Council, first promulgated on April 12, 1936, revised 9 times, the last amendment on March 1, 1947.
Electoral Law of the National Assembly, May 14, 1936.
Organic Law of the National Defense Advisory Council, August 10, 1937.
Organic Law of the National Military Council, January 17, 1938.
Regulations to Unify Administration in the War Areas, May 31, 1938.
Law governing the Election and Recall of the Delegates to the National Assembly, March 31, 1947
Law governing the Election and Recall of the Members of the Legislative Yuan, March 31, 1947.
Law governing the Election and Recall of the Members of the Supervisory Yuan, March 31, 1947.
Law governing the Election and Recall of the President and Vice President, March 31, 1947.
Organic Law of the National Assembly, March 31, 1947.
Common Program of the Chinese People's Political Consultative Conference, September 29, 1949.
Organic Law of the Central People's Government of the People's Republic of China, September 29, 1949.
Organic Law of the Chinese People's Political Consultative Conference, September 29, 1949.
Electoral Law of the People's Republic of China for the National People's Congress and Local People's Congresses of All Levels, March 1, 1953.
Organic Law of the National People's Congress of the People's Republic of China, September 20, 1954.
Organic Law of the People's Courts of the People's Republic of China, September 21, 1954.
Organic Law of the People's Procuratorates of the People's Republic of China, September 21, 1954.
Organic Law of the State Council of the People's Republic of China, September 21, 1954.
Amendments to the Organic Law of the State Council of the People's Republic of China and to the Organic Law of the Local People's Congresses and Local People's Councils of the People's Republic of China, July 30, 1955.

C. Laws and Regulations dealing with the Local Government

Electoral Law of the Provincial Assembly, July 22, 1908.
Organic Law of the Provincial Assembly (Tse-I Chu), July 22, 1908.
Electoral Rules for Local Self-Government in Cities, Towns and Villages, January 18, 1909.
Regulations for Local Self-Government in Cities, Towns and Villages, January 18, 1909.
Electoral Rules for Local Self-Government in the Imperial Capital, February 3, 1910.
Regulations for Local Self-Government in the Imperial Capital, February 3, 1910.
Electoral Rules for Legislative Councils of Counties and Districts, February 6, 1910.
Regulations for Local Self-Government in Counties and Districts, February 6, 1910.
Electoral Law of the Provincial Assembly, September 4, 1912.
Membership Chart of the First Provincial Assemblies of the Various Provinces, September 25, 1912.

Rules for the Application of the Electoral Law of the Provincial Assembly, October 2, 1912.

Regulations governing the Organization of the Office of the Military Governor, January 8, 1913.

Regulations governing the Uniform Organization of the Districts, January 8, 1913.

Regulations governing the Uniform Organization of the Local Government under Shun-tien Fu, January 8, 1913.

Regulations governing the Uniform Organization of the Prefectures, January 8, 1913.

Regulations governing the Uniform Organization of the Provinces, January 8, 1913.

Regulations governing the Uniform Organization of the Special Areas Directly under the National Government, January 8, 1913.

Temporary Organic Law of the Provincial Assembly, April 2, 1913.

District Government System, May 23, 1914.

Prefecture Government System, May 23, 1914.

Provincial Government System, May 23, 1914.

Regulations governing the Office of the Military Commissioner, July 6, 1914.

Regulations governing the Administrative System of Ching-tsao, October 4, 1914.

Experimental Regulations of Local Self-Government, December 29, 1914.

Procedural Rules for the Application of the Experimental Regulations of Local Self-Government, April 14, 1915.

Temporary Regulations concerning the Establishment of the Departments of Education and Industry of the Provincial Government, September 6, 1917.

District Self-Government Regulations, September 8, 1919.

Electoral Rules of the District Assembly, June 18, 1921.

Procedural Rules for the Application of the District Self-Government Regulations, June 18, 1921.

Regulations governing the Provincial Consultative Council, June 23, 1921.

City Self-Government Regulations, July 3, 1921.

Village Self-Government Regulations, July 3, 1921.

Chekiang Provincial Constitution (also known as "9/9 Constitution"), September 9, 1921.

Hunan Provincial Constitution, January 1, 1922.

Procedural Rules for the Application of City Self-Government Regulations, September 9, 1922.

Organic Law of the Provincial Government, first promulgated July 1, 1925 and revised many times.

Organic Law of Municipalities, July 3, 1928.

Organic Law of Special Municipalities, July 3, 1928.

Organic Law of Districts, September 15, 1928.

Procedural Rules for the Application of the Organic Law of Districts, September 15, 1928.

Rules for the Classification of Districts, December 23 1929.

Organic Law governing Municipalities, May 20, 1930.

Temporary Regulations concerning Provincial Administrative Inspectors, August 6, 1932.

Electoral Rules of the *Municipal Assembly*, March 12, 1933.

Organic Law of the Municipal Assembly, March 12, 1933.

Electoral Rules of the District Assembly, March 13, 1933.

Organic Law of the District Assembly, March 13, 1933.

Principles for the Improvement of Local Self-Government, February 21, 1934.

Temporary Regulations governing the Office of Administrative Inspectors, October 15, 1936.

Organic Law governing the Provisional Municipal Council, September 26, 1938.

Organic Law governing the Provisional Provincial Council, September 26, 1938.
Outline of the Organization of the Several Levels of the District (Hsien) Government, September 19, 1939.
Provisional Organic Regulations of Village or Township Council, August 9, 1941.
Provisional Organic Law of the District Council, May 5, 1943.
General Regulations for Provincial All-Circles Representative Conferences, December 2, 1949.
Organic Law of the New Regional Government Committees (Councils), December 16, 1949.
General Regulations for the Organization of the Provincial People's Governments, District People's Governments, and Municipal People's Governments, January 16, 1950.
Decisions (Regulations) on Measures for the Establishment of Local Democratic-Coalition Governments of Nationalities, February 22, 1952.
Decisions (Regulations) on the Protection of the Right of All Scattered National Minority People to National Equality, February 22, 1952.
Organic Law of the Local People's Congresses and Local People's Councils of the People's Republic of China, September 21, 1954.
Revised Regulations for the Enforcement of Local Self-Government of Districts and Municipalities in Taiwan Province, November 5, 1954.
Organic Law of the Provincial Assembly, August 26, 1959.

D. Other Documents

Manifesto of the Second National Congress of the Communist Party, July 1922.
The Constitution of the Nationalist Party, first promulgated on January 25, 1924 and revised many times.
Manifesto of the First National Congress of the Nationalist Party, January 1924.
Principles underlying the Period of Political Tutelage, October 3, 1928.
The Nationality Law of China, February 5, 1929.
The Confirmation of Dr. Sun Yat-sen's Writings as the Fundamental Laws of the Republic of China during the Period of Political Tutelage, March 21, 1929.
Rules concerning the Exercise of Governing Powers, July 10, 1929.
Rules governing the Party Supervisory Committees in Their Examination of Policies and Records of the Governments of Corresponding Levels, December 19, 1929.
Land Law of the Chinese Soviet Republic, November 7, 1931.
Manifesto on Anti-Japanese United Front, April 15, 1933.
Letter of the Central Committee of the Communist Party to the Nationalist Party, August 25, 1936.
Declaration of the Communist Party, July 15, 1937.
Non-Aggression Pact between China and Soviet Russia, August 21, 1937.
Program for the Federation of Chinese Democratic Parties, March 25, 1941.
National General Mobilization Act, March 29, 1942.
Examination Law for Technical Personnel, September 24, 1942.
Regulations for Safeguarding the Freedom of the Human Person, August 1, 1944.
Advocate Act, April 5, 1945.
The Constitution of the Communist Party of China, June 11, 1945, revised September 26, 1956.
Sino-Soviet Treaty of Friendship and Alliance, August 14, 1945.
Joint Statement of Chiang Kai-shek and Mao Tse-tung in Chungking, October 11, 1945.
Sino-American Economic Agreement, July 3, 1948.
Farm Rent-Reduction Regulations, 1949.

The Sino-Soviet Treaty of Friendship, Alliance, and Mutual Assistance, February 14, 1950.
Marriage Law of the People's Republic of China, May 1, 1950.
Trade Union Law of the People's Republic of China, June 28, 1950.
Agrarian Reform Law of the People's Republic of China, June 30, 1950.
General Regulations governing the Organization of the Peasants' Associations, July 14, 1950.
Decisions concerning the Differentiation of Class Status in the Countryside, August 4, 1950.
Statute on Punishment for Counter-Revolutionary Activity, February 20, 1951.
Labor Insurance Regulations of the People's Republic of China, February 26, 1951, revised January 2, 1953.
Provisional Statute on Penalties for Undermining the State Monetary System, April 19, 1951.
Statute on Penalties for Corruption in the Chinese People's Republic, April 21, 1952.
Temporary Regulations for the Surveillance of Counter-Revolutionary Elements, June 27, 1952.
Decisions on Employment of the Government Administration Council of the Central People's Government, July 25, 1952.
General Programs of the People's Republic of China for the Implementation of Regional Autonomy for Nationalities, August 9, 1952.
Land-to-the-Tiller Act, January 1953.
Provisional Regulations on Awards for Inventions, Technical Improvements and Rationalization Proposals concerning Production, May 6, 1954.
The Equalization of Urban Land Rights Act, August 1954, revised July 1958.
Regulations on Labor-Reformation, September 7, 1954.
Sino-American Mutual Defense Treaty, December 2, 1954; *Exchange of Notes*, December 10, 1954.
Decisions on Agricultural Cooperation, October 11, 1955.
Model Regulations for an Agricultural Producers' Cooperative, March 17, 1956.
Regulations governing Safe Working Conditions in Building Construction and Installation Projects, May 25, 1956.
Regulations on Factory Safety and Sanitation, May 25, 1956.
Model Regulations for Advanced Agricultural Producers' Cooperatives, June 30, 1956.
Provisional Regulations of the State Council concerning the Granting of Home Leave to Workers and Staff Members and Wages to Them on Such Leave, February 6, 1958.
Provisional Regulations of the State Council concerning the Retirement of Workers and Staff Members, February 6, 1958.
Constitution of the Trade Unions of the People's Republic of China, May 10, 1958.
Tentative Regulations (Draft) of the Weihsing (Sputnik) People's Commune, August 7, 1958.
Resolutions on the Establishment of People's Communes in the Rural Areas, August 29, 1958.
Regulations for the Collection of Provisional Special Defense Assessments, May 1, 1962.

II. BOOKS AND PAMPHLETS

There are numerous publications on Chinese history, civilization, politics, philosophy, and other special subjects. A comprehensive list of all these works with particular relation to the present subject is neither permissible in consideration of space nor necessary because the reader can always refer to the bibliographies in the field of his interest. Among the valuable bibliographies on modern China are those contained in the following books: (1) Ch'ien Tuan-sheng, *The Government and Politics of China;* (2) Chen Chih-mai, *The Government of China;* (3) Li Chien-nung, *The Political History of China, 1840–1928* (translated by Ssu-Yu Teng and Jeremy Ingalls); (4) C. Martin Wilbur and Julie Lien-Ying How, *Documents on Communism, Nationalism, and Soviet Advisers in China, 1918–1927;* (5) Conrad Brandt, Benjamin Schwartz, and John K. Fairbank, *A Documentary History of Chinese Communism;* (6) Richard L. Walker, *China Under Communism;* (7) W. W. Rostow, *Prospects for Communist China;* and (8) Peter S. H. Tang, *Communist China Today.* Some bibliographical guides are extremely useful even though they are not up to date. They include: (1) John K. Fairbank and Kwang-ching Liu, *Modern China: A Bibliographical Guide to Chinese Works, 1898–1937* (Cambridge: Harvard University Press, 1950); (2) Charles S. Gardner, *A Union List of Selected Western Books on China in American Libraries* (Washington: American Council of Learned Societies, 1938); (3) L. C. Goodrich and H. C. Fenn, *A Syllabus of the History of Chinese Civilization and Culture* (New York: China Society of America, 1946); (4) *Basic Bibliography on China* (New York: China Institute in America, 1956); (5) Yuan Tung-li, *China in Western Literature* (New Haven: Yale University Far Eastern Publications, 1958); and (6) the United States Joint Publications Research Service, *Contemporary China: A Bibliography of Reports on China* (Edited by Richard Sorich, prepared for the Joint Committee on Contemporary China of the American Council of Learned Societies and the Social Science Research Council, New York, 1961). The lists of works contained in the *External Research* of the State Department and in a number of periodicals are most informative on current publications. Among these is the *Journal of Asian Studies,* which contains bibliographies on Asia in general and China in particular, published as an extra issue in September each year.

For the convenience of Western readers, English sources are cited whenever possible. Otherwise, Chinese materials are used, especially those of the pre-War period. The following list is selected from books and pamphlets referred to in this work. Those mentioned only occasionally in the footnotes are not repeated in this bibliography because of limitation of space. In the list below, sources in English are marked with an asterisk and all others are in Chinese.

*Agrarian Reform Law of the People's Republic of China and Other Relevant Documents.** (d) Peking: Foreign Languages Press, 1959.

Ballantine, Joseph W., *Formosa: United States Foreign Policy.** Washington: The Brookings Institution, 1952.

Band, Claire and William, *Two Years with the Chinese Communists.** New Haven: Yale University Press, 1948.

Barnett, A. Doak, *Communist China and Asia.** New York: Harper & Bros., 1960.

Blaustein, Albert P., *Fundamental Legal Documents of Communist China.** (d) South Hackensack, New Jersey: Fred B. Rothman Co., 1962.

Boorman, Howard L., *et al., Moscow-Peking Axis.** New York: Harper & Bros., 1957.

Brandt, Conrad, *et al., A Documentary History of Chinese Communism.** (d) Cambridge: Harvard University Press, 1959.

Brzezinski, Zbigniew K., *The Soviet Bloc: Unity and Conflict.** Cambridge: Harvard University Press, 1960.

Cameron, Meribeth E., *The Reform Movement in China, 1898–1912.** Stanford: Stanford University Press, 1931.

Chang, Chia-sên (Carsun), *The Third Force in China.** New York: Bookman Associates, 1952.

Chen, Chih-mai, *The Government of China.* Chungking and Shanghai: Commercial Press, 1944–45. 3 vols.

Chen, Ju-hsuan, *The Constitutional History of China.* Shanghai: World Book Co., 1933.

Chen, Theodore Hsi-en, *Chinese Communism and the Proletarian-Socialist Revolution.** Los Angeles: University of Southern California Press, 1955.

Ch'en, Jerome, *Yüan Shih-K'ai (1859–1916).** Stanford: Stanford University Press, 1961.

Cheng, Chu-yuan, *The People's Communes.** Hongkong: The Union Press, 1959.

Cheng, Fang, *A General Course on Chinese District (Hsien) Government.* Changsha: Commercial Press, 1939. 2 vols.

Chiang, Chung-cheng (Kai-shek), *Soviet Russia in China.** New York: Farrar, Straus & Cudahy, 1957.

Chiang, Kai-shek, *China's Destiny.** New York: The Macmillan Co., 1947. (an authorized translation by Wang Chung-hui)

Chiang, Kai-shek and Madame Mei-ling (Sung), *General Chiang Kai-shek; the Account of the Fortnight in Sian When the Fate of China Hung in the Balance.** Garden City: Doubleday, Doran & Co., 1937. (originally published in Chinese under the title, *Sian: a Coup D'Etat.*)

Ch'ien, Tuan-sheng, *The Government and Politics of China.** Cambridge: Harvard University Press, 1950.

Ch'ien, Tuan-sheng, et al., *History of Political Institutions under the Chinese Republic.* Shanghai: Commercial Press, 1939.

Chou, Ching-wen, *Criticism on People's Communes.** Hongkong: Continental Research Institute, 1961.

Chou, Ching-wen, *Ten Years of Storm.** New York: Holt, Rinehart and Winston, 1960.

Chou, Fu-hai, *The Theoretical System of "The Three People's Principles."* Shanghai: Hsin Sheng Ming Press, 1928.

Chow, Tse-tung, *The May Fourth Movement: Intellectual Revolution in Modern China.** Cambridge: Harvard University Press, 1960.

Chu, Teh, *On Guerrila Warfare.* Shanghai: Chien-she Publishing Co., 1938 (2nd ed.)

Chu, Teh, *On the Battlefronts of the Liberated Areas.** Peking: Foreign Languages Press, 1952.

Clark, Gerald, *Impatient Giant: Red China Today.** New York: David McKay Co., 1959.

Collected Laws and Regulations of the Republic of China, The. (d) (Edited by the Legislative Yuan) Shanghai: Chung-hwa Book Co., 1934.

Collected Manifestoes of the Nationalist Party, The. (d) Nanking: The Special Committee of the Mass Meeting at Nanking on the Memorial Day of Dr. Sun Yat-sen, 1928.

Collected Works of Sun Yat-sen, The. Shanghai: New Cultural Press, 21st ed., 1929.

Collected Works of Sun Yat-sen, The. Shanghai: San-min Book Co., 1937.

Collected Works of Sun Yat-sen, The. Shanghai: Tai Chuan Co., 1929.

Collection of Laws and Decrees, The. (d) Peking: Government Printing Office, 1912.

Communism in China.* Hongkong: Union Research Institute, 1959.

Complete Collection of Laws and Regulations of the Republic of China, The. (d) Shanghai: Commercial Press, 1936.

Conlon Associates, Report on Communist China and Taiwan.* *Congressional Record*, Proceedings and Debates of the 86th Congress, 2nd Session, 1959.

Current Laws of the National Government. (d) Nanking: Bureau of Legal Affairs of the National Government, 1928.

Degras, Jane, *Soviet Documents on Foreign Policy.** (d) London: Oxford University Press, 1951. 3 vols.

Dr. Sun Yat-sen: Commemorative Articles and Speeches by Mao Tse-tung, Soong Ching-ling, Chou En-lai and Others.* Peking: Foreign Languages Press, 1957.

Electoral Law of the People's Republic of China, The.* (d) Peking: Foreign Languages Press, 1953.

Fairbank, John King, *The United States and China.** Cambridge: Harvard University Press, revised ed., 1958.

First Five Year Plan for the Development of the National Economy of the Chinese People's Republic 1953–1957, The.* Peking: The People's Press, 1955.

Fischer, Louis, *The Soviets in World Affairs.** Princeton: Princeton University Press, 1951. 2 vols.

Fitzgerald, Charles Patrick, *Revolution in China.** New York: Praeger, 1952.

Fo, Chi-hsüeh, *The Chinese Government.* Taipei: Cheng Chung Book Co., 1956.

Garvey, James Emmett, *Marxist-Leninist China: Military and Social Doctrine.** New York: Exposition Press, 1960.

Ho, Kan-chih, *A History of the Modern Chinese Revolution.** Peking: Foreign Languages Press, 1959.

Ho, Ying-chin, *A Description of the Eight Years' War of Resistance.* Nanking: Chinese Ministry of Defense, 1955.

Hornbeck, Stanley K., *A Brief Study of Some Facts and Many Not-Facts Regarding "China" and United States "China Policy."* * New York: American-Asian Educational Exchange, Inc., 1961.

Houn, Franklin W., *Central Government of China, 1912–1928.** Madison: University of Wisconsin Press, 1959.

Hsiao, Wen-che, *A Study of the Chinese Administrative Inspectorate System.* Chungking, 1943.

Hsieh, Pao-chao, *The Government of China, 1644–1911,** Baltimore, Johns Hopkins Press, 1925.

Hsieh, Ying-chou, *A Study of the Organic Law of the National Government.* Shanghai: Hua-tung Book Co., 1933.

Hsü, Ch'ung-hao, *An Outline of Chinese Political Institutions.* Chungking: Commercial Press, 1943.

Hsü, L. S., *Sun Yat-sen: His Political and Social Ideals.** Los Angeles: University of Southern California Press, 1933.

Hsü, Yung-ying, *A Survey of the Shensi-Kansu-Ninghsia Border Region.** New York: Institute of Pacific Relations, 1945. (Mimeo., 2 vols.)

Hsüeh, Chün-tu, *Huang Hsing and the Chinese Revolution.** Stanford: Stanford University Press, 1961.

Hu, Ch'ang-tu, *et al.*, *China: Its People, Its Society, Its Culture.** (Edited by Hsiao Hsia) New Haven: HRAF Press, 1960.

Hu, Chiao-mu, *Thirty Years of the Communist Party of China.** Peking: Foreign Languages Press, 1959.

Hu Hua, *Source Materials of the Chinese Revolution under China's New Democracy.* (d) Shanghai: Commercial Press, 1951.

Hu, Tz'u-wei, *The Self-Government in District (Hsien) and Township (Chen).* Chengtu: Szechwan Training Corps, 1942.

Hua, Lin-i, *A History of the Chinese Nationalist Party (Kuomintang)*. Shanghai: Commercial Press, 1928.

Hudson, Geoffrey, *et al.*, *The Chinese Communes.** New York: Institute of Pacific Relations, 1960.

*Important Labor Laws and Regulations of the People's Republic of China.** (d) Peking: Foreign Languages Press, enlarged ed., 1961.

Isaacs, Harold R., *The Tragedy of the Chinese Revolution.** Stanford: Stanford University Press, 2nd revised ed., 1961.

Jao, Jung-ch'un, *The New District (Hsien) System*. Chungking: The Independent Press, 1942.

Kan, Yiu-lan, *Mao Tse-tung and His Clique*. Hongkong: Freedom Press, 1954.

Kao, I-han, *The Evolution of the Chinese Supervisory System*. Shanghai: Commercial Press, 1926.

Ku, Chung-hsiu, *A History of the Establishment of the Chinese Republic*. Shanghai: Tai-tung, 1914.

Ku, Tun-jou, *The Legislative History of China*. Soochow: Mutuhsintseng Tang, 1931.

Kuan, Ta-tung, *The Socialist Transformation of Capitalist Industry and Commerce in China.** Peking: Foreign Languages Press, 1960.

K'ung, H. H., "A Memoir of the Sian Incident," in *The Collection of Speeches of H. H. K'ung*. (New York: Chinese American Institute of Cultural Relations, 1960. 2 vols.), Vol. II, pp. 657–704.

Kuo, Ping-chia, *China: New Age and New Outlook.** New York: Alfred A. Knopf, 1956.

Kuo, Shao-chen, *A Complete History of the Chinese Revolution*. Shanghai: Commercial Press, 1912.

Li, Chien-nung, *The Political History of China, 1840–1928*. Shanghai: The Pacific Book Co., 1938. (Translated in English by Ssu-yu Tang and Jeremy Ingalls. Princeton: D. Van Nostrand Co., 1956.)

Li, Choh-ming, *Economic Development of Communist China: An Appraisal of the First Five Years of Industrialization.** Berkeley: University of California Press, 1959.

Li, Tsung-huang, *The Contemporary Pao-Chia System*. Chungking, 1943.

Li, Tsung-huang, *The Theory and Practice of the New District (Hsien) System*. Chungking: Chung-hua Book Co., 1943.

Liao, Kai-lung, *How the New China Was Born*. Shanghai: Hai-yen Book Co., 1950.

Lindsay, Michael, *China and the Cold War; A Study in International Politics.** Carlton, Melbourne University Press, 1955.

Linebarger, Paul M. A., *The Political Doctrines of Sun Yat-sen, an Exposition of the San Min Chu I.** Baltimore: Johns Hopkins Press, 1937.

Linebarger, Paul M. A., *et al.*, *Far Eastern Governments and Politics.** Princeton: D. Van Nostrand Co., 1954.

Liu, Shao-ch'i, *Internationalism and Nationalism.** Peking: Foreign Languages Press, 1952.

Liu, Shao-ch'i, *On the Party*. Peking: Hsin-hua Book Co., 1950.

Liu, Shao-ch'i, *Report on the Draft Constitution of the People's Republic of China.** (d) Peking: Foreign Languages Press, 1954.

Liu, Shao-ch'i, *The Training of the Communist Party Members*. Hongkong: Hsin-min-chu Press, 1949.

Lo, Chih-yuan, *Local Administrative System in China*. Chungking: The Independent Press, 1942.

MacFarquhar, Roderick P., *The Hundred Flowers Campaign and the Chinese Intellectuals*.* New York: Praeger, 1960.

MacNair, Harley Farnsworth, *China in Revolution: An Analysis of Politics and Militarism under the Republic*.* Chicago: University of Chicago Press, 1931.

Mao Tse-tung: Selected Works.* New York: International Publishers. Vols. I–III, 1954; Vol. IV, 1956; Vol. V, 1962.

McLane, Charles B., *Soviet Policy and the Chinese Communists, 1931–1946*.* New York: Columbia University Press, 1958.

Minutes of the Legislative Assembly. Nanking: The Provisional Government, January 31, 1912.

Minutes of the National Emergency Conference, The. Nanking: The Executive Yuan, 1932.

Minutes of the National People's Convention. Nanking: Central Headquarters of the Nationalist Party, 1931.

Minutes of the Third Plenary Session of the Fourth National Congress of the Nationalist Party, The. Nanking: The Secretariat of the Central Headquarters of the Nationalist Party, 1932.

Newman, Robert P., *Recognition of Communist China?*.* New York: The Macmillan Co., 1961.

North, Robert Carver, *Moscow and Chinese Communists*.* Stanford: Stanford University Press, 1953.

Pan, Wei-Tung, *The Chinese Constitution: A Study of Forty Years of Constitution-Making in China*.* (d) Washington: Institute of Chinese Culture, 1946.

Payne, Robert, *Mao Tse-tung, Ruler of Red China*.* New York: Henry Schuman Inc., 1950.

People's Communes in China.* Peking: Foreign Languages Press, 1959.

Price, Frank W. (tr.), *San Min Chu I: The Three Principles of the People*.* Shanghai: Commercial Press, 1927. (an English translation from the tenth edition of the Chinese text)

Quigley, Harold S., *China's Politics in Perspective*.* Minneapolis: University of Minnesota Press, 1962.

Research Project on the Chinese Communist Party Line.* Cambridge: Harvard University., Russia Research Center, Docs. 1 & 4.

Riggs, Fred W., *Formosa under Nationalist Rule*.* New York: Institute of Pacific Relations, 1952.

Rosinger, Lawrence K., *China's Wartime Politics, 1937–1944*.* Princeton: Princeton University Press, 1944.

Rostow, W. W., *et al., The Prospects for Communist China*.* New York: John Wiley & Sons, 1954.

Schwartz, Benjamin I., *Chinese Communism and the Rise of Mao*.* Cambridge: Harvard University Press, 1961.

Selected Works of Mao Tse-tung.* Peking: Foreign Languages Press, 1961, Vol. IV. (The English translation of the first 3 vols. is under preparation.)

Shih, Yang-cheng, *The Chinese Provincial Administrative System*. Shanghai: Commercial Press, 1947.

Sih, Paul K. T., *Decision for China: Communism or Christianity*.* Chicago: Regnery, 1959.

Snow, Edgar, *Random Notes on Red China, 1936–1945*.* Cambridge: Harvard University Press, 1957.

Snow, Edgar, *Red Star over China*.* New York: Random House, 1944.

Snow, Helen (Foster), *Inside Red China*.* New York: Doubleday, Doran & Co., 1939.

Stein, Guenther, *The Challenge of Red China.** New York: McGraw Hill Book Co., 1945.

Strong, Anna Louise, *The Rise of the Chinese Communes.** Peking: New World Press, 1959.

Sun, Yat-sen, *The International Development of China.** New York: G. P. Putnam's Sons, 1922.

*Sun Yat-sen: Commemorative Album.** Peking, 1956.

Supervisory *Yuan*, The, *A Sketch History of the Supervisory System.* Nanking: The Supervisory *Yuan*, 1936.

Ta Ch'ing Hsüan T'ung New Laws. (d) Shanghai: Commercial Press, 1909.

Ta Ch'ing Kuang Hsü New Laws. (d) Shanghai: Commercial Press, 1908.

Tai, Chi-t'ao, *The Philosophical Basis of the Theory of Sun Wen.* Canton, 1925.

Tang, Peter S. H., *The Commune System in Mainland China.** Washington: The Research Institute on the Sino-Soviet Bloc, 1961. (Pamphlet series No. 2.)

Tang, Peter S. H., *Communist China Today.** Vol. I, revised ed., 1961, by Washington D. C.: Research Institute on the Sino-Soviet Bloc. Vol. II (d), by New York: Frederick A. Praeger, 1958.

T'ang, Leang-li, *The Inner History of the Chinese Revolution.** London: G. Routledge & Sons, 1930.

Teng, Hsiao-p'ing, *Report on the Rectification Campaign.** Peking: Foreign Languages Press, 1957.

Thomas, S. B., *Government and Administration in Communist China.** New York: Institute of Pacific Relations, revised ed., 1955. (Mimeo.)

Tsao, Wen-yen, *The Constitutional Structure of Modern China.** Victoria, Australia: Melbourne University Press, 1947.

Tsou, Lu, *The Manuscript of the History of the Nationalist Party of China.* Shanghai: Ming-chih Book Co., 1929.

Tung, Shih-ching, *Reminiscences of the Communist Area.* Hongkong: Freedom Press, 1951.

Tung, William L., *China and Some Phases of International Law.** New York & London: Oxford University Press, 1940.

Tung, William L., *The Government of China.* (d) Shanghai: World Book Co., 1941. 2 vols.

Tung, William L., *Imperialism and China.* Shanghai: Kuan-min Press, 1929.

U. S. Congress, Senate, Committee on the Judiciary, *Nature of Communism in Occupied China.** Washington: Government Printing Office, 1957.

U. S. Department of State, *The Republic of China.** Far Eastern Series 81, released October 1959.

Vinacke, Harold M., *Modern Constitutional Development in China.** Princeton: Princeton University Press, 1920.

Walker, Richard L., *China under Communism.** New Haven: Yale University Press, 1955.

Walker, Richard L., *The Continuing Struggle: Communist China and the Free World.** New York: Athene Press, 1958.

Wang, Ching-wei, *China's Problems and Their Solutions.** Shanghai: China United Press, 1934.

Wang, Shih, *et al.*, *The History of the Communist Party of China: A Short Course.* Shanghai: The People's Press, 1958.

Wang, Shih-chieh and Ch'ien Tuan-sheng, *Comparative Constitutional Law.* Chungking: Commercial Press, 1942. 2 vols.

Weale, B. L. Putnam *(pseud.* Bertram Lenox Simpson), *The Fight for the Republic in China.** New York: Dodd, Mead & Co., 1917.

Wedemeyer, Albert C., *Wedemeyer Reports.** New York: Holt, 1958.

Wen, Chun-t'ien, *The Chinese Pao-Chia System.* Shanghai: Commercial Press, 1935.

Whiting, Allen S., *China Crosses the Yalu.** New York: The Macmillan Co., 1960.

Wilbur, Martin and How, Julie Lien-ying, *Documents on Communism, Nationalism, and Soviet Advisers in China, 1918–1927.** (d) New York: Columbia University Press, 1956.

William, Maurice, *Sun Yat-sen versus Communism.** Baltimore: Williams & Wilkins, 1932.

Willoughby, Westel Woodbury, *Constitutional Government in China; Present Conditions and Prospects.** Washington: Carnegie Endowment for International Peace, 1922.

Willoughby, Westel Woodbury, *Foreign Rights and Interests in China.** Baltimore: Johns Hopkins Press, 1927. Rev. ed., 2 vols.

Wittfogel, Karl A., *From Marx to Mao.** Seattle: University of Washington, 1960.

Wittfogel, Karl A., *Oriental Despotism: A Comparative Study of Total Power.** New Haven: Yale University Press, 1957.

Wu, Ching-hsiung and Huang Kung-chiao, *A History of the Constitution-Making in China.* Shanghai: Commercial Press, 1937.

Wu, Tsung-chih, *Constitutional History of the Republic of China.* Peking, 1924.

Yakhontoff, Victor A. *The Chinese Soviets.** New York: Coward-McCann, 1934.

Yang, C. K., *The Chinese Family in the Communist Revolution.** Cambridge: Harvard University Press, 1959.

Yang, Yu-chiung, *Legislative History of Modern China.* Shanghai: Commercial Press, 1936.

Yen, Fu, *The Secrets of the Chinese Communist Party.* Taipei: Tung-nan Press, 1950.

Yen. Hawklin L., *A Survey of Constitutional Development in China.** New York: Longmans, Green & Co., 1911.

III. OTHER SOURCES

The yearbooks on China were published under different titles in different places: *The China Year Book*, published in London, Tientsin, and Shanghai, from 1912 to 1939, edited by H. G. Woodhead; *The Chinese Year Book*, published by the Commercial Press, Shanghai, from 1936 to 1945; *China Handbook, 1937–1945*, published by The Macmillan Company, New York. After the War, the title of *China Handbook* was first used but now has been changed to *China Yearbook*, published in Taipei, Taiwan. *The Handbook on People's China*, published in Peking, contains some basic information on Communist China. Students interested in the recent development on the Mainland are advised to read the following important publications by the American Consulate General in Hongkong: *Current Background, Survey of China Mainland Press, Review of Hongkong Chinese Press, Selections from China Mainland Magazines,* and *Extracts from China Mainland Publications.* Other materials with divergent views are published by different organizations in Hongkong, including the Union Research Institute and Continental Research Institute.

Source from various articles and periodicals, referred to in the footnotes of this work, are not repeated here. Among the periodicals valuable for research on contemporary China are the following: (1) *The Journal of Asian Studies* (formerly the *Far Eastern Quarterly*), (2) *The China Quarterly* (London), (3) *Pacific Affairs* (formerly New York and now Vancouver), (4) *Foreign Affairs*, (5) *Journal of International Affairs*, (6) *The Annals of the American Academy*

of Political and Social Science. There are numerous periodicals issued on the
Mainland and Taiwan, but most of their contents are strongly opinionated one
way or the other. Only a few contemporary newspapers are used in this research.
They include *The New York Times*, *China Tribune* (in Chinese, New York),
Central Daily News (in Chinese, Nanking and Taipei), *People's Daily* (in Chinese,
Peking), and *Ta Kung Pao* (in Chinese, Tientsin, Chungking, and Hongkong).
Other daily papers, published in the United States and England and used only
for occasional reference, are not listed.

INDEX

Aborigines in Taiwan, 235
Absolute monarchy, 1, 8
Administrative Conference (Yüan Shih-k'ai's), 51
Administrative Court, 41–42, 43, 69, 121, 132, 133, 209
Administrative inspector, 44, 138, 142, 143, 192; regulations, 142, 143
Agrarian reform, 265, 311; laws and regulations, 159, 200, 273, 282
Agrarian revolution, 241, 242, 243
Alice Memorial Hospital in Hongkong, 3
All-China Congress of the Soviets. See Chinese Soviet regimes
All-China Federation of Democratic Youth, 238
All-China Federation of Labor, 151, 158, 238
All-China Federation of Writers and Artists, 239
All-China Students' Federation, 238
All-China Women's Congress, 238
All-Circles Representative Conferences, 268, 275–276, 285; regulations, 275
All People's Party, 38
Amoy, 215, 227
Anfu (or Anhwei) clique, 66, 68, 69
Anhwei, 23, 108, 145, 150, 156, 159, 166, 188, 195, 274, 286
Annihilation campaigns. See Chiang Kai-shek
Anti-Comintern Pact between Japan and Germany, 164, 172
Anti-Japanese Military and Political College in Yenan, 244
Anti-Japanese People's United Front, 163
Association for the Advancement of Republicanism, 38
Asylum, political, 161, 268, 284
Auditing Yuan, 69
August First Uprising in Nanchang, 155
Autonomous areas or regions, 267, 276, 277, 281, 286, 287, 295, 299, 306–308; general programs of regional autonomy for nationalities, 277

Autumn Harvest Insurrection in Hunan, 155, 241

Bandung Conference, 316
Blooming and contending (or thought contending) campaign, 309, 310
Board of Political Affairs (Yüan Shih-k'ai's), 55, 56, 61, 62; Presidential order, 55
Board of trustees (cities, towns, and villages), 14, 15
Borodin, Michael, 93, 95, 107, 109, 110, 155
Boundary delimitation and disputes, 21, 316
Boxer Uprising or Rebellion, 6, 21
Cabinet system, 11, 27, 41, 62, 65, 79
Cairo Conference, Declaration, 171, 235
Cantile, James, 4
Canton, 3, 72, 74, 75, 76, 77, 78, 88, 93, 95, 96, 108, 115, 123, 140, 147, 150, 151, 152, 153, 154, 156, 170, 215, 216, 240
Canton Commune. See Chinese Soviet regimes
Central Military Government of the Chinese Republic in Wuchang, 22
Central Party Academy in Yenan, 167
Central People's Government Council, 239, 240, 260, 268, 269, 270, 274, 278, 285
Central People's Government of the People's Republic of China, 239, 240, 246, 259, 260, 263, 269–273, 274, 276, 286, 287, 312, 315, 317; Organic Law, 239, 263, 264, 269, 285
Central Planning Board, 181, 182
Central Soviet District. See Chinese Soviet regimes
Central Studies Association, 33, 34
Ch'a-lin (Tsalin), See Chinese Soviet regimes
Chahar, 58, 139, 148, 168, 170
Chamdo Area, 161
Chang, Carsun (Chun-mai), 176, 177, 179, 199